I0104485

The Monster Collector

Shay Lawless

Monster Collector— Copyright © 2016/2025 by Shay Lawless

ISBN-10: 1-940087-16-3
ISBN-13:978-1-940087-16-0

21 Crows Dusk to Dawn
Publishing, 21 Crows, LLC

All rights reserved. No part of this book may be reproduced or transmitted in any form or by any means, electronic or mechanical, including photocopying, recording, or by any information storage and retrieval system, without permission in writing from the copyright owner. This is a work of fiction. Names, characters, places and incidents either are the product of the author's imagination or are used fictitiously, and any resemblance to any actual persons, living or dead, events, or locales is entirely coincidental. This book was printed in the United States of America.

It started with a letter. The envelope was generic and white. The print was nondescript except for each lower case letter 'i' was dotted with a heart. It was sent from the Danville Station, West Virginia post office. There was no return address, no name to identify who had written it. It had been sent to an old address and had been forwarded twice. The letter was two months old by the time it got to her:

To Austin Jackson:

I think you should know that your ex-boyfriend and your daughter are in big danger. If somebody don't stop what is going on at Canaan Mountain, we're all going to die.

Chapter −1

It was two in the morning when the knock came—three raps, soft and perfectly spaced. Brandon Tremaine sat bolt upright in bed, blinking into the darkness. The taste of sleep was still thick on his tongue. For an instant, he thought it was the pat-pat-pat of his three-and-a-half-year-old daughter's bare feet, her shadow flickering at the doorway. He looked around, heart drumming in his ears. He waited for the mop of Tessa's deep brown hair to appear. No one was there.

Then—another rap of knuckles against the door. A surge of anxiety twisted in his gut, sharp and sudden. Heart racing, Brandon scrubbed a hand through his short dark hair, a nervous habit. The bristly feel made him shiver. He tossed off the worn sheet and slipped out of bed. The air smelled stubbornly of old wood, the kind of musty, lived-in scent that clung to the walls no matter how many Rain Fresh air freshener plug-ins his mom brought over, determined to cover up what she called his house's "old" smell.

As he made his way toward the stairs, he glanced right and saw Tessa's little bed: the pink princess comforter sliding toward the floor, the lump of blankets wrapped around her tiny body. The soft smell of strawberry shampoo lingered in the air. A glint off her too-thick glasses on the bedside stand reassured him. She was tucked in, safe and sound—her eyesight so poor she wouldn't go two steps without them.

The farmhouse was ancient—a white-painted wooden structure with too many rooms and a sagging picket fence outside. Each cautious step sent a creak through the chilly floorboards beneath his socks.

He glimpsed a form shifting across the porch. Brandon hesitated, considered grabbing the baseball bat under his bed, palms slick with cold sweat—then abandoned the thought and descended the stairs. The knock didn't come again, but Brandon's unease lingered, doubt gnawing at him as he held his breath.

He moved to the bay window beside the front door and gingerly pulled back the thick, dusty curtain, the fabric gritty beneath his fingers. The porch and lawn glowed in bright moonlight all the way to the driveway. Beyond that, the thick oaks lining the drive swallowed the light.

He spotted the faint silhouette of an old, battered truck merging with the darkness—paint flaking, one headlight opaque with grime. Someone lurked at the edge of the trees, almost swallowed by shadow, moving with a caution that made Brandon's skin crawl.

Brandon opened the wooden front door—its paint was cool and slightly tacky under his hand. He wasn't sure why he didn't feel threatened. Not yet. His mind wrestled with confusion—shouldn't he be more afraid? The screen door was the only barrier between him and whatever prowled beyond the porch—though he couldn't remember if he'd latched it. The night breathed in through the seam: dew, grass, a fading curl of wood smoke—scents so familiar, so homelike, he almost relaxed. Too comforting. And that was dangerous.

"Hey!" he called out, his voice cracking the silence. The shadow seemed to dissolve into the trunk of the tree, as if it had never been there at all. There was a hushed, wispy sound near the front door. A sniff. Brandon's eyes dropped. His breath caught. Someone stood not a foot from him, close enough for him to see the shine of rain in their hair.

"Hey, Five." Five. Nobody called him that anymore.

"Cripes!" Brandon jumped back. *Five—High-five*—from when he was a lanky, fourteen-year-old on the Danville Station High basketball team. His team had won a game against rival Jenkins one Friday. Brandon and his teammates had come to school on Monday, all haughty and high-fiving everyone down the hallway. A tiny girl at her locker had turned just as he passed, tapping her fingers on the metal over and over and over. He remembered her big blue eyes going wide. He'd heard her mutter something like, *"I'd have to get on a ladder to high-five that dude."*

He'd stopped everyone, turned, and taken two steps back.

"Okay, a low-five for the spazzy half-pint back here." *Spaz*. Austin Jackson. Hell, everybody knew Austin Jackson had ADHD. She was always staring out the window, tapping out a beat on anything nearby, or driving teachers crazy with her banging.

"Spaz?" he muttered now, shaking the old memory away. His nickname had stuck through high school. The tiny firecracker Austin Jackson had stuck with him long after.

"Yeah. Folks call me Austin now."

She shifted on the porch, voice low: "Me and some friends need a place—just tonight. I've been driving three days, no sleep—could we crash here?"

"I don't know." Brandon's voice sounded distant even to himself, shock tightening his throat and uncertainty rising in his chest. He blinked a few times, struggling with disbelief and the flood of old memories triggered by seeing her after so long.

"Okay, thanks anyway."

"Did you call your dad?"

A long pause, then a breath. "Yeah. He hung up."

Just like that, she turned and made her way down the porch steps. At the second-to-last step, she did a skip-jump on both feet—just like she always used to. Brandon stopped in mid-thought, a pang of bittersweet nostalgia mixing with a sudden ache of longing—how much it resembled the same two-footed skip-jump his daughter had done that afternoon. It was a strange, mirrored movement that made his chest tighten with emotion. Austin stopped, turned. "How is Tessa?"

"She's fine." *Not that you helped,* Brandon thought, bitterness stabbing at him before he could push it back. He forced his tone to sound neutral, swallowing a swell of anger and disappointment he didn't want to reveal. Three and a half years ago, Austin had called him from the hospital, her voice barely a frightened whisper.

Her father was forcing her to give up *their* little girl for adoption—he'd kicked her out of the house, told her to leave town. Would Brandon take Tessa until she could figure something out?

The call had been a shock. He and Austin had broken up months earlier. He hadn't even known she was pregnant.

Now, Austin hesitated as if to say more, but didn't. Brandon watched her scrawny form head to the battered truck, long black hair bouncing in the moonlight. She looked tiny—barely five feet and hardly a hundred pounds, the night making her seem even smaller. He heard the truck door grind open. Even from here, he could tell it was a rustbucket. His gaze swept across the truck bed, where four figures sat huddled. They slid back down as the engine coughed to life.

"Shit."

Brandon swung open the screen door with a loud creak and then a bang. He made long strides from the porch and yelled across the expanse. "Hey!" He didn't think she heard him at first. The truck just sat there. But as he crossed the dark span between truck and porch, he could see her sitting in the driver's seat, her thumb and forefinger pinching her temples. He pounded on the hood to catch her attention.

"Yeah, fine." He raised a single finger. "Just one night."

He regretted his words instantly when he saw the passenger—a giant of a man stooped to avoid hitting the truck's roof, eyes fixed silently on him. Brandon's gaze flicked to the truck bed: four more people—a lanky man, two young women, and a boy of about thirteen or fourteen.

"We can sleep in the barn if you've got blankets." Austin's voice was raspy and worn—like weathered leather between finger and thumb. Exhaustion clung to every word. She avoided his eyes. He could barely trace her features, the flash of blue eyes, and the faint tang of motor oil and road dust on her clothes. For a moment, he wondered what she was fleeing—or who.

Austin always had that funny way of looking downward, then flipping her head up like she was waiting for some awe-inspiring word from God. Brandon had seen her do it a thousand times, but now—right now when she did it—it hit him different. A strange tightening in his chest. A deeper pull he hadn't expected.

He realized, in one sharp, breath-stealing moment, that first love never really leaves you. It lingers. Years pass, and still, that first rush—the dizzy hope, the impossible longing—seeps into the edges of your days. Even when you think you've outgrown it, a flash of laughter or the familiar curve of a smile pulls you back. The old ache softens, but it never disappears. *Bam.* Something inside him cracked open, flooding him with the truth he'd been sidestepping since high school. The feeling overwhelmed him—so sudden and fierce he couldn't even swallow it back.

"No," he blurted. "You can sleep in the house."

He didn't bother explaining that the barn might not be safe. Preacher Abel Martin lived just over Canaan Mountain, wedged between Brandon's land and Crazy Jack's campground. Tourism folks liked to call his place the *Clan at Canaan Mountain*—a neat little rebrand meant to keep visitors from getting spooked. Locals weren't fooled. Most just called them a cult. Not the violent kind, supposedly. Just the kind that kept to themselves...until they didn't.

Abel hadn't caused Brandon much trouble personally. Not really. He'd dammed up Turtle Creek between their properties, leaving only a thin trickle for the cattle, but it wasn't worth a fight. Now and then, his kids stole eggs or tools from the barn. If Brandon yelled, they'd pelt him with rocks or wave around a BB gun like it meant something. Harmless stuff, he told himself. Annoying, sure. But harmless. Still... he wasn't stupid enough to wonder what those kids might do if they startled someone sleeping in the barn at night. And he really didn't want Preacher Martin angry with him. The man had bought three cows and a pair of pigs last year—good money for a struggling farm.

Even so, after the sun went down, people whispered about the Martins. Always in low voices. Always with a glance toward the mountain. Brandon tried not to think too hard about why.

"Thank you." She said it simply and turned off the truck. "I just need a couple of hours' sleep. We'll be out of your hair before the sun's up." Brandon nodded, unaware of the way her words brushed against something old and waiting in the dark beyond the barn.

Chapter −2

Brandon tried not to stare when they filed through the front door, but his eyes kept drifting back to Austin. She stood in the center of the room, framed by the yellow porch light, clutching a pile of his grandma's old blankets against her chest—her knuckles white and thin as bone. The air smelled faintly of mothballs and the spicy pine of the cedar trunk where the blankets had been stored, softened by the lingering trace of last night's coffee.

Austin. Holy hell, she'd changed.

There was an edge to her now—a tension in her jaw. He remembered Austin as that beautiful, awkward girl from the summer they hooked up. Now her black hair tumbled to her back, her arms were lean, and as small as she was, her presence was magnetic and drew the whole room. The piercing blue of her eyes held him captive, anchored to the floor.

He had known Austin all his life—just never paid attention until that summer. She'd even tutored him in math in high school. Judge Jackson's youngest, she was geeky, scrawny, and always shoving thick glasses up her nose. She had a laugh that made you join in, even if you didn't get the joke. *Remember, one plus one equals three.* She used to tease him with that. He'd pretend to roll his eyes, but her laughter always got to him—she could make even the worst day seem lighter just by grinning at you.

At Danville Station High, she'd been the girl in the back of the room. Austin knew all the answers but never raised her hand. She was shy, quiet, and self-conscious. Brandon had always gravitated toward tall, sassy redheads—the uncomplicated girls who didn't expect much and didn't stick around. But that summer, something about Austin finally caught his attention. He never really noticed her—until she started working nights at Mister Salty's Gas & Carryout. There, beneath the buzzing fluorescent lights, she seemed transformed: confident, quick with a joke, talking easily with customers, her laugh ringing out in the small pizza place and store.

Maybe it was the way she changed her hair, or how she suddenly dared to look him in the eye. Or maybe he'd just been too wrapped up in his own world until then, but now he couldn't look away. She was different from everyone else he knew—sharp, bold, always hiding a secret smile. Back then, his life was all impulse and no consequence.

If he'd known how she'd upend his life, maybe he would've run.

But he hadn't. Tonight, though, she looked like she'd been dragged through hell. A fresh bruise darkened her right eye, a thin cut traced her cheekbone, and the skin beneath her oversized jacket was mottled with angry red marks. He opened his mouth to ask if she was okay, but the sharp creak of the screen door sliced through the thick, quiet air. The metallic tang of worry lingered at the back of his throat. "Stats, you get the floor this time," Austin said, slipping toward the door as she handed out blankets.

The first man through was nearly seven feet tall, with a bleach-blonde ponytail on top, sides shaved down to the skin. Tattoos in spirals of blue and red wrapped his neck and arms.

"I had the floor last time," he grumbled. "It isn't good for my sciatica. And I think I have a degenerative spine condition from riding in that truck." His accent was thick—maybe Italian, maybe Greek.

"No, you didn't," Austin shot back, grinning now. "If you want a bed, out-charm Golem. Tall order."

Brandon's eyes climbed upward as the next man entered. He had to twist sideways to fit in the doorway. He was feigning air punches at Stats. All muscle. Arms like a triple-sized pro wrestler. A golem was right. "Golem, don't start." Austin poked him in the arm. "Save the wrestling for tomorrow. I've had it up to here." She waved a blanket over her head. "You two are like eight-year-olds fighting over Legos."

"Big-ass eight-year-olds." The teenage boy who stomped in behind them had a thick accent—maybe Mexican, maybe something else—but he looked like any worn-out fifteen-year-old with black hair and tired brown eyes. "And a bunch of pussies," he added.

"Stop, Hutch. Change your attitude." Austin held out her hand.

Brandon blinked. Another man slid up beside Austin—quiet, watchful, like a German Shepherd guarding its owner. His face had a certain canine quality; the lean lines, keen eyes, and perpetually earnest look reminded him of a loyal retriever. Austin's head barely reached his shoulder. He leaned in protectively, touching her with his arm while he studied her face, reading every flicker. He spotted a blanket slipping from her pile and, with a careful, almost shy gesture, scooped it up and handed it back to her. Austin flashed him a grateful smile.

"Roo, it's alright," Austin murmured, firm but gentle. "He's just tired. We're all wiped." She gave Roo a soft smile—the kind you'd give a faithful old dog. "Go sit, okay?"

"Oh, console Roo," Hutch muttered, knocking Roo on the head with his knuckles. Roo only looked at Austin again, reassured by her smile, and obeyed. He lumbered to the couch, never taking his wary eyes off the boy, plopping down with a deep sigh of relief.

Austin turned back to Hutch. "Do you know what it means to call someone churchy?"

Hutch smirked. "Yeah." He puffed his chest, sliding into a mocking southern twang. "Someone who puts on a show of being religious and righteous, but doesn't actually live by those values—like some of those Evangelicals."

"You're half right. There *are* those kind of churchy people, but this family is from good stock—kind, generous, patient." Austin leaned in hard. "God help them, because they're about to meet you. And charitable or not, they haven't met your brand of smart-mouthed chaos. So, unless you want another night in the truck bed, rein it in. And quit mocking my accent, you little turd."

"Yeah, Pet," he said, back to her, shoulders tipping in a haughty wiggle. "Whatever you say. I guess since the boss ain't around anymore, you're taking over. You're five feet tall, maybe a hundred pounds, and look twelve. I could knock you over with one finger."

"I'm sorry." Austin spun toward Brandon with a tight smile. "Excuse me a minute."

Hutch clearly knew the soft spot to jab. Brandon remembered how much it bothered Austin—being small, looking young, never being taken seriously.

She shoved the blankets into his arms and strode across the room to snatch Hutch by the arm. Austin tilted her head, voice turning low and razor-clean. "Do you want the job, Little Bird?" Hutch bristled. "Because I swear," she continued, "I've been searching for an exit ever since they saddled me with you. Should I call your dad to come pick you up? You've spent three years sticking a knife in my back every chance you get." But her eyes stayed on him—a little too steady, a little too knowing—as if she already suspected the bird wasn't so little after all. The boy's mouth twisted, then faltered as she tightened her grip. "You don't think I know that?" she whispered. "I do. And for the record—I never wanted to be his *pet*. You could've had him heart and soul. But you spent so much time trying to get him to hate me, your annoying whining only made him want me more. He's gone. I'm here. I've got a phone. I can call your daddy. And you're gone."

"Don't," Hutch rasped, cheeks flushing. "Please."

Two young women slipped in quietly behind Brandon as the tension thickened.

"Hi, I'm Aina," said the smaller one—thin, short black hair, cat-green eyes rimmed in heavy makeup. She jabbed a thumb at the tall girl behind her. "And this is Starr." Aina was all dark colors and sharp lines, except for the wry, tiny smile tugging at her lips. She smelled faintly of peppermint and smoke. Starr, by contrast, was long-limbed, willow-graceful, with nearly white hair half shielding her wide blue eyes. She moved like a doe—beautiful in a way that didn't feel quite real.

"Pet, you're going to hurt him," Aina said sweetly in a thick Irish lilt. The tone was soft as church organ music behind closed doors. She slipped her fingers over Austin's, gently prying them from Hutch's arm. Hutch yanked his arm away dramatically.

"Damn you," he spat. "That hurt like hell."

"Learn your place."

"Like your lap dog, there?" he muttered toward Roo, his lip twitching. Roo let out a low, warning growl, eyes never leaving Hutch.

Starr stepped up behind Aina, giving Hutch a gentle shove toward the living room. She looked scared, her hand trembling slightly as she touched Austin's shoulder, but her eyes were full of quiet strength and loyalty.

"You're tired. Let us get everyone settled," she murmured.

Austin blinked, her nod wobbling. "I need you, Starr," she muttered.

"I know, baby."

"I mean, I need to talk to you." Austin's odd little smile appeared as Starr's fingers trailed down her arm, hooking their fingertips.

"I know what you're saying." Starr laughed softly, their shared smile lingering like a missed kiss. "I was just teasing."

"Yeah, I don't know," Austin said, smiling more shrewdly this time as she looked at their intertwined hands. "Then let go, please."

"Who's staying up first for the watch?" Golem boomed.

Everyone flinched at the sudden rumble of his deep voice.

Brandon's eyes flicked toward the stairs, half expecting Tessa to appear, sleepy and disoriented from the commotion. The cold floorboards pressed against his bare feet, grounding him in the middle of the chaos.

"Oh God, just go to sleep," Austin groaned. "It's safe here." Her eyes flicked to Brandon, searching his face. "Sorry. It's been a long three weeks—" she let out a shaky laugh, waving toward the ragtag group behind her, "—hauling this circus across the border. No passports, no papers, just luck and bad decisions. I did not plan on becoming a one-woman human-smuggling operation in Mexico."

"Oh, so we're baggage now," Aina muttered, puffing her bangs away from her eyes before ruffling Austin's hair.

"Pretty baggage," Austin shot back. "But still a traveling circus full of clowns." She jabbed a finger at Aina. "And absolutely no fires. Don't test me. I'm running on fumes and spite."

"No fires," Aina echoed. Then, with a conspiratorial wink at Brandon, she added, "Not unless you're cooking breakfast, boss."

Austin dragged her gaze to Brandon. "Hey, you got someplace private I can talk with Starr?"

Brandon nodded, pulse thundering. He caught Aina's anxious glance and offered a reassuring nod—he hoped it would help. He stared at the unfamiliar crowd gathered in his living room—a mismatched, weary bunch led by the mother of his daughter, missing for three years, now standing in his home with bruises, secrets, and a look that said everything was about to change.

Whatever this conversation would be, he felt it in his bones:

It would change everything.

Chapter −3

Austin sat in the chair, elbows on her knees, shirt pulled up to her collarbone. She'd asked to see Tessa, just to peek in while she slept, and Austin had expected Brandon to deny her. When he entered the kitchen, his suntanned face turned red at the sight of Starr tending Austin's wounds. He hesitated in the doorway, awkward and anxious, rubbing his hand through his hair as if he wanted to vanish. The kitchen still carried scents from last night's bacon and coffee, mixed with the faint antiseptic of Austin's bandages.

Until then, she'd always believed Brandon was a player— someone with girlfriends on every street corner, and herself just one more name. Looking back, she thought she'd been naïve the night they slept together. By the time he came to the hospital to pick up Tessa, he already had a new girlfriend. Hands in pockets, chin tucked, he could barely meet Austin's eyes. She remembered how handsome, tall, and skinny he'd looked, hair falling over his eyes as he nervously shook it away.

Still, those feelings lingered—then and now—stale and heavy in her belly. Shame and regret twisted inside Austin as she looked at Brandon. Brandon looked as inexperienced as a small town twelve-year-old caught spying on his sister's cute friend, wide-eyed and embarrassed.

"It's okay. She's a healer," Austin said, her voice low as she pulled her shirt down. As soon as she spoke, she realized how strange that sounded. Brandon's family was as homegrown farmer as they came. They probably still went to Doc Huntley. He'd been in that same office since landlines were cutting-edge technology. But if Brandon thought it was out of the ordinary, he didn't let on. He just turned around again as if trying to will the red out of his cheeks. She did see him wince at the cuts on her back, the welts on her shoulders.

"That looks—um, rough. Do you need to go to the hospital?" he asked.

Austin had told him no, they were healing just fine. He didn't ask what had happened. She figured he didn't care, and she wasn't offering anything. Resentment and disappointment simmered in her. His distance didn't hurt as much as the reminder of who they'd become. He stayed the hometown boy. She'd become someone else entirely—her life shaped by miles and danger. She'd traveled too far, seen too much, to ever fit that version of life again. That's when she asked to see Tessa. Because that wound, she knew, would never heal. And she may never have the chance to see her baby again.

Austin knew the rules. She'd signed the adoption papers lying in a hospital bed at Mercy Medical three years ago. *No contact*, it stated clearly. She knew he figured she was selfishly trading the kid for a college degree, a life. That wasn't the truth at all. Signing those papers had ripped her heart out.

Her dad had told her bluntly he'd take the baby, put her up for adoption, and wouldn't let Brandon touch her. He'd find a way to get "the idiot" put in jail for the rest of his life. He'd told her if she didn't do as she was told, she was dead to him, dead to the family.

Maternal instincts kicked in like a rabid dog. She did what it took to keep the newborn safe. It didn't matter. In the end, she was dead to her dad anyway. But she signed the papers. Her daddy left Brandon alone and left Tessa alone.

That night, Brandon had only nodded and said he figured she'd want to see Tessa. Austin stood outside the bedroom door, watching the little girl sleep for almost an hour. The room was filled with the scent of Tessa's baby-shampooed hair and the fresh, just-laundered smell of her comforter. Austin was desperate to engrave the image in her mind. Even if she tried, she knew the memory would fade, no matter how hard she fought to keep it. "She wears glasses like me?"

"Yeah, like you used to wear. The thick ones."

Her nose was Austin's. She couldn't see much more in the dim light. But every inch of her was like a mirror image of herself at three and a half years old.

"Is she—is she like me?" Austin asked cautiously. "I mean, is she hyper and stuff?"

"She's really easygoing," he'd said, voice soft as silk.

Austin had exhaled in relief, her nerves releasing the tension that had knotted in her shoulders.

Later, she sobbed herself to sleep—quiet, desperate tears she tried to muffle against the musty, scratchy couch. Grief, guilt, and longing sliced through her chest, raw enough to steal her breath. Starr climbed beside her, encircling her in warmth, holding Austin until exhaustion claimed her at last.

Austin awakened to Brandon's girlfriend scream-whispering at him outside his upstairs bedroom two hours later—around seven in the morning. The fight continued down the stairs and out the front door. The girlfriend was a fake redhead with long hair tied back in a ponytail, wearing blue nurse scrubs. She had a frayed, store-brand white sweater hanging sloppily over her arm.

Who the hell was the creep sitting on the porch? And what the hell was going on downstairs? It looked like a freak show had blown up in the living room.

Brandon's footsteps kept going when the screen door slammed behind him, but their voices still carried across the porch.

She's Tessa's mom, Lyndsey. She's got a right to see her.

Some mom. She handed her over at the hospital and ran like hell. And all of a sudden, she's come back? How do you know she's not here to steal her, huh?

Austin knew nobody suspected the truth about her dad—the man everyone thought was the always-the-good-guy type. Instead, she would always be the bad guy for leaving the kid. Maybe she was. Living in a car wasn't the life for a newborn. Brandon hadn't wanted to marry her.

She sloughed it off and headed toward the porch. The "creep" on the porch turned out to be Golem. Austin swore he never dozed more than an hour on any given night. He'd devour buckets of fried chicken wings and cheesy bread without a second thought—then spend half the night groaning with a belly ache.

Starr always tried steering him toward low-calorie salads at restaurants. He'd dutifully eat the salad, then calmly order three burgers, two fries, and four sides of scrambled eggs. Now he sat on the steps, massive and unbothered, quietly chuckling at the chaos while digging into a bag of potato chips like he was in a theater watching a comedy. Austin stepped outside into the crisp morning air. "Hen-pecked or fighting?"

"Yep." Golem's voice was deep, and his vocabulary ragged at best. He came from the Czech Republic and often struggled as English words tangled with Czech in his mind. But what he lacked in fluency, he made up for in charm. He was incredibly gentle by nature—protective, and quick to offer a sweet smile.

"Let them have some privacy," Austin told him. She had tied her hair back, still in last night's clothes—jean shorts and a T-shirt—but after a shower, she felt clean again.

"No, no fighting," he corrected her. "I don't like fighting."

"People fight, Golem," Austin whispered, tugging at his seat. It wasn't easy—he was a giant, seven foot five and over five hundred pounds, all dense muscle. "They argue. It's okay. That's how people work things out. She's fine. He won't hurt her."

"I'm not afraid for woman. I am afraid for man," he said, nodding toward Brandon's back. Austin sighed. Fair enough.

"You fight," he said. "You didn't work things out with those men who attacked us on the boat."

"They had guns, knives, and big fists," she replied. "Look at Brandon's girlfriend. She's just got little fists, and she's not even using them to hit." Austin glanced up, catching Brandon and his girlfriend staring at her from the driveway. "Come inside, big guy," she said softly. "Please. I don't want to talk about it now. Remember what we talked about? We don't tell anybody what happened. I was protecting you. It is my job."

"You didn't protect Paolo."

Austin drew in a slow breath, then let it out. "I did my best. But there were a lot of people to fight—"

"No, I saw you—"

"Golem," Austin said, her face flushing. She hushed the man with a pat on his arm. "You're fighting with me now, don't you see?" she continued with a warning twist of her head. He blinked slowly, chewing on her words until the realization hit. His face sagged with sadness she instantly felt mirrored in herself.

"I'm sorry."

"Do you miss Paolo?" she asked softly.

"The happy side of Paolo."

"Yeah, me too. Come on. Let's go inside, wash up, and get ready to leave." Austin grabbed his arm and playfully pulled the huge man to his feet. He came easily. "We're going to find us a place to live happily ever after."

"Happily ever after. All of us together."

"Yep."

But she'd promised Brandon she would leave before Tessa woke up. Really, he'd asked her to go before his girlfriend got off work at eight at Mercy Medical and drove thirty-two minutes to his house. Lyndsey had come early, bringing a bag of breakfast biscuits for him, and slammed them on the kitchen table before storming out.

~

Austin dreaded waking the bodies sprawled across the living room. She stood in the doorway, shoulder against the cool wooden frame, breathing in the smell of old blankets and the earthy tang of freshly cut grass blowing in from the open window. She watched them, lost in the deep, safe sleep they hadn't known in weeks.

Aina snored contentedly, face pressed into the couch, a tiny clutch purse resting at her waist. Her breath carried the peppermint tang of the gum Starr gave her for anxiety and acid reflux, mingling with the old, dusty upholstery. Austin eyed the purse. She certainly did not remember Aina buying it. Odds were good it was stolen. Aina probably had a lighter tucked somewhere within; she loved to steal and set things alight—grass, T-shirts, and, to Roo's endless irritation, his fuzzy fluorescent yellow tennis balls.

Still, Austin let her sleep. She'd regret the momentary lapse in judgment later; there was probably enough hay in the barn for Aina to ignite half of West Virginia. Her eyes drifted left. Hutch was smiling in his sleep, hands pressed together and tucked under his cheek. He didn't look fifteen—more like twelve lying there. Still, she could see the growth spurt coming; with the way he'd been eating, he'd shot up two inches in the last month alone.

"You want to talk, let them sleep?" It was Brandon who came up behind her. Austin heard the door close quietly, then listened as his steps stopped just short of her bare feet.

"Sure." She nodded at the shadow stretching across the living room. In truth, her stomach lurched; she wanted to run, not talk. Fear and dread churned inside her, but she said, "I'll buy them all the time I can get."

Brandon sniffed a laugh, crossed the room quietly, and picked up the bag of Mister Salty's sausage biscuits. The greasy, savory smell filled the air, making Austin's empty stomach twist. He waved her toward the kitchen. She wasn't intimidated by anyone—except, perhaps, Brandon. "Sit," he told her, pointing to the ragged wooden chair at the kitchen table.

She did so slowly. The worn wood creaked beneath her, cool against her thighs. She felt more like a third grader who'd been told by the teacher to sit in the chair outside the classroom for punishment.

"I'll make you breakfast." He held up the bag as if it were an offering. "You drink coffee?"

"Sure."

"You haven't changed. You get right to the point," Austin declared. She rested her chin in her palm and leaned forward. "I haven't changed either. I can lie to you or not say anything at all."

"Oh, yeah, you've changed." He had started to put a filter in the coffee maker. He came to a standstill, turned, and leaned his rear against the counter. "It's not that the glasses are gone—it's the way you stand there and look me right in the eyes. Where have you been, Austin? Tell me the truth." He breathed in deeply and eyed her.

23

"Two days ago, if you'd walked in here, I would've sworn to everybody I'd send you packing. I wouldn't let you talk to our kid. I'd figured you were dead, maybe drugged out, buried off some highway. Maybe you finished college, changed your name. I'd had a thousand things go through my mind about where you were. I can't tell you how many missing person advertisements I've read. A thousand. It becomes obsessive. I'd sneak down here at night, trying to find you. Lyndsey, she thought I was looking up porn. You know what? It was easier telling her that's what I was doing than telling her I was trying to find my kid's mom so—"

"Dead?" Austin laughed harshly in objection. "*Dead* people don't deposit money in *live* people's accounts." And she'd been doing that for Brandon for the last three and a half years.

That was bullshit and felt like a knife in her gut.

"That's nice, Spaz. Real nice." Brandon grunted at her eye roll.

Austin didn't say anything more. It just irritated her. "If I tell you, I would put you in danger."

He laughed at her then, a warm chuckle with his eyes crinkling at the corners. "You sound like one of those Tuesday night dramas on TV. Please don't tell me you're being chased by the feds—or—or you're a terrorist."

"I told you. I will lie to you. I don't want to, so please don't ask."

"Okay, let me put it this way." Brandon brought his hand up and rubbed it against his chin.

Austin smiled, looking at the table. She knew he was smiling too. He wasn't flirting with her now, but he was so accustomed to that smile, he probably didn't even realize he was doing it. "Do you want to see Tessa? Do you want to stay here a couple of days and get to know your kid?" Brandon asked. "Because if you do—and I think you do—you'll tell me if you're putting Tessa and me in danger. You'll tell me why you're dragging a delegate from every country in the world into my house."

"I can't."

"No, listen. I've been dating Lyndsey seriously for a few months.

She's sweet. She's nice. She's a hard worker and a smart gal. She's the marrying type. I'm putting my relationship on the line here. She's pissed I let you in. She's even more pissed I didn't stop her from leaving. It's not for you, okay? It's for Tessa. I think she needs to know who her mama is. She asks about you—"

"What did you tell her?"

"Her mama needed to *find her way home*." He shrugged. "Maybe she's lost. It probably isn't the most normal thing to tell a kid, but I'm winging it here as a single dad."

Austin stared at Brandon. For a moment, she let her soul show—something she never did for anyone else. "I'm scared," she admitted softly. "What if she doesn't like me? What if I'm not pretty enough, or I say the wrong thing?" His hair was slightly askew, like he'd been rubbing his hand through it with worry. He just looked like an anxious kid to her, gentle and kind. Austin's eyes stung with unshed tears. She didn't tell Brandon how beautiful that sounded—*her mama needed to find her way home*—instead of telling Tessa that her mama had just disappeared, didn't care, just walked away.

"She'll like you. You look like her. You act like her."

"I want to stay," Austin said. "You have no idea how long I've dreamed about coming here, seeing her. But I'm begging you—let me keep my secrets."

"Nope."

"Brandon, please let me see her." Austin stood up. "You don't need to tell her who I am." She wasn't inexperienced with men anymore. She knew the right look; the right touch could sway them at least briefly. She stepped across the room, reached out, and grazed his arm with her fingers. Austin let her gaze—wide-eyed and sad—find its way slowly up to his. "Let me keep my friends safe for a few days, keep the secrets. Until I leave. Then I will tell you."

Chapter −4

When Brandon was in third grade, the playground was his battlefield. Dodgeball was his weapon—dart, twist, survive Eric Tyler's red rubber missiles. Eric, the playground's golden boy and future quarterback, never missed. Tug of war was the other game he loved. He hardly ever ended up on the winning team, but he liked the feeling of everyone pulling together.

His life with Austin had always been dodgeball—quick, unpredictable, sharp retorts flying from all directions. But with her misfit crew, he felt tug of war: one rope, everyone straining together, for better or worse.

Fear radiated off Austin now as Tessa slipped down the stairs. Each step was slow, cautious. Austin's knuckles blanched. Her group moved instinctively—Roo nudging her shoulder, Starr brushing her arm, Stats lifting his head in quiet alertness.

"Daddy?"

He rounded the corner. Tessa's hair stuck up every which way, her fairy pajama shirt faded, and her pink pants were on backward. Thumb in her mouth. Brandon's stomach lurched—did Austin think he hadn't taken good care of her?

He lifted Tessa, masking nerves with a grin. "We had some visitors while you were sleeping. Want Daddy to make your toast with honey?"

"Yeah, toast with honey," she murmured against his shoulder, peeking at the strangers.

The kitchen smelled of burnt toast and coffee. Stats hunched over Brandon's ancient laptop, tattooed fingers tapping like a woodpecker. Someone whispered about groceries. Someone else about wiring money. Brandon ignored Lyndsey's eighth text vibrating on the counter.

The kitchen noise faded behind Austin as she slipped outside.

"Here, I'll take her for a minute." Starr appeared beside him, hands out. "Austin's freaking out."

And now Brandon had handed his daughter to a perfect stranger. But something about the woman named Starr—her calm voice, her steady eyes—made it feel okay.

Outside, Austin paced, the sun too bright; every crunch of gravel an alarm. Roo sat on the truck hood, fingers tapping a frantic rhythm, watching as if she might bolt.

"She's perfect. I don't deserve her." Austin's voice cracked. "I shouldn't be here. I came back for reasons I can't even explain—not to her, not to you. I could've stayed gone."

"You sent money," Brandon said quietly.

Austin stared past him at the barn.

Memories rose unbidden—blank envelopes with crumpled bills, then twenties and fifties. Later, a thousand every two weeks. And the Christmas deposit of six hundred that had kept his truck legal and the lights on. He never asked how she'd gotten his account number. He didn't want to know.

"When I left, I lived in a two-hundred-dollar car," Austin said softly. "I ate dollar-store cereal for every meal. I panhandled outside a gas station once for a hamburger." Her voice thinned. "I told myself if I couldn't be her mom, I could at least keep the lights on here." She chuckled like it hurt. "That first five I sent was from selling my suitcase to a pawn shop, mailed with a borrowed stamp." She drew a shaky breath. "I worked bars. Restaurants. Then I gave blood for extra cash and signed up for medical trials. I got a few grants. A philanthropist helped me finish school in two years while I worked for him; that's where I met this crew. Everything he gave me, I pawned if I could. I sent it to you." She swallowed. "I sold a diamond ring worth twelve thousand dollars for four hundred. He asked why I wasn't wearing it. I said I lost it. He bought me another. I sold that too."

"Who...was the philanthropist?" Brandon asked.

"It doesn't matter." Her eyes flickered. "He's dead."

She forced a small smile. "I just didn't want you thinking I didn't try."

Before Brandon could answer, the screen door slammed. Starr set Tessa on the top step. Tessa held a piece of toast in her fist, jelly smeared across her cheeks. "She wants her daddy," Starr said. Tessa ran to Brandon. Arms out. Austin flinched. Hope and dread crossing her face. Tessa peered at Austin over Brandon's shoulder, uncertain and wary. A low rumble broke the moment. Tires on gravel. Austin stiffened. Her eyes found the road.

"Roo!" she called out to the man lounging on the truck hood. "In the truck. Stay." A Danville police cruiser pulled up, its blue-and-silver decal glinting in the sun. Austin exhaled through her teeth. "Why does everything have to be so complicated?"

"You don't have a reason for the cops to be here, right?" she asked Brandon.

"No," he muttered.

She tried a smile. It faltered. A small blue pouch emerged from her pocket—soft from years of use. She dangled it gently toward Tessa. "These are Worry Dolls from Guatemala," she whispered. "If you tell them your fears before bed, they hold the worries for you. Maybe your daddy can show you how they work while I talk to the police?"

Brandon didn't take more than two steps before the officer—Ben Jackson—was out of the car. Austin's brother. Mid-twenties. Brick-built. Eyes sharp as broken glass.

"Hey, little sis," he said, looming, shadow swallowing her. "I bail you out in Texas, you keep moving. That was the deal. Instead, you burn through my favors, drag in guns and lawyers—and now this circus?"

Austin stared past him, jaw tight. "I had things to take care of."

Ben scoffed, moved his gaze to Brandon. "Did she tell you she stole a truck in Mexico and drove it through the checkpoint sideways? Gas tanks blew. I'm surprised she isn't dead."

"Um... no," Brandon muttered.

Ben jabbed a finger at her chest. "I could've left you there. Should've. And now you're standing here like nothing happened?"

"Yeah," she snapped. "It was a blast for me too—sitting in jail thinking you left me there to rot."

"Don't mouth off." His laugh was a growl. "Mom doesn't want you. Dad hates you. Nobody wants you here. Especially not him." He pointed at Brandon. "You're trouble. Get in that truck and drive." The door slammed behind them. Austin flinched. Golem filled the doorway, enormous and tense.

"What the hell is—*that*?" Ben's hand drifted to his holster.

"It is *who*," Austin corrected. "His name is Josef."

"He's got a gun, Pet," Golem murmured.

"He's my brother," Austin said softly. "His name's Ben."

Golem tilted his head. "Like *my* Konrad? Or *my* Petr?"

Austin blinked. "Which one's Petr again?"

"The brother who locked me in the chicken pen when I sat on his cat. Konrad was the one who tried to trade me for a car."

"Oh." Austin nodded. "Yeah. He's definitely a Petr."

"Ah." Golem nodded with grave understanding.

"Shit on a stick," Ben scowled. "Where do you dig up these freak friends?"

Tessa perked up like she'd been handed a new vocabulary word. "Shit on a stick. Ew. What *is* that?"

Brandon rubbed his forehead. "Tessa, honey... that's a big-people phrase we do *not* repeat."

Ben sneered. "You're done here, Austin. Dad said forever. Three hours. If that stolen heap of junk is still here, I'll check the plates myself. I'll haul all of you in." His eyes wandered to Brandon. He poked a finger in his direction. "Including him."

"That's harsh," Austin whispered, voice breaking despite her best efforts.

"You've done plenty to earn it." Ben leaned close. "Remember steal-the-flag? You cried and ran to Dad. Lost the whole game for your team. You made messes then—you're making bigger ones now."

Austin's shoulders curled inward. "We haven't eaten in two days," she said quietly. "We're wearing the same clothes we had when we left. Let me give them breakfast. Lunch. Supper. Then we'll go."

"No," Ben said flatly. "Three hours."

Austin swallowed, nodded once. "Fine."

But her chin trembled. "Ask Dad about Papaw's necklace," she said. "Please."

"He's not giving you anything." Ben's jaw tightened. "You're dead to him. Leave it."

Before anyone could respond, tires screeched on the gravel again, sending a cloud of dust rolling up the road. The wind pushed it aside—and Austin froze, eyes locked on the tree line.

A dark outline stood between the oaks. Motionless. Watching.

The whole porch went silent.

Tessa pressed her Worry Doll bag to her cheek and whispered, "Daddy... I don't like that."

Brandon pulled her closer. The wind rattled the fence.

And in the quiet that followed, Austin heard only one word echo in her mind—Run.

Chapter −5

"So—" Austin waited for Ben to drive off in a spray of gravel and dust. She turned to Brandon, mustering a small smile even as her stomach twisted with anxiety. "Can I play dolls with Tessa for two hours and fifty-five minutes, or until she gets sick of me?" Brandon shrugged, barely looking at her, indifferent as ever.

"I don't have to work until four," Brandon replied. "Take two hours and fifty-eight minutes if you want."

She forced a laugh but felt like crying. She spent an hour on the porch step with Tessa, who sat on Brandon's lap while they sorted the tiny rag dolls from the pouch again and again. Brandon leaned back in the sunlight, phone in hand, texting or occasionally glancing up at the sky.

"Do you want me to tell you a story?" Austin asked Tessa. Tessa only blinked at her from behind her oversized, round glasses—her blue eyes magnified beneath the thick lenses. "How about I tell you a story my papaw told me when I was your age?" Austin didn't wait for an answer. She settled back on the step, picturing her papaw in his old wooden chair, gazing at the night sky. She remembered playing with her toys at his feet, half-listening, half-playing, until her mom would disappear inside to wash supper dishes. About ten seconds after the door slammed, her papaw would crane his neck and clear his throat. That was always the sign—a scary story was coming, and Austin would inch closer to his feet. She loved those stories, even if her mom complained they kept her awake at night.

"My papaw used to tell me stories about his people—the Ani Yunwiya, the First People," Austin whispered. "They call them Cherokee now, but back then, they were simply The First. My papaw would say, 'Sit down, Little Turtle Girl, I will tell you a story.' He called me Little Turtle Girl because of my thick glasses—he said they made me look like a turtle." Austin pointed to her own eyes. Tessa looked up, blinking shyly behind her own thick lenses.

"Nice," Brandon said dourly, peering at Austin.

"He didn't mean it to be mean," Austin retorted quietly. "He liked turtles. And I was little, and I did look like one to him. It isn't any worse than me calling you High Five." She shrugged. Then she turned back to Tessa. "One day, huge birds called the Tlanuhwa began swooping down and stealing little boys and girls from their village and taking them to their caves." Austin watched Tessa's eyes blink twice. She'd caught her attention. "The warriors, the fighters of the village, set out to find the children, and they found them inside the Tlanuhwa's caves along with the big bird's eggs. But just as they rescued the little boys and girls, the Tlanuhwa returned with more children."

"Did the big birds eat the little girls?"

"No, because the warriors began throwing the bird eggs down into a river below to get their attention. And the Uktena, a huge snake with giant wings and horns that lived in the river, came up and began eating the eggs."

"Did the snake— Uktena—eat the little girls?" Tessa asked softly, trying hard to make her little lips say the words just as Austin said them.

"No, so angered by the snake eating their eggs, the Tlanuhwa dropped the children and began fighting the huge serpent. The children were rescued, and the big birds flew far away." Austin raised her hand in a fist, then opened it wide to wiggle her fingers like wings.

"Don't tell me we're leaving." There was a sudden burst of footsteps from inside the house. "What the hell did you do this time?" It was Hutch slamming the front door.

Austin was so sick of Hutch's bellyaching that she just wanted to scream at him. She didn't remember being this whiny when she was fifteen.

"Well, the scary stories she's telling Tessa aren't helping," Brandon murmured, barely looking up from his phone.

"Oh God, you're not telling her those stories you used to tell me, are you? The ones your papaw told you? Those are freaking terrifying."

Austin ignored Hutch's remark. Far be it from her to bring up the fact that his Aztec history seemed far more violent than her own. "Your ancestors offered human sacrifices, Hutch," Austin tossed at him. "What could be more terrifying than having your stomach ripped out? And yes, we are leaving. I told you not to get comfortable unless I tell you to get comfortable."

"You always throw that in my face, Pet, as if I had any control in what my parents or their parents did. You need to come up with something else. You know how much I hate you, right?"

"Yeah, because I got to hear it all the way up the coast, all the way from Texas to West Virginia. At every rest stop and every diner, you made it quite clear."

"You know I get treated like royalty in my country, right?" Hutch ran his hand through his hair. Thick, dark, perfect. Austin figured he could probably pass as an Aztec deity if he wanted to. "You'd be arrested," he went on. "And I'd suggest they use you as a sacrifice except we all know you aren't a virgin, so the gods would be mad and spit you back out. You know how much I hate you, right?"

"I do." Austin watched him start to sit down. She pushed her hair back. "I need some time with Brandon and Tessa. Go inside. Get something to eat."

He made a show of getting up. Austin waited until he closed the door behind him. "He's hungry," she murmured. "He gets so grumpy when he hasn't eaten, even though I know he's gotten into just about everything in your refrigerator. I'll pay you back."

"You don't have to give me money. There wasn't much in there. I haven't been shopping this week yet."

Austin didn't answer. Yes, she did. She knew he didn't have much money. He'd used every penny she'd sent.

"Yeah, he's a bit spoiled. Always gets what he wants. And it isn't just because he's pretty. His mom and dad are rich and bought him everything. They just weren't good at giving him guidelines. His village—they worship him. He's the seventh son of the seventh son. When Paolo found him, he bought him everything but the sun to keep him from running away—"

"Paolo?" Brandon asked.

"I guess I told you I'd tell you some things before I left." Austin looked up. Brandon was still staring at the sky. Maybe he didn't really care. "Paolo was the one who took me in. He funded the projects at Southern West Virginia State College. He liked to collect *things*. I helped him find those *things*." She opened her mouth to say more, then paused. "But the more stuff Paolo bought, the more stuff Hutch wanted. I just don't think he wants material stuff. I'm not sure how to show him that, so he's a work in progress."

"Okay... so what *thing* is Hutch?"

"Oh God, you were listening." Austin groaned.

Brandon looked at her from the corner of his eye.

"Well," she went on. "You were looking everywhere but at me." She sighed. "Hutch is short for Huitzilopochtli, the Aztec warrior god. The god is often shown as a hummingbird, which annoys Hutch because his mom branded her clothing line with a tiny hummingbird logo. Hutch wants to be seen as a fighter, not something delicate. Paolo used to say Hutch was a descendant of the real warrior behind the legend, and that his family kept their lineage pure. His real name is Frederico. We clash sometimes—he's got a strong personality."

"And Golem?"

Austin laughed. "He's from outside Prague. Big farm boy like you. It was whispered in his village that he was a Golem since the day he was born. His mother was almost seventy when she had him. They said he weighed fifty pounds when he was three weeks old. He's not a golem. He isn't even Jewish." She sighed. "And Stats— what he lacks in socialization, he makes up for in intelligence. His IQ is like 160. He's from Greece and is descended from Apollo, per original records from 1868."

Austin snuck a peek at Brandon. He was looking at her—and then looked away. "I know you think we're weird. I usually have a kiwi fruit for this moment so I can talk about everyone's sweet inside and the strange fuzzy outside—"

"Who's weird? I don't think you guys are weird." Brandon looked at her, and by God, his furrowed brow and curious eyes were genuine. "They're all just from different places, have different accents. I'm not used to that here."

Austin went still. Her eyes flicked up, startled; she hadn't heard someone defend her people in years. Warmth rose too fast, too sharp. Instinctively, she braced for the joke, the jab, the inevitable backhanded dig. But none came. Just sincerity—simple, steady— and it rattled her more than any insult ever could.

"Oh," she murmured, barely a breath. She turned quickly before the moment could grow roots.

"Tessa, can I get a hug before I go?" she asked.

Tessa scooted deeper into Brandon's lap instead.

"How about a smile, then?" Brandon offered.

Tessa grabbed a swatch of his shirt and gave a shy smile.

Austin smiled back—but then the distant grind of tires on gravel shattered the quiet morning. A harsh metallic sound echoed through the stillness. The faint smell of exhaust drifted in through the screen, mixing with cut grass and yesterday's rain. Turning her head, she watched as a dark car—or rather, six of them—slipped single file into Brandon's driveway. "You aren't expecting anybody, right?" Austin knew how stupid the question sounded the second it left her mouth.

"No," Brandon said. His eyes lifted. He tipped his head upward.

Austin looked west. She heard helicopters—big ones—riding the horizon. "Aw, crud, what else could go wrong?" She stood up, shoved her hands on her head, and turned toward the reverberation of helicopter blades. The deep thrum vibrated in her chest, rattling the windows. The oily tang of aviation fuel hung in the air.

"Do you want to take Tessa inside?" She didn't smile. She just puffed out her cheeks and walked to the door.

"What can I do? Austin, how bad is this?"

"You're fine." She rose with him, listening to the cars grind to a halt as she stuck her head inside.

She saw Starr starting to rise. "Did Hutch go back and get his phone after I tossed it?"

"Yes."

"Shit!" Austin stomped her foot. "You know it's really difficult to protect all of you when you're constantly stabbing me in the back." She narrowed her eyes at Starr, then at Aina, who was nervously chewing on a fingernail.

"He was homesick. All his pictures were on it," Starr said softly. "And... he just wanted to play his games."

"If he's homesick, he can go home," Austin groaned. "We've dealt with—and survived—more danger in the last month than any of his action-adventure games could dream up. Where is he?"

All eyes went to the kitchen. Roo hopped up and pointed a thumb at Hutch standing by the table. "How do you know it's me?" Hutch growled.

"The United States Air Force just scrambled jets to keep this from becoming an international incident. If not, your daddy is in his helicopter sending Mexico's idea of Navy SEALs to get you," Austin told him. "Come on. While I play delegate, you're going to—"

"Don't make him go." That was Stats, head bobbing over a game of Solitaire. "There's a ninety-six percent chance he will never finish school. Only four percent of dropouts return. There is an eighty-two percent chance he will—"

"Stop, Stats," Austin said. "I get it."

She looked at the others. Each nodded in support of Hutch.

"What the heck?" Austin threw her hands out. "I don't have a choice. If we don't go out there, they're coming in here." She turned to Hutch. "What were you thinking? You know they can track you by your phone. You should have thought it through. Come!"

"Pet, stop it!" Starr swept across the room and wrapped an arm around Hutch, pulling him slightly behind her.

"Why are you coddling him?" Austin snapped. "You're not the one stuck between the bad guys and the good guys, taking hits from both sides while everyone else scatters like scared rabbits.

Sometimes I think you set these situations up just so you can watch me take the—" She stopped abruptly when she caught Brandon watching her, one brow raised. Austin blew out a sharp breath. "Whatever. Hutch, come on. I cannot stress this enough—you have got to start living up to your name at some point—"

"A hummingbird?" Starr snorted.

Austin shot her a look sharp enough to freeze the floorboards. As much as she wanted Hutch to sit with the sting of that—because humiliation was sometimes the only thing that got through to him—she reined herself in.

"It's not the bird," she said, jaw tight. "It's the symbol—Huitzilopochtli, the god of war. Until he learns self-control and how to follow orders before acting on his own, he'll never grow into the strength he deserves —nor will he be bequeathed that honor."

They barely made it to the porch when three well-armed men in black suits stopped at the steps. Brandon followed her out—minus Tessa—his eyes wide. Eight more men in riot gear formed a semicircle in the yard.

"Are you Austin Jackson?"

"I am." Sweat pooled at her brow. She swiped it away and caught the acrid scent of gun oil as one man shifted his rifle.

"None of us have guns," she said, raising her hands.

"And this is Frederico Arias?" a second suit asked.

"Yes." Austin nodded. Hutch looked like he might leap off the porch. Austin raised a hand to hold him back.

"We have Marco Arias landing in the field adjacent to the barn. We need the young man to come with us."

Hutch froze. Like a bear cub caught in a leg-hold trap. "I don't want to go," he grunted. He nudged Austin's shoulder with one knuckle. "Please and thank you."

Austin drew a slow breath. "Mister Arias prefers to meet with his father in private. We will prepare a meeting area in the house."

"Miss Jackson, you know we can't do that. Frederico Arias must come with us."

"No. Señor Arias insists." She rested her hand on Hutch's shoulder. "And the respect of the property owner must be taken into consideration." She gestured toward Brandon—pale, blinking at the sight of his lawn covered in tactical gear.

"You can tell Marco Arias," Austin continued, "that if he visits this property as a delegate of Mexico, he is either considered a guest of this home or an enemy. In West Virginia, guests enter the home and sit at the table for coffee to discuss concerns. Enemies stand in the cornfield with guns and call the owner outside. It is a sign of hostility. A readiness to battle."

The man with the headset relayed the message. Silence followed.

He finally nodded. "Señor Arias agrees. He will meet inside the home."

~

"Coffee. We need coffee. And toast. And jelly." Austin rushed inside. "Brandon, I swear, I owe you my left kidney."

"I'll take your right kidney. Lyndsey will take your left," Brandon muttered, grabbing the coffee from the freezer. "I saw her out there. The men in black were gutting her car. She might want both your kidneys and part of your heart."

"Do you want to go out there with her?" Austin sighed. "I'm sorry. I was preoccupied with Homeland Security." She turned to him. "I bet you hate me now. Can you add jelly to the toast and cut it into quarters?"

"Right now, I should probably get your toast," Brandon said. "She can wait. I'd hate to think I caused a war with South America because my girlfriend was mad at me."

"You're right. You understand you should sit in on this, right? You own the property." Austin wanted to kick herself for coming here. "All you have to do is stand and nod—*crap*—"

She stuck her head into the living room. "How exactly do we greet your dad? Handshake? Bow?"

Hutch gave her a saucy scowl. "How do *you* usually meet him on your little rendezvous—*in a nightgown*?"

Austin narrowed her eyes. He relented with a sigh. "Fine. Shake his hand."

"Yeah, yeah. Makes sense," Austin said. "We're in West Virginia. Our territory."

"Territory?" Brandon said as she re-entered the kitchen. "You make it sound like a battlefield."

"Uh-huh. Wait until you meet Marco Arias. You'll understand why my brain is running a hundred battle strategies. And you, lucky man, are on the frontline."

"Is Tessa safe?"

Austin froze.

The question sliced deep.

She dropped her gaze.

"So, you still have trust issues," she said quietly. "Still always on guard." She exhaled. "Let me confide something."

She met his eyes.

"Sometimes late at night, when I can't sleep, I try not to count on my left hand how many people ever believed in me. Not my dad. Not my mom. Not my brothers. My teachers only paid attention because I was the judge's daughter." Her voice thinned. "And then there's you, Brandon. You noticed me. And for that short time we were together, you made me see things I never saw before. You became the one damn person I wanted to impress. To prove I wasn't a complete idiot." Her throat tightened. "Don't question my judgment. Don't—don't question me. I don't know what I'd do if I didn't have at least one finger to hold up for the only person I ever thought believed in me."

Chapter −6

Three days ago, if someone had asked Brandon where his life was heading, he would have said he planned to keep working at Gent's Hardware. His dream was to pay off his family's five-hundred-acre farm—a legacy spanning over a century and a half. With the debt gone, he'd raise cattle, maybe a few pigs, and finally make enough to stay home with Tessa instead of sending her to strangers for babysitting.

"I know what makes your life easier," Austin was saying to him. "But what's your real dream—the thing you've always wanted to do but that feels just out of reach? I think that's what Señor Arias wants to know. He can have anything he wants; he was born to money. He's curious about the gap between what's possible for people in America and what's actually attainable. You've got to understand—many of his peers get a lot of flak for not doing anything about the poverty in their communities."

Brandon stared at Austin. What the hell? Was she really calling him out as poor, right in front of everyone?

"I'm not poor," Brandon said, careful and wary.

He scanned the crowded kitchen table: two bodyguards in matching suits flanking the doorway, a heavyset interpreter with a nervous habit of tapping her pen, a slender assistant clutching a notepad, and Marco Arias himself. Marco's black hair and chiseled features were unforgettable—but it was the way he watched, eyes flat and unblinking, that unsettled Brandon far more than his looks.

Marco looked just like he had in the magazine Lyndsey flashed at Kim in the grocery store three weeks ago. "Now that's drop-dead gorgeous," she'd whispered, grinning, and both women had giggled like teenagers.

Even Brandon had to admit the guy was striking—slim, well-built, probably in his forties. The memory flickered, quick and sharp, then vanished beneath the tension in the kitchen.

"Of course not. I didn't mean to imply that," Austin said firmly.

She sat up straighter, all business, even in her T-shirt and shorts. Somehow, the grungy clothes vanished beneath the weight of her presence. She spoke slowly for the interpreter. "Your family farm is huge compared to most in South America. But you work. You don't live off your daddy's paycheck. You're part of a community. You dig your hands into the dirt. Historically, that's blue-collar. But the point is this—"

She leaned closer, voice steady.

"Here in the U.S., if you wanted to start a record company, or open a business, or do anything like that, there's at least a path to try. In Señor Arias's country, even with money, those kinds of opportunities haven't always existed. People in his position get a lot of criticism for not doing more to help their communities climb out of poverty."

She motioned toward Brandon.

"That's why you're an enigma to him, Brandon. You work. You choose your own direction. You aren't handed anything. Back to his question—what is your dream?"

Nobody had ever asked him that.

And now fourteen strangers were watching him in his worn-out kitchen. The air felt tight—someone shifted their feet, a chair leg scraped over the linoleum, and one of the guards coughed behind a fist. Most were guards, with two interpreters and a few assistants. He'd dragged in every lawn chair and battered dining chair he owned, but eight people still had to stand. Brandon felt exposed— the hardware clerk trying to keep his head above water each month.

"I guess I'd like to be my own boss. Raise a real cattle herd someday, not just work at a hardware store," he answered carefully. "It sounds possible, but when you're juggling bills, paying off old family debts from a president who messed with tariffs, and raising a little kid... dreams start to feel out of reach."

"Yes, thank you," Austin said, nodding at Brandon. "That's exactly what I'm trying to help Señor Arias understand. My whole point was that you're a good man—a hardworking man, but that is not enough. You dig yourself out of bills and debt every day.

Meanwhile, like most U.S. politicians, neither he nor his son have ever had to worry about health insurance, childcare, food on their table, or losing their home because their paycheck simply is not sufficient."

"I have learned more than you think." For the first time, Hutch spoke. He tugged one earbud out, held it in his fist. Brandon had assumed the kid was zoning out, but apparently, he heard every word. "I do all my schoolwork. I'm learning to drive. Austin—I mean, Miss Jackson—gives me chores like washing dishes and cleaning my room—"

"Taking out the trash," Austin added.

"He takes out trash?" Señor Arias's translator said.

"That is despicable," Marco declared, his tone calm but edged with ice. "No son of mine will shame our family by touching someone else's waste."

Hutch's big eyes drifted toward Austin. She cringed, shrugged.

"It's a rite of passage, isn't that what you call it, Miss Jackson? It's what makes a man." Hutch said. "Boys take out the trash—a reminder that every role has value and deserves respect. No job is *beneath* anyone. It fosters respect for every contribution. Makes them a better leader."

He said something in Spanish—fast, low, aimed at his father alone. Marco lifted a hand to halt the interpreter.

Austin tugged on her lower lip. Hutch's face went white.

"No." He turned rigidly to Austin. "I don't want to marry yet. I don't want to go into the military."

Austin straightened. "He needs guidance. He needs self-control. He's too young to marry. Surely you're joking," she muttered. "At some point, he will lead politically. Do you want him to be a dog on a leash like your leaders now?"

"But he doesn't need any of this," the interpreter blurted. "He has money."

Austin's eyes sharpened into a storm. "Bullshit. That's an easy out. Money doesn't buy everything. What has it gotten him so far?"

She rose, palms braced on the table. "Where was he when Paolo Bertinelli and I found him? Twelve years old, drunk, held hostage by terrorists. He wasted your money, wasted your country's money. Ran away every time you dragged him home. Lied, cheated, stole. Do you really think the people in your region want to be ruled by a slack-jawed drug addict? No. *That* is outrageous. Despicable."

She stabbed a finger in Hutch's direction, her voice trembling with barely checked fury. "Now he's homeschooled. Prepping for college. Wants to try a real high school like a real American kid. He's smart, and he works. He washes dishes with me on Tuesdays. You can't run a country and babysit him. Think of me as his nanny."

Marco Arias rose with deliberate slowness, fury simmering beneath his polished exterior. He shouted so fast the interpreter struggled to keep up. "You say I don't watch over him! The things he did were boyhood mischiefs. I saw what was left of the ship after it was hijacked! Your Paolo died! I don't want him involved in any of this—whatever you do!"

"For God's sake, you want to send him to the military!" Austin shouted back. "His only injury that day was a bruise on his elbow! They were pirates looking for money, not people after us! I protected him. Do you think he'd be safer fighting in your country?"

"Perhaps! Better than here!"

Austin lurched forward, but one of the guards—a tall woman with a scar on her chin—stepped between them, stance wide and hand hovering near her belt. Austin's breath came hot and sharp.

"Are you deliberately trying to piss me off, Marco? Because you're getting under my skin. If you disrespect your host because you're angry at me, I swear—"

Brandon's attention bounced with the translator's back-and-forth, but then Señor Arias slipped into flawless English—his lips curling into a sly, knowing smile, as if he'd been listening and weighing every word all along. "Crazy mad," Señor Arias declared. "Isn't that how you say it, Austin?"

The entire room froze. Even the guards traded glances, the sudden switch catching everyone off guard.

For a moment, there was only the faint hum of the refrigerator. Austin stopped mid-rant, a surprised smile tugging at her own. She tilted her head, never looking away from Marco, her expression softening as if warmed by a sip of hot cocoa on a cold night—a comfort that felt almost shocking after the tension that had just filled the air.

"See, it is not just my son who is trying to impress someone, hmm?" Marco said, his voice smooth as glass. "May we speak privately?"

Chapter –7

"I guess you took one for the team."

Austin skidded to a halt just inside the front door, duffel bag swinging from her hand. Starr stood nearby, arms folded, a smirk creeping across her face. "Back so soon? I expected at least a few battle cries. Was it hand-to-hand combat, or did you skip straight to the surrender? Don't worry, I won't tell the others how valiantly you fought for... diplomacy. If you need an ice pack—or a high five—I'm available." She finished, deadpan: "Oh, great warrior."

The screen slammed behind Austin. The sharp scent of the two overgrown evergreens flanking the steps filled her nose. Heat flushed her cheeks. Helicopters roared outside, their noise pouring through the open windows—along with Aina's laughter.

"You're just jealous," Aina joined in.

"What does that mean, 'took one for the team'?" Golem asked in his deep voice. Austin shook her head, tried to get them to lower their voices a bit. Brandon and Lyndsey were on the front porch. Tessa wanted to watch the helicopters take off.

"It means she sacrificed something for our benefit." Aina gritted her teeth—way too loudly—to keep from laughing.

"He didn't hurt her, did he?" Golem scooted up on the couch and pushed a fist to his knee. Austin decided he'd have run across that pasture, jumped twenty feet into the sky, and jerked the helicopter to the ground if he thought Marco Arias had done her harm.

"No." Hutch glared angrily at Austin. "It means she whored herself out to my father so I could stay."

"Can you guys please be quiet? My love life doesn't need to be broadcast to everyone," Austin said, her voice low. "And no, baby. I think it was the other way around. It wasn't me on the table, begging for more."

Well, actually, that wasn't quite true.

They had cleared the kitchen in less than two minutes, guards stationed on the far side of the door, backs turned for privacy.

Austin knew the moment they were alone, they weren't going to fight it out. Not this time.

He thought she was so damn hot—told her that in perfect English. She thought he was hot, too—told him that in perfect Spanish.

Marco didn't hesitate. He grabbed her around the waist, quick and sure, and pulled her against him. His mouth crushed onto hers, a hard, hungry kiss that sent her heartbeat slamming against her ribs. He had to feel it. His own pulse hammered against her chest—fast, heavy, desperate.

Was this love? Austin's mind spun. *Was it?*

Usually, things would get physical quickly—sometimes right there in a kitchen. It was always a little out of her comfort zone. He liked that about her. He liked all her edges.

But something hit her. Hard. Like a sharp knock from inside her own chest. Her hand shot up between them.

"No. Stop. Marco—stop."

He froze immediately, eyes narrowing, breath hot on her lips.

"I can't," she whispered. "I won't. This isn't right."

A step backward took her out of his reach. Marco's jaw clenched—those jaws had broken men's careers, men's confidence, hell, maybe even men's ribs. His eyes flashed, *How dare you defy me.* No woman ever defied Marco Arias. But Austin did.

Even when her emotions begged her not to.

"This is not for the right reason."

"Not even for my son?" he blurted.

That alone told her how rattled he was. Marco Arias never spoke without calculation. Her refusal had knocked him off-balance.

"That's why I won't do it," she said softly. "Marco... no."

For a heartbeat, he stared at her—furious, wounded, turned inside out. Then he stepped back. Because she was right. And she'd never been more drawn to him—and hated herself for it—than in that moment.

But Hutch did not know all that. "You're sick," Hutch told her now. He looked a little green and rolled his eyes.

"And you're staying. And I'm this close—" Austin walked around the couch and pinched her fingers almost together. "—into talking him into letting you go to a real high school." She dropped the duffel bag in Stats' lap. "We'll need this." Then she strutted over to Hutch. "So, I'm sorry if it bothers you. But a thank you will suffice. You do realize that the world doesn't owe you, right? I had a confidential meeting with your dad to solve the problem."

"Confidential meeting, that's a joke. How much money did he give you?"

"You mean your ransom money or the money I get for being your nanny? You know, you better be nice to me." Austin spat at him. "I might be your next mother. And since you are the seventh-born child, I could knock you off with a snap of my fingers, and nobody would miss you."

"I am the seventh son of the seventh son going back eight generations," Hutch folded his arms across his chest. "The world might implode if you murdered me. Besides, you'd miss me. And I detest you."

"Yeah, I like all of that teenage angst you torment me with." They stood inches apart, jaws tight like they were about to fight. Austin's hand hovered on his chest—about to shove him—while Hutch's fist knotted. Then she leaned back and gave him a playful slap to the shoulder. "Hey, it wasn't me who impressed your dad with my beauty, charm, and of course, my classy elegance," she said with a soft smile, waving her arms in front of her T-shirt and jean shorts. "It was you, Frederico. You acted like a well-dressed man in the kitchen. You were respectful, not rebellious. You made valid points without interrupting. You made me proud."

"You told my dad I took out the trash. He thought I had to eat it or sit on it when I was bad or something. There were some translation issues with your dorky accent."

"Yeah, I thought that was strange. Maybe he needs a new interpreter."

"What he needs is a *new you*," Hutch grumbled.

~

"Hey, what are the odds I could convince you to let us stay a week?" Austin stepped out to the front porch and closed the door behind her. Sadness pooled low in her stomach after Marco left. Rubbing at it with her fingers didn't help. He wasn't much of a boyfriend. More of a one-night stand every now and again. Maybe Austin loved him. Maybe he loved her. It didn't matter. What they had was all they would ever have. He was obligated to marry within proper bloodlines for purity's sake. But he was the closest thing to a friend, a lover, she'd ever had. He didn't expect anything from her. Still, it hurt.

The quiet road stretched ahead, empty. A car passing by with unfamiliar headlights wouldn't have surprised her a bit. Porch boards creaked under her feet, making her feel exposed.

Brandon leaned against the railing, watching Tessa play on a blanket in the grass. Lyndsey stood near him. "Like five days being a week," Austin went on when he didn't answer. "Before you say anything, I—I know that's a long time, and I know there's a lot of us, but we need a place to land long enough for me to get some good food in everybody, buy clothes, take showers. Okay, honestly, I have no idea in hell where we're heading."

Lyndsey's shoulders slumped. She was wearing her nurse scrubs again. She shook her head and rolled her eyes. "You aren't serious, are you?" she asked Austin. "Haven't you caused enough trouble?"

"What about your brother, the cops, and stuff?" Brandon listened to Lyndsey, then turned to Austin. "Austin, I can't jeopardize the farm. I don't want Tessa in any danger."

"Yeah," Lyndsey added. "You might be leaving, but Brandon, he's got to stick around. He doesn't need trouble."

"Well, Marco's handling it—"

"*Marco*," Lyndsey huffed with an eye roll. "You mean Señor Arias. They'd *behead* you in his country for talking like that." Jealous? Maybe. The comment hit Austin sideways.

"Uh... pretty sure they don't behead people there anymore," Austin muttered. "But what I was saying is that he's used to paying off cops, border guards, all that. I'm just waiting for Homeland Security to call and confirm it's squared away. It was a misunderstanding. I'm in charge of Hutch—pretty much his nanny—, and I thought his dad knew we were coming here," Austin lied, and felt the weight of just how easily the lies were coming now. "He didn't. He panicked and assumed I was kidnapping his son for ransom. I didn't realize crossing borders could get that complicated."

"Homeland Security." Lyndsey sniffed a sarcastic laugh. "Really? So much for trying to fly under the radar, babe." She said to Brandon, "Now you are probably one of the FBI's Most Wanted, along with the freak show."

"Don't, Lyndsey." Brandon looked a bit sore, maybe a bit uncomfortable. "Enough with the name-calling."

"You know what she did when you left the meeting, right?"

Brandon leaned into the stairway handrail, elbows planted, clasping and unclasping his hands. "Yeah, that was a bit much."

"Okay, I get it." Austin sighed, heart sinking. It hurt to see Brandon with someone else—and, worse, that it still mattered after all this time. Every lonely moment was a what-if: what if he hadn't turned away when she got pregnant?

When they were together, she'd been sure he was her soulmate. The One. She wished she could tell him—how every argument, every silence, still meant something. But she buried it, too proud or too scared. "Yeah, it wasn't my usual response to seeing Marco." Austin shrugged, lied. She did not want to explain what really happened. She was still taking it in herself. "It's just been a while. What is that saying? Absence makes the heart grow fonder. I'm sorry about that. It isn't often we get to see each other. It's complicated. He's like trying to run half the world, and I'm a workaholic. We're from two different worlds and can't even speak each other's language enough to have pillow talk afterwards. My life is complicated. His life is complicated. We un-complicate it together when he can."

Rambling spilled out of her before she could stop it. She also knew she was rubbing it in a little—proof she was worth something to somebody. Even if Marco didn't love her enough to give up his world.

"Well, don't un-complicate it on my kitchen table again."

"It was the counter, sink, and the floor. But, okay," Austin spat, then wished she had held her tongue. She was grumpy. Exhausted.

"Well, she won't because she's leaving, right?" Lyndsey tossed her arms into the air. "Right, baby?"

"Yeah, we're leaving." Austin nodded. She looked to Tessa, decided not to make a big deal of leaving. Turning quickly, she headed for the door.

Her phone was already out—checking for something from Marco, anything. Then she thumbed through hotels to see if she could book rooms. She almost ran headfirst into Roo, who was pacing in front of the door, waiting for her.

"Roo, please stop pacing. I'm fine." He'd been walking to and fro like a caged wolf upstairs the entire time they were dodging security. She'd heard every heavy step.

"He's driving everybody nuts, Pet," Aina said with a giggle. "So is Golem. It took everything we had to stop him from getting up. His steps are really loud." She pushed her dark hair from her eyes and peered from the couch. "Roo almost went through the door when Hutch's dad came. I think he almost peed in the corner to mark his territory."

"My dad has that influence on people," Hutch muttered.

"He didn't—pee, right?" Austin asked, way too seriously. Laughter burst from the group. They looked comfortable now—TV blaring, Starr sprawled across the couch, Golem leaning hard on the recliner to hear the movie. Stats with his hands on his ears trying to tune everybody out. Aina and Hutch were playing cards.

"Something's the matter," Roo said. His Cajun drawl was thick, but Austin had learned to sift through it easily.

He sensed her dread.

All she wanted was a soft bed and three days of sleep. Not a restaurant full of staring strangers. Not a hotel where half the guests would complain about the huge, weird guy or the creepy little Irish girl peeking around corners.

"We just have to find another place to stay. No big deal." She tried to sound upbeat, but silence answered instead.

Roo's brow furrowed. "It's not safe out there. Not for us."

"He doesn't like us, does he?" Starr asked quietly. "Brandon thinks we're a freak show, too? Did you do the kiwi fruit thing for him?" The kiwi fruit thing. Austin smiled faintly.

Starr's voice softened. "I wish people could see that about us." Her words hovered, drawing a hush from the room.

"No, no, no. It isn't you guys," Austin told them. Maybe she was lying. Again. She couldn't tell. Brandon always stared at everybody the same way—bored, aloof, detached. When she was younger, it had seemed cool. Now it just looked like he didn't care. Austin crossed the room, leaned over the couch, and hugged Starr around the neck.

"For God's sake, I don't know anybody who doesn't like you guys. It's me." She lied. "I screwed up again. I insulted him during the meeting with Hutch's dad. Hell, my own kid doesn't even like me. But let's not focus on the negative. On the good side, we've got nothing to pack, we've got money now, and we can go shopping and stay at a classy hotel." Austin sat, phone in hand, staring at the blank screen. Her reflection hovered ghostlike on the glass. Outside, dusk crept over the empty road.

She waited for Marco's name to light up the screen. Only silence answered.

Chapter −8

"Hey, you remember Becky Wilson?"

Austin slumped at the kitchen table, forehead pressed to her arm. Starr checked the stitches on her shoulder and back—hastily sewn, moonlit, in a grassy field their first night ashore.

The kitchen was washed in tired morning light, everything pale and quiet except for Austin's shallow breathing. Starr's fingers pressed the stitches, hot and electric. Austin gritted her teeth, fighting not to flinch. When Brandon's voice came from the kitchen door, she forced her face blank.

He leaned against the frame, hands in his pockets.

"Becky Wilson," Austin repeated. "Yeah, vaguely. Math class, I think. Dated one of Abel Martin's boys. Why?"

"Just thought it might be someone we both knew." He moved to the fridge and popped open a soda. "Her dad owns Gent's Hardware. He's a commissioner now. Want a soda?"

"No—"

Starr pressed hard on a bruise, stabbing with her fingernail. "Cripes almighty, Starr! What the hell? That hurt." Austin jerked upright. Starr only rolled her eyes. "Starr's descended from a Norse healer goddess, allegedly," Austin muttered. "But I think she's just a sadist with a medical license."

"If you were really a warrior, you wouldn't whine like a four-year-old." Starr nudged the stitch again.

"A warrior?" Brandon snorted. "What part of this screams anything but girly-girl?"

"Don't be fooled by the pretty clothes and scrawny legs," Starr murmured. "She's got tough roots, even if she whines at my stitches."

"My great-grandpa fought a giant serpent," Austin grunted. "If he could do it, so could I."

Starr grumbled a laugh, and Brandon joined in. "Screw you both," Austin hissed. "But I probably shouldn't say that. Starr's on the hunt, Brandon, so be careful."

Starr smirked, then jabbed Austin with her nail.

"Ow!"

"I put the damn things in you. I'll take them out if you don't quit being a baby about it."

"Damn, that's a lot of stitches." Brandon peered over Starr's shoulder. Austin's cheeks burned.

"She got it with a butter knife here," Starr said, poking at the shoulder.

"Ow."

"And a piece of a boat stairway banister here." She poked another finger along a bruise on her shoulder.

"Ow."

"A gun barrel, fist, and a boot." Poke, poke, poke.

"Ow, ow and dammit, ow!" Austin leaned back angrily. She slapped Starr's hands away with her fingers. She could hear a loud thump in the living room. She knew it was Roo jumping to attention at her yowls even before he came running around the corner with the anxious eyes of a German Shepherd after hearing a loud bang in the dark.

"It's alright, buddy. Just Starr and her *miracle* hands." Austin waved Roo away, but he narrowed his eyes at Brandon, who shrugged.

"I didn't touch her, dude. Somebody did, though," Brandon muttered. "What did you do, fight off an army?" Brandon asked with a soft laugh. Austin didn't laugh. Her glare made it clear she didn't find it cute.

"No, pirates boarded our ship," Austin said. "Not the silly hat kind. The kind with guns and knives."

"Butter knives, apparently," Starr added. "Not sharp at all."

Austin groaned. "It was mine. The guy chased me into the galley. I grabbed it from a drawer. Kind of wish I hadn't now."

"I'm sorry." Brandon dropped the smile and looked uneasy. "I didn't know you really meant it. I guess, I just figured you'd done it skiing or something."

Silence returned. Starr pressed Austin's head back down and worked, her touch a strange mix of warmth and sting. Austin caught the whisper of a prayer.

"I'm going to college," Brandon said quietly. "Mostly online." He looked embarrassed and turned to Starr for support. "Austin and I started hanging out after I got sent to the principal's office. She was always helping out—brown-nosing. The principal told me I'd never amount to anything." Brandon grinned at Austin. "Austin said, '*Brandon isn't failing the system, Mister Peters—the system failed him. Kind of like it failed when it let you teach.*'"

"I almost got suspended for that," Austin said. "My punishment was tutoring this idiot." She jabbed a thumb at Brandon.

"You should have been suspended. But Peters knew you were a spaz. Well, and your dad is the town judge."

"Spaz?" Starr asked. "I don't know that word."

Austin's gaze worked up to Brandon's. "It means hyperactive."

"Well, you do have a mild case of ADHD. You'd spot an ant crawling in Texas from Ohio."

"Yeah, well, it sucks being small and hyper while Starr's all legs and curves." Austin wiggled her fingers at Starr, then slipped from her grasp. "Thanks for the drive down memory lane, Brandon. We should go before dark." She nodded at Roo. "You're riding up front."

"Hey. You could stay, if you want."

Starr's hand squeezed Austin's shoulder. When she looked up, Starr's eyes were pleading. They were all too road-weary to keep moving. Austin wanted this—more than another night in a sterile hotel room.

"I thought Lyndsey didn't want us here," she prodded Brandon.

Brandon paused. "If Lyndsey trusts me, she'll get on board. She's just worried about me and Tess."

Austin pressed her lips together to keep from laughing.

Lyndsey worried, sure—but mostly about losing her grip on Brandon. "What about my dad? My brother?"

"I don't know that either, Austin." He sighed, shrugged his usual shrug. "We'll figure it out. I told you. Tessa needs to know she's got a mom. It's important to me that she knows she's got one that—that gives a crap."

A distant engine rumbled outside, making Roo's ears perk. Austin glanced through the blinds, heart thumping, but saw only a car creeping past the driveway before speeding up again. The sound lingered, unsettling, until it faded into the dark.

"I do—give a crap," Austin mustered barely above a whisper. "I—I mean, more than crap."

"Then show her. Spend time with her, Austin. She's three. Read to her. She just wants you." Brandon's voice stayed quiet but firm.

Austin bristled. She barely had time to keep Golem from wandering off, stop Aina from lighting the bathroom on fire, throw Roo's tennis balls, and stop Stats from pulling up porn on Brandon's laptop.

"Yes, sir."

Brandon tipped his head sideways. He looked more confused than amused. Starr chuckled. "Did you just call him *sir*?"

Austin's stomach twisted. Even here, she couldn't quite settle. She wondered what she'd risk by staying—or by leaving.

"Yeah, I did." Austin ran her hands through her hair. "I just need sleep. Or an hour to myself without babysitting." She glanced at Starr and Brandon—blank faces. "Never mind."

"Then stay. I get paid tomorrow. I can see if I can get my check early. My truck payment can wait. As soon as I get my paycheck, we'll buy food."

As Brandon spoke about paychecks and food, Austin tried to focus on hope. But something outside—the flicker of headlights, or maybe just her nerves—made her shiver. She told herself it was nothing, but deep down, she knew trouble had never been far behind.

Chapter −9

"What do you need, daddy?" Austin held up her phone, showing the missed call from the city offices. "They said you wanted to meet me here." The crossroad between Bakersville and Warren Roads was wrapped in the last smear of evening sun. Gold light slashed across cracked blacktop and a battered stop sign. The air smelled of rain, and the hip-high corn in the nearby field rustled in the wind. Somewhere a dog barked, the echo swallowed by the hills.

Austin stood in the middle of the intersection, halfway between her battered truck and a sleek, dark sedan with tinted windows. Her father, Judge Jackson, sat inside—his face masked by the glass and the last smear of evening sun.

By six-thirty, she'd spent seven hundred dollars on groceries, dropped them at the house, taken Starr and Golem to the mall for clothes, loaded the car with bags—and then Francis Maynard clerk for the city offices called, summoning her here.

Her father didn't get out. He cracked the window instead. Same thick white hair, same jowls, same black suit. "A Ned Gunderson from the American Embassy called," he said. "Courtesy request: we're to make your stay...*comfortable*." His stare burned. "I don't know what trouble you're mixed up in, but you'd better keep it out of this town. One misstep from you and that dumbass boy and his people will pay for it."

"You lay one finger on that *dumbass* boy or anyone with me, and I'll come after you myself."

"Is that a threat?"

"It is."

"I don't know where you got that mouth."

"You always said the apple didn't fall far from the tree."

"You should've stayed gone. Nothing here for you."

"And you shouldn't have made Ben dump me in Columbus three days after I had a baby."

"You should've put that baby up for adoption. You shamed our name. Do you know what you did to your grandfather when you hooked up with that boy whose family took his land?"

"It was two hundred years ago, Daddy. They didn't steal anything."

"You might as well have stabbed your ancestors in the back. I figured once you ran off, you'd crawl home with your tail between your legs." He squinted at her dress. "What the hell are you wearing?"

"It's a dress." Austin lifted her chin. She wasn't that scared little kid anymore. "Let's end this. I'm not your daughter. You want to see me? Treat me like a stranger. My life isn't yours anymore." Austin shivered. "And don't talk to me about shame. Ray Jackson, I know exactly what you've done in this town. Marta Givens. Bob Gilford— six DUIs, you let him off until he killed Kayla Harley. Tickets waved for your friends while everyone else paid. Forty years of corruption. And you want to clutch your pearls over me having a baby?"

Her father's lip twitched.

"I'm not your problem anymore," Austin said, voice low. "But I can sure as hell be yours. You threaten anyone near me, and I'll call the feds myself. Fraud. Extortion. All of it. Don't test me."

"Shame on you for talking to your daddy like this."

"And shame on you for treating your daughter like dirt," Austin fired back, voice low and steady. "And I want my necklace. The one Papaw left me."

"Necklace?" He scoffed. "Papaw lost faith in you the day he learned who you were seeing. Even if I had it, you wouldn't get it. He gave it to someone faithful to the family. Someone you're not."

A shadow fell across the crossroads as her father's cruiser idled, headlights flickering once. Austin stared him down, but he just rolled up his window, face unreadable. She didn't move until the car finally pulled away, gravel hissing beneath the tires. As the dust settled, Austin turned—and saw a second set of headlights cresting the hill behind her, slowing just out of sight. Then it vanished.

Chapter –10

Hell broke loose over a damn burger.

They'd forgotten Hutch's fries, burgers, and chocolate shake when Austin, Golem, and Starr ran to town to shop pants for Golem and pick up ice cream for a treat for everyone. They were halfway home when the smell hit—smoke, grease, meat. A flicker of neon from a roadside bar. Austin's stomach dropped.

"Bam. Hutch's food," she muttered.

"The ice cream is going to melt while we wait for it to cook," Starr protested. "He can go one night without clogging his arteries with junk food. Just come back later."

"I'm exhausted. It has been a long day." Austin grunted. "And once I park this piece-of-crap vehicle, I'm not dragging it back onto the road."

She made the mistake of turning around.

Inside, the place was dim and sticky, the kind of bar where time clogged in the corners. Men stared openly at Starr as they walked in—she always drew eyes the way a flame drew moths, but in places like this, something about her made drunk men crazier, bolder, meaner. Austin felt the old, familiar prickle of unease settle in. They took a grubby table and waited for the order, nerves quieting just long enough for Austin to hear it—the slow scrape of a chair behind her.

A voice followed, close enough she felt the heat of it on her neck: "You ignoring me, sweetheart?"

Then everything snapped. A hand shot out, fisting in Starr's hair. Another hand—another man—flashed a gun, shiny and stupid in the bar's dirty yellow light. Austin didn't think. Didn't breathe.

She moved. Wrist. Shoulder. Twist. A sharp **POP** as bone gave way. The gun blasted into the ceiling—BOOM—dust raining from above. Someone screamed. Chairs scraped violently across the sticky floor, and glass shattered underfoot as people scrambled away from the fight.

The sour tang of spilled beer mixed with the heavy scent of sweat and old fryer grease. Over the chaos, the jukebox whined and cut out, leaving a ringing silence punctuated by panicked shouts and the crash of bodies tumbling into tables.

A beer bottle shattered against Austin's shoulder—white-hot pain ripping down her arm in a wave that took her breath.

Golem's boot landed like thunder, smashing the gun to the floor and pinning it under his heel. "Austin—GO!" Starr shouted, voice cutting through the chaos. But the room tilted. Her fingers went numb. Blood was sliding warm down her arm.

Austin blinked—once, twice—and suddenly she wasn't fighting anymore.

She was falling.

Down into noise and smoke and pain. Golem's enormous shadow bent over her, shoulders heaving, jaw clenched with something like panic in his eyes. Starr's voice, hoarse and trembling, called her name—once, twice—as if trying to pull her back. Austin felt fear, regret, and a strange, floating relief as the world went soft and dark around the edges.

Then came the sirens.

Chapter −11

Brandon figured that when he got off work at nine, he'd come home to an empty house. All he wanted now was peace—a chance for things to settle down, for Tessa to feel secure. Austin looked like she was ready to bolt when he told her to step up to bat with Tessa. It was killing him to watch his little girl doing everything but somersaults to get her mama's attention, while Austin completely ignored her. The only thing worse than not knowing your own mama, he figured, would be one that cast her off like a dirty, ragtag washrag.

What he did not expect was his mom sitting at the kitchen table in her Thursday church dress and flat pumps, sipping on a cup of coffee and watching intently as Stats was poking at her phone.

"Mom, I thought you and Dad were still in Tennessee on that bible study trip," he said reluctantly, looking around. He set Tessa on the ground and watched her little legs pump toward his mother. Hutch was stirring something over the stove, the wooden spoon clinking against the pot. Aina was staring intently into the too-full refrigerator, shuffling past the cheddar cheese and two bottles of Golem's spicy pickles. The scent of sizzling onions mingled with the sharp tang of an open jar of pickled eggs on the table.

"And I didn't know you had company. So, we're even," Olivia Tremaine replied thoughtfully. "I had to hear it from your girlfriend." She had a strangely calm look to her eyes while she poked her brown hair with one finger, which meant she was not cool with this situation at all.

It occurred to him that they cut their road trip short to see what all the fuss was about. "Felix, here, is setting up my phone for me. He's adding some—"

"Apps." Stats didn't even look up to acknowledge Brandon. "I'm adding some music software so she can practice her church hymns at home. I'm setting her up on some social networks, finding her friends from her bible study class and her book club."

"And you said you could fix all my contacts, didn't you, Felix?" His mom looked up at Branden. "I don't know how I did it, but I put last names first, and I can't find anybody's phone number quickly."

"Eighty-two percent of phone owners don't complete their contacts properly," Stats told her, barely skimming a gaze at her. "You are in the eighty-second percentile. You are quite normal."

"Normal is having lamb at the grocery," Aina muttered. "My auntie would faint dead away if she knew I made shepherd's pie with beef. That said, nobody here is normal as far as I'm concerned."

Brandon almost laughed. She was so laidback, didn't care what anybody thought of her. She kept bending down so Tessa could touch her hair. There was something about it that caught her attention, and she giggled every time Aina dipped and shook her head on her little fingers. Her accent was deep and rolled off her tongue. His mom almost seemed mesmerized by it and kept saying how cute her little accent sounded. Aina rolled her eyes. He could hardly see the ocean green retinas underneath with all the mascara caked on her lashes.

"It's her comfort food," Hutch added. "If Pet ever gets home, she's supposed to bring me mine—burgers and fries, and a chocolate shake."

"Where is Austin anyway?" He almost hesitated asking. He saw his mom's eyes roll at the name. Something about the silence that followed made his skin prickle, as if everyone was avoiding the real story.

"She went clothes shopping and dropped off the groceries a few hours ago. Couldn't find pants for Golem," Hutch said, leaning against the sink. "She figured she'd try Bigley Farm and Country— said farmers are usually big. On the way back, she was going to pick up ice cream and grab my burgers. But knowing Austin—and a fat wallet full of my dad's money—she won't be back for a week. She'll find another strip mall and try on every dress in every shop."

"Well, surprise, surprise," Olivia muttered, studying Hutch. "She's nowhere to be found and shopping. So, your father is married to Austin?"

"No. She's just one of his mistresses. He can't marry her—wrong bloodline. And, you know...he already has a wife."

That shut up his mom for a moment. She just stared at Hutch, who hadn't even looked up from his phone.

Brandon watched Aina slowly turn and look at him, as if he should say something in her defense. When he didn't, she gave his mother a flat-lined gaze. "The stores will probably close soon. Regardless, she's never going to find anything for Golem. She's probably sitting in the car now, ordering something specially made online." Aina tugged out some butter. "He's like trying to fit an elephant into mouse shorts." She turned to Brandon. "I made everybody a pie. I hope you're hungry."

He was. His stomach had been growling since six o'clock. He usually skipped supper until he got home at night, then put Tessa to bed real quick and made a peanut butter and jelly sandwich. If Lyndsey were here, he'd pick up some burgers and fries at Big Bill's Diner. The pot pies that Aina was taking out of the oven with an oven mitt that nearly covered her all the way to her elbows smelled like heaven. She plopped one in front of everyone and even had a tiny one for Tessa, who was sitting on his mom's lap. Brandon watched his mom look at the odd array of people around the table as she smiled at Aina, who was laying the dish in front of her. Hutch moved in and sat down. Roo slipped in the doorway, eyes darting back and forth before he slinked around the corner. "I'll wait until Pet gets back." He was almost crazy with anxiety whenever Austin wasn't around.

"Pet?" Brandon's mom watched Roo slip out of the room and seemed to listen as he paced in the living room again.

"That's what we call Austin," Hutch told her.

"Oh," his mom said curiously. "How do you get a nickname like Pet?" She looked up at Hutch.

"You belong to Paolo." He looked up enough to shrug and laugh a little. "Well, and you get housebroken."

"Is that where she has been for the last few years, with *Paolo*?"

"Mom, stop!" Brandon turned and snatched up forks for everybody. He held them out, and passed them around. Of course, asking her to stop and having his mom stop asking questions were two different things, especially when Hutch had absolutely no reservations about dishing out information on Austin. Most of it, however, Brandon assumed was being made up by the boy.

It was only twenty minutes into the late-night supper when the front door opened slowly. Brandon could hear Austin's voice telling Roo to go help Golem clean up the melted ice cream in the truck. *No, I'm fine. I'm fine. Can you tell Aina to meet us upstairs?* She said that twice, then he could hear two sets of footsteps going upstairs. Roo had come to the door. He didn't say anything at all, just nodded behind him. Aina had looked up from her meal. Her face had paled when she stood.

"Can you see if she picked up my burgers?" Hutch asked. Aina had tossed him a flaming glare, told him to go check for himself.

Five minutes passed, and then ten. Hutch left a few minutes after Aina and Stats just dug harder into his pot pie. Brandon could see his mom's eyes wavering toward the kitchen door. "Where did they all go?" she asked. "Maybe you should go put Tessa to bed and see if everything is alright."

It was strangely quiet at the top of the stairway. Brandon walked past the first time, slid into Tessa's room, and helped her into her pajamas. He watched intently while he laid her into bed. "Book, daddy," she kept asking him. He shook his head. "Not tonight, baby. It's late." He always read her a book.

He never closed the door when he left her room. He could see her still sitting up in bed when he walked out. She wasn't happy when he tugged the door partway and slipped down the hallway.

He had a bad feeling in his gut. It wasn't just the feeling of apprehension in the air. It wasn't that his mom was downstairs and wasn't at all crazy about the situation with Austin and her friends here. It was the fact that Austin had come at all that disrupted his and Tessa's lives. Everything was going smoothly. She shows up. By God, just like her dad used to say, trouble came right after.

Hutch and Golem were leaning against the wall outside the bathroom. Both gave Brandon a cautious gaze. The door was slightly ajar, maybe an inch. Roo was pacing back and forth, stopping at the door and pushing his hands against it, "Is she alright? Answer me."

Inside, he could hear gentle sobbing, then the sound of Starr's placid, but forceful tone: "Be still, be still. Dammit, be still!"

"What happened? I take it Austin got hurt." Brandon's eyes met Golem's, who made an awkward shrug of his shoulders. He sighed, walked to the door, and used a knuckle to make three loud knocks.

"Hey, let me in a minute." Silence.

"Let him in," Starr said. "Because Aina is not doing her job, and I can't do mine when you are fighting me."

"I'm not fighting you," Austin muttered.

"Liar. Everything's a fight with you. You even kick in your sleep."

Suddenly, the door swung open. It was Starr's hand pulling the knob. "Yes, come in and help." She stepped back like she was expecting Austin to stop her. In one hand, she was holding a needle. He saw Austin jump up and try to grab the door with her free hand. The other was holding on to the top of her dress, which was slipping down her side.

A line of blood dribbled down her shoulder and arm.

"What the hell?" Austin hissed, her eyes angry. "I said *no*!"

Aina jumped at her snapping voice; her cheeks were red, tears still flowing. Suddenly, Starr's hand came out and slapped hard across Austin's cheek. The sharp crack echoed in the small bathroom, making the air thrum for a split second.

Complete and utter silence filled the air. Aina's eyes were as wide as fists. Starr's glare was defiant as heck, but it was wide, too, when she stepped back. Austin's hand went up to her cheek, touching the red palm print there, her fingers trembling.

Had a giraffe climbed up the stairway behind Brandon right then, he wouldn't have expected a more surprised expression than the one he saw on Austin's face. "You slapped me."

"You won't listen to me. This will take five minutes if you sit still. I am the boss when I have to fix you. You are not being a good warrior. You're making Aina upset."

"You've never slapped me before."

"Well, she's making up for all the times she wanted to and didn't, I guess." Hutch came up behind Brandon and peered over his shoulder. "Ow."

Austin hadn't shed a tear until this moment. But Brandon saw one tear slip down her cheek, quiet proof that Starr's action had stung. Without looking away from Starr, she swiped it aside. "Alright. But I'm mad at you. You're a healer, not a fighter. How would *you* like it if I tried to heal you?"

"I'm going to be a spanker and not a hitter if you don't sit your ass down on the toilet and let me finish," Starr muttered.

"Holy shit, I want to see that," Hutch mumbled with an eager look to his eyes. "Please, Starr, please."

"I'm going to kill him," Austin muttered, slicing her gaze toward Hutch. "Can I do it before I sit? Because right now I want to rip his tiny hummingbird head off. I'm dying over here, and he's acting thirteen."

Starr waved Hutch out. "Shoo!" The boy made a show of slamming the door behind him.

"Dammit! Don't close the door all the way," Austin hissed. Brandon watched Aina jump up and open it just a bit again. Austin seemed to relax, but her eyes kept flicking to the hallway, as if she expected someone—or something—else to appear.

"She likes to fight," Starr said quietly to Brandon. "However, she's a little girl and doesn't like the consequences of fighting bigger boys than she is."

"I do not like to fight. I was defending you. You need to ugly yourself up, so I don't have to keep idiots away from you, princess. Were you looking to date that jerkoff? If so, sorry."

Brandon ignored Austin and turned to Starr. "Would you rather take her to a hospital?"

"Don't offend her," Austin muttered. "She's a doctor."

"Okay," Brandon said pensively, jerking his head to Starr. Damn, she was almost as pretty as Austin. "I'm sorry. Where was the big guy while all this was going on?"

"Golem doesn't fight. He's like—a pacifist," Starr answered. "She didn't need help anyway. There were only three of them. And I don't think she expected one of them to fight like a little girl and grab her hair."

"Yeah, what was up with that?" Austin grumbled.

Brandon laughed, thinking she was kidding. The three women looked at him curiously. "What can I do?" he asked in the awkward silence. "Because whatever needs to be done, it's got to get done before my mom comes up the stairway."

~

"You have to admit, this is better than Aina blubbering a minute ago. Golem holding you down the last time, right?" Starr asked.

"It hurts to watch," Aina muttered. She was kneeling down beside the toilet, rubbing Austin's leg. Starr hovered over top. Brandon was sitting on the toilet with Austin on his lap, facing him. She'd set her face against his shoulder for lack of a better place to lay it. Her arms, he was holding tightly against her sides while Starr deftly wiggled the needle into the soft flesh of Austin's shoulder just above the bone. It would have been a hell of a sexy position in any other circumstance. But the cut was about four inches long and deep and he could feel Austin's belly tighten with every stitch. For a moment, he wondered how long he could keep holding all this together—for Tessa, for himself. If Austin fell apart, would the rest of them follow?

"Yeah, I'm not so sure about that," Austin grunted. "Sitting on my ex-boyfriend's lap and watching him smile smugly every time I wince is so much healthier for my ego than being bathed in tears and squeezed like a toothpaste bottle every time I grind my teeth."

"That was your teeth grinding?" Brandon teased her. "It sounded more like whining to me."

She didn't say anything in return for a moment. He could see the reason. Starr was pulling the stitch through the center of the cut. She was, however, cursing hard beneath her breath. Her fingernails were cutting past the pieces of shirt she held in her fists and heading straight into the soft flesh of his ribs. He cringed, and Aina sniffed a giggle.

"Okay, laugh," Brandon declared. "You're going to have to explain the scratches on my back to my girlfriend when we're done, Aina. I know she's not going to find it as amusing as you are."

"That you are laughing at all about this is less than comical to me, Aina," Austin grunted. "And you, Brandon, should take pride in being one of the few men who have had their backs scratched by me. I'm rather hard to please." She sounded like she was going to say more, but her words fell away.

Starr was working the needle in again. This was hard. His stomach was aching for her.

"Here's something that will take your mind off of it," Brandon said casually. "My mom's downstairs and wants to see you."

"I wondered whose car that was. Could this day get any worse?" Austin pushed back and looked up at him. "What does she want with me?"

"Be still," Starr mumbled. "I'm almost done."

"I don't know. She was here when I got home. Stats was fixing her phone." Brandon reached up, pushed her head back to his chest to get a better balance. "Be quiet so she can finish."

Starr acknowledged him with a smile. "Maybe this will help. Let's play the game," she said softly. "What's your biggest fear, Pet?"

"That you will leave me."

"I won't ever leave you. I promise. Where's the place you feel the safest?"

She didn't answer. Even in the stagnant air of the bathroom, Brandon didn't realize he was hushing her like he comforted Tessa when she skinned a knee, whispering she'd be alright, rocking her between pokes until Starr patted his back. It was just automatic.

But she was limp, lifeless when he leaned back. Her head lulled forward clumsily.

"Geez, did you kill her?" Aina giggled.

Starr snapped forward, tipped her head to the side. "Well, shit, she's asleep."

Outside in the hallway, a floorboard creaked. Brandon looked up, heart skipping, wondering if it was his mother—or someone else—coming to change everything again.

Chapter −12

"Mrs. Tremaine, sorry about that. I had a bloody nose. I'd like to say I shopped so hard, I had to fight my way through the boxes. I didn't. I hit it on the car door." Austin knew the fine art of lying. She used to be a horrible liar—blinking, stuttering, looking anywhere but the eyes. Now she started by pretending to clean a fingernail, glancing up just long enough, then smiling. It was hard. Her shoulder pain was excruciating.

"You are pale. It took all of you to fix a bloody nose?"

"Well, everybody had their own idea of how it should be stopped." Brandon pushed around her. She rubbed her cheeks. She was so embarrassed that she'd fallen asleep right in the middle of getting stitched up. Starr's laughter and Aina's hands tickling her sides had woken her. She blinked at Brandon, wondering where the hell she was and why she was staring up at him.

Olivia Tremaine was sitting on the living room couch, chubby but well-muscled, legs crossed, fingers rolling gently through Tessa's hair. "She came downstairs. Said it was too noisy. She should be in bed, Brandon." She nodded to Tessa, who was sucking her thumb and staring at Golem. Golem was making peek-a-boo faces. Tessa giggled softly.

Olivia wore a flowered dress and pink flats. She kept eyeing Golem like she was waiting for him to tromp across the room and gobble Tessa up in a single bite.

"Have you met Josef?" Austin asked her, carefully sitting beside Brandon without bumping her shoulder. "He's from the Czech Republic. His family had a farm like this one."

"Not so big," Golem reminded her. "Just chickens and sheep. And lots of sisters, brothers, cousins, and grandmas and grandpas."

"What made you decide to leave your farm, Josef?" Silence. Olivia looked around, curious, while Starr dropped her chin.

"It is hard feeding such a big man in a big family," Austin said quickly without losing a beat, fingers tapping rapidly at her waist.

"He came to live with us. Now I'm the one buying the twelve boxes of powdered donuts and eighteen hot dogs with catsup and onions a day."

Golem smiled at her. It made her heart hurt—because he missed his father's farm, and because she knew he was terrified there wouldn't be enough money, and he'd have to be sent away.

"And you? How did you find Austin?" Olivia asked Starr.

Starr's gaze snapped to Austin.

"Paolo paid my family—"

"—lots of money to come live with us," Austin jumped in, heart lurching. "We needed a doctor while we were traveling. Starr's a healer—a doctor from Sweden. Paolo was eccentric and a raging hypochondriac."

Olivia sifted every detail like she was sorting beans before a church potluck.

"You know, we're really tired," Austin added. "Haven't slept much. We should get to bed."

She knew it was coming.

"Honey, will you walk with me to my car while Brandon puts Tessa to bed?" Olivia asked.

"Do you want me to find a kiwi fruit?" Golem blurted, jumping up. "Then she'll understand."

"No, sweetie, it's okay," Austin said, patting his arm. "Out here in the country, the stores close early."

She didn't have a choice but to face Olivia alone. She thought she was sweating more bullets now than when Starr told her the guy at the bar had a gun.

"Why did you come back? Is it money?" Olivia asked as they neared the car. "Because Brandon doesn't have much. But if it *is* money, I talked to his father, and we have a small amount in our savings—"

"No." Austin pushed her hands out. "I don't need money."

"What is it?" Olivia asked softly. "If it's Brandon, you need to understand—he was young—"

"We both were young and naive," Austin said sharply. "It was just as much my fault as his."

"He's got a chance with Lyndsey. Don't mess that up. Like Brandon always says, Lyndsey, she's sweet. She's nice. She's a hard worker and a smart gal and the marrying type. Tessa needs a mama who is around. Not someone who shows up once in a while—"

"You're right," Austin admitted.

"Then leave. Don't come back. It's been hard, sweetie."

"Yes. It has."

"Now what do you know about hard?" Olivia gave a small, sarcastic laugh. She laid a hand on Austin's arm. "You abandoned that newborn. Tossed her at my son and ran before heading off to college—something Brandon couldn't do because he was raising Tessa. Leave him alone. Leave them both. Go away. Don't return."

Austin bit her lip. Olivia was wrong—painfully wrong. Austin had never wanted to abandon Tessa. She'd had no choice. Her father would have tracked her like prey—relentless, connected, armed with every law-enforcement ally he'd cultivated. He would have taken that baby from her, by force or by paperwork or whatever else he could weaponize. But he could not tear a child away from its biological father. Brandon would fight tooth and nail, and her father couldn't touch that. That was the only reason she had even told Brandon Tessa was his—"You're right," Austin whispered. "But I'm not the bad person you make me out to be. Yes. I'll leave."

~

"Hey, Roo."

Austin sat on the steps. It was eleven at night. Crickets chirped. Frogs called from the creek. Roo slipped outside as soon as Olivia's car pulled away. He plopped beside her.

"You're hurt," he said softly. "Can I do anything? I should've been there. Why didn't you take me? I like riding in the truck."

Austin snatched his hand and squeezed it. It was warm—comforting. "You're my best friend." She pressed his fingers. "But I just needed to shop."

71

"Is it because I look weird? Or act weird?"

"It's because girls like to shop without guys sometimes."

"You took Golem. He's a guy."

"I had to get him measured for clothes. I know *your* size."

"Will you toss the ball with me?"

"It's dark. You see it better than I do. You hit me in the head every time." She sniffed the cool night air—grass, pigs in the barn, and the faint sweetness of summer.

"That man, Brandon, gave you a room upstairs. Can I sleep on the floor?"

"Yes."

Roo sighed. "I love you, Pet. So much."

"I love you too."

"I know you're hurt."

"I'm fine. Just stitches."

"No. Inside." He thumped his chest. He probably heard every word Olivia had said. "What's your biggest fear, Pet?"

"That you will leave me."

"I won't ever leave. I promise."

"Just don't—" Too late. He licked her shoulder. "—lick me."

"I'm sorry." And he was. His huge brown eyes were so mournful she couldn't stay mad.

"Give me ten minutes to soak in the night, and I'll come to bed."

~

She just wanted silence—finally. But a shadow crossed her bare feet only minutes after Roo left.

"I brought you some tea to make you feel better," Aina said. She stood above her with a chipped teacup. "Starr's herbs. And a little of my magic so it tastes good."

Austin took it, sniffed. Honey and strawberries.

"I got Brandon one, too. You two need to talk."

"What about?"

"I don't know. You just do." Aina flicked a glance at the porch. "He's coming. I'm going to bed. Can I sleep on your floor?"

"Roo's in there, too. He snores."

"I don't care."

"Aina... did you take anything from Brandon?"

Silence.

"Give it," Austin said, palm up.

Aina reluctantly pulled something from her pocket and placed it in Austin's hand.

"A ring," Austin sighed. Just a simple gold band with a tiny diamond. "Stay out of his room."

"Uh huh."

"And burn incense instead of lighting fires in the sinks," Austin said, tugging the hem of Aina's shirt as she walked away. "If you stay out of trouble for a few days and don't burn the house down, we'll light you a bonfire."

Chapter —13

Austin looked up again, and Aina was gone already. She heard Brandon greeting her when he passed.

"Hey, Austin." His voice was soft, subdued in the darkness. There was a bit of moon peeking out of the fluffy clouds floating overhead, casting silver shadows across the worn wooden porch steps. Austin could see Brandon's face in that moonshine. It was so damn beautiful. He had the perfect nose with just the right slant and the kind of lips Starr called angel lips because they curled up at the corners. She could see why the girl inside her fell so madly and deeply in love with him that summer. Even now, her heart was making a thump-thump-thump in her chest when he sat down next to her on the step, elbows on knees and a coffee cup in his fingers.

"So, did my mom rip you a new one?" he asked Austin. "Because I'm apologizing for it right now."

"Yes, she did. No need for apologies." Austin sipped the tea. It was heavenly, fragrant with a floral, earthy scent, and it made her shoulders relax. "She told me to get my ass out of town and not to leave my glass slipper anywhere around for you to find. I'm supposed to leave you and Tessa alone so you could have a long and wonderful life with Lyndsey and live happily ever after."

"Are you comparing my mother to a wicked stepmother?"

"Um, I'm more inclined to want to compare myself to a princess. But if the shoe fits—" She nudged Brandon with her elbow, smiled softly up at him. "I'm teasing. In her defense, she did it with the grace and charm of any mama watching out for her son and granddaughter."

"This tea is good."

"It is. But I'm warning you of one thing before you gobble it up." Austin listened to the crickets chirp when her words ebbed. "Aina's father swore she was a changeling, a fairy, when she came to stay with us. She's supposedly a descendant of the goddess of love.

We call her a fairy-angel. She was raised by a religious father to believe that the fairies were fallen angels, cast out of heaven by God for their role in the battles of heaven. Her aunt said she was a true fairy, a goddess. We can't quite agree on the truth, so we settle on a little of both."

"What?" Brandon drew out the word, let it trail off in a sing-song way. "You're kidding. There's no such thing as fairies, right?"

"Sure. I believe in them. I've seen Aina do too many things to write it off. And you don't have to believe. But I'm warning you, I don't know what she put in that tea. You just might fall in love with me or her or Roo, for that matter."

Brandon stared at his tea. He nibbled on his lip, then shrugged. "I don't think she likes me. She wouldn't poison me, would she?"

"No, that she wouldn't do. You saw her. She was gagging and crying the entire time I was getting stitched up. She wouldn't hurt a fly. The worst thing she does is light a few fires and—" Austin held out her hand, palm up to expose the ring. "She steals stuff. You'll probably find a little trinket where the ring was."

Brandon leaned over, squinted in the dim light, before he plucked the ring from Austin's palm. "Yeah, that was my grandma's engagement ring. I had it in a box in my underwear drawer because I was taking it up to get it sized."

"Your grandma's ring. Ah, don't tell me you are getting ready to ask Lyndsey to marry you." Austin sniffed a laugh.

"Yeah, actually, I am." He mumbled, low. "What's so funny about that?"

"It isn't funny." No, it wasn't funny at all. But Austin didn't let on that her heart just dropped. "I was just thinking about—" She wiggled up her finger, started pretending to clean her nail. "I must stay vigilant with Aina. I'm sorry. Fairies are funny creatures."

"That's alright. A fairy, huh?" Brandon seemed to still be chewing on the idea. "What's with Roo? I passed him on the stairway. He growled at me."

"Roo is short for Rougarou. He's from the bayous of Louisiana.

He grew up there deep in the woods. His dad was afraid somebody was going to shoot him, take him away. He never bonded with him and couldn't get Roo to listen. Roo was always out in the cypress swamp, feet muddy, chasing will-o'-the-wisps, drinking from mason jars."

"Rougarou. I've heard of that before," Brandon muttered. "I saw something on some late-night show about idiots hunting one down."

"It is said in some parts of Louisiana that there is a beast that lives in the swamps that has the body of a man and the head of a wolf. He was cursed by a witch. Roo's father believed Roo was that creature."

"Do you believe it?"

"If you look at him in the moonlight, his eyes really glow red." Austin looked up at Brandon. His expression was lackluster at best. He was still staring at the ring. She didn't care if he believed her or not. He was probably just holding up the conversation and wasn't really hearing it. She'd like to think it didn't matter to her. However, it did. "He's my best friend. I don't care either way. He knows me better than anybody and knows when I'm sad or feeling sick."

"Do you love this Marco guy?"

It was so out of the realm of the immediate conversation that Austin sat there silently for a moment, trying to tie it to what they were talking about so she could answer correctly.

"Um, I do love him," she said. "I think he loves me in his own way. It doesn't matter; he's married."

"That's what Hutch said."

"Yeah, Marco is kind of—an institution. His family has followed many of the old Aztec traditions for centuries. I suppose it is like your mom and dad's church practices, but in their own way. The customs are burned into his mind. Their bloodlines are believed to be pure. I'm just an American mutt. Fun to play with, but not on the teeny tiny list of women he can marry and bear purebreds like Hutch to continue the bloodline."

"And that's okay with you?" Brandon asked slowly, deliberately. "Being somebody's toy?"

"Are we here to discuss my love life? Maybe he's *my* toy," Austin grouched. "Because it really is none of your business."

"You asked about Lyndsey."

"I didn't ask if you loved her. I didn't try to pry into the intimate details of your relationship."

"I'm just worried about the mother of my daughter, alright?" Brandon said gruffly, and took a swig of his tea. "I can leave if you want."

"You might as well bail. That's your type's signature move—guys like you say sweet things, get the screw, then run off to marry Miss Nice and Normal."

"Guys like me? What the hell does that mean?" He sniffed a loud laugh, threw one hand up. "Why would you say that?"

"I didn't say it first. Your mom did a half hour ago."

Brandon swallowed hard. "Well, it's not true. Don't listen to my mom. And I'm not the one who left."

"I had nothing to stay for. You were *in love*," Austin raised her hands, made quotation marks with her forefingers and middle fingers to stress her point, "with your next girlfriend."

"I had no clue, Austin, you were pregnant. I had no clue you even liked me. I figured you were using me to get back at your daddy when you stopped coming over. Then he told me to stay away from you. The only reason I had another girlfriend was that she was there. You weren't. I really liked you."

"Liked."

"Well, I don't know you anymore. You come back here looking like a prizefighter and dragging along a half-dozen friends. Running. It's like you're running from something, and that kind of scares me. No, it scares me a lot."

"I mean, you didn't love me. You said *liked*."

"I don't know," Brandon was drinking his tea more out of being nervous about the conversation. Austin could see that.

His hands were shaking. He'd nearly downed the entire cup. "I felt something. Like I'm feeling now. I don't want that feeling to go away. You're alright. I look at you the same way I did four years ago. You're beautiful. You're smart. You've got that pretty geek thing going. And now you dress like this—" He waved a hand from head to foot. "I don't see girls in sexy dresses. I don't see girls at all with the eyes I'm seeing you now. And I haven't felt the feelings I'm having right now since I saw you last. And I'm seeing you in a whole new light. I don't care if you hear me say it or not. I'm being open and honest. I'm stepping out of my comfort zone and feel like my foot is landing in cow shit. But I'm saying it really bothered me, that thing you did with Marco. I'm feeling the pain. Like you ripped out my heart."

Austin was staring at him. He was being open, really open. He was never one to expose what was beneath the thick armor he always seemed to wear. He looked like he was waiting for her to say something.

"I'm not sure what this means," she said softly. "A minute ago, you told me you were getting ready to propose to your girlfriend. Now, you're telling me you've still got feelings for me?"

"Yeah, I think so." He was puffing a little bit on the last drink of tea. It was hot, and Austin tried to squelch a smile.

"Did you burn your tongue?"

"I did. It would have been easier telling you that if I had a beer or two in me." She felt his hand come out, slip around her good shoulder. "And this would be a lot easier too if I'd had a drink." He leaned in and pulled her toward him.

Austin felt his lips on hers. Warm from the tea, sweet. It was like breathing in the scent of cotton candy for the first time, tasting it with her lips, and feeling the realization that she'd been missing *this* perfect sweet all along.

Her belly jumped, wiggled with a thousand butterflies. He gave her two, gentle swipes with his lips, then came in for the big one.

Holy hell.

It was like nothing she had ever felt. Her arms tingled with goosebumps; her heart jumped like a runaway basketball down a hillside. She didn't remember his kiss being so good, no *great*.

Austin pushed her hand on his chest. His T-shirt was soft beneath her fingertips. She felt his fingers lost in her hair, barely touching the skin of her neck. This seemed so easy. Why hadn't she just walked up and kissed him the first second she'd been standing on his front porch? She was dizzy with him. Dizzy. *Dizzy.*

"Aw, no," Austin gave Brandon a gentle push backward with her palm. "Hey, stop."

"I'm sorry. I am so sorry." Brandon stood up quickly. "I don't know what I was thinking. It just happened."

"It didn't just happen." Austin stood up, pushed in front of Brandon, and stomped her way to the front door.

"Uh oh." It was Aina who stepped back from the door when Austin threw it open.

"Yeah, *uh oh*," Austin hissed. "You spiked the tea."

"In my defense, you said this was your safe place. I just thought I'd maybe get you guys together—"

Austin's hands trembled around her cup, knuckles white. "Holy shit." Austin had her hands on her head, eyes smashed tight, and face toward the ceiling. "The reason I felt safe here is that it was only what I conjured up in my mind, like—like a fantasy. Do you understand? It is what I dreamed, not what is really here. Reality sucks. Reality is a guy dumping you for a prettier girl and finding out you're pregnant with his kid. I don't want reality. It is easier to make stuff up in my head than to know I'm going to get dumped again and again and again," Austin yowled softly to the air. "You can't drug people's drinks. Do you think I don't know you guys will leave me too? As soon as you get the chance, you're gone. Because I'm not pretty enough, smart enough, or strong enough. Because, for some reason, I pissed you off, and no amount of sorries will Band-Aid the skinned heart I made. I'm hoping to God you don't dump me at a mission in the middle of Columbus like my dad did because you're mad I undermined something you were doing.

Or leave me stranded in some foreign city without money like Paolo did when he had one of his spells. Brandon Tremaine doesn't love me. He's got a girlfriend, for God's sakes! He doesn't like me. No potion poured into him will last longer than two hours when he gets his head screwed on straight. He'll see me for what I am, the *broken* me that nobody ever keeps around, and the same one he never liked in the first place, other than the fact that I was an easy lay. Stop it!" She turned, opened her eyes. "Oh, my God! Do you understand what you have done?"

"Pet, stop, would you stop for a second?" Starr walked up, snatched onto Austin's upper arms, and shook her. "You are ranting."

"She's ranting because I put something in her drink."

"You what?" Starr asked.

"One of my grandma's truth serum drinks," Aina told her. "It's really just something to calm the nerves, an herbal sedative."

Austin turned. She knew what Aina was capable of, and she fully believed the girl had something in her that could make a man love anybody.

But it wasn't right, and it wasn't fair to the one who was on the receiving end without knowing. And *he* had just come into the living room, was standing at the door, peering into his cup.

"I'm so sorry, Brandon. She roofied our drinks." That's all Austin could say when she turned to him. She turned and shook her head. "I was just kidding out there. I didn't think Aina would really do it. It was a joke. Please don't be mad."

Austin turned. She didn't want to look at anybody, didn't want to be reminded that it took drugs to have some guy profess his love or like or whatever that was out there. "I'm going to sleep this off, and in the morning, I am going to murder in cold blood the first person who mentions this—this event."

"For the record, I said I put something in *yours*," Aina muttered as Austin stomped up the stairway. "I didn't put anything in *his*."

~

At twelve-thirty, there was a soft knock on the bedroom door. Austin could hear Roo rustling around in his blankets on the floor. She untangled herself from Aina, who had slipped in beside her. Austin was in a daze, kicking her feet over the edge of the bed. She peered toward the crack of the door. She could barely make out a shadow, but knew from the stature that it was Brandon. "Yeah," she whispered. She just wanted to go back to sleep in her bed.

"There's some guy at the front door for you."

"What?" Austin rubbed the sleep from her eyes. She stepped over Roo, opened the bedroom door, and looked out into the dimly lit hallway.

Brandon was standing there in a pair of flannel sleep pants and a worn T-shirt.

"There's a guy outside from the bar tonight. He said he works for the fire department," Brandon whispered. "He had somebody run your car tags because he was worried about you. He was getting a beer with his buddy when the fight broke out. He said he was the one who gave "the big guy" a towel to hold on to your cut, but you all left right after. They called the police station in town, and somebody told them where you were staying."

"Can you tell him to go away?" Austin mumbled, halfway asleep. She hardly remembered anything, much less a man with a towel. Her shoulder ached, throbbing where Starr had sewn the stitches.

"Maybe you should, Austin," Brandon said as he scrubbed the top of his head. His hair was askew, and his eyes were bloodshot from sleep. "He didn't seem to trust me. I don't need the cops out here tonight because they think I beat you or something."

"Why would they think that? He was literally *there* during the fight."

Brandon sighed. "You had bruises on your face when you left. You get what I'm saying?"

Austin swung her head impatiently right to left. "It was dark in the bar, but yeah, alright," she whispered, pushing out of the bedroom door.

"Um," Brandon dropped his chin, made a little point toward Austin's feet. "You might want to put some pants on or something."

Austin's eyes dropped. She was standing in a short T-shirt and her black panties. Another reason to never drink anything Aina gave her anymore. "Yeah, I'm sorry."

"You don't have to apologize to me." Brandon didn't smile, just turned. "I'll sit up at the top of the stairs until you're done. Not that you need backup or anything. You just look a little out of it."

Austin threw on a pair of shorts and slipped around Brandon on the stairway. He was doing exactly what he said, plopped down at the top with elbows on his knees and rubbing his hand through his hair sleepily.

He was right. There was a man at the door. Short, blonde, and buff. She remembered him—a stranger's face half-lit by the porch lamp, one of the two men eating when they had stopped at the bar. Her pulse quickened.

"Okay, you're alright," he asked, and laughed a little when Austin opened the screen door between them and took one step outside.

"Yeah, I'm fine. It's nice of you to check on me. I think. Unless you're a pervert or something."

"No, no, I'm not," he said quickly. "I'm Trevor Bentley. I live right over in Concord. You were bleeding pretty badly when you left. I couldn't tell if he shot you or if it was the beer bottle that got you."

"Beer bottle."

"That was Billy Tate. I guess he'd been swinging that gun all day at work. They made him take it out to his vehicle. The guys told the cops that. He's actually under arrest at the hospital. Where'd you learn how to fight like that? The military?"

"Kind of." Austin yawned into the cup of her hand, took a step back toward the door frame. "Listen, I appreciate you checking in on me, but I'm really tired. I've had a long, very cruddy day, and I want it to end."

She started to close the door between them. Trevor's hand came out, stopped it gently.

"Was that guy who answered the door your boyfriend?" he asked. "I mean, if not, do you want to go out sometime? Tomorrow?"

Austin looked at him. "I'm sorry. I've got a boyfriend in Charleston."

"Maybe just dinner."

"Buddy, she said she's got a boyfriend. He's about seven feet and two hundred pounds of meaner than shit. I would just walk away right now."

Austin hadn't even heard Brandon stride down the stairway in his bare feet. He stood there towering over the other man.

"Well, if you break up with that boyfriend, just give me a call." He shoved a piece of paper at Austin. She stared at the paper a beat too long, wondering why every stranger she met wanted something from her before they even knew her name. She automatically took it from him while Brandon stepped in front of her, closing the screen door between them.

"You weren't playing hard to get, right?" Brandon muttered while he locked the door. "I didn't just screw up a date with the dude, did I?"

"No."

"Yeah, he didn't seem your type." Brandon was wearing a baby-blue T-shirt. It was tight on his shoulders, and Austin was having a difficult time not staring at him when he turned to the steps. She could see Golem peering out of the shadows in the hallway upstairs.

"My type? I have a type?" Austin yawned again.

"Yeah, you like to hit and run. He was the kind of guy who liked to stick around, I'd bet. You know, *a nice guy.*"

"Ouch." She stopped behind him on the bottom step.

"Just saying."

Austin stared up the dark stairway. He was right. The truth landed like a punch she didn't dodge. She was exhausted—tired of running, tired of pushing people away, tired of being the one who bolted first before she could get hurt. But worse than all of that was being tired of not knowing how to stop.

Chapter –14

Lyndsey showed up at six-thirty in the morning, the scent of peppery sausage and flaky biscuits from Big Bill's Diner curling through the kitchen as she nudged open the door. Brandon sat at the table, cool wood pressing into his forearms, Tessa curled in his lap, squinting against the watery blue light spilling across the linoleum. The hush was broken only by the low hum of the refrigerator and the distant cluck of chickens outside.

He'd accepted years ago that he wasn't a morning person, and it was nice to know he wasn't the only one. Starr was slumped in a chair, her head buried in her arms, muttering about how the country silence was louder than city noise. She'd threatened to make breakfast three or four times, but never moved.

Austin locked eyes with Aina across the table, her glare sharp enough to cut. She winced as her shoulder stitches tugged when she shifted, but she held the stare anyway.

Aina responded with exaggerated eye-rolls. "These are stink eyes," she announced, pointing back at her face. From the open window drifted the raucous cackling of chickens and the faint scent of cut grass. Outside, Roo darted behind the barn in pursuit of the hens, his brown hair a blur in the morning haze. Golem slumped at the table, rubbing his stomach and grumbling in his thick accent about starving to death before breakfast. The spicy tang of sausage lingered in the air, mixing with the sharper note of brewed coffee. Hutch was still missing in action—Starr claimed he never surfaced before one in the afternoon.

Brandon glanced over at Stats. His gray suit and navy-blue tie made him look like an insurance salesman who'd stumbled into a barnyard sitcom—crisp and formal in a room full of sleepy faces, pajamas, and morning hair. "You look nicely dressed," he said.

"Men who wear ties five days a week earn more than men who don't," Stats divulged to him.

"You're going to a job interview today?" Brandon joked.

Stats shook his head, stared hard at Brandon. "No, studies have shown that twenty percent of women are more attracted to men who wear suits and ties."

"So, you've got a date then?" Brandon asked. He figured the man wasn't unattractive, just maybe a little too tall and too skinny and too tattooed for most local women.

"No."

"Oh."

"I got you your favorite breakfast," Lyndsey said, her voice just a little too bright for the hour. Brandon looked up, smiling despite the heaviness in his eyes, his stomach growling at the scent of sausage biscuits.

"You're a babe," Brandon told her. But he was eyeing the small bag she was holding. Surely she got enough for more than just him. "But did you happen to grab some for everybody?"

"I figured they'd be gone." Lyndsey was smiling a little too hard. "I'm taking the day off. We're dropping Tessa off at your mom's. I already talked to her. I've got a surprise planned for you."

"Oh, oodles of fun, can I go?" Aina teased.

"Uh, no," Lyndsey said flatly. She tugged on Brandon's shirt. "Come on. We're going to be late." And he followed her outside.

"You didn't have to be rude," Brandon grunted as he snapped Tessa into her car seat. She clutched a picture book to her chest, swinging her legs with nervous energy. "Come on, Lynds, they'll be gone in a day or so." He paused to ruffle Tessa's hair, noticing the light catching on her green sundress with pink flowers, her pink sandals a cheerful splash against the truck floorboards—Austin had picked those out at the mall. "And did it occur to either you or Mom that it might have been nice for Tessa to stay with Austin?"

"Yeah, it had. We both laughed at the idea." Lyndsey waited for Brandon to jump in the truck. "I'm sorry," she went on. "I didn't have enough money to feed that army. I think you're crazy for even thinking she'd be safe with her. I think one of those men beat Austin up. If I had a kid, I wouldn't leave her with any of them."

"Austin read me a book last night."

Brandon caught Tessa's reflection in the rearview mirror, her small feet thumping a restless rhythm against the seat. She lifted the book, its sparkly cover catching the morning sun. "It was about fairies. I like fairies."

Brandon narrowed his gaze. "Sweetie, I don't think she read to you. You were asleep when I went to bed."

"No, I wasn't," Tessa disagreed. "I wanted a drink. I went to your bed. You said to go back to bed. No drink. I'll pee the bed. I woke up Austin. I plugged up her nose with my fingers." She held up a finger and thumb, pinched them together. "She said: Are you trying to kill me?" Tessa made her voice sound deep. "She got me a drink. And she read me the book she got me so I wouldn't kill her."

"Great," Lyndsey said, rolling her eyes. "Your kid is going to go to Sunday school and tell everybody she tried to kill somebody." She turned to stare out the window. The truck rolled forward, tires crunching over gravel, the only sound in the cab Tessa's off-key song drifting through the air.

"I love you, you know," Lyndsey finally said softly. It wasn't the first time she'd said it. It always seemed like a big deal to her. Brandon liked her. He really did. She was pretty, smart, and worked hard at her job. But he knew in his heart he was going through the motions expected of him. Having a relationship with Lyndsey was like driving to work every day. He took Tremaine Road to the stop sign, then turned left on County Road 14. It eventually turned into Main Street in town. He went there every day. He came home. He was going to date her, marry her, have kids, and get old. He felt old right now, just thinking about it.

"I know."

"I know?" Lyndsey asked. "Do you feel anything for me? I mean, one minute you tell me you really like me too. The next, you're like *I know*. Are you just saying it to say it so you don't hurt my feelings? Or do you really feel that way?"

"Baby, you know how I feel. Do I need to say it?"

"Well, yeah, kind of."

"Okay, I love you." Oh, his voice always sounded so dull and flat when he said those words.

Lyndsey stared at him hard. "Is something bothering you today? You're quiet."

"No. I'm tired."

"Is it Laura?" Lyndsey's voice was softer now, her fingers tapping a nervous beat on her knee.

Brandon cringed inwardly, wishing Lyndsey hadn't brought her up. Still, Laura was a convenient excuse to keep the memory of the kiss at bay. Kissing Austin was all he'd thought about since last night—the cool slip of her skin beneath his fingers, the faint strawberry scent of her hair, the way her eyes flashed up at him with anger and heat. She was unpredictable, sharp, and soft at once. Nothing like the quiet routine of Lyndsey or the girls in town.

Austin moved differently. Thought differently. Being around her felt like trying to catch butterflies in a field—you never knew which way she'd dart.

"Baby?" Lyndsey interrupted him.

"Yeah, it's Laura," he lied.

"They'll find your sister. You know that. We have ways of finding people even if she is—gone." Lyndsey scooted closer, her shoulder brushing his as the truck bumped down the rutted driveway toward his mom's house. "She's out there somewhere, just waiting to be found. I mean, look at Austin. Everybody thought she was gone for good, but she came back."

"Sure." The tires crunched on loose gravel as they pulled into his mom's driveway. Brandon reached for the door handle just as his phone started to buzz.

"Hey, Brandon."

"Is this—Austin?" How the hell did she find his number?

"Yeah, Stats dug around and found your number. I know. Sorry to bother you. But we've got a bit of a *predicament* here at the farm, and we don't know how to take care of it."

"The house isn't on fire, is it?"

There was silence for far too long. Then Austin had forced a laugh. "Oh, good. I am assuming that is the far end of the worst-case scenario. A fire." She actually sighed. "No fire. Just—just a—a misunderstanding."

~

"Okay, you'll think this is funny later, right?" Austin called from the end of the driveway, but Brandon's gaze slid past her, snagging on the sight of fourteen cattle trailers stretching down the road. The lowing and shuffling of cows filled the morning, drowning out almost everything else.

"Well, here's the thing," Austin was saying while she tried to focus on Brandon. He was sure Lyndsey was churning her jaws right then, next to him. She'd had reservations for two at the Concord Day Spa for a couple's massage. The appointment was at ten. It was nine-forty-five. "You know, there's kind of a translation issue between Marco and me, right?"

"*Marco*?" Lyndsey was looking from Brandon to Austin.

"Yeah, remember the dude from the other day? He's my dad." Hutch was standing behind Austin. "And Austin's lover." He'd said lover with a sexy tone. If he was there for moral support, he wasn't doing a good job. He kept rubbing his belly and laughing.

"Don't listen to him," Austin went on. She looked kind of pale, but she always seemed to lose a bit of luster when Lyndsey was around. "Okay, you remember the discussion we had about cattle? I was trying to make him understand that in the United States, you had the ability to prosper if you really wanted to prosper, right?"

"Yeah, you made me sound like I was poor."

"Well, his translator misunderstood some of the conversation. He thought I was requesting—"

"No, *demanding*," Hutch interrupted. "When Austin wants something, my father cowers like a bunny under a wolf paw. What Austin wants, Austin gets."

"That's not entirely true." Austin rolled her eyes, shook her head.

"Don't listen to him. It's just that he thought, when I was giving him the analogy, that I was asking for a couple of hundred head of cattle as a gift for you, for taking us in, so you could prosper. Not that you *aren't*—doing well—" She stumbled through the words. "You're not poor." She threw out a hand toward the trailers. "Oh, hell. Surprise."

Brandon's eyes followed the line of trailers. The truck drivers were standing outside, looking impatient. "I can't accept these." Brandon pushed himself out of his pickup truck in a daze. "This is more than a hundred thousand dollars' worth of cattle," he muttered, scratching his head. He wasn't sure how to react. Yeah, he could take them. The dollar signs were banging off his head. He'd be an idiot *not* to take them. He didn't think there was enough water in the creek that Abel had dammed to support this number. No, no, it would be like taking a coat from the poor box at church. He was not going to accept a donation of cattle.

"Austin," Brandon said. "I don't have enough water, hay, and grain. I haven't checked the fences yet. It costs a lot for the veterinarian to come out—"

"Um, the hay and grain are coming. Golem and I can check fences; he grew up on a farm. I've got some money to help with the veterinarian." She reached out a hand and laid it softly on his arm. "Please, Five, don't hate me."

He couldn't stop staring at the trucks until she touched his arm, her fingers warm and uncertain. He dropped his gaze, rubbing his jaw, the grit of stubble rough under his palm. He looked hard at Austin. "I don't hate you."

"Babe, what's going on?" Lyndsey called out from the truck. Brandon turned and saw her leaning toward the door. "I don't get my money back if we don't show."

"It would be crazy to take free cattle, right?" He turned back to Austin. Brandon could see Hutch tapping his phone. He knew he was listening to the conversation, so Brandon waved Austin to the back of the truck. He saw Lyndsey twisting in her seat, her gaze wary. "Okay, what's the cost to you if I take the cattle?"

"There isn't a cost," Austin said, leaning into the bed of the truck.

"Although it might be considered an insult if you sent the cattle back, I don't think it would start a world war."

Brandon's mouth dropped. "I hadn't thought about that."

"I didn't want to bring it up," Austin said, "but refusing a gift can imply it's not good enough for you. It comes off very disrespectful. And Marco gives me things all the time for taking care of Hutch. He's a humanitarian—very kind. He helped me save turtles."

"Marco Arias saves turtles?"

"Sure. When I ask him to save turtles, he saves turtles." Austin shrugged, reached out, and poked Brandon. "It was fun. He likes our adventures. Can I say something? I mean, you heard what I said last night. As stupid as I feel, I'm not taking it back. You gave me something to dream about for the last three years, something to—to get me through hard times. Let me pay you back, even if it wasn't my intention for Marco to buy you cows. You said this was your dream, to farm as your dad did, and so you can be with Tessa."

"Abel Martin's dammed up Turtle Creek that runs between our properties. I don't know if there's enough water for all of them."

"You could talk to Abel Martin, ask him to release some water, or you could have some water tanks brought in."

"Yes, but, Austin." Brandon waved an arm toward the fields and barns. "This is outside my realm of things that are normal. Things like this don't happen here."

Austin gave a short laugh. "Normal? Brandon, look at our lives. Talk to Golem's parents. Or Aina's dad, who tried to burn the 'fairy' out of her. People do crazy things because everyone's got a different idea of what normal is."

She stopped beside the truck, leaned into the bed, and wrapped her fingers around the bumper. "Look," she said softly. She glanced around to make sure no one was watching. Then she lifted.

The back of the truck creaked upward in her hands—a few inches, but enough to steal the breath out of Brandon's throat. He froze, eyes wide. Lyndsey glanced frantically around in the cab, trying to figure out whether the truck had rolled.

Austin set it down gently and stepped back.

"Brandon," she said, her voice steady, "sometimes the world hands you something that makes zero sense. You get to choose whether you accept it or pretend it isn't happening."

He stared at her. "Did you—actually lift the truck?"

"Yeah," Austin said simply. "Because sometimes life is bigger than 'normal.' And you can't talk yourself out of reality just because it feels impossible."

Brandon swallowed. "So… the cattle?"

"That's the point." Austin nodded. "Strange things happen for a reason. You get to decide what to do with the gift — not whether it should have happened."

"Babe, alright, I've had it," Lyndsey was stepping out of the truck, leaning over the door. "We're too late to go. I've spent half my paycheck to do this for us." She turned to Austin whose eyes were still locked on Brandon's dazed stare. "You know how rude this is, right? I know you planned this. You come back, think you can flirt it up with my boyfriend and—"

"Lyndsey, stop." Brandon forced himself to look away from Austin. He wiped sweat from his brow, feeling the heat creep up his neck. "Come on. It was a mistake. But I can't leave these cows in the trucks. I'll call the spa, get a refund—or I'll pay to have it done another day."

"With what money?" Lyndsey spat out. She cringed right after she said it.

Brandon's cheeks burned. Lyndsey was blunt, sure, but he'd never seen her this jealous. The look she shot him was pure feral—like the barn cats he'd watched fighting over a fresh-caught mouse, eyes sharp and unblinking, ready to defend what was hers.

"I'll do it, but only if we can look at it as an investment," Brandon turned to Austin.

"Whatever you want to do, Brandon."

"And you're a part of the investment, and we pay Marco Arias back if it succeeds."

"Well," she laughed, didn't look at Lyndsey. "I know you're going to succeed." She'd rolled her eyes like he was being silly. "Come on, dumbass, you can't fail at something you haven't even started yet."

Brandon was standing there thinking of all the what-ifs, ready to take a nose-dive already. She'd said the same thing when she had tutored him in math when he had the horrible gut feeling he was never going to make it through high school. God, he'd hated math since third grade. Why? Because he'd never memorized the stupid times tables. Then she said, "*Hey, dumbass, you haven't failed high school yet because you're not done.*" But he'd gone home and studied the stupid things all weekend just to please her. Why, again? He didn't know. It almost embarrassed him that he cared what she thought. Because she was the only one who ever expected him to be anything more than a guy who just went to work and came home.

"Yeah, I'll do it," Brandon said.

Lyndsey just tossed her hands into the air. "This is crazy," she groaned. "There's no way they are going to release water from the dam, Brandon. The town up there needs all of it. There's no way you or I can request it. They'll say it is not for the good of all, just a waste for you and this farm."

"Well, I know there's a spring down there," Austin offered. "It wouldn't impact the amount of water Mister Martin needs for his compound if his people are difficult to deal with. If you put in a well, then perhaps Mister Martin could use it in emergencies, too. It comes from a different source than Turtle Creek."

Brandon had taken in her smile, soft but assertive. It was a diplomatic approach. She'd obviously dealt with sensitive issues before and with belligerent people.

"*His* people, as you call them, aren't difficult," Lyndsey grunted.

"Of course not. I didn't mean to imply—" Austin was trying to be considerate. But Brandon knew from past experiences with Lyndsey that it wouldn't happen.

"Yes, I think you did," Lyndsey spat at Austin, pivoted on her feet, and glared hard at Brandon. "This is nuts," Lyndsey hissed, jaw tight. "Nuts."

Chapter −15

"Okay, so my cattle fiasco bought us a few more days." Austin had slipped out to the pasture and came up behind Golem, who was sitting on a four-foot-high round bale of hay. After her run, sweat slicked the back of her neck. She lifted her hair, letting the cool, prickling breeze send a shiver down her spine.

Eight miles. It felt like forty. She'd run along Tremaine Road and, against her better judgment, headed up to the top of Canaan Mountain Road—a newer dirt road. The county had covered it in gravel for a couple of miles, then the gravel abruptly ended. Austin stopped. In front of her loomed a huge electric gate with TRESPASSERS WILL BE SHOT signs bolted to the rails. She scanned right to left before spotting a camo-colored game camera aimed at the road.

"Shit," she cursed beneath her breath, made a quick turn, and took a few steps back before triggering the cameras. It usually took them a second or two to start up. She looked to the left. There were two more cameras attached to thick cables and bolted to the trees.

Austin slipped back into the trees. She could hear the camera click as it took a picture. Hopefully, they just got the ground where she was standing. Carefully, she glanced around, stepped up to a small oak, and clambered up the branches.

"Holy hell." When she climbed high enough, she could see out over the mountain. Below sprawled a complex—a small city: nicer homes to her right, mobile homes to the left, rickety houses scattered everywhere in between. The sharp scent of pine needles mixed with the distant, acrid tang of smoke from somewhere below. The hillside with the homes had been nearly stripped of trees, except for a few near a massive house at the very top. Austin guessed a thousand people must live in the compound.

The sound of a truck coming from inside the compound, heading toward the gate, forced Austin to slip down from the tree and cut back along Brandon's property, winding through forest and fields.

Oddly, the closer she'd gotten to the compound, the heavier her limbs had felt—fatigue seeping in until she barely wanted to run at all. The air tasted metallic, thick, and her skin prickled with every breath.

Where had she felt this before? Oh, when Lyndsey was nearby, she remembered—the same strange heaviness creeping in. Though she'd chalked that up to stress, not anything real. When she came up next to Golem an hour later, Austin rubbed at the slashes in the thighs of her legs from the tiny barbs the patches of briars had left on her skin. Curiously, she noted she felt more awake again. The fatigue she had felt near the compound had eased.

"Did you take a shortcut?" Golem asked. He was tugging off the makeshift barn gloves Starr had sewn with Brandon's grandmother's old sewing machine and an old pair of leather chaps from the barn. He needed them to shovel a trench and divert some water from the old spring along Turtle Creek into a makeshift pond they had all taken turns digging.

"You know me," Austin smiled. "Always looking for another adventure." He grinned, leaned over, and stretched out his hand. Austin latched on, letting him pull her up beside him. He was warm against her shoulder, smelling of earth and sweat. For a moment, all was quiet—the cows contentedly munching on the grain and hay Golem had laid out. "Stats is having a heyday with the books. He's come up with a business plan for Brandon that is almost five pages long." Austin smiled. "I don't think I've ever heard Stats giggle. He was having so much fun crunching the numbers, he was getting goosebumps."

"This reminds me of home, Pet." Golem didn't seem to hear her. He just made a deep, deep sigh. Austin craned her neck to look up to him. He really was a giant, a huge hulk of a man. "I miss home."

"Do you want to go home, Golem?" Austin asked. He was a little hard of hearing with quiet things, and she had to step up her voice a bit—but she knew he always heard emotional things too well. "I can take you home now that Paolo's gone."

"No."

Austin could see tears in his eyes. He could go home. Yet she knew life there was difficult. His family was poor. They couldn't feed him or take him to the doctor when he got sick.

"Do you want me to go home?" Golem shifted a bit in his seat, like he just might have realized maybe she didn't want him around. "I can eat less."

"Hutch eats more than you. What is my biggest fear, big guy?" Austin banged Golem with her shoulder. He looked down and smiled.

"That I will leave you."

"You're right."

"I won't ever leave you, Pet. I promise." Golem gave her his most wide-eyed gaze to let her know he wasn't lying. Austin swallowed against the sudden tightness in her throat. "Where's the place you feel the safest?"

"Here. Right here."

"Brandon is nice to you. Nicer than Paolo." Golem seemed to decide.

"Brandon has a girlfriend, Golem. We just share Tessa. His girlfriend is nice and pretty."

"Yuck. She's ugly." Golem wrinkled his bulbous nose, pushed up two fingers, and pinched his nostrils. "She smells bad."

Austin laughed out loud. "You're my biggest cheerleader. I'm going to get you a couple of pom-poms and a little skirt to wear," she said. Then she let her smile drop. "Do you miss Paolo?" Austin asked him. She didn't want to bring up the fact that they would have to leave. Brandon had a girlfriend. Paolo wasn't her boyfriend, so she could see through Golem's eyes that her relationship with the two men was somewhat alike. Golem contemplated her question a moment. "I miss his good side. I don't miss his bad side. I miss his good days. I don't miss his bad days."

Austin nodded. "It was always hard getting up, not knowing if he'd—"

"—hurt you?" Golem finished.

She pinched the bridge of her nose. "That was the worst. Let's not talk about Paolo. I hated and idolized him, and now he's gone."

"Hey." It was Brandon's voice following the sound of boots swishing through grass. Austin turned to her left, scooted on the hay bale to see him. His face looked tired and worn, but he was smiling contentedly as he tugged off his work gloves.

"Your ears must be burning—we were just talking about you."

"All good, I hope." Brandon's shirt was smudged with hay and dirt. When he wiped his face, he left a muddy streak on his cheek. "There is an envelope on the kitchen counter for you."

Half listening, she eyed the skinny boy turned well-built man—muscles evident even beneath his jeans. When he leaned over the hay bale, his musky scent hit her.

"What?" Brandon had looked up and smiled, caught Austin staring at him. She felt her cheeks burn, shrugged.

"You've—you've got dirt on your face," she mustered, sounding like an idiot.

"Oh." He tried to swipe it away, but made it worse. "Did I get it?"

"No," Austin said, and Golem laughed next to her.

"You're not going to put some spit on a used tissue and wipe it off, are you?" he asked. "That's what my mom used to do."

Austin let her shoulders drop, leaned in, and gently scrubbed her fingers over his cheek. He shifted toward her touch, surprising her. Maybe she left her hand there a second too long. He swayed back, his smile flattening—like the old man at the grocery store who lit up thinking a local had walked in, only to shut it off like a light switch the second he realized he didn't recognize Austin.

"I've got a girlfriend, you know that, right?" he'd said suddenly.

Austin had nodded. "Yeah, I didn't grab your butt. I just wiped off your cheek."

"Like you were making love to it."

"Oh, screw off, Tremaine." Austin snapped her fingers away. "If I made love to you, you'd be lying dead on the ground. I'm way too much woman for you."

"In your dreams."

"No, baby," she'd said, her voice soft and hoarse. "In *your* dreams." Austin tried to look cool as she shifted forward, but leaned too far, almost toppling. Embarrassment flushed her cheeks, but before she could fall, Golem reached out, grabbed her shoulder, and tugged her back to her seat. "Another adventure?" he asked quietly.

Austin chose to ignore Brandon while he stifled a laugh. To compensate for her clumsiness, she turned to Golem. "You're always saving my ass, Golem. What am I going to do with myself?" she said.

~

Later, back at the house, a plain white envelope lay on the kitchen counter. Austin picked it up, turning it over in her hands. She asked Starr and Aina, who were watching TV in the living room, if they knew who had left it. They didn't know. Austin didn't recognize the cursive. It was fairly nice print.

"It's been there all day." Stats looked up from the computer. His gaze went right to left before he nodded for Austin to come over toward him.

"What's up?" she asked. He peered around her shoulder as if making sure no one could hear.

"The stuff you wanted me to look up. I got a satellite view of the compound." Stats always talked in a jerky voice, words coming in short sentences like he was making an effort to dumb up what he wanted to say to everyone else. "The compound is prodigious, Pet, circumambient to the north-facing and south-facing side of the mountain."

Talking to him sometimes was like deciphering a foreign language. He had a huge vocabulary and a compulsive need to try every word at least once.

"English, please," she muttered to Stats.

But when Stats turned the computer sideways, Austin was staring at a satellite view of the compound. He didn't need to explain his words.

"Yeah, dumb it up for her," Hutch muttered from across the room.

"English. Dumbed up. Alright." Stats eyed Hutch, then turned his attention to the computer. "The compound encompasses the entire mountain. From what I can uncover so far, it is owned by a man named Abel Martin. He has a brochure that states he is an ordained minister. It is not with any traditional churches. He lists many credentials, including a college degree in theology and business management. None has any support to back them up. He was born James Hill. He has at least six aliases, each with a different wife and children. He has a rather large following online, advertising himself as a faith healer and spiritualist who has heard the words of God directly. He was arrested in Utah and Colorado for falsifying records to rob families of their dead parents' estates. He was brought in six times for conspiracy to murder—do you want me to go on?"

"What's your take on him, Stats, other than he's a fake?"

"I believe he is describing himself as a prophet to his followers. A false one, of course. He has several other names. Over the last 43 years, he has been building these compounds across the United States and has recently expanded into Mexico. He has twenty-three small communities like the one on the other side of the mountain. The one adjacent to this property is his home base and his largest."

"Ah, yeah," Austin muttered. "My grandma used to tell me this: beware of the false prophets, who come to you in sheep's clothing, but inwardly are ravenous wolves. It's from the book of Matthew in the Bible."

"Beware of wolves in sheep's clothing." Stats nodded. "Yes. Like Paolo."

Austin's eyes darted up to him. He had turned quickly back to his computer. Had he really said he hadn't trusted Paolo?

She didn't make a note of it aloud. Didn't want anyone else to think Stats was not to be trusted. "And the envelope?" She held it aloft for Stats to see. "It just appeared out of nowhere?"

"It was there when we got back from the fields this afternoon."

Hutch was listening to music when he popped one earplug out to look at Austin. "Nobody saw anybody come in, so we don't know who dropped it off."

"I'm sure it's fan mail." Austin feigned indifference and dropped it in her purse when she passed. She yawned, watched the shadow slip into the living room. She knew it was Brandon. He'd looked a bit peeved that his mean retort hadn't bothered her.

"How about I have Stats order a new set of books so we can get back to work on your school, huh?"

"How about we stop long enough that I can be a real teenager and go to a real American high school?" Hutch had retorted.

"Is that what you want?"

"Girls. That's what I want." He yawned into his hand. "You guys are old. I would like to date before I'm thirty. I can't meet girls here. I'm going insane hanging out with old people."

"I think your daddy has different ideas for your dating situation." Austin turned. "A genetically tested Aztec of child-bearing age."

"Who is thirteen, probably weighs six hundred pounds, and has pimples. Come on, Pet," Hutch scrubbed a hand across his hair. He needed a haircut. It was getting long. "Can we at least land long enough that I can go to a real American high school?"

"What have you been doing up to this point?" Brandon walked into the kitchen, opened the refrigerator, and grabbed a bottle of water.

"Austin homeschools me."

"I wouldn't have guessed that."

"I have a teaching degree, Brandon," Austin muttered.

"A teaching degree?" Brandon said, twisting the cap off. "You haven't even been gone that long. I thought it took at least a bachelor's and certifications. I never pictured you as the teacher type. Though... you did stop me from flunking high school."

"I fast-tracked my degrees," she deadpanned. She flicked a look at Hutch. "This farm-raised genius over here was my inspiration. Shocking, I know."

"Really, hmmm. I suppose if you could get me through high school and shame me into going to college," Brandon had chuckled. "You could probably teach anybody."

"Pet, you need to come here a minute." It was Starr who caught her attention. Strangely, she looked ashen when she stood up from the couch and called out to the kitchen.

Austin scooted around the table, headed to the living room. Aina had her finger on the TV remote. As soon as Austin stopped just short of the couch, she pushed the play button.

The private superyacht of eccentric Italian businessman Paolo Bertinelli, called the Lady Dreams, was found gutted and empty and has been brought to port off the South American coast. Authorities believe it drifted aimlessly for weeks. All those on board are presumed to have perished in a fire. The yacht had left Chile months earlier. Pirates are suspected of having boarded the boat. Nineteen unidentified bodies were found decomposing on deck. Paolo Bertinelli was best known for his charitable work with people with disabilities in many countries. He will be missed...

Austin wavered, dizzy.

"Are you okay?" Starr flitted up beside her, snatched her arm.

"No. I don't think so," Austin answered, her voice sounding flimsy. She watched as a helicopter view of the yacht skimmed blurry across the TV screen. White tarps covered bodies on the deck.

"I'm going for a run."

"Baby, you're running a lot," Starr said softly, reached out, and tugged on a few strands of Austin's hair lying over her shoulder.

"Obviously not enough," Austin muttered. Her hands were shaking. Not as much as Aina's, though.

"They said they didn't find Paolo's body on the boat," Aina whispered. "I told you before—I could feel he wasn't gone. Now they don't know where he is. What happened to him?"

Chapter −16

Austin sat down on the bed in the room Brandon had given her and sighed. It was a real bed, not a hotel cot or a boat berth bunk. The worn quilts and comforters were handmade and homey.

She didn't open the envelope right away, just sat and soaked in the scent of the farmhouse and the hush of the room. She'd dreaded this moment. Finally, she slid her finger beneath the envelope flap and eased it open. Inside was an eight-and-a-half by eleven sheet of paper, handwritten in pretty cursive. Austin skimmed it, listening to footsteps on the stairway outside the closed door.

TO Austin Jackson:

Don't trust Brandon Tremaine. He's lying. He's friends with Abel Martin. He might kill you. You should leave.

There was a knock—three gentle taps of a knuckle. Austin looked up, waited for Roo to come bolting through the door. He didn't.

"Yeah?"

"Um, can I come in?"

It was Brandon's voice. Austin folded the letter, stood up, and opened the door.

"It's your house."

"Well, I know. But I'm not walking into a room without asking." He was standing there with bags dangling from his fingers. He lifted one up while Austin sat back down on the bed. Her phone dinged. A text. She snatched it up.

"What are these?" Brandon asked, nodding toward the bags.

Austin's phone buzzed.

Stats: *Are you alright? Do you need me?*

"Clothes," Austin said, eyes still on her screen as she tapped back, *No. I'm good.*

"Three pairs of jeans and three shirts. I went shopping, and everybody got new clothes. I figured you might feel left out, so... I picked some out for you."

"You didn't have to do that."

"I know. I like spending other people's money frivolously. That's what Starr tells me. There's a bag over there for your girlfriend." She nodded toward the dresser. "I got on her social pages. Her favorite color is baby blue. She likes dolphins—"

"Dolphins?"

"Yes, dolphins. You should know that, Five." Her nickname for him tugged a faint, involuntary smile to his mouth.

"Inside is a dolphin stuffed animal, a bracelet with baby-blue stones, and a couple of country music CDs. And there are two gift certificates to the Burn Mountain Spa and Inn."

He looked at the bag, drew in breath, let it out slowly. "That's really nice."

"I know. Not my money, though—I just like spending it. Tell her you bought them. And if she asks—again—how you afforded it, just say we're paying rent."

She shot Brandon a small, knowing grin, the burn at Lyndsey's expense still hanging in the air. "Hey... what do you know about the Martin Commune?"

The grin wiped from Brandon's face instantly. His shoulders tightened. "Why?" he asked. "Did somebody say something?"

"Not necessarily." Austin shook her head. "When you said Laura had left, you didn't mean she left your family, did you? You meant she left the commune."

Brandon didn't speak. His eyes went blank, defenses sliding into place.

"Let me rephrase," Austin said carefully. "She's out. You're in. How deep are you—and your mom and dad—into Abel Martin's family?"

Brandon swallowed. "Lyndsey is his daughter."

"How long have you been dabbling in this—"

"It isn't me." He ran a hand down his face. "Well, I guess it is me, right? I'm doing what I can to keep my mom and dad from getting hurt. That said, I'm marrying Lyndsey."

"Abel Martin wants this side of the mountain," Austin said quietly. "He built that dam, so he controls your water. He'll take your land or let you keep it by marrying Lyndsey. One tactic? Shutting off your creek. Has he done that recently?"

"Yeah," Brandon admitted. "I noticed the creek was down."

"Do you want to marry her?" Austin asked. "I mean, that's the big question. If you want her, this is different. But if you don't—"

"I don't understand what you mean."

"If you loved her," Austin said bluntly, "you wouldn't care if her father absorbed the property. Do you love her? Tell me the truth. This isn't about how I feel. This is about *you*. If you could walk away from her and keep your farm, what would you choose? Right now."

Brandon stared at the floor. "I wouldn't marry her. I'm just not... there. Everybody's pushing me to marry her—Mom, Dad, Gill at the hardware store." His voice grew tight. "But I'm stuck. If I want to keep the farm and my job, I'm going to have to marry her. If I want my parents safe, I'm going to have to stay on Abel's good side. Everybody else around here has done it. "If you don't, he bans you from the stores, the gas stations— even the church. The whole town shuts you out. I've seen it. People who don't fall in line lose their homes, their property... or they fade out of the community like they were never here."

"Where do they 'fade away' to?" Austin asked, pinning him with a stare. He didn't answer. Austin let the silence stretch. "People don't just fade away. They don't just vanish, Brandon," she said softly. "Not around men like Abel. They get taken off the map."

She didn't mention the twenty-two other compounds Stats had found. He didn't need that part yet.

"I know you're going to take Tessa," Brandon whispered. "That's why you're here, right? You found out I'm getting married. And... God, I know it's the right thing. I just love her so much. It would kill me to lose her."

"I'm not here to take her," Austin said, smiling faintly. "The boat got attacked. I needed somewhere to get my head straight."

"You should've gone to some exotic beach or something."

"Yeah, well," Austin shrugged. "I didn't."

"You know what kind of life she'd have," Brandon murmured.

"Yeah," Austin said. "But you also know I wanted you to keep her. The day I put her in your arms, something in me almost died. The only thing that kept me going was knowing you'd fight to the death for her—whether it was my dad coming after you or the devil himself. You already beat my dad. Now I'm hoping you've got it in you to take on Satan wearing Abel Martin's face. Just like before... you were the only one I trusted."

Brandon blinked slowly. Honest confusion flickered behind his eyes. "I don't want her ending up like I did," he admitted. "Doing what I have to do just to keep everybody alive. I don't want her marrying some old man she hates someday because Abel Martin tells her to. I know I should take her and leave, but—"

"No more absurd than a father chasing his daughter through three states, flashing lies and badges the whole way, then trying to dump her in a psychiatric hospital just to keep her away from—"

"People like me?" Brandon finished wearily.

Austin let out a breath. "Nobody stopped it because nobody realized how deep it went until it was too late." Austin's stomach twisted. "Here's the thing. You tell me you don't love Lyndsey. You don't want to marry her. What if I can help you stop this?"

"You could help me? How?"

"That's what we do," she said simply. "Stats is a savant. Before I found him, a casino practically held him hostage to calculate cheat systems. He weighed 115 pounds when we broke him out. He stops eating when he gets locked into something. Six days without food. Nobody even cared when he was there."

Brandon tipped his head, something wounded in his eyes. "I don't know. At what cost?"

You could lose the farm," Austin said. "You could lose everyone tied to Abel. I rebuilt a family after mine threw me out. It's lonely. It's scary. Starting over is hard." She rose, touching his arm gently.

"But you'd be free. And you'd have Tessa. And us. My new family likes you."

"But not you," Brandon murmured.

Austin froze. She knew her answer mattered more than anything she'd said so far. "That might be up to you, Brandon," she said softly.

"You sound like a politician." He leaned back. "I know you've got this whole 'don't ask, don't tell' thing. But can I ask one question?"

"Yeah," Austin said. "Not promising to answer."

"Shocker," he muttered. "So... was it really an optical illusion when you lifted the truck?"

"No." She didn't flinch. "I could really lift it."

Brandon waited for the punchline. When none came, he let out a small exhale.

"I think you're an amazing dad," Austin said.

"You do?" He looked surprised. "What makes you say that?"

"I see you with her," Austin said. "She's confident. She cuddles. You talk to her like you're actually listening. You make breakfast with her. You never get mad when she grabs your face and demands attention. You tuck her in. You read to her. You wipe her nose without gagging. You don't dump her off on someone else because she's too much work. You're the best thing she's got. I'll never take her from you. But at some point, you're going to have to fight for her."

"Fight?" he repeated. "Yeah. I will."

"I'm not sure," Austin said. "Because it looks like you gave up a long time ago. If you don't even like Lyndsey, why'd you bother dating her?"

"There aren't that many girls here, Austin," he snapped. "Ben at the hardware store pushed and pushed—"

"Why not quit the hardware store?" Austin shot back. "Why give up your farm? If you marry her, everything goes into Abel's name. You understand that, right?"

"No, it won't," Brandon muttered. "It's still our farm."

"Right," Austin said gently. "Until he ships you to Mexico to run one of his compounds. Or worse."

"You're funny," Brandon laughed nervously. "Martin's a lot of things. But he's not a murderer. And Lyndsey—she's sweet. She's nice. She's a hard worker and a smart gal. She's the marrying type."

"'A smart *gal*? The marrying type?'" Austin lifted a finger like a gun and aimed it at him. "That sounds prerecorded—and it's the second time you've said those exact lines. Nobody our age says *gal* or *the marrying type* unless someone planted those words in your head. Boom. That's the problem. Brandon, you have no idea what these people are capable of—"

"Yeah, I do," Brandon snapped. "They're good, kind people, Austin. You know what? I think you just came back to get revenge. I don't have to listen to this. Take a couple of days. Then get your friends. Leave."

Chapter –17

Austin wiggled her rear on the faded vinyl seat of the truck. There was something sticking to her leg, and she leaned over to expose a small, tattered sticker with a kitten on it affixed to her thigh.

"This truck is disgusting," she said, holding it aloft and smashing it between finger and thumb. It was dirty and in even worse shape than the truck she'd driven into town a week ago, with her friends piled in the back. But folks in Danville Station already recognized her truck, which was parked in Brandon's driveway. She had to buy a different one outside the area and stash it at the all-night grocery before Starr came to pick them up two blocks out of town.

"Can trucks have bedbugs?" she asked Stats, who was sitting in the middle.

"Yes," he answered. He was poking at the new computer Austin had ordered for him. He had been clutching it like a newborn babe since the moment the postman delivered it to the back steps of Brandon's house.

Austin shivered at the thought, her skin prickling as if something crawled beneath it. The stale truck air pressed heavily with the scent of old vinyl and sweat. She opened the window a little more, hoping for a breath of fresh air, and scratched her arm, the rough edge of a scab catching under her fingernail.

"Can you open your window more, Aina?" she asked. "I can't breathe in here."

The headlights from a car coming down the highway caught her attention. She pushed the truck into gear and got ready to turn left at the stop sign, as if she had just pulled into it. She watched it pass while Aina rolled down her window a bit more. It was an old red minivan. Austin sighed and pushed it out of gear again. It was not even close to the brand-new green truck she was waiting for so that she could pursue it in secret down the roadway.

"This piece of shit is going to stall as soon as he drives by." Austin shook her head.

"You paid eight hundred dollars for it, what did you expect?" Aina asked, leaning forward and poking her forefinger at a dent in the dashboard. "Is this a bullet hole?"

"You're in West Virginia. The odds are good it would be just the right size pellet for a 12-gauge shotgun," Austin mumbled. She was a bit jaded with sitting still in the truck for the last three hours. They were waiting for Abel Martin to drive by so they could follow him. "Why couldn't I get a job in a nicer part of town so I could drive a Porsche, huh? Trying to be unobtrusive in an old truck sucks big."

"You were the one who headed like a bat out of hell toward your hometown," Aina reminded her.

"Really?" Austin snapped her head to the right, took in the green eyes staring back at her in the dim glow of Aina's cellphone. "Because Danville Station was right at the top of my list of places I'd like to come back to after being kicked out three years ago. Is that what you're saying? It's a stupid hick town. I could have chosen a million other places that included a white sand beach, tequilas, and—" Austin waved a hand lazily, "Pretty cars with sunroofs so I can see the blue sky and smell the suntan lotion. What makes you think I would want to come here to old barns filled with pig shit, creeks with mine drainage, and a seventy-percent chance it will be twenty degrees below zero for half the year?"

"The average low in West Virginia is actually between 26 and 29 degrees in the winter—"

"Shut up, Stats," Austin spat at him.

"You wanted to come home because it's home?" Aina cringed. "And because of Brandon? I mean, you always said he was your safe place. What else were we to think?"

"You did say that," Stats added. "Whenever we all sat around and talked about where we wanted to be if we had a choice, you said: *I would be lying in Brandon's arms on a soft bed—*"

"Please do not repeat that to him, you hear me? Brandon has a girlfriend," Austin interrupted. "And do I appear to be welcome here?"

Austin rolled her head back, peering at Aina, and groaned. She caught Stats watching them, as if calculating odds. "I'm not an idiot, alright? I know you used your hocus pocus on me." She lifted her hand and wiggled her fingers. "It pisses me off. I don't want to be here. I'm not mentally ready yet. And I don't want to start a national incident with creepy commune people. Let them take over the area. It's what they do. They'll inbreed to extinction sooner or later."

"Because it's more than that, Pet, and you know it," Aina said quietly. "Or you wouldn't be sitting in this truck right now with— bedbugs." She giggled.

"Shit, now, don't do that," Austin muttered. "Roll down your window more. And I don't really give a rat's ass. I hate it here."

Aina winced, looked out the window. "Screw you, Pet. If you had a choice, we'd still be with Paolo." Beneath all the black eyeshadow and the curtain of bangs, she was beautiful—perfect jawline, stunning eyes. "But it wasn't so great with him, you know? Not all of us were his favorite. Only you. We were just his freak show."

"And I wasn't?" Austin jerked her gaze away. "Just because I don't look like it on the outside doesn't mean I don't feel the freak too." She didn't deny Paolo liked her best. She was easiest to manipulate—at least that's what he thought.

"Listen," Austin reached out and flicked Aina's arm. "I know you guys want me to be happy. I get it."

"No, not really," Aina muttered. They watched another car come down from Canaan Mountain Road — a beat-up silver SUV with one headlight flickering. "You were just the only one who could go home," Aina added quietly.

Austin had looked away, but her head snapped back. "You're kidding me, right?" she snapped. "What makes you think my backstory is any better than yours? We were all dragged through hell."

Aina didn't answer. She didn't have to. Even Stats shifted uneasily in the dark. Because that was the truth Austin didn't want to look at: They all had places on the map. Hometowns. Families. Histories.

And every one of those places was stained, broken, or haunted in its own way — just like hers. She hadn't come back because she was the only one who could. She'd come back because something here still had its claws in her—and she was done running from it.

Headlights slashed across the dashboard, cutting jagged shadows over the cracked vinyl. It was the twelfth vehicle. Austin had been keeping count. Heart pounding, she pushed the truck into gear, let it roll forward at the stop sign—and waited.

"That's it." Aina nodded as the olive-green truck rolled past. It was new and shiny.

Austin pulled out onto the roadway.

"Holy crap, that thing's got gold tire rims. No wonder Brandon wants to marry Abel's daughter. Hell, I might marry her for gold tire rims. Write down the license plate number," she told Aina, who was already jotting it down. "Stats," she said next, "are you good to go once they stop?"

"Yes." Stats nodded, lifting a palm-sized plastic box. "One GPS tracking device. I simply have to place it in the dashboard. Then we'll know exactly where he is. It's quite uncomplicated. I have the directions in my head." He tapped his temple twice. "Abel Martin will stop at Hills Family Restaurant for a minimum of forty-eight minutes if he is eating. If he is just grabbing a piece of apple pie and two cups of coffee, he will be inside for forty-one minutes. It will take me thirty-two minutes to install the GPS on the dashboard. I will have nine minutes to spare. I did take into account people coming and going."

"If you're so sure he's going to stop there, why didn't you tell me? I could have parked in the lot."

"You didn't ask, Pet." Stats sniffed. "But the waitress who brought me coffee said Martin and his three sons have eaten out there three times this week." He pointed as Abel Martin's taillights bounced into the far corner of the parking lot. "You need to go around the block twice to give him time to get out."

"It sucks when somebody's smarter than you, isn't it?" Aina giggled.

"It isn't Pet's IQ that is so low," Stats added. "It is the fact that she isn't able to utilize her mind to the highest degree. ADHD symptoms vary. However, from past experience, Pet's indicators tend toward the inability to consistently sustain attention, losing much-needed items, and being easily distracted."

"Enough, Stats," Austin interrupted while Aina laughed.

Then she poked Aina's arm. "And you have no room to talk about issues. I saw what Golem dragged out of your pockets when he did the wash yesterday. A pair of my favorite panties, Hutch's cell phone cord, and one of Brandon's bank cards."

~

Stats needed thirty-four minutes to place the GPS tracker inside the truck dashboard. Austin kept time on her cellphone, sweat trickling down her spine, the humid air clinging to her skin. Rain began to hammer the windshield harder, blurring the neon lights outside. With each passing minute, a deep fatigue settled in her limbs—a heaviness she always felt in Abel Martin's orbit, as if the world itself pressed harder when he was near.

There was one close call when one of the sons came out to smoke. He pat-checked his pockets like he was going to head for the truck. Austin thumbed an emergency text to Stats—but then the man reached behind his ear, found a cigarette tucked there, and wandered back to the porch.

Stats slipped into the truck minutes later, rubbing the snake tattoo on his right arm—a good sign. He flipped open his computer and, within seconds, showed Austin the satellite image of the parking lot, the little blinking arrow marking Abel's truck. "Nice job, Stats," Austin said. "You're damn good at what you do."

"Do you have to pat me?" Stats asked warily. "I know you're going to."

"You want a hug instead?" Austin teased.

"No." He huffed, so she gave his back a quick, gentle pat.

"Are you done?" he asked, watching her hand retreat.

"Done," she said.

"We need to find out where he's going," Stats continued. "And we don't tell anyone else, right?"

"Nobody," Austin promised.

He tapped his pen once and let it drop into the cupholder. "Remind me again why we aren't just leaving?"

His voice was flat, unblinking, deceptively innocent. Austin knew better. He wasn't really asking — he was griping about the unwanted pat and the fact that they still hadn't settled somewhere safe.

She could have lied. But she didn't.

"I felt drawn back here, Stats," she said softly. "Like the ground itself was screaming at me to come home. I've never felt anything like it. And now that I'm here and I see the danger... I can't just leave Tessa to be eaten alive by those monsters."

"At least this time, somebody else gets to be the monsters," Aina giggled, even if her eyes didn't budge from the restaurant.

Stats drummed his fingers once more, then let the pen drop. "You know this doesn't mean we're safe," he said quietly. "If anyone saw us—"

Austin managed a faint smile, but her eyes stayed locked on the doorway. She leaned back in her seat; the warning letter was tucked inside her jacket like a hot coal. For a moment, she let herself imagine it—driving away, starting fresh, not getting pulled into this place, this man, this mountain, this danger. But the truck stayed in park. The engine idled. Rain drummed steadily on the roof. She stared at the restaurant, every shadow stretched long.

"Now we wait," she murmured.

Chapter –18

Sunlight slashed across Lyndsey's face as she stood on Brandon's porch, one hand clamped white-knuckled on the railing. She had been in the kitchen fourteen minutes—long enough to glare at Stats, glance through the crayon chaos where Tessa colored, then storm out without a single greeting. The screen door had rattled after her outburst, still vibrating when Brandon followed her out.

"What the hell, Brandon?" she snapped.

"What's wrong?" he said, letting the door slam. The boards creaked under his boots. "I don't get it."

"You don't get it?" Her voice cracked. "You're following her like every other dog here. Like she's in heat. I can't take you chasing Austin while I stand here, like I don't matter."

Brandon blinked, stunned. He shouldn't have smiled—it was reflex, disbelief—but he did, and Lyndsey's eyes went hotter.

"You're kidding, right?" he asked. Except... he wasn't so sure anymore. He *had* followed Austin from the kitchen to the living room, lingered at her doorway, and waited at the stairwell. He had hovered because he couldn't seem to stop orbiting her, even though he didn't understand why he was drawn to her instead of focusing on Lyndsey.

Lyndsey's chin trembled with fury. "You didn't even know I was here."

Well... no. He hadn't. Not really. He'd heard a door, but she hadn't said hello or called out for him.

"I put up with a lot," Lyndsey continued, lowering her voice, as if wanting him to hear the consequences if he kept going down this path. "There are six guys who'd kill for a chance with me the second you screw this up. And you're screwing it up *right now*."

Her words landed like gut punches, one after another. Inside, the memory sharpened—Tessa's drawing on the table.

"This is daddy," she'd said earlier, tapping a stick figure. "And this is Austin. Look, you're holding hands."

There were two stick-figures with hands touching, and a rainbow drawn behind Austin. "The rainbow looks like it's coming out of Austin's butt," Tessa had added with solemn confidence.

Starr had dissolved into laughter. Austin had made a victorious fist pump. Lyndsey must have seen that drawing. Must have watched the scene. And maybe heard more than she'd let on.

Now she spun, stomped down the steps, and slammed her car door so hard that dust puffed into the air. The tires skidded across gravel and spit the truck into the road. Brandon stood there in the settling quiet, throat tight. Behind him, the porch door creaked open.

"Did your leash get caught in the door?" Hutch asked dryly, squinting into the sun.

"What?"

"Nothin'. She just has you on a tight leash."

"No, she doesn't. It's called a relationship."

Hutch raised both hands. "Dude, I'm fifteen. I barely know what a relationship *is*. I was just joking." He pulled out his phone, scrolling through at least a hundred girl names. "My relationships last as long as it takes for us to move on again."

Brandon stared. Hutch shrugged.

"I figured that's what you were like," Hutch added. "From the stories Austin told us."

Brandon's pulse spiked. "Austin talked about me?"

"All the time." Hutch plopped down on a porch chair. "We've all been through crap. Aina got beaten half to death because her family thought she was a changeling. Her dad tried to burn her to 'fix' her. Golem's family tried to sell him. We were all messed up. Austin— she's our safe place. Yours too, I guess."

Brandon swallowed. That hit deeper than it should have.

"She said you were a player who liked the ladies," Hutch continued. "You never held her hand where anyone could see. Except when nobody was looking. She said it felt like a secret code. That's why she never forgot."

"That wasn't my fault," Brandon muttered. "Her dad hated my family."

"Whatever." Hutch's gaze softened for just one second. "When she was with you, she told us it felt like nothing could go wrong." He pushed up from the chair. "Enough old-people talk. I'm nauseous."

Inside, the house buzzed softly—Starr humming, Aina teasing, Tessa giggling between cookie bites. The smell of crayons and chocolate drifted through the air.

Austin sat at the kitchen table, watching Tessa color.

"Hey," Brandon said, leaning in the doorway. The room quieted. "You know I loved you back then, right? Before you left."

Austin stiffened. Starr raised her eyebrows. Aina froze mid-bite. Even Tessa paused, crayon suspended.

Austin flushed. "I—I never really thought about it."

"It doesn't matter," Brandon said, suddenly wishing he could kick his own shins. "Never mind."

He pivoted—and then pivoted back, heart pounding. "No. Wait. It *does* matter."

Starr choked back a grin. Austin yanked her gaze away from everyone. "Let's go to the other room," she muttered, rising and brushing past the table.

Brandon followed her to the living room, the curtains blowing with the warm breeze. "What is up with you?" she asked as he ran his hand through his hair over and over.

"I don't know." He stopped abruptly near the couch, and she bumped into him. He steadied her by instinct. "I still have feelings for you, Austin. What we did—it felt right. But I'm not the guy who cheats. I hate that I hurt Lyndsey, and I don't want to be the reason she gets hurt. She knows something's going on. She wants you gone."

Austin's hands flexed at her sides. The weight of the warning letter tucked in her jacket pressed like a stone.

"I won't tell her," she said quietly. "I won't mention the kiss."

"What?"

"We won't do it again," she insisted.

He tapped her lightly on the top of her head. "You're not listening. Focus."

"Okay."

"I'm in a relationship with Lyndsey," Brandon said slowly. "I want to be in a relationship with you."

Austin froze.

Wind rustled the grass outside. Somewhere inside, the floor creaked—a house settling, or someone moving. His heartbeat thudded in his ears.

Austin didn't move. She just stared at him, studying his eyes like she was searching for the lie. "I don't know what twisted picture you've built of me from whatever gossip you've heard," she said, voice flat. "I don't do being anyone's second choice or their pretty little distraction. I'm not a *pet*. I'm not your dirty little secret. And I'm sure as hell not the affair you sneak around with." She looked like she was going to say more, but from the porch window behind them, the scent of cigarette smoke wafted in... a shadow shifted—watching. Waiting.

Austin pushed past Brandon. He followed her with his eyes as she stopped at the window, her posture stiffening. She didn't speak at first—just stared into the sunlight, unmoving. A trace of her hair's scent drifted back to him, distracting him, tugging at his attention even as something outside held hers.

"Someone was listening to us," she said at last, her voice barely above a whisper.

Brandon moved in behind her as she lifted a hand and pointed.

The rocking chair on the porch swayed gently, creaking—moving on its own, as if someone had just risen from it.

"They were sitting there the whole time," Austin murmured. "Listening."

Beneath the chair, a cigarette butt still smoldered, a thin ribbon of smoke twisting up and disappearing into the breeze.

Chapter −19

"Hey, there are kittens in the barn," Brandon said from the kitchen doorway, eyes red, a sneeze catching mid-sentence. "Can you tell? I'm allergic to cats."

Everyone at the breakfast table looked up at once—each of them tensed for danger, expecting the next crisis—only to be met with the ordinary promise of kittens.

Aina muttered, "We can't even keep Tessa from eating crayons—now kittens?"

Stats' gaze flicked around like he was already adding "kitten protocol" to their disaster planning.

"Kittens!" Starr shrieked. "Baby kittens!"

They all bolted up at once like a stampede of cattle, knocking each other around to get through the doorway. Tessa giggled as Aina tried to shove Golem out of the way with both hands, only to ricochet off his hip.

Austin snagged a bit of Stats' shirt. "Baby kittens. Normal people like to play with kittens, Stats. They want to hold them and feel their soft fur, listen to them purr, and kiss their little noses. You must come."

"I don't want to go. I'll play with my *baby* computer."

"You remember what you promised me, right?" Austin tugged harder.

"Yes. I said I would interact with other human beings. These are *kittens*."

"You will be interacting with humans," she corrected, knocking her knuckles on his laptop. "By pretending you like kittens more than your computer."

"Don't hurt her," he whispered while Austin shut the laptop gently. "Come on."

"You're mean to me, Pet," Stats sighed as she dragged him toward the door.

Tessa hopped down, grabbed Austin's free hand, then turned to Brandon and gave him a stern thumbs-up—his cue to keep the plan going. Austin didn't notice she'd been set up. Brandon had told Tessa that lonely people needed someone to hold their hand. Tessa had taken that to heart.

Lyndsey's empty chair at the table felt like it was watching them, too. No one mentioned her, but her absence was a taut string in the room, ready to snap. Outside, a shadow lingered near the porch— just visible at the periphery, daring anyone to acknowledge it.

The barn erupted with soft sounds—purrs, squeaks, whispers of straw. Golem held a kitten in his massive palm and sang to it in a deep, raspy voice. Tears shimmered in his eyes as the tiny creature stared up at him.

Starr scooped up the runt—a calico with mismatched paws—and whispered to it like it was her own heartbeat. Stats stood rigid until Austin and Tessa shoved a gray fuzzball into his hands. Austin took a picture to send to his computer.

Brandon sat on a stall door, pretending to fiddle with his phone. Really, he watched Austin. She smiled once at him—soft, tired, edged with something wary. The yellow barn light glimmered in her eyes as she guided Stats's hand in a gentle stroke across the kitten's back. God, he loved her.

Even now, with all the walls she'd built. Even after the mistakes. Even with Lyndsey's rage still echoing in the back of his skull. He tried to detach from her, but every time he pulled away, something in him ached harder.

She used to leap into his arms, wrap her legs around his waist, kiss him everywhere while he pretended to roll his eyes. Now she gave him distance, and it hurt more than he expected.

Brandon drifted into the memory of Sunday dinner. Abel Martin's big house on the hill had been...overwhelming. Nearly fifty people crammed around long pine tables; wild packs of feral barefoot kids tore through the rooms, screaming, shoving, hitting each other as they went. The laughter didn't sound joyful—more like people forcing themselves to sound normal.

Tessa was taken by the swarm instantly, swept along like a beagle pup tossed into a current of Rottweilers.. Brandon tried to fold himself down into his chair. Abel's cobalt eyes moved over the room like searchlights. Lyndsey's gaze never left her father's table—eager, hungry, desperate for notice. The moment Abel crooked a finger in her direction, she gripped Brandon's hand and pulled him toward the head table with an almost feverish joy—as if being summoned by him was a blessing straight from the angels, a chance to sit at a throne.

"You've got company on your farm," Abel said. "Family?"

"Tessa's mother and her friends," Brandon answered.

"And Tessa's mother... she is Ray Jackson's daughter?"

"Yes."

"Interesting." Abel had studied him with a strange smile, like weighing him on a scale. "I wonder," Abel murmured, "if it would be better for them to stay at one of our hotels during her visit. For my daughter's sake."

Brandon's stomach had knotted. "Yes, sir."

Then Abel leaned closer, voice low. "My daughter says there were helicopters and police at your home."

Brandon had stuck to the lie he'd rehearsed—Austin as a nanny, misunderstanding with the boy's father, nothing serious. Abel's smile never changed. His eyes never blinked. When Brandon added that Austin had a Homeland Security meeting, Abel's brows twitched—barely—but the tiny movement made Brandon's chest tighten. Brandon's voice faltered as regret crawled up his spine—he couldn't believe he'd told Abel that.

Afterwards, Lyndsey whispered, "Don't look him in the eyes like that. It'll make him think you're challenging him."

Brandon had snickered. "It's what men do."

"Not in our home. Do what everyone else does. Don't look at him. Eyes down. For us. For the good of all."

He'd nodded. "I'll do it. For you. For us. For your dad." His eyes, thereafter, had snapped downward, as if trained into submission.

Only now standing in the barn watching Austin playing with the kittens, did the unease scratch at the back of Brandon's skull.

"Hey, butthead." Austin's voice snapped. She rubbed her forehead. "Thanks for showing us the kittens. However, you could've warned me about the beam." She'd run directly into it— twice—then stood staring at it as if the beam had jumped in front of her.

"The beam's been here for two hundred years and is six inches thick. You passed it six times today—I'd have thought you'd notice."

"Obviously, I did the first six times. The seventh and eighth, I didn't. Asshole."

"You know," Brandon rolled his eyes. "I'd forgotten how irritating and caustic you were with those little razor-sharp teeth."

"I know, right?" She laughed. "Just makes you want to keep me around longer, doesn't it?"

"Not really." But he looked at Tessa, who stared at Austin like she was something magical. "*She* wants you here."

"That's not what you said the other night." Austin's smile thinned and disappeared. "Before you went to eat at Martin's."

She watched him carefully—the barn door, then the window, then Brandon again, her gaze flicking like she expected something to move behind him.

"Why are you looking over my shoulder?" Brandon asked, uneasy.

"Watchers," she murmured. "You don't feel it? Like someone's always hiding around a corner listening?"

He rolled his eyes, brushing it off, but she didn't blink. "You're the one acting like you've been in a cult, Austin," he muttered— projecting without even realizing it.

Austin didn't rise to it. Didn't flinch. "I suppose there's nothing I can say that will make you see Abel Martin for what he is?" she asked, low and calm—as if she already knew the answer.

"He's just an old guy with a big family and a community to look after," Brandon retorted, but his voice had that soft, reverent edge.

"God told him to make a place for people the world rejected."

Austin blinked. "Wait. I'm sorry—God *Himself* said that to Abel Martin's *face*?" She held out a hand like she needed him to stop and rewind.

Brandon didn't. Instead, his tone shifted—gentle, patronizing, like he was explaining something to a stubborn child.

"I know people like to throw around words like *commune,*" he murmured, "but that's not what this is. Abel's a good man. A shepherd. He's been nothing but kind to my mom and dad. His grandkids adore Tessa."

He shoved his hands in his pockets and dropped his gaze, as if looking her in the eye might break something inside him. When he finally looked up again, his expression tightened— something defensive, something rehearsed.

"You show up out of nowhere and start stirring things up," he said, voice sharpening. "Just like you used to." He snapped his head away when he caught her watching him. His words took on a rhythmic, cultish cadence—Abel's cadence. "I've got to look out for my family. My community." He drew in a deep breath, puffed out his chest. "My community comes first. My family comes after. Maybe your dad was right," he said quietly. "You need to make a quick visit... and go."

"Oh. I get it." Austin nodded. "Yes. We'll leave. One more night."

"One night," Brandon said. "For now, we need to talk. You want to take a sit?"

She grinned suddenly, eyes lighting like a lantern switched on inside her.

"Are you laughing at me?" Brandon snapped, bristling.

Austin shook her head. "No. God, no. I just—those words. *'You wanna take a sit?'* You remember that?" Brandon blinked. "We were at the old swimming hole behind your dad's woods," she said. "I was there with Janey Fitzpatrick—remember her? Red hair, little lisp. I had so much Sweet Summer Coconut Suntan Lotion on I smelled like a beach in Fort Lauderdale on spring break."

Her voice softened as if the memory pulled her in. "The sun was brutal that day. We were lying on the rocks, half melting, and Bradley and Blue Martin came barreling up on their ATVs..."

Brandon's breath hitched—the memory slamming into him like heat off pavement. The scent of coconut lotion. The sharp glare of July sun. Austin's laugh echoing off the water. It was four years ago, but it hit him like now. He'd been cutting hay in his dad's tractor. Stopped for a dip. Heard the girls giggling as he stepped through the trees. And there she was—Austin—standing in that tiny black bikini with the little roses on it. Dark hair. Blue eyes. Sun on her skin. He remembered the gut-punch of wanting her so hard he couldn't breathe.

Then the Martins had shown up, swagger loud as their engines. Austin and Janey sat up fast, towels clutched to their chests. Blue had stepped in front of Austin and said something gross like, "Look what we got here," voice dripping with that ugly kind of hunger.

Brandon had stepped out of the trees behind them.

"Yeah," he'd said. "A couple of trespassers riding around on my dad's land. Get out." And for whatever reason, they had.

Janey, flustered and grateful, had turned to Brandon afterward and blurted: "You wanna take a *shit*?" Her lisp mangling "sit" into something awful. Austin had burst into uncontrollable laughter—falling sideways on the rock—

"Oh my gosh," Austin interrupted his memory. "I teased her for *days* about that. She had such a huge crush on you."

Austin was still smiling at the memory when she looked back at him. Brandon wasn't smiling. He looked... stunned. Like someone had ripped back a curtain in his mind and let the sunlight in.

"That was..." his voice broke. He swallowed. "That was the best day of my whole damn summer." Brandon dragged a hand through his hair, eyes darting like he was trying to reconcile two versions of reality. "I remember you laughing so hard you almost fell in the water," he said. "And Janey tried to pretend she meant it. And you— you couldn't breathe. You were—"

He cut himself off, jaw tightening as a surge of emotion flickered through him. For a moment—just a moment—he looked like the Brandon she used to know. Warm. Protective. Awake.

Then something shifted.

His gaze drifted—far, distant—like someone pulling a chain around his neck. His shoulders rose and fell sharply as Abel's voice—Abel's cadence—pulled back through him like a tide.

He blinked hard and the softness vanished. "Anyway," he muttered, clearing his throat, forcing his expression flat. "That was years ago. Things are... different now." The light in his eyes dimmed. He shoved his hands in his pockets again—the posture of someone sliding back into a script. "I've got responsibilities. I've got people relying on me," he said, voice tightening. "My family. My community. I can't just—"

The shift hit him hard. His eyes went unfocused.

"I have Lyndsey. She's sweet. She's nice. She's a hard worker and a smart gal. She's the marrying type."

The words came out flat. Automatic. Like someone had hit *play* on a tape recorder inside him. Brandon flinched the moment they left his mouth. He shook his head violently—like a dog shaking off water—then scrubbed a hand across the back of his neck.

"Man," he muttered. "My head hurts."

Austin tilted her head. Quiet. Watching him too closely. "Are you okay, Five?"

He didn't know if he was. He didn't know *anything* in that moment. He just nodded—lying out of instinct—and pushed past her toward the door. The instant he stepped out onto the porch, the light shifted. Something moved.

A flicker of motion at the tree line. A shadow pulling itself back into the woods. Brandon froze. Austin wasn't paranoid. She wasn't imagining things.

Someone had been listening. Someone had been right there.

And they'd just slipped away.

Chapter –20

The night air tasted like wet iron and wild garlic as Aina stood on the buckled asphalt of Old Grossman Road, stamping her heel into a pothole just to hear something familiar break the silence. Or maybe it was because when she got nervous, it always made her have to pee. Mist crept out of the woods in pale sheets, carrying the smell of rain-soaked soil and old timber. The railroad tracks cut across the road like scars—dark, slick, and humming faintly under the chill of early June.

Behind her, Austin sprawled across the hood of the truck, knees drawn up, one headphone dangling. Austin kept pretending she wasn't scanning the treeline, but every rustle in the woods made her shoulders tense. Roo paced beneath her, teeth flashing whenever the wind shifted in the wrong direction.

"This is even more fun than sitting four hours in the rain waiting for Abel Martin to show up at that restaurant," Aina muttered, black mascara starting to smear beneath her eyes in inky trails.

Austin slid down the hood an inch, grit scraping under her palms. "We're in the right place. Stats said the GPS pinged here twice—unless Martin's people jammed it." Her gaze flicked toward the dark barn at the edge of the lot, its heavy smell of hay and old oil seeping from its gaps.

"Then help me look," Aina shot back. "Standing there singing off-key isn't helping."

Austin made a face. "It was one song."

"You butchered it."

Austin didn't argue. She just tapped her thumb against the truck's hood, restless, eyes following every shadow like she expected one to peel loose and start walking toward them. The dread here wasn't normal. It clung. It pooled. It pressed in. Aina dug a hand into her pocket until her fingers curled around the silver dog charm she'd lifted from Golem's suitcase. Cool metal. Solid weight. Something real to hold onto when her lungs felt tight.

The last time she'd felt this particular brand of fear, she'd still been living in Fernhill then—locked in her room most nights, beaten for trying to warn folks, and blamed for every strange thing that happened in the village. Her da said she was cursed. Her gran said she was a changeling. The neighbors whispered she was evil.

A soft wind curled up the road, and Aina closed her hand around the little silver dog charm—letting the cool metal pull her back to the moment everything in her life changed. She remembered the girl sitting in the back booth of her brother Ryan's pub where Aina worked—dark hair, restless fingers, American accent that didn't belong in that old stone room. When Aina growled at her to leave, Austin had only leaned in and asked, "Are you the girl who burned down the sheds last night?" And then she'd pulled out the blurry satellite photos—little scabby red creatures climbing walls, squeezing out cellar windows, bent over the fence with long-nosed, human-like faces. Aina had dropped a glass. It shattered at her feet.

"How... how did you know something was in the sheds?" she had whispered.

Austin had shrugged in that maddening way of hers. "Somebody posted about the incident on social media. I believe you. Those creepy little bastards are called Bloody Bones, right?"

Aina had felt her throat close. "They were trying to steal the boys next door. Nobody believed me." And she was beaten for it.

"And you saved them," Austin said. "And people still treat you like trash for it. That's not fair."

It was the first time anyone had ever said she wasn't a monster.

Seconds later, Ryan's shadow had filled the doorway, hand raised to strike—and Austin caught his fist mid-swing.

"If you want out," she'd told Aina, "grab your things. I'm getting you out of here." Aina had set her room on fire before she left. And Austin didn't flinch. Now, three years later, the same Bloody Bones instinct prickled the back of her neck. Something was wrong.

"I'm going to light a couple of candles," Aina said. "See if there's anything supernatural hanging around."

Austin didn't tease her. Didn't grin. Just nodded stiffly. "Okay. Do it."

That alone told Aina everything she needed to know—Austin smelled danger, too.

Fog rolled low over the ground, swirling around Austin's boots as she hopped down from the hood. She circled the truck with a practiced sweep of her gaze that never looked frantic, but Aina knew the signs: the tightening jaw, the tapping thumb, the little hitches in breath when Austin thought she heard footsteps where there weren't any.

"So, my fairy friend," Austin said, voice too chipper to be real, "are you going to do your mojo tonight, or should I serenade whoever's watching us?"

The humor cracked at the edges. A faint whiff of cigarette smoke drifted from somewhere unseen, seeping between the trees. Roo's growl deepened.

Aina reached into her pocket and pulled out a small glass vial sealed in wax. Mugwort, oak leaves, cloves. A charm she hadn't given anyone in a long time.

"Pet," she said, holding it out. "Take this. It will protect you. Make Roo get in the vehicle. He can't be around the charm either."

Austin hesitated. "Why? Protect me from what?"

Aina's voice dropped to a whisper, carried thin on the cold air. "From me."

Austin froze.

And somewhere in the dark—between the trees, near the barn, or perhaps right on the tracks—a shape shifted. Watching. Waiting.

"Roo! In the truck! Now!"

Then the night held its breath. So did they.

Chapter −21

"Starr—get Starr. Aina's hurt!"

Austin never took anything for granted. Not safety, not normalcy, not the illusion of control. But she never expected to look up—five minutes after Aina finished arranging a small circle of pink candles scavenged from Brandon's pantry—and see Aina standing twelve feet tall, magnificent and terrible, drenched in gauzy black wings that breathed with the wind.

"Don't look at me."

The words were a hiss, shaking the leaves.

Austin remembered the moment before: Aina kneeling, striking a match, cursing because the breeze kept blowing the candle out. Austin sliding off the hood to help. And then—nothing. Aina was gone.

"Aina?" Austin called, irritation fading to confusion. She backed up two steps. "Where'd you—holy hell—"

Her spine hit something tall, warm, and moving. She turned upward until her neck protested. Roo growled in the truck, low and guttural. Crud. When Roo got scared, he tended to shift, and a half-changed Rougarou was nearly impossible to control.

"Stay, Roo," Austin grunted. "Shush."

"Don't look at me." The voice came from above. Austin snapped her gaze down to the mud. Sweat slicked her forehead and crawled down her back. Something warm dripped onto her arm.

Saliva.

"Aina... are you okay?" Austin whispered. Her voice rang thin, hollow. Her pulse hammered through her teeth.

"There's been something bad here," Aina murmured above her, voice deep as a cave mouth. "Something really bad happened on this ground. Don't look at me. I can't—control it."

A claw—soft skin stretched over something curled and sharp— slid beneath Austin's hair and roughly grazed the base of her skull.

A tremor rippled through her. "You know," Aina said gently, "I could kill you right now. You're scared. I smell it. It fills me up."

"I...I know," Austin breathed, unable to swallow the panic. Begging Roo did not burst from the truck to save her. "You won't," Austin said. "Because death isn't my biggest fear. What's my biggest fear, Aina?"

"That I will leave you."

Austin closed her eyes. Aina made a soft chuff behind her. "Ask me yours."

Austin swallowed. "What is your greatest fear, Aina?"

"That right now..." Aina's voice dropped to a whisper. "I'll kill you."

Warm breath washed across the back of Austin's neck. The claw pressed in—sharp enough to bruise, not break skin. Pain shot down her spine in a white-hot line.

"I'm going to leave," Aina whispered. "So that I don't hurt you."

A sudden gust slammed into Austin and drove her to her knees. She didn't look up—she knew better. She stayed bowed to the dirt, trembling, waiting. Seconds crawled past like an hour before the enormous presence finally withdrew. Behind her, Roo let out a series of low, wounded whines.

"Stay, Roo," Austin whispered between clenched teeth. "Stay inside the truck."

The night collapsed into silence.

Austin pushed herself upright. Her hands shook so violently she had to grip the truck just to steady them. Her neck throbbed where the claw had grazed her—hot, burning, already swelling.

Aina didn't return.

"Roo," Austin called, voice tightening. "Come. Find Aina. Now."

Roo exploded out the doorway, nails scraping the metal. Tracking was second nature to him—nose lifted, reading currents of wind only he could decipher. He could follow a creature for miles.

A fairy's scent was no exception.

~

Roo found her at four in the morning—crumpled behind an old hunting stand, limbs twisted like a discarded doll, blood smeared under her nose and a gash on her chin. Austin gathered her up and drove straight to Brandon's, heart pounding the whole way.

Starr, Golem, and Roo had been awake, waiting. Golem carried Aina upstairs, cradled her like she weighed nothing, then Starr shut everyone out of the room.

Twenty minutes later, Starr reappeared, pale and exhausted. "She's just sleeping," she whispered. "She'll be fine."

Then her gaze cut to Austin. "We need to talk. Now."

Roo, sitting on the floor, pressed himself against Austin's leg—worried, watchful. Austin stroked his head once, then whispered, "Everyone, go to bed. Quiet. Don't wake Brandon or Tessa."

Roo didn't move. Not until Austin nudged him away.

"You know you dropped us right in the eye of a storm, right?" Starr's voice was low as she sat at the kitchen table. Austin stood at the window, staring out into the black yard. The wind tugged at the trees, as if something unseen was brushing past them.

"Maybe," Austin murmured. "It wasn't my intention."

"That's a lie," Starr said softly. Not cruel—just tired. "Is anything ever *your intention*? Because it feels like we go from one disaster straight into another. No breath. No pause. We can't even blink."

"I don't know." Austin rubbed the heel of her hand against her forehead. "You guys were different. I was building a family. Paolo was having me—"

"Collect a curiosity shop of monsters and misfits?" Starr raised an eyebrow.

Austin winced. "Yeah. Maybe."

She turned, Austin. Starr's voice slipped quieter. "Full fairy. That's what did this to you." She nodded at Austin's neck.

"Yeah."

"She was terrified she hurt you. Terrified you'd hate her for it."

Austin huffed a sound between a laugh and a sigh. "She should know better. If anything... I like her more. She was well-restrained."

"Then tell her." Starr scrubbed her hands over her face. "She felt something awful in that place you took her tonight. Something that left a stain in the air. And Stats tracked Abel Martin somewhere else tonight. He'll tell you in the morning."

"I didn't plan this," Austin said. "Whatever happened to her wasn't part of anything I envisioned. You know Aina's been desperate to unlock whatever fairy's in her—taste that power now that she's finally free to chase it. But I had no clue it was tonight."

"I know," Starr said. "But now that you understand what happens when she turns? You need to stop letting her do it. Her body can't take it. If she tries that again too soon—it could kill her."

Austin swallowed hard. "Okay. I'll do what needs to be done."

A loud slam hit the porch.

Austin flinched. Something moved past the glass. A flick of shadow—too quick to catch, too real to ignore.

"They're watching us," Starr murmured.

Austin nodded, breath tight. "Like a storm on the horizon," she hissed. "Peeking through the night sky."

And the storm was close now—close enough to taste. But it wasn't the only thing closing in. Someone stood on the porch in the silvery dark. Not knocking. Not calling out. Just... waiting.

Chapter —22

Secrets. Sometimes Austin had so many she thought her head would explode—confetti bursting from her skull, scattering across the floor for everyone to inspect, dissect, and finally learn who she really was. And then there were the *borrowed* secrets—other people's truths she held because she had to.

One of them was Aina's. Aina had whispered it only once, voice barely above breath: "Golem makes me feel soft. When I feel soft, I lose myself. Love makes me weak."

Austin had scoffed gently. "Love doesn't make you weak."

Aina's emerald eyes had flickered, almost ashamed. "For fairies, it does. Please don't tell anyone. It is a secret."

Austin had promised. And like every promise she made to this crew, she meant it. That secret, among many, sat heavy in her chest now as she stood in the loft of the barn, the upper doors flung wide to drink in the chill air and the raw sprawl of pasture. Far beyond, fires burned on Abel Martin's side of Canaan Mountain—yellow at dusk, now a violent orange bruising the horizon at two in the morning. Smoke drifted thick and bitter through the fog, a chemical tang that stung her sinuses and made her eyes water. She pressed her knuckles to the bridge of her nose, fighting the ache creeping behind her eyes.

She held her phone to her ear. "Daddy, this is Austin." She'd poked the number in her phone, bracing herself for the always-angry voice. Gravelly. Coarse. Familiar in a way that hurt. "Brandon said we can't stay here anymore. We don't have anywhere else to go. Can we please stay with you just a couple of days?"

"No."

That was it. No hesitation. No kindness. Just a slammed door in the shape of a word. Austin paced, boots scraping the old boards. She stopped against the far wall, leaning into the warm timber still holding yesterday's sun. "Two days. I'm begging you. One of my friends is sick. She shouldn't be moved."

"Why do you keep calling me, Austin? It will always be the same answer. Go away. Go far away from this place. You aren't safe here. Danville Station isn't safe with you here."

Austin swallowed the sharp sting. "Before I go, can I stop and get Papaw's necklace?" Silence—too long, too stiff—and she opened her mouth to press the issue when a faint scuffle in the hay behind her made her spin around. Someone had climbed the ladder into the loft without her noticing.

"Hey." Brandon's voice, thick with sleep, cut through the hush, making her jump. She fumbled to hang up. He was barefoot, in a faded blue T-shirt and jeans, hair ruffled like he'd run a hand through it a dozen times on the way up the ladder.

"Sorry—did we wake you?"

"It's okay." He yawned, covering his mouth as he crossed the loft. "What are you doing?"

"Just...winding down. Aina had a seizure." Austin rocked on her heels, bumping her back against the wall. "It scared me."

"Oh—does she have them a lot?" Brandon glanced at her phone. Marco's name flashed for a second before she locked the screen. She didn't call him. There was no space for her with him—not the others, not her mess. She pocketed the phone.

"No. Usually it's just nosebleeds."

Brandon stepped closer. "You know, I don't want you to go. Not that it's up to me." He smiled a tired, crooked smile, one that tugged at something deep in her chest. "It's been good having you here. Seeing you."

"Yeah, we're a total delight." Austin snorted. "Could you make a list of our wonderful assets for the next seven people I call to bum a place to sleep? Because the seven I already called think I'm—"

"Trouble. Yeah, you are." His grin softened.

"A pain in the ass," Austin corrected, looking at the rafters. "Remember Haley Brighten? Student council with me?"

"Yeah."

"She laughed when I asked her."

"What happened?" Brandon tugged a curl of Austin's hair, letting it fall against her neck. The touch sent a ripple across her skin. "You used to be so quiet."

"I got picked up by Paolo Bertinelli and what Starr calls his curiosity shop of mutants, monsters, and beasts."

"Paolo Bertinelli, the Trillion Dollar Twit?" Brandon blinked.

"Tabloids said that. He preferred 'eccentric.' I called him crazy."

"You're one of his...what? *Things*?" Brandon asked gently.

Austin didn't answer. She stared at her hands.

Brandon's voice softened. "You don't trust me, do you?"

"You're dating Abel Martin's daughter."

"You're being paranoid," Brandon murmured. "Again, he's just some old guy trying to keep his family together. And Lyndsey—"

"I know. Don't say it again," Austin groaned.

"Say what?"

"She's sweet. She's nice. She's a hard worker and a smart gal. She's the marrying type."

"Don't do that. It's not *that* serious yet."

"That's what you were going to say, wasn't it?" Austin shot back, rolling her eyes. "And a ring isn't serious?"

"I haven't given it to her yet." He moved closer, crowding her space. Her pulse spiked. She hated being boxed in. "Why do you think I haven't dated anyone seriously for four years? Why I haven't given her the ring?"

"The same reason you dumped me," Austin said sharply. "Attachment issues?"

His brow shot up. "I have attachment issues? You said it would hurt too much to keep going out and then leave. You were the one who broke it off."

"I said it would hurt to leave," Austin snapped. "I would've stayed. But you—Brandon—you changed your number. Blocked me. Your sister told me to bugger off."

"I never told her to say that," Brandon said quietly. "I liked you."

He sighed. "Until you tore my heart out and left me with a little mirror image of you walking around every day."

"Tessa." Austin's anger faltered. Her voice went soft. "Does my family ever ask about her?"

"Your mom texts me all the time. Wants pictures. She asks if I know where you went."

Austin sighed. "Enough sad stuff. Let's get mad again." She reached up and slapped his cheek lightly. "You're an idiot."

Brandon immediately laughed—too loud for the quiet barn—and it startled a cow into a low complaint outside. Austin laughed too, nerves unraveling into something warm and dangerous.

He stepped closer and touched her hair, lifting it gently. "Holy crap, are you alright? Your neck...did Aina do that?"

"Yes. During the seizure."

"Why do you always have to get hurt?" he murmured, letting her hair slide through his fingers.

Austin opened her mouth, but Brandon leaned in, bracing an arm behind her, and caught her chin in his hand. He kissed her— hard, desperate—a kiss that stole her breath, her balance, her sense of what she came up to the loft to do.

He paused, forehead against hers. "Can I kiss you?" he whispered. "I should've asked first."

"Yes," she breathed.

He kissed her again—slower this time, searching, relearning her. His hands framed her face, then settled at her waist, steady, warm, grounding her.

Austin's thoughts tangled. She didn't trust him. His family didn't want her here. Abel Martin was a threat. Everything was a trap waiting to spring. But for one reckless heartbeat, she let herself stop thinking. When she tugged him closer, his breath stuttered, and he whispered that he loved her—raw, almost painful. Maybe he meant it. Maybe he didn't. Austin didn't let herself decide. His shirt slid over her fingers, rough from farm work, warm from sleep. Then his hands lifted her shirt a few inches before he froze, breath unsteady.

"Austin," he said quietly. "I don't know if we should keep going. The consequences...think about them first."

She flinched. "You know how to kill a mood."

"You're going to walk," he admitted. "I don't know if I can handle that again."

"That's your choice," Austin said softly. "You're telling me to leave."

"Okay...then stay. At least a couple more days."

She exhaled, tension draining. They leaned into each other again, kissing—slower, deeper, full of history and hurt and something neither dared name.

The barn felt small around them, warm, humming with the storm rolling over the mountain.

Brandon's hand cupped her cheek. Her fingers slid up his spine. Their breaths braided together.

But when his fingers brushed the hem of her shirt again, Austin caught his wrist gently—not a push, not a refusal, just a quiet boundary. He understood.

They sank to their knees on the hay-dusted boards, foreheads touching, lips brushing, sharing the same thin breath—but the moment stopped there. Held. Sealed. Safe.

Outside, thunder cracked across the ridge, shaking the rafters.

Austin closed her eyes.

For a little while, with Brandon's arms around her, secrets stayed quiet. But only for a little while.

Chapter −23

"Where have you been? Roo said you were taking another for the team."

Austin made it three steps into the kitchen before Hutch blurted, the overhead light flickering across scratched linoleum, the scent of burnt coffee clinging to the air. He looked both offended and thrilled to have ammunition. If he'd known Brandon was right behind her, he probably would've said it louder.

Austin went eight shades of red. Brandon didn't comment—just shot her a look that said *Really*? and headed upstairs with an eye roll. Stats waited until Brandon's boots creaked out of earshot. Then he leaned in and poked Austin's hand with his pen. "There was a town where you and Aina visited last night. Terrytown. The population was 258 in the 1880s. Coal camp. Rail junction."

Austin rubbed her face. "Stats, start small. Pretend I'm an idiot."

"A train wreck," he said simply. "1891. The freight train was fifteen minutes late picking up coal. Dispatch forgot to warn the passenger train coming the opposite direction. They collided on the curve. Thirty-two people died."

A breath snagged in Austin's throat. Aina's terror, her wings scraping wild grooves in the night sky—shrieking on the wind, feathers flashing in the moonlight—*Yeah. That fit.*

She slid closer and laid a hand on Stats's forearm, her fingers trembling. He scooted away, the chair scraping protest across grimy tile.

"Sweetie, you've got to let people touch you."

"No. Actually, I don't."

"Studies show lack of human touch increases violent tendencies."

Stats blinked once. Twice. Then—very faintly—his eyebrows lifted. "Oh," he said slowly. "You're using statistics on me." A tiny flicker of pride tugged at the corner of his mouth. "Appropriately."

Austin squinted at him. "So... are you insulted?"

"Moderately," he admitted. "But also... impressed."

She groaned. "Are you ignoring the violent tendencies part?"

"Oh, I heard it," he said, lips almost smiling. "I'm just choosing to focus on your academic progress."

Starr cackled from the living room, the harsh sound bouncing off the peeling wallpaper like a threat barely contained.

Austin groaned. "I'm trying to make you a better person, and you're weaponizing science."

"You are implying I'm a *bad* person?"

"No. I'm telling you outright that you need to feel loved. Now hold still. Thirty seconds." She pressed her fingers to his wrist. Stats lifted his watch to time her—because of course he did—but for a split second, his hand twitched beneath hers. Not pulling away. Not leaning in. Just... pausing. Like the unfamiliar warmth startled him in a way he didn't hate as much as he wanted to.

"Twenty-nine," he muttered, a little too quickly.

"So," she said, "why do you think Abel Martin spent two hours at the scene of a disaster?"

"No idea." Stats dropped his watch hand and froze, staring at her fingers on his arm like they were radioactive. "If he were seeking historical information? One-percent probability. Paying respects? Zero—no relatives deceased. But if you acquire a DNA sample—"

"No DNA samples."

"Blood would also work."

"No *blood*, Stats."

He leaned closer to the screen, eyes glowing. "Maybe he was simply smoking a joint in a remote location."

Austin snorted. "Right. Abel Martin, king of the creeps, hotboxing a Victorian ghost site."

"THAT theory," Stats said, "I can test with blood."

"Stats."

He sighed in defeat.

Then she softened. "Look at me when I talk to you."

He grimaced but turned, locked eyes with her, and forced a smile so wide it was unsettling. "There," he said. "Happy?"

"Ecstatic."

It *was* a milestone. Two years ago, Stats insisted emotions were just chemical illusions.

She stood to leave. In the doorway, Golem appeared, anchoring the room's energy as the next moment unfolded. His huge hands tapped together like muffled thunder.

"Aina wants to see you," he rumbled. He kept glancing over his shoulder, waiting for Starr to step outside. Austin's pulse jumped; every nerve alive, a sense that something would go wrong. That look—Golem only got that look when something was *wrong*.

She nodded. "Take me up."

Chapter −24

Aina was sitting up. Her cheeks were ashen—a strange, pasty shade made even paler by the black hair framing her face. Her eyes, bright as emeralds, tracked Austin across the room.

The walls were white, lined with faded family photos. A cheery side table by the bed glared in its brightness. All of it made Aina look even more out of place—a tiny black bead lost on immaculate white sheets. The air felt brittle; every detail was too sharp. Austin's skin prickled, cold sweat gathering at her hairline.

"There is something wicked going on there." Aina's voice was barely a whisper. "Last night's place. Something's wrong. You need to know." She glanced at the window. "Starr told me to rest, not think about it. I can't." Her hand trembled on her chest. "I smelled something—bitter, burned, catnip, and sandalwood. I hoped I was wrong. But I wasn't."

Austin's heart hammered against her ribs. The walls seemed to close in, suffocating her. Cold sweat trickled down the back of her neck as dread tightened its grip.

"I followed the scent back to the compound over the hill. There's a trail of it, a trail of darkness. Not just one pathway—so many, I got lost. I couldn't find my way out." Aina's fist clenched. "The smell, it was enough to make me feel—like melancholy. It set me off, set—"

"Set your fairy into coming out of hiding?" Austin smiled softly. "It's okay."

"Starr says it *isn't* okay. I have to be careful."

"Starr just wants us safe, sipping milk on the porch like stray cats—pretending everything's fine, even when the milk's laced with poison," Austin muttered, rolling her eyes.

Starr stood in the doorway, arms folded. "I told you to leave Aina alone. Get out, Austin."

"You're not my boss." Austin turned to Aina, who watched her nervously.

"I am when it comes to Aina's health and well-being."

"You're never my boss. Say what's best for Aina. I'll decide what's good for us."

"Another reckless decision—typical you. It's always about you."

"Escaping the yacht? I had no options. I brought you to the only safe place I knew."

"The place you ran *from*."

"The place *I was taken away from*."

"Yes, exactly. The place that didn't want you, that spit you out. "See? The place you think is safest is the place you're actually least safe. Does that register?"

Austin gritted her teeth. "You got a better idea?"

"Yes, anyplace but here," Starr murmured. "Because I even feel the evil here baking on my skin." She held up her arm, displaying a reddish glow, a tiny rash from wrist to elbow. Austin stared at Starr. Frustration seethed inside, hot and razor-sharp. Every nerve tingled with electric irritation.

She'd had Starr's back from day one with Paolo—had all their backs since the start. Why did they always turn against her? Why now, when every raw instinct inside begged her to shield them, even if her methods weren't popular? Jaw clenched, heart pounding wildly, she felt the sting of betrayal and desperation.

Austin clenched her teeth. "I'm done bickering. You're alive because of me. I need to find Roo—he ran off."

"He follows you like a goddess. Why'd you upset Roo?" Starr rolled her eyes. "You can piss off anyone."

"Well, for your information, he peed on my leg when I came down the ladder of the barn this morning, Starr," Austin stared hard at her. He had.

She'd come down first, and Brandon was coming down right after her. When she had taken one step toward the door, Roo had come out of the darkness, scaring the crap out of her.

She gasped, followed the sound of trickling to the floor, and Roo just stood there and peed on her. "He can't start peeing on all of us to mark territory. He can't pee on me every time I have a friend."

She'd yelled at him, told him it was not appropriate on any level to display his loyalty, claim his turf like they were fenceposts. Brandon was her friend. Roo's suddenly haughty air just fell from his face, and his eyes had widened. He hated being admonished by Austin.

Then, he had taken off into the darkness.

"It was probably a wise decision on his part. I'm assuming you were up in the barn with Brandon."

"None of your business."

"It is if it gets us all killed." Starr marched closer. "He has a girlfriend from the commune. Don't trust him. Is there anything in that head of yours—?"

Austin listened, but every disapproving remark from Starr tangled with old voices—her father, her brother, Paolo—all balled up in her chest. Her lip twitched. She tasted the metallic tang of adrenaline. Warning. Her pulse skipped. A bead of sweat rolled down her spine.

"Stop, Starr," Austin said, voice raw. "Talk to me before you make decisions for everyone."

"No."

"Okay," Austin said, and she felt a smile flicker at the corner of her lips. She reached up her hand and closed her eyes softly. She imagined her hand pushing Starr to the wall with tiny poppy wallpaper, shoving her up along the wood so she rolled and rolled, with jerky bangs, toward the ceiling.

"Austin—" she could hear Aina grunting her name. "Please don't. Please!"

A shudder twisted inside her belly when Starr screamed—a hot, giddy rush, electric and wrong. It flared up her throat, flushed her cheeks, and buzzed in her fingertips. Sweat poured along her scalp. She felt alive with dangerous power.

Starr's angry words only fueled it.

"Bitch gonna screw with me still?" Austin opened her eyes and looked up at Starr, now pinned awkwardly to the ceiling, arms bent, legs straight. Her own hands ached with tension.

"Please don't hurt me, Austin."

"I'm not hurting you. Then do as I say."

"I—I can't. You don't think things through. My conscience won't let me."

"I'm not evil. I am making you do as I say."

Austin smiled at her. She told herself it wasn't wrong to want a reaction—to show Starr she couldn't undermine her authority. She wanted Starr to feel enough discomfort to stop questioning her decisions, just enough so maybe next time, Starr would trust Austin's leadership—because deep down, Austin believed her choices kept them safe. As Austin looked at her fingers, she imagined them gripping Starr's shoulder, asserting the control she felt slipping away.

"You need to choose soon," Starr hissed. "Or you'll turn into one of them—the little dark things that crawl into your mind and feed you bad thoughts."

Austin was teetering on the edge, becoming like those dark things that once in a while popped into her dreams. She knew Starr hoped her plea would pull Austin back, away from the temptation of power and toward her humanity, because she believed Austin was losing herself to the same darkness she feared.

Them. The dark things from her dreams, the ones with all the power. *Girl, do you want to ride with us in the wind?* In dreams, she said yes. They took her to places she'd never been. Austin would awaken, bathed in sweat, never remembering exactly where they had taken her.

She just knew she liked it—the feel of *power*. Like now. She saw them wiggling out of the corner of her eyes, tiny shadows flitting around the throw carpets on the wood floor.

Maybe they'd ask her to ride with them now.

"Ask me," Austin said to the shadow right now. She felt something cool and wet on her arm. She saw the shadow there, wriggling fingers touching her. "Ask me."

"No, don't do it!" Starr's scream tore through the air.

Aina's voice rose, desperate: "Please, Austin, let bygones be bygones. Please!"

Footsteps thundered up the wooden stairs. The sound hit Austin's chest like a fist. Golem's shout.

Brandon's warning: "What is happening!"

Austin shivered, panic crashing in her chest, jagged and cold. The shadowy presence vanished, but her skin crawled, and her breath hitched with leftover terror.

"You'd better move, Aina." Austin stared hard at Aina, watched the girl make a jerky dive off the mattress. Then Austin winked up at Starr. "Prepare for a landing."

She wiggled her fingers like she was shaking off a spider web. Starr made one last scream as she fell downward and landed with a flop on the bed, then bounced off onto the floor on her rear. "Umph." Austin felt Golem's arms wrap around her. He flipped her on her back and sat down hard on top. She bucked a little just for show, kicked out at Starr because she wanted that warm, fuzzy tingle to come back.

"Alright, Golem, get off!" Austin grunted. Twenty minutes had passed. Golem was sitting on her. Hutch had her hands held together in a death grip. They were all staring down at her with fearful, wide eyes. Starr was holding her head between her hands, cooing at her like she was two years old. Austin felt humiliated.

"I can't feel my arms and legs," she grunted at Golem. "And I can't breathe, you tub of lard."

"Let her up," Starr said softly. "Her eyes aren't black anymore." Golem grumbled like he enjoyed sitting on top of her. She gave him a bit of a shove with her hands and pushed herself to her feet.

"Daddy?"

"Stay back."

That was the worst part.

Tessa stood at the bottom of the stairs, wide-eyed, terror carved deep into her young face. Austin's stomach turned to ice. Her skin prickled with dread, shame crawling up her spine.

Brandon told Tessa to keep her distance from Austin, then hurried to their daughter before Austin could pass. The way he looked at Austin—guarded, disturbed—reminded her of someone staring at a mangled opossum on a July highway: horrified, unable to look away.

Shame burned in her chest, hot and raw.

"It's alright, they fight like that all the time." Stats was calm, standing at the top of the stairs, looking at Brandon.

"No, it's not alright. Not in my house," Brandon had answered, passing him. He was shaking his head like he couldn't believe what he just saw. "It's not normal. *She's* not normal. Who does that kind of stuff?"

"Nice going, Pet," Hutch muttered from the corner.

Austin rubbed her wrists. They ached. She said nothing, just watched as Brandon scooped up Tessa and disappeared into the other room.

The second they were gone, she bolted from the house, shame burning behind her eyes, breath fast and shallow.

Chapter –25

Roo waited until dark to slip up under the wire fence. He could hear the dogs baying and howling, lots of dogs barking. He followed their chatter in a low run-jog until he saw the shadow of one of them stop, a huge Rottweiler that growled low beneath its breath.

"Come." Roo squatted down. He patted the grass at his knees. He made a soft huffing sound and sat still, letting the dog come up and sniff him. Roo rolled to his back, letting the dog sniff him again. Then he lay there while all twelve dogs—a mix of Rottweilers, hound dogs, and mutts—gave him a snuffle with their wet muzzles. "Good boys," he said softly to each of them. Roo rolled back over and petted them, rolling with them on the ground while they nipped and licked his face and arms.

The Rottweiler, he knew, was the alpha. The lead dog was somewhat confused by his position and took it lightly, allowing Roo to roll him over and scratch his belly, claiming the pack. Then the dog jumped up, put its nose to the wind. The sound of someone's voice called out for the dogs far away.

Roo breathed in the air too, caught the bitter scent of something burning, something like old truck tires. It was pungent, hurt his nostrils, and gave him a headache. He shoved a hand in front of his nose and stood up. The dogs came and lounged down next to him. Another voice called out to the dogs, and the alpha whined up at Roo.

Roo waved him away with his hand. "Go," he muttered.

He crouched, the night's damp seeping into his jeans. It wasn't silent—Pet's voice echoed through the trees, ragged with worry, her scent sharp and anxious on the air. His hearing caught her from impossibly far away—her breath, her words, the wild rabbit stutter of her heartbeat when she was scared. He should have gone home hours ago.

The guilt prickled under his skin, but he let her fret.

It was easier than facing her with all the anger tangled up inside.

The thought of her with Brandon burned a bitter taste in his mouth. It wasn't a lover's jealousy, but the blunt, animal kind— protective, territorial, pack-deep, the instinct of a creature guarding its person. Roo didn't know how to make her happy, didn't want to share her, and didn't want her to settle for Brandon just to stay safe. And Brandon—he smelled wrong, like the commune: earth, rot, old secrets. Roo clung to the anger, letting it mask how much he wanted to run home and bury his face against her shoulder. The resentment simmered—hot and sour in his gut. He didn't let it go; he just packed it away, tight and hidden.

Roo trotted down the hillside. Mobile homes lined the dirt road below, and he could smell them—mungy carpet, damp wood paneling, mildew clinging to every wall.

Little lights twinkled inside. The scent of beans, cornbread, and ham wafted to his nostrils. He knew better than to stop and ask for a meal. He knew he shouldn't be seen. He couldn't look in the windows. No, that wasn't good. He'd done that before, and that's when the trouble started the last time.

He'd been hunted before. The very thought hurt. It made him stop and hold on to his head with both hands. He'd actually been caught and caged in a makeshift chicken wire cage. Roo had been out and about like he always was on the bayou near his town of Little Key Swamp in south Louisiana. He rarely went home. His grandpa, who had raised him, died two years earlier. Roo had set off on his own, fished, and hunted the land around him. Then one night, he'd been sleeping on the ground. The sound of a boat spooked him, and he rose up, only to hear a gunshot. Roo had bolted, jumping into the water. When he finally found a bit of land jutting out, Roo had run for the shore. He felt a snap in his ankle and screamed out in pain— a wolf trap.

"Boys, I think we got a Louisiana swamp monster." He remembered the man who found him there, trying desperately to unlatch the trap. "A real Rougaroo."

The next day, people came to take pictures. Nobody seemed to care that he was hurt, his ankle swollen.

He'd been poked and prodded for two days while people with cell phones recorded his howl.

Rougarou.

He didn't like to remember it, the big lights flashing in his eyes, the men with guns, the trap cutting into his ankle. Taped his mouth so he didn't bite. Austin told him later they were three dumbass monster hunters with a TV show that started it all: *Louisiana Swamp Boy: Lord of the Swamp*. That's what the episode was called. It ran three times the first week, and that's when people started coming from all around the United States to find the Louisiana Swamp Boy, see his eyes glow. They had guns, knives, explosives, and traps. They came in airboats and canoes, cars, and even a helicopter.

Hush hush. Shhhh. Roo would never forget that sound, so soft and like his grandmother's sing-song tone when she made her humming sound to help him sleep. He'd fallen asleep in the pen, had smelled her scent long before he saw her sneak into the room. "I have cheeseburgers," she had whispered. "Fast food was all I could find open this late at night. I'm starving, are you?" He'd just stared at her while she climbed right into the pen with him. She'd handed him a burger and stuffed fries into her mouth. "I came a long way to find you. I don't like airplane food. I can take you someplace safe where they won't put you in a cage."

The woman had smelled sweet and safe, a mix of cheeseburgers, vanilla, and pine.

"Okay." That's what Roo had said. Now, missing her pressed in on him sharp as hunger. He remembered her hands on the cage, the smell of cheeseburgers, and the softness of her voice.

"Pet," he whimpered, guilt thick in his gut for getting angry. The pee thing—he'd deal with that later. He needed to get home, let her see he was alright. Roo snuffled the air, her scent already fading.

But something else hit him—a rank, animal stench: moldering meat, sour milk, old feces—dead-dead, long dead. It curled in his nostrils and pulled him off course.

He followed the smell.

For now, Pet was forgotten, just sitting in the back of his mind as something secondary to do. Find what is dead. Go home to Pet. She would have to wait. Roo worked his way up one hill and down another. He came to a small clearing in the trees below and stopped.

Men were digging. There was a cemetery.

He saw three raw holes in the earth. Men moved like shadows, splashing gasoline that stabbed Roo's nose, making his eyes water. He stayed crouched, choking back coughs. When flame caught, burning chemicals filled the clearing—hot, plastic, wrong.

Roo shivered, hair prickling down his arms. Every sense screamed to run. And deep in his Rougarou instincts, something clicked sideways: *They weren't burying bodies. They were hiding something about themselves.* Only when the men left did Roo slip away, heart thudding, heading for the porch to wait for Pet.

"Crap." That was her voice. He smiled when he saw her drive up late into the night. She got out of the car and stood above him.

"What the hell, Roo?" she declared, voice hoarse, eyes raw from worry. "I've been out calling for you all day and half the night, scared something happened—and you're just sitting on the porch?"

She plopped down next to him, leaning into his shoulder, tension radiating off her. "What's my biggest fear, dumb butt?"

"That I'll leave you. But I didn't," he said, voice wobbling. He tried for smug, but guilt and relief tangled in his chest. Her hand shook when she stroked his head—he felt the tremor in her fingers. She smelled like rain and electricity, happiness laced with fear. "I'm here. See?"

"Did you get something to eat tonight?"

"No."

"Alright, come inside, I'll cook you a steak."

"They were burying people on the other side of the mountain," Roo blurted, the words tumbling out too fast. His accent thickened when he was nervous. "They'd been dead a long time."

"Say it slower."

"They were burying people on the other side of the mountain. They'd been dead a long time."

"Dead people?" She froze. "At Abel Martin's place?"

"Yeah."

"I'm scared, and I'm tired, Roo," she whispered, her voice splintering at the edges, as if she might shatter. "Will you watch over me tonight?"

For a heartbeat, Roo felt bliss—her needing him made everything else fade. He lived for the hush as her breath slowed, the soft hitch in her chest as she settled beside him. He'd stay awake, muscles coiled, senses flaring outward—holding the shadows and strange scents at bay until morning.

"Yeah, uh-huh."

But as Roo stared into the dark beyond the window, a shadow slipped across the porch—quick, silent, putrid. It did not carry the scent of his safe place: cheeseburgers, vanilla, pine, and Austin.

Something cold and electric crawled up his spine.

It left the scent of burning dead.

Tonight, he wasn't sure even he could keep the monsters out.

Chapter −26

Austin was dancing in the kitchen behind Starr that morning, her earphones on and eyes closed as she sang quietly to herself. Brandon could tell Starr was not enjoying it.

Austin kept grabbing Starr's hips, bumping against her with exaggerated, silly-sexy moves, waving her hands over her head like she was trying to shake off the tension.

"Stop it! That's enough!" Starr snapped, pulling an earphone off.

"Ow. I was just messing around." Austin yanked her hand back, voice brittle.

"You're always teasing, Austin. If you're not serious, quit it."

"Why can't *you* just *like* me? Be my friend?" Austin shoved her earbud in and turned away.

"Why can't *you* have a crush on me?"

Austin groaned, staring at the ceiling. "Because I like men."

"Not the right kind of men," Aina muttered, voice small.

Brandon hovered on the stairs, half in shadow, not ready to be seen after last night. Austin spun, her eyes going glassy-hard on Aina. "And you're an expert on men and relationships, Aina? Really?"

Aina flinched.

Austin's voice sharpened. "You want to lecture me on choices when you're terrified of your own? Didn't you just tell me that Golem 'makes you soft' and soft makes you weak?" Her hands fluttered in agitation. "At least when I screw up, I don't hide behind fairy excuses." She barked a brittle laugh. "Maybe just admit you love King Kong instead of making the excuse you can't because he steals your power. He doesn't. You do."

Austin sighed and drifted toward the kitchen, peeling herself out of the moment like she needed distance. The room felt different the second she stepped away. Brandon felt Austin's words punch Aina in the gut, the impact echoing straight through his own heart.

He was drained after a week of emotional whiplash. Austin had seemed like a flicker of hope—until he saw her pin Starr to the ceiling, haunting his sleep.

Lyndsey could storm in furious at any second, but Brandon still wanted Austin to be the version of herself he remembered. That tiny hope soured with her last words. She was the mother of his kid, and he couldn't deny he was still drawn to her—but moments like this reminded him why everything between them was so damn complicated. And God, she made it hard to stay on her side.

Brandon muttered under his breath, "Holy crap, I'm justifying sending my whole family to hell in a handbasket because she's got a nice ass." He said it softly, more to himself than anyone else—until a shuffle in the darkened living room made him freeze.

"There's nothing wrong with that." Hutch's voice drifted out, followed by a long yawn as he stretched his arms overhead. Damn teenagers and their freakish hearing. He was smiling, hair sticking up everywhere. "I won't tell Austin you said that if you fix me up with somebody. I don't even care if they're from the creepy commune, as long as they're cute."

"Bro code," Brandon muttered, flustered. "Abel's place is a 'cooperative.' Everybody chips in. It's a community of equals."

"Abel Martin lives in a mansion on the hill; everybody else gets shacks," Austin said, stepping back in with one of Brandon's grandma's tarnished 1960s silver cups clenched in her fist like it was armor and not full of juice.

"Not everybody lives like that."

"You mean *Abel's family* doesn't live like that."

"No, not necessarily," Brandon said, confronting her head-on. "It is *his* property, and he has every right to live in a nice house. And if the people who live there work hard, they get more. And if you're talking about the little houses going into the property, those are families that have just moved into the community. Good God, he buys them a mobile home and has it moved to the property. Free housing. What more could you ask for?" Why is she looking at me like that?

Austin's eyes bore into him. She just nodded. "Freedom," she said quietly. "The ability to make their own decisions."

"That makes no sense at all. Everybody in there is free to come and go as they please," Brandon grunted. "Sure, Abel makes decisions for people there. It's in the community's best interest. He's like the—the mayor."

"And the gates and security cameras?"

"There are gated communities everywhere," Brandon sighed.

"Does that mean I can just walk right in there, knock on somebody's door?"

"Well, if you ask and they give you permission."

"Maybe I'll do that today," she said slowly. "Brandon, why are you defending him?"

"I'm not. You're making it a bigger deal than it is. Everyone in town's on board with him."

"What is that saying you always tell me, Pet?" Hutch said slowly. "If your friends jump off a bridge, are you gonna jump with them?"

"Pretty much summed it up, Hutch," Austin said, voice low as she fixed Brandon with a searching look. "Are you going to jump, Brandon? Or do you feel like you don't have a choice? You told me that you felt trapped into marrying just to save the farm. What happens if you refuse to jump? Does Abel push you?"

"I'm doing it because I like him. He's done so much for Danville Station. He bought a playground and helped start a soccer program. Let's see, he paid for a water and sewage system for the entire town so they could get fresh water out at the property," Brandon told her.

He remembered last spring: the storm that knocked down his fence, flooded his pasture, and caved in his barn roof. The next morning, twelve or fifteen men from Abel's community were at his door, chainsaws and tools in hand. "We're fixing up the neighborhood," one said. "You're next on the list."

"Austin, you don't get it," Brandon muttered. "It's nice having neighbors. I couldn't have fixed that stuff on my own. They rewired the electricity at my house, too."

"Rewired your house," Austin repeated. "Why?"

"To be nice. You need to be less cynical. He's just a nice guy. I can't say it enough." Brandon shot at her.

"Ever check the wiring? For cameras?"

"Oh my God, you're crazy." He laughed, aggravated. "You are the most suspicious person I know. Everything is a conspiracy to you."

He almost jabbed a finger upward—almost asked if she wanted to "earn a few more days of rent"—because she was pissing him off. But he choked it back. Instead, he sighed. "That's why I wouldn't mind marrying Lyndsey and sharing the farm. We're all family."

"And you will be in the *big house* by marrying Lyndsey, Abel's daughter. Makes perfect sense."

He shot Austin a pointed look.

"What's stopping you?"

What *was* stopping him?

"Daddy." Tessa bumped down the stairs on her rear, clutching her glasses to her face. Brandon scooped her up, kissed her hair.

"I don't know what's stopping me," Brandon shrugged. "Maybe last week I would've answered differently. I think I was waiting for something special to jump out at me, but now... I don't think love works like that. I want something stable. Someone who'll read Tess a story and tuck her in." He sighed. "I guess I just have a certain level of *freak* I can tolerate. And you—" he nodded at Austin "—hit the threshold. Sending Starr up the wall—"

He froze. The words were out. Cutting.

Austin's eyes widened, wounded. She glanced at Hutch. Hutch's face was unreadable.

"Yeah, okay, I get it," Austin whispered. "I blew it. Any chance I had with you guys is gone."

"Pretty much."

Her smile died, face crumpling. "Guess it freaks people out when I do that. Not what you wanted to jump out at you."

Brandon felt his chest cave. "Austin, wait—"

"Turn around, Pet," Hutch said, waving a hand in the air.

"Turn around?" Austin blinked at him. "What? Did you see a bug?"

"No. Just buying some insurance."

He brushed past her, winked at Brandon, and walked into the kitchen.

"What is he talking about?" Austin asked, holding her arms out helplessly. "Did he put something on me?"

Brandon couldn't help but laugh. "No."

He wanted to say something else. Something that would pull her back from the edge. But—the whine of ATVs growled into the driveway. Tessa leaned harder into him, staring at Austin.

"That'll be Lyndsey," Brandon muttered. "I'm supposed to go riding with her brothers. I've put her off for a week. She thought you'd be gone by now."

"Do you want us to leave?"

Brandon stared at her, leaned back, and looked at the ceiling like it could give him answers. "What do you want me to say, Austin? It's complicated."

"Stay," she whispered, trying to sound tough. "Just say *stay*. I'll forget all the weird stuff. You're not a dork. I missed you. You were better than any girl I've dated. Prettiest woman in the world. Did I mention *stay*?"

She rattled it so fast it disarmed him.

"Okay," he breathed. Tessa's thumb-wet fingers tickled his neck. "Let's see. I wish you weren't an idiot. And yes, you are a dork." He watched her eyes lift, terrified—so he softened. "I missed you. I liked you. I still do. You're beautiful."

"You forgot: 'You're better than the other girls I dated,'" she whispered. "And stay," she added.

"You know I can't do that, Austin," Brandon finally said. "I'm sorry." He wanted her to stay. He didn't want to lose Lyndsey. *She was sweet. She was nice. She was a hard worker and a smart gal. The marrying type.* He couldn't reconcile either.

"Well," Austin said, voice turning sharp, "when things start going south for you—when you find out Abel Martin has a motive behind his madness, or maybe he's hot-selling Tessa online for a tractor—you let me know."

"Hot-selling? What does that even mean—?"

The front door banged open. Lyndsey walked in with Brenda and Kim—her cousins, her cavalry. Austin's practiced smile trembled.

"I thought she was leaving," Lyndsey said flatly. She looked Austin up and down like she was mold on a newly opened bar of cheese. "I'm not comfortable with this. Just being honest. It's weird."

"Okay," Austin whispered. Her eyes darted like a cornered animal.

"Can I say it clearer?" Lyndsey stepped forward. "Get out."

"Funny thing," Austin said, smiling too brightly, "your boyfriend just said the same thing before you walked through the door. I'm sorry we imposed. We'll pack. Aina got sick—"

"Well, good," Lyndsey cut in. "Easier than I thought."

"Aina," Brenda giggled. "Like *anus* but plural. Is she plural-anus?" Kim and Lyndsey laughed.

"They're all illegals," Lyndsey sneered. "Not our kind."

"Want help packing?" Kim said. "The boys outside will load the truck."

Austin had gone pale. Kim swooped in and grabbed Tessa.

Tessa yelped, reaching for Brandon. "Daddy?!"

Kim cooed, carried her upstairs. Brandon looked at Austin. She looked out the window. Fourteen ATVs in his driveway. Twenty men drinking beer. All watching.

"Just like old times," Austin whispered.

It didn't fit. But Brandon suddenly felt sick.

She headed up the stairs to pack. And Brandon knew—deep in the place he ignored most—he was making a mistake. A big one.

Chapter −27

"Two more days. Please don't make me kick them out. They've got nowhere to go."

"I'm sick of hearing that, Brandon." Lyndsey's voice cracked like a whip. "You don't think it's weird your *ex* is staying here while you're going out with me? It's just not right. I want her out. I'll settle for nothing less."

"There's a whole house of people, not just her."

"Exactly—the freak show. If people think we're connected to them, I'd die. Make her go. If you don't, I'll tell Daddy. He'll do something."

"Why would you tell your dad?"

"Because you don't listen to me, but he'll make you listen. I know you'll do what he says. She's no good for you or Tessa. Even her own dad wouldn't take her—that should tell you everything."

"She's got nowhere else to go, honey, sweetie. Be reasonable—"

"Me? Be reasonable? Get her out, or else."

"Or else, what?"

"Or else I'm telling Daddy."

~

Austin yanked her dresses from the closet, plastic hangers snapping, the stale smell of dust and old fabric rising around her. Sweat beaded on her temples. She shoved the clothes into paper bags—fast, frantic movements that scraped her knuckles. The air felt thick, too hot, the walls pressing inward. The argument downstairs bled through the floorboards, every harsh syllable a reminder she wasn't wanted here.

She stuffed Hutch's shirts and Roo's thin pants into another bag. More voices joined Lyndsey's—the cousins, loud and sharp. Then Tessa's scream pierced the house. A tantrum, loud enough to rattle boards. Brandon tried calming her; someone shoved the child into his arms, muffling her sobs against his chest.

Austin's throat burned. Her hands shook as she shoved another shirt into a bag.

"I'm sorry." Starr stood in the doorway, looking torn—half guilt, half helpless compassion. "I shouldn't have provoked you the other day. It is my fault, Pet. Maybe if he hadn't seen you do that thing, he wouldn't be making you leave."

Austin shook her head hard, heart pounding. Outside the window, Roo waited, shoulders rigid, eyes anxious. She gave him the smallest closed-lipped smile—anything wider, and he might mistake it as a challenge. She needed him calm.

"You piss me off sometimes. But I am responsible for my own actions." Austin dragged a shaking hand through her hair. "But you had it coming. At least he saw the real me now. I can't hide this anymore—can't pretend for people I love, even if it makes them stop loving me back."

"Like your dad."

"Yeah," Austin whispered. "Like Paolo. Like Marco will, too. People always end up quitting me. Easier to blame myself than wonder why. I just...wish I was someone who made people stay."

"Because you're not pretty, smart, funny—or because you piss people off?"

"Pretty much."

"Before you found me, I was dirt." Starr's voice dropped. "You know that, right?"

"You were never dirt." Starr sank onto the bed. Outside, Lyndsey's brothers thudded across the porch; Austin recognized Bradley's voice. She stiffened. "You showed me I was more than dirt," Starr murmured. "When I was fifteen, I ran away. My stepdad wouldn't leave me alone. I survived two years selling myself. Hospitalized and half-dead—then you appeared. You breathed life into me."

Austin hesitated. Starr had healed a child at that hospital, and that miracle had drawn Paolo in. And while it had looked like he swooped in to save them, that was the lie that fooled everyone.

He pretended to protect them, but that wasn't what he did. Paolo collected them. *He made Austin his monster collector*. He wanted them the way a man wants rare animals—beautiful, useful, and caged. The words were so ugly she almost couldn't push them out. "I'm never sure Paolo's intentions were as good as you believed."

"*Your* intentions were." Starr smoothed the blanket beneath her fingers. "You saved all of us." Then her tone shifted, casual but pointed. "Stats said we only have a few thousand dollars left. How are you going to support us now?"

There it was—Starr placing the weight on her again, the expectation that Austin would somehow keep them all afloat. Not out of trust. Out of habit. Austin had never been given a choice.

"I don't know," Austin admitted. "I'll find a job. We'll stay in a cheap hotel."

"You're walking away from this one?"

"I don't have a choice. No money, no place left—I'm out of options." Her voice cracked. "We came here for home. Safety. And yeah, maybe to see if Brandon loved me."

"Did he?"

Austin half-laughed, half-choked. "He never loved me. Just liked me enough to mess around. I needed to see the truth. Mostly...I wanted to see Tessa."

"And the necklace you mentioned? Papaw's?"

"It's not a necklace—it's a pouch he carried," she said. "Leather. Red-dyed thumbprint. Papaw gave it to me. My grandparents wore them around their necks with whatever was sacred—things meant to guard them. When they died, the pouch was supposed to be buried with them. But Papaw left his to me, which... almost never happens. I know it means something," She she said quietly. "In my dreams, I'm standing where it's hidden. When I find it, the shadows in my nightmares stop trying to swallow me—the same ones that make me go rogue, like I did to you the other day. Angry. Irritated. Not myself." Austin's voice thinned to a whisper. "I was told if the wrong person ever got ahold of it... I'd do bad things."

"You're from the Indigenous people here?"

"Papaw was Cherokee. He told me I'd know what to do with the pouch when the time came. I carried it everywhere because my father didn't follow the old ways—none of us kids were taught anything about medicine bags except what Papaw whispered to us. My dad thought it was all nonsense. When I went to the hospital to have Tessa, the nurses took my things and made me remove the pouch." Her throat tightened. "My dad took everything but my clothes. Purse, pouch... all of it. Could be anywhere now." She pressed her palm to her chest. "But I hear it calling me."

"You hear it?"

"Right now." Goosebumps lifted across Austin's arm. "It's like electricity crawling inside me—hot and cold."

Roo slipped in, settling against the bed. Starr's face softened.

"He adores you."

"And I adore him." Austin hugged him. Roo's tongue slid warm up her arm. "Don't do that!"

Starr giggled. Roo laughed too—until footsteps hit the stairs. The laughter died.

"Hey, can you finish up?" Kim leaned in the doorway, adjusting the messy bun on her head. Austin thought she just looked cheap. "We want to lock up the house. Hard to do that with you guys still here."

"Kim, stop. Don't rush them." Brandon's voice drifted up the stairs.

Kim giggled behind her hand. "Go play with the boys, Brandon. I'll handle Spaz and her circus."

Austin shoved the last clothes into a grocery bag. Starr's eyes were full of sympathy. Austin despised it.

"There. Done," Austin told Kim, then whispered to Starr, "Don't pity me."

"Goody," Kim smirked. "We'll escort you out."

Austin passed the bag to Roo and followed Starr downstairs. Brandon waited at the bottom, looking lost, torn in half.

"I'm sorry," he whispered. "Lyndsey said her dad would call the cops if you weren't out—and she would."

"That's odd." Austin blinked. "Why would *he* call the cops? This is *your* house." Then her eyes widened in mock understanding. "Oh. Right. The 'not-a-commune' thing. Got it." She plastered on a bright grin. "Thanks for the stay. When I get money again, I'll send it."

"You don't have to send money, Austin."

"Yes, I do. Because once you marry her, she'll push you to sue me for child support. I'm trying to stay ahead of the game."

"Stop. You know I wouldn't."

"Really? But you'll let them bully us out?" Austin shrugged. "Maybe I don't get it. Or maybe *you* don't."

Brandon paled. He caught Austin's arm, voice fraying. "You'll still see Tessa, right? I'll call you tonight. After they leave, we'll fix things. Please."

The screen door banged open downstairs. Brandon jerked his hand back like he'd been burned.

Austin stepped past him. "Grow a spine, Tremaine. When you do, maybe we'll talk."

Outside, twenty ATVs crowded the driveway. Lyndsey's brothers lounged around them, drinking, laughing.

"I hope you planted seeds with him," Starr whispered.

"Yeah," Austin muttered. "But honestly? I don't know if there's anything left to reach. He's as stubborn as a mule. Whatever used to light him up—it's gone. I tried, Starr. God, I tried. But looking at him felt like looking at an empty house—lights off, nobody home."

"You've never really lost somebody, have you?" Starr murmured.

Austin stared at the porch boards. Her jaw tightened.

"I'm not losing Tessa." Her voice was steel wrapped in fear. Her fists curled until her nails dug into her palms. "I can't. No matter what they do—I won't let her go."

Chapter −28

Seeds. Austin had sown them in his head, and yes, she was right—Brandon was obstinate, blind to what was unfolding all along. Not until a week later, when Lyndsey graciously invited him to "go with the guys fishing." Which meant angling with Abel Martin and his sons. According to Lyndsey, it was a huge deal. And the perfect time to ask her dad for her hand in marriage.

"Well, I was wondering when you were getting on board, son." Abel Martin sat on an old green-and-white folding lawn chair at the edge of Turtle Creek, which split the two properties. "My Lyn, she thinks a lot of you. She's sweet. She's nice. She's a hard worker and a smart gal. She's the marrying type."

Brandon shifted, those words—*she's sweet, she's nice, she's a smart gal, the marrying type*—looping in his head as Abel waited for a response. Abel was a burly man with thick gray hair and a proud demeanor, which he could flaunt because of his size. He gripped a fishing pole in one hand, the other repeatedly reaching for a battered plastic water bottle with the label torn off, spitting tobacco into it. "What the girls don't know, don't hurt them a bit," he'd told Brandon the first time he pinched out a thick wad from the little can in his pocket. "Let's talk—*things*."

"Things." Brandon had chuckled, lowering his eyes like Lyndsey taught him to do. "Yes, sir."

He knew what was coming. He and Lyndsey had ridden ATVs for three hours with her family, then stopped at the pond to cool off. She'd tugged him away from the others, a sly twist to her lips. *I am so ready to get married, Brandon. So ready. Let's just do it. Let's just have my dad marry us in a couple of weeks.*

He wasn't prepared for that, but he'd managed a smile.

Marry? It's kind of a quick notice. My mom and dad don't have a whole lot of money, and they need to save up—

We'll do it on the cheap. We'll just have our honeymoon here, and Kim can take Tessa—

She went on endlessly about the wedding dress, the bridesmaids, quitting her job, and starting a family. A large family—because every child was another rung up the ladder in her father's eyes. Another way to be seen. Another way to matter.

Brandon had only mumbled, *I'll think about it.* He knew why. Lyndsey wasn't what preoccupied him anymore. He kept seeing those red circles around Austin's eyes when he'd called her a freak. She wasn't a freak. He didn't even know why he'd said it. The word hadn't felt like his—it had pushed its way out, foreign and heavy, as if someone else had been standing in his thoughts. He pictured the cornered-kitten look Austin had when Lyndsey and her cousins ganged up on her at the house. Ganged up on, dammit. It was not normal. His house. *My* house. Only now Brandon realized— Lyndsey had already laid claim to it.

"Well, I'm glad that little group of freaks is out of there." Abel nudged Brandon with a fat elbow. "No good having the cop's sister hanging out, keeping watch on everything we do, right?" He waited for Brandon to nod. "There was a minute I wasn't sure if it was that Lyndsey wasn't enough for you, or if you were getting cold feet." Another nudge.

"No, sir."

"Because I've got other girls. Let's see, there's Lilly. She's the pretty one with the blonde hair and the big tits. Kind of young. She's sixteen. She's ready to be assigned."

"Assigned?" Brandon was creeped out that Abel had mentioned his daughter's breasts in a conversation, much less as a way to get him to marry her.

"Well, married. Nobody wants their kids marrying just anyone, right? I lend a hand—a bit of matchmaking now and then. Should've done it for Lyn years ago. I waited too long. She was her mama's darling. Gotta do it before they get too old and stop listening to their daddies. Or start eyeing younger men. If Lyndsey's not right for you, we'll send up a couple of others to try out. Gail's the one with the wide hips. Some men prefer that. You like big butts?"

"That's a song, Dad." One of the young men laughed heartily.

It was Bradley. They all looked just like Abel, meaty boys with too-small eyes, thick hair, and bulbous noses.

"Yeah, you're right," Abel said, spitting into the crinkled water bottle. "But let the boy decide."

He leaned over and patted Brandon's leg like he owned him.

"Hell's bells, you can keep Lyndsey or Lilly," he drawled. "And we'll find you two more girls to help around the place." He flashed a grin as he lifted his fingers in lazy air-quotes. "Cleaning. Company. You know how it is."

Abel settled back, smug as a king handing out favors.

"A man deserves a few women to match his moods. And the Lord provides, son—we'll bring in more girls to tend the house." His fingers made the air-quotes again. "Help with the *'cleaning.'* One for comfort. One for labor. One for obedience. That's how a household prospers."

Brandon felt his face flush. Austin's words—hot-selling—echoed in his mind, and now he understood what she meant: Abel was pitching him a wife like a tractor. Had Abel had more than one wife? Brandon hadn't heard of that in the community. *Come ride this one a while, break it in. If it isn't enough, we'll get you another.*

"Lyndsey is just fine, Mister Martin."

"Abel. Call me Abel." He nodded to the son on his right. "If we meld our properties, we can really expand our game. You've got prime farmland, Brandon. You're sitting on a gold mine of oil."

"Oil?" Brandon muttered. "Our land doesn't have any oil."

"Sure it does," Abel said. "Good thing that land's in your name."

~

Later, at Lyndsey's cabin, Brandon enjoyed the view. Sitting together on the front porch, they could look out over a little pond where her horse grazed. Early evening brought peace; the mosquitoes hadn't started biting yet. This side of the mountain felt empty—the cabin perched on a clear hill, distant hills rolling away.

I wonder where Austin is now?

"What's that, baby?" Lyndsey asked, scooting in closer to him.

She tucked her legs beneath her. She'd tossed a blanket over herself, though it wasn't chilly. He liked it. It usually meant she wanted to fool around. That was fine with him, even if they couldn't do much with Tessa playing in the yard.

"Have you ever thought about leaving Danville Station?"

"Leaving?" She laughed under her breath. "No. Never. I lived in Texas with Daddy at the ranch—nothing but brown and the smell of paper factories. In Florida, the bugs were awful." She sighed deeply. "I take it he asked you about managing one of his properties in Mexico or Texas?" Lyndsey went on. "He told me to be ready to move away from Mommy. But I don't want to go. Anywhere you go, I'll go. You're going to be the man of the house. You'll make the decisions. I'll just have babies. We'll get some girls to clean."

It had never really occurred to him that when she said she wanted a family, she meant *now*. Brandon was only a few months into the relationship.

"I guess I meant leaving your dad's—place. The whole scene."

"Oh, God, no." She looked up, almost horrified. "I get everything I want here. I've got my family, I've got you. If I need anything, they're here."

"Your dad isn't making you marry me, right?"

"That's a strange thing to ask," she told him. "No. Why would he do that?"

"He said something about assigning girls to men."

"Well, not *his* girls with my mom. That's for the old guys that don't have wives. He tries to find young women so they can take good care of them. I mean, no. No, he wouldn't do something like that. I'm sure he was kidding." Lyndsey clamped her mouth shut and waved a hand in the air. "So how long do you think Tessa's going to have to wear those ugly glasses? She looks like an ant."

"Lyndsey, don't," Brandon said with a sigh, wanting to push her away. She'd said that before, even called Tessa "Ant-girl" in front of her. "And I don't know. I doubt she'll grow out of them. I saw Austin putting in contacts. Probably forever if she's like her mama."

"Have you ever thought she'd be better off with Austin?" Lyndsey said softly.

Brandon looked out, watching Tessa play with the little worry dolls Austin had given her—lining them up in a row, tucking them into the little bag again and again. "She is like her, you know. I just don't get her."

"She isn't like Austin. I mean, she is, but she isn't," Brandon muttered.

Why was Lyndsey being so mean? Why was he afraid to tell her that Tessa was just like Austin? "And even if she was better off with Austin," Brandon stated. "I would not give her up. Ever."

"Okay. She's just not sociable—doesn't get along with Kim's kids. We were all talking the other day. Brenda knew a lady in another community whose kid was, you know, *slow*. When I ask Tessa things, she just stares at me. She stared at us while we talked about her—didn't even seem to care. Have you ever had her tested for that? Maybe she could go to a special school."

"She's fine."

"Okay. Don't you remember in high school when my brother made fun of Austin? I remember him coming home from school, telling Mom all about it. You called her Spaz because she looked so goofy and scatter-brained. Those funny glasses made her look so stupid, remember?"

"I don't remember that," Brandon said. Just like old times. But he did remember Austin saying something like it. He wondered if that was what she meant. Maybe they did make fun of her a lot. But she deserved it, didn't she? She was always kind of stuck up.

"I remember when he taped her to the bathroom wall in the teacher's lounge with duct tape," Lyndsey said, rolling her eyes with a soft laugh. "I see where this is going. You slept with her four years ago, so you feel obligated to defend her. But stop. I'm here. Forget her." She winked and leaned in, lowering her voice. "Here, let me show you a little taste of married life." She latched onto his hand, tugged it under the blanket, and pressed his palm to her breast. "How else can I please my husband-to-be?"

Chapter −29

The Cherry Grove Hotel sat forty-eight minutes from Danville Station, its brick façade painted a faded, blushing pink that caught the evening light. A battered sign read: **ROOMS BY DAY OR WEEKLY RATES**. Two stories tall and hunched beside the highway, it looked like a building trying to run away. A cracked swimming pool shimmered a tired blue in the heat. Brandon found it a week and two days after Austin had left his house—though, he told himself it was coincidence. It wasn't. He still had Hutch's number from calving season. One text later:

How are you guys doing?
Good. U?
Staying out of trouble. U still in WVA?
I think. Not far. Cherry Grove. Hotel. Sucks. Has a pool. Fun stuff. JJ.

A picture came through—murky pool water, a pregnant lady bobbing with two kids, an old woman dangling her feet over the edge.

Another picture: Starr and Austin in sunglasses and bathing suits, stretched in lounge chairs, beers in hand, laughing with a couple of guys nearby. His stomach tightened. Hutch texted once more, then went silent. Brandon should've known Austin would come to Cherry Grove—cheap weekly rates, a pool, and Crazy Jack's Pizza Barn right up the road. She'd worked there every summer during high school. If she needed money, she'd find a job fast.

Two days later, he strapped Tessa into her car seat and drove the winding mountain roads. He pulled into the hotel lot just after five. Heat still clung to the sky. Austin's truck was parked crookedly near the end. At the pool, a grill smoked. Music tumbled across the pavement. Austin sat at a picnic table with Aina and Golem, sunburned cheeks, faded T-shirt, flipping her keys as she laughed with a woman he didn't recognize. She looked alive—lighter—like something uncoiled in her since leaving Danville Station.

Brandon watched for almost an hour before Austin got up and walked to her truck. He followed at a distance to Crazy Jack's Pizza Barn. He drove past once. Then again. Austin didn't come out with food. She must be working.

"Daddy, I have to pee."

He muttered under his breath, glancing back at her. Tessa blinked at him behind her thick lenses, clutching the book Austin had given her. He thought about driving up the road and letting her pee in the grass—but he'd come this far.

Inside Crazy Jack's, Austin was behind the counter—ringing up orders, answering phones, moving like someone who'd been doing this since high school. He could've ducked into the bathroom and left without being seen. But he hadn't driven forty-eight minutes just to lurk.

When they stepped out of the cramped restroom, Tessa pointed. "Daddy. There's Austin."

Austin glanced up mid-transaction. Her eyes snapped to them. Her hand didn't stop sliding the credit card.

"Are you stalking me, Five?" she asked, a half-smirk pulling her mouth. The man she was ringing up stared at Brandon as if he were trouble.

"No," Brandon said. "Tessa wanted you to read her the book. She misses you reading it."

Tessa lifted the book as if presenting an offering.

Austin leaned over and plucked it from her hands. "Okay. But I don't get off until midnight."

"We'll wait."

She jerked her chin toward the road. "We're staying at the Cherry Grove Hotel. The owner knocks off the rate if I clean rooms before my shift."

"Yeah, it's the only place in town," Brandon muttered.

"I'll text the girls you're coming. Hang with them until I get back." Then, softer, eyes flicking to Tessa: "Hey. Thank you."

He swallowed. "Yeah. I get it."

~

Austin had her own room. Roo was watching TV when she got back just after midnight; she shooed him out and flicked on the lamp. Tessa refused to sleep, curling against the pillows as Brandon lay beside her.

"This kid should be asleep," Austin muttered, rubbing at her eyes. She disappeared into the bathroom and returned in thick glasses that made her look sixteen and exhausted. She crawled into the bed, sandwiching Tessa between them.

Tessa didn't look at the book. She just stared at Austin's face—drinking her in, memorizing every line like she was afraid Austin would vanish when she blinked.

"Again," Tessa whispered after the first reading. Austin looked up. Brandon nodded. She read it again. And again. Brandon dozed somewhere around the fourth time.

"Again," Tessa murmured. Austin began the story for a fifth time. A buzz cut through the dark. Austin's phone. Three-thirty. Maybe four. Brandon opened his eyes to her silhouette sitting up.

"Yes, sir," she said groggily. "It's four a.m.... I can't get to the airport in twenty minutes... Senator who? Is that his first name? Oh—a senator. Dude—I just called you dude. No, I can't get to New York in three hours. We're in some piddle-dunk town in West Virginia. How'd you even—fine. Send a car. But I must be back by noon. I have a shift." She hung up, sighed, and turned to Brandon.

"Stay as long as you want. I won't be back until late morning."

She dressed fast—tight black skirt, blazer, heels that clicked like she was stepping into another life. Her lipstick was deep cherry; she finished applying it in the doorframe.

"Five," she said, one hand braced against the jamb. Her voice softened. "Thank you. Really."

She kissed Tessa's forehead without waking her. Brandon watched her silhouette disappear into the hallway, her heels tapping like a heartbeat down the corridor. He heard her wake Stats and Starr. Muffled voices. A low rumble of Roo in the background.

Twenty minutes later, a car pulled up outside—expensive engine hum—then doors opened, voices murmured, and Austin left again.

He lay awake staring at the ceiling. What job took her away at four in the morning? What world was she walking into? And how had he ever believed she was the one who wasn't enough?

Chapter —30

Austin sat hunched in a cracked vinyl booth at an all-night diner, neon lights flickering against rain-streaked windows as she absentmindedly traced a pattern on her chipped coffee mug. The hum of old fluorescent bulbs mixed with the clatter of dishes and the hiss of the coffee machine. Everything smelled faintly of burned grease and over-brewed coffee, the kind that stuck to the back of your throat. The world felt cold and distant—forty minutes from New York City, but it could have been a thousand.

She realized—never once had she set foot in the city, not even when the jet dropped her at the airport. Only glimpses of the skyline from above before they circled back to this nowhere town, each mile feeling like a wall. New York, sprawling in all directions, hid more forgotten places than she'd ever imagined. Tonight, Austin felt swallowed by them.

"You're Austin Jackson?"

"Yes, sir." She faced a pasty-faced man of about sixty, sitting beside his wife. Both were pretty, but a bit frumpy. She'd seen him on TV—some generic government official from the eastern United States. Not that she paid any attention; she didn't follow politics, didn't care who was pissing on who in Washington.

Eight bodyguards blended awkwardly among truckers and insomniacs, their eyes flicking toward Austin every few seconds. The static of their radios crackled under the low hum of the diner.

Yet it was not them, but the young man four booths down, who unsettled her most. He wasn't a guard—he looked too raw, too brittle—and *he* was being watched. Shoulder-length hair curtained a face so delicate it seemed almost beautiful, but his eyes darted, always wary, never settling. He looked desperate to vanish.

"I'm Don Madison. You've seen me on TV and social media. Sorry about meeting here." He looked around the diner. It was old and tired. "I must be discreet. I need someplace without reporters. I was told you find people, confidentially. Nothing leaves this table."

"Of course."

"I'll get to the point." He reached into his jacket, pulled out a creased sheet of paper, and slid it across the table to Austin. "My daughter, Jenna, is eighteen, a college student. We thought she was on campus, but two weeks ago, this letter came."

Austin studied the senator's face—lined, haggard, his eyes rimmed raw and anxious, jaw clenched to dam back despair. The sour tang of sweat and cut-rate aftershave hung on him.

She dropped her gaze to the letter:

Daddy, please come find me. I am at a farm in West Virginia. They keep moving me. Phil Turner runs the farm. There are three girls with me—

"Phil Turner." Austin rubbed her face. "Phil Turner is an alias. You know that, right?"

"No."

"They're at one of Abel Martin's farms," Austin muttered.

"A farm? She was heading to Florida for spring break, and then the texts stopped. We thought she was just... having fun." His wife's voice cracked. "We filed a missing person report. Police told us that she's an adult. She can do what she wants. Then we got the letter. She's been abducted. What do they do with the girls at this farm?"

"It's a commune run by Abel Martin. Calls himself a prophet. Has over twenty more. The place reeks of human trafficking. He's probably shopping for wives for his men—*or something uglier.*"

"Oh, God," the wife moaned, jabbing a tissue at her eyes.

"Can you get her out?" the senator asked, eyes bloodshot.

"That's what I do, Senator. But the timing's bad. I'm not taking jobs right now. I don't even know how you found me."

He didn't answer. Then: "I'll pay you anything you want."

"It isn't the money—"

"She's my baby." His wife sobbed, twisting the tissue in her hands. "She's our only daughter. She's a good girl. What if she's dead—?"

"I'm sorry." Austin shook her head. "I can't—not right now."

"I thought you might say that," he murmured. "I might be able to sweeten the deal." He nodded to a bodyguard, who obeyed and stepped aside from the booth where the young man sat. He stood slowly, brown hair falling into his eyes, cuffs glinting around his thin wrists as he hesitated before approaching.

Austin's gaze darted from the metal to the senator, unease prickling down her spine.

"His name is River Hatathli," he said. "He was originally from Colorado. Native American. You might have seen his story in the tabloids."

"No. Why is he wearing handcuffs?" Austin asked. He had cuts on his face and was wearing pajama pants and a white T-shirt.

"He is supposed to be a *character* of some sort."

"A Skinwalker," the young man murmured.

Austin met his gaze—eyes so dark they swallowed light, unreadable and haunted. Shapeshifting was a myth, she told herself. Still, doubt gnawed.

"I know—you collect these things," the senator said. "You're a monster collector."

"These *things*," Austin echoed, eyes hard. "Senator, people aren't *things*. And I don't collect monsters. These people end up in my lap—misunderstood, sometimes dangerous, but people."

"Do you want him or not?"

"I don't buy people. I don't trade services for them."

"That's your loss," the young man murmured. His hands shook despite his attempt to look tough.

Austin felt something twist in her gut. Nobody that young should look that scared. "My loss," she muttered. "What could you possibly offer me except another mouth to feed?" She looked him over. Tall, thin, fragile. "Why is he in handcuffs?"

"It's a long story," the senator said. "He can allegedly turn into an animal over time. Bastion Enterprises in California was utilizing him—"

"They kidnapped me—"

"—from prison," the senator finished sharply. "Regardless, we have contacts there. He can go back."

Austin reached out, fingertips brushing River's warm, feverish skin as she gently turned his arm to examine it. She noted the track marks, bruises, and yellowing skin.

"You don't want to go back," she murmured. It wasn't a question.

He shook his head.

"Skinwalker, right? Navajo?"

"No. And yes. Naaldlooshii."

"How old are you?"

"Eighteen. I just turned eighteen. At least that is how old my family said I was—"

"You don't murder people or hurt them?"

"No." A whisper. "What I am—I had no choice."

"We're holed up in a motel off the highway. The pool's green, beds squeak if you breathe. River... you're free to come or go. No chains. If you stick with us, I'll protect you. It's not fancy—I'm just the one dumb enough to keep everyone moving."

"Yes. I want to go with you."

Austin's gut clenched again. He was the kind of deal you regretted the instant you made it. Sometimes you had to take the deal anyway. "I need money," she said.

The senator's wife slid her purse across the table, hands trembling. "There's a hundred and fifty thousand dollars in there. Cash. That's one-third. You get her out, you'll get the other two-thirds."

Chapter −31

"Alright, everybody, this is River."

It was early lunchtime when Austin finally got back to the Cherry Grove Hotel. The lobby's old carpet reeked faintly of mildew and lemon cleaner. A tired ceiling fan rattled overhead. She led River through the faded corridor. Outside, the sun turned the pavement into a white glare. Stepping into the courtyard felt like plunging into half-shade. The air was heavy with chlorine and cut grass. Rickety tables, sun-bleached chairs, and the electric hum of cicadas filled the space.

As soon as Austin spoke, the shift in the courtyard was immediate—like a flock sensing a predator. Conversations dulled. Shoulders tightened. Even the cicadas seemed to hush.

"He's the new kid on the playground, so play nice," Austin said, her tone lighter than she felt. "He's going to be with us for a while, like the rest of you. I'm going to go get him a room. Aina, can you make him a sandwich?"

She plunked her battered brown purse onto Stats's lap. Inside were three thick brown envelopes—Jenna Madison's file and the police/FBI printouts. Her hand trembled once as she slid them to him—just once—before she locked it down. "We'll talk later," she murmured.

Brandon and Tessa sat off to the side. Tessa's hair stuck to Brandon's arm as she rested against him, already folded into the group's rhythm. "Surely somebody's got a trick up their sleeve to get handcuffs off?" Austin prompted. She tugged the skull bandana around River's wrists—the only thing hiding the cuffs. "Nobody seems to know where the key is."

River's eyes darted across the courtyard. He kept his back to the wall, mapping exits rather than people. Aina's sandwich hung frozen halfway to her mouth. Roo's nostrils flared—fast, sharp—cataloging River's scent, threat, and origin in one breath.

Starr watched with narrowed eyes.

"Well?" Austin muttered. "Are you all asleep? Because I'm the one who got up in the middle of the night and flew across the U.S. and back again before lunch. You probably slept in until ten." She jabbed a finger at Aina. "You. Ham sandwich for the man."

Aina rose, but River shook his head. "I'm not hungry. I'll go with you."

River trailed her to the front desk, clutching his borrowed backpack like a lifeline. The motel lobby was stuffy and over-bright, smelling of old coffee and faint cigarette smoke. Inside his room, thin curtains let in sickly yellow light. He perched there like the space might bite.

Back in Austin's room, Roo glared at him from the corner. The shower hissed. Stats and Brandon worked a bobby pin into the cuffs until disengaging the internal locking bar, popping it open. Tessa watched, eyes wide. Austin paced with her on her hip, sweat sticking her shirt to her back. When Austin left to clean rooms, River lingered in the doorway, flinching whenever Roo edged closer. Bleach and cleaning chemicals filled the hall as the vacuum droned. Aina watched from the second-floor balcony, arms tight across her chest—not curious, but calculating. She didn't trust River. Not yet.

"Hey, I've got to get back and feed the cattle, then go to work," Brandon said, catching her on the first floor as she lugged a bucket of cleaning supplies. The hallway was muggy, the walls water-stained, a bulb flickering overhead. He sneezed—hard—and waved at the air like he could push the allergic tickle away.

"Missus Smythe has a cat," Austin guessed.

"Yeah." He wiped his eyes. "Sorry, I didn't get more time with Tessa. But I can bring her back later. You want Austin to read to you again?"

"Yes," Tessa whispered.

"Can you give her a kiss before we go?"

Austin leaned down; Tessa pressed a warm, soft kiss to her cheek.

"Brandon, you don't have to drive an hour—"

"I know I don't have to. I want to."

"Thank you. For what you're doing."

He shrugged, looking down. The door clicked shut behind them—soft as a sigh. And that was all it took.

"Oh, God." Her knees nearly buckled. Tears rushed hot and helplessly to her eyes. She pressed her fist to her mouth to choke the sob. The room was too quiet: the buzz of the old fridge, the distant slam of a door somewhere down the hall.

"Is that little girl yours?" River asked.

"Yes."

"Why does she call you Austin?"

"She doesn't know I'm her mama yet." Austin wiped her face with her sleeve.

"Why aren't you married to him?"

"Because he has a girlfriend."

"Why do you work while they all sit around? I thought you were in charge."

The question hit harder than expected.

"Wow, you have a million questions." Austin stepped into the sun-blasted walkway. "My job is to protect them. That's what I do. However, I have to. We were out of money and had nowhere to go, so I worked. I make sure we have shelter and food. There is more to the story. But for now, that's what matters."

"But who watches over *you*?" River asked quietly. "What if the people who had me—what if they come?" He looked terrified. Truly terrified. "I just want to sleep," he whispered. "Without getting jerked awake every two hours. I'm freaking out. I'm afraid they're going to come for me."

"I'll protect you."

He gave a soft laugh. "I'm sorry. You're about an inch tall. My five-year-old sister is bigger than you."

"How about if I get Golem to sit in the chair and watch TV outside your door tonight?"

"That big man? Where will you be?"

"In the next room. And if you get scared, you can sleep on my floor next to Roo."

"Roo?"

"Behind you."

River turned—and nearly stumbled. Roo stood inches behind him, silent as a shadow.

"Geez!"

Austin touched River's arm before Roo could react. Roo's eyes snapped away.

"It's normal to be jumpy," Austin said. "We've all been there. Every single one of us."

"You?"

"Yes." She held his gaze. "You're safe."

For the first time, River's shoulders eased.

"I believe you," he whispered. "I don't know why—but I do."

Chapter −32

"He has to kill someone in his immediate family to become a Skinwalker, you get that, Pet?"

Aina was in rare form—amped, jittery, meaner than she meant to be. Her words tumbled out sharp as she slapped Stats' monitor, the computer's electric hum thick in the room. Her palm left smudges on the glass. Stats winced every time she thumped the screen.

"Please stop," he murmured, fingers tapping nervously at the sticky keys.

"Look—right here," Aina pressed, stabbing at a grainy PDF scan. "River stabbed his grandfather. Up on a mountain. With a steak knife. The cops wrote he was 'believed to be a Skinwalker.' Witch. Monster. Bad news."

Austin leaned closer, squinting past the smudged text. Half the paragraph was cut off; the rest looked like a fax someone spilled coffee on ten years ago. "Aina... this isn't evidence. It's gossip. The charges were dropped two days later." Austin scrolled. "That's from a tabloid. A word in a story doesn't make it true."

Aina threw her hands up. "Pet would think a rabid dog was as timid as a kitten."

"Until it ate her," Hutch muttered.

"Exactly." Aina crossed her arms. "I say he goes."

Austin flicked the page away. "That word?" she said sharply. "It doesn't mean what they think it means. And it isn't our word to throw around." The room went quiet. Heat pressed in from the open door; cicadas buzzed like a live wire.

"Why did you pick him up?" Hutch grumbled. "We barely have money."

"He needed us," Austin shot back. "He's been through the same hell."

"I didn't kill my grandpa," Starr yawned behind her hand. "Just saying."

Aina snorted. "Skinwalkers are creepy."

"Aina." Austin's warning slid low, her eyes darkening.

"I'm just reading what the page says," Aina snapped. "Skinwalker equals murderer."

Austin's jaw tightened; her breath came slow and controlled. "Stop calling him a Skinwalker, like you know what that means," she snapped. "It equals outsiders mislabeling something they don't understand. That's all it equals, *Miss Fairy*."

Aina's smirk faltered.

Starr glanced nervously between them. Roo stayed quiet in the corner, his shoulders rising and falling with slow, deliberate breaths.

"Alright, I've had it." Austin stood so fast her chair skidded. "Listen to yourselves. Judge him after you know him. Not before."

"And that's why we're living in a dump," Starr muttered.

Stats let out a short laugh. Austin snapped her head toward him; he ducked his gaze instantly.

"I'm still hiding the knives," Aina added. Golem stayed silent, refusing to back her.

Austin exhaled hard. "Stats, we have a few minutes before Brandon—"

"If he comes," Hutch interrupted without looking up. "You piss people off. They don't come back."

"You're still here," Roo rumbled softly. "She pisses you off. Brandon will come."

Everyone laughed. Austin groaned. "Listen. If we get Jenna Madison out, we get paid. That's our priority."

"Money so you can buy more clothes?" Hutch muttered.

"Emergency mode," Austin snapped. "Paolo isn't funding us. I'm working two jobs to keep us fed and sheltered. Don't help? Say goodbye to your phone."

"Dad pays for it." Hutch shrugged. "Why don't you have him fly in and give you a little love? He'll leave a nice tip."

"I think he just called you a whore," Aina laughed.

Austin's lip twitched. A tremor ran through her jaw. She stared skyward, blinking against the glare. Rage flickered sharp and hot. Starr saw it immediately. Golem leaned in and tapped her chin gently. "Pet. Your lip is bleeding."

"She's gonna flip out," Hutch whispered.

Austin's hand shot out. She pinched his shoulder with two fingers—hard enough to make him squeak.

"I suggest you go to your room, Frederico, before I make you a hummingbird."

"Can she do that?" Roo whispered.

"When Aztec warriors die, they turn into hummingbirds," Starr whispered, inching forward. "Pet—let him go. Just breathe."

Austin forced a slow exhale and released Hutch. "It is not a joke to call someone a whore," she said, voice shaking with restraint.

"O-okay." Hutch rubbed his shoulder. "I'll go study."

"Do that. No TV." He slunk down the hall. Austin turned to Aina.

"And you? If you can't respect me the two times a week I ask for help, then go to your room too, like a four-year-old."

"I'm not your kid," Aina snapped. "Hutch was being a jerk. My fault. I didn't light anything."

"Aina—stop talking."

"I'm just saying—"

The table flipped with a hollow crash. Paper plates skittered. Sandwiches tumbled. Mustard splattered across Austin's ankles. The sharp vinegar tang hit the air. Everyone froze.

"You know what?" Austin exploded. "Screw all of you! Figure it out yourselves. I give respect. I deserve it too."

~

Twenty minutes later, Brandon knocked on River's door. Austin was hunkered in with him watching TV.

"Rumor at the pool says Austin—" He raised his voice in a high-pitched Aina imitation—"—just lost it tonight."

"Oh, it's you." Austin groaned. "You sounded just like her."

River lay on the bed, nerves twitching beneath the motel's stale chill. Golem sat silently on the other bed. Roo stretched out on the floor, nose twitching at the musty carpet.

Tessa reached for Austin instantly. Brandon placed her in Austin's lap.

"Hey, Golem," Brandon said. "Find a swimsuit yet?"

"Austin's having one made."

Austin half-listened, eyes locked on Tessa's solemn face. The bleach tang from the sheets mixed with the AC's droning hum.

Tessa climbed higher and wrapped her arms around Austin's neck. Austin didn't move. Neither did Tessa.

Ten minutes later, Brandon chuckled. "She wouldn't nap—kept worrying I'd leave her if she fell asleep. Rolling eyes, jerking awake. But now—she's out."

Austin brushed Tessa's hair. "Feels like I wasted our time."

"No," Brandon said. "She feels safe with you. Better than any book I read her."

"Is that why you almost failed Harper's English class?"

"And why you didn't stick around," he teased.

River mumbled, "You knew him well enough to make a baby."

Austin glared. River flinched.

"Great," she muttered, smiling slightly. "Another comedian."

River sat straighter. "I'm following you like a baby calf. I'm the one with attachment issues. You—" He swallowed, words slipping uncontrolled. "You've got... daddy stuff. Something he took from you. Something he won't give back. You left to get it, didn't you?"

Silence.

River paled. "I—I was just guessing."

Austin snorted. "Great. An eighteen-year-old who thinks he's both funny *and* qualified to psychoanalyze me."

"I got ten bucks," Brandon said, handing River a bill. "Explain why she gets spicy over nothing."

Roo and River laughed.

"Don't give him money!" Austin barked. "He'll start charging me. I'll be broke."

"See?" Brandon nudged her foot. "Spicy."

Austin didn't move it away. She tucked Tessa under her chin and reached to switch off the lamp.

"Go to sleep, River," she murmured. "You're safe now. We'll watch over you."

River hesitated.

Then—quietly: "People call it 'Skinwalker.' That's not what it is. That's just the word outsiders use when they don't understand."

Austin cracked one eye open. "Then what are you?"

River swallowed. "Just... tired."

Austin nodded.

"That," she whispered, "we can work with."

Chapter −33

"I've been inside the Canaan Mountain commune."

Roo had said the words, then immediately shrank back, glancing at Austin like he'd been caught peeing on the floor. Two days later, Austin was grumpier than ever—stretched thin, running on fumes, poring over satellite maps late at night, neck stiff and eyes gritty. The blue glow burned her skin as she searched for angles she hadn't checked, snapping at Stats to figure out what her exhausted brain couldn't. Her head lifted slowly.

"What did you say?" She turned fully toward Roo, one hand still planted on the map spread across the sticky hotel table. Stats hovered with a pen, waiting for her next mark.

"I've been in the commune...a couple of times." Roo drew in a breath through his nose. "Maybe every night when I go for a walk. Maybe." His voice dropped lower. "There are lots of dogs. I played with them. Sniffed around overflowing trash cans, nosed through the candy wrappers, peered at the houses—watching the flicker of TVs behind curtains. I chased a cat. Caught it. Let it go up a tree. I peed on every corner until I had none left." He swallowed hard.

Austin's shoulders sagged, disappointment tightening her eyes. Roo felt guilt press down heavily on his ribs. He hung his head, throat tight, trying not to cry. Her anger was palpable—he hated it, hated disappointing her.

"What have I told you time and time again, Roo, about listening to what I say?"

"To... listen to what you say."

"And I said: don't go near the commune."

"I'm sorry. I went near the commune." He edged toward her, trying to lean against her side, pressing his head into her hip. She gave him a gentle push away. The rejection stung like a slap. His eyes burned.

"No. You went *into* the commune," she corrected, voice sharper. "Don't do that, Roo. You could've gotten shot. This isn't a game."

She tapped three red-marked spots on the map. "These? All trail-camera clusters. Anything that moves triggers them—people, deer, dogs, shadows. They record everything."

"Okay." His voice cracked. She angled his face toward hers with two fingers. He looked away instinctively—submissive pack behavior he couldn't control. "Don't." Then she turned to the others. "Stats dug up something else. Abel Martin's been driving out to certain areas outside the compound. Every place he visits? Something bad happened there. Murders. Disappearances."

"It was my theory," Stats said quickly. "That he's collecting negative energy. Using it."

"Can he do that?" Hutch asked. "Like catch a ghost in a bottle?"

"We don't know," Austin said, rubbing her forehead. "We're guessing. But the point is: it's dangerous to go anywhere near that place."

"We are an hour away," Roo whined.

"Roo, go lie down on the bed. Seriously. You're getting on my nerves tonight."

He sulked to the far corner stiffly. After a minute of trembling frustration, he stomped out the door and let it slam behind him.

Outside, cool air tinged with cigarette smoke hit him. He paced the balcony, nails clicking, peering over the railing at headlights flickering in the dusk. He spat over the edge, glancing back at the door—hoping she'd call him back. She didn't.

Finally, he slunk in again, huffing, and dropped heavily into the chair beside Austin. His hair prickled with leftover irritation. Hutch scooped cereal loudly, the crunch echoing across the cramped room.

"This complex is huge, Stats," Austin said, pointing at the map. "More houses than a Charleston subdivision. Ten separate trailer clusters. A damn water tower. And this satellite image is from last fall. Leaves are still brown. Everything could be different now. There's no way to walk in blind and find this girl. I'm watching fifty grand evaporate."

"Do you want me to stop eating these chips?" Golem asked gently. "I can save them in case we're out of money."

"No, Golem. We're good. I'm just being—"

"Whiny," Aina cut in. She leaned over the map, reeking of chocolate. Roo's nose twitched. She tore another piece off her candy bar.

"I want a bite," he whispered. Aina flicked a chunk toward him. Roo caught it mid-air, jaws snapping shut with satisfaction. He sank lower in his seat. If no one saw his trick, maybe he needed a bigger one. "I've been in the commune," he repeated.

"And I'm still mad at you for that," Austin warned, not looking up. "Don't push your luck tonight."

"No, Pet. I know where things are."

That finally got her attention. Austin's gaze lifted slowly— measured, wary. Roo grinned, relieved.

"I know who lives where. It's a pack. Abel's the alpha—big house. The closer your house is to his, the more he likes you. If you're in a trailer, you're a worker. Some get dropped at highway exits with cardboard signs for food and diapers—I've seen them. Some work at the lumber yard. He's got a mine too."

Hutch's spoon clattered. "So, dude—were you gonna sit on that for two days and wait for someone to toss you a bone?"

Roo didn't answer. He looked at Austin instead. Austin's eyes softened—not with forgiveness, but with calculation.

"I swear, Roo," she murmured, fingers tapping a quick rhythm on the table, "if you can tell me who lives where? I'll drive into town and buy you a big steak bone."

Roo's eyes widened. Yes. Yes, yes, yes. Steak bone time.

But as he licked his lips, something in the night air shifted. One ear cocked toward the window. A faint crunch of gravel in the parking lot. A scent he didn't recognize—cold and not right.

Roo stiffened. Whatever was out there did not smell like a stranger or a neighbor or a dog. It smelled like trouble.

And tonight, he wasn't sure he'd be fast enough if it came.

Chapter −34

A single rose lay on the gritty asphalt when Austin pulled into the hotel parking lot. The dashboard clock glowed 9:15 p.m.—the summer storm had just cleared, and the air was thick and muggy. She rolled down the window, letting the scent of cut grass and the dampness of the night drift in, swatting at a cloud of persistent bugs. Headlights caught the red bloom. Austin eased the truck to a stop, got out, and crouched to pick it up. The rose's stem was cold in her hand—out of place. Exhaustion pressed in, arms heavy, legs trembling, the world tilting. She straightened, blinking. *Trap*, her mind whispered. She was already too late to run.

"Cute, smart, naive."

A shadow merged with her own. Footsteps scraped across the rain-buckled asphalt. The man's voice slid in behind her—gruff, soft, almost greasy—words curling around her like smoke. She shivered, bile rising as she forced the image away.

The arrogance in his tone made Austin stiffen. She turned, slow as mud, fatigue dragging at every joint. The rose felt suddenly leaden in her palm. A whiff of something rotten drifted up—she fought a gag. Abel Martin stood close, the threat in his bulk and posture unmistakable.

She'd never met him, but she didn't have to. Even an hour away, people lowered their voices when his name came up. Rumors about the commune's strange practices spread quickly—children kept out of sight, homeschooled and half-wild, piling off a bus after dark to raid donation bins like scavengers.

Adults drifted along highways with cardboard signs, picking through thrift-store dumpsters and trying to resell whatever others had thrown away. All of it shrouded his reputation in secrecy and unease.

He was thickset, gray-haired, his belly pushing against his shirt, his small eyes shifting over her with predatory interest. Every breath from him left a residue on her skin—a crawling, oily dread.

"She's everything a shabby, small-town, horny boy craves," Abel Martin continued, glancing toward the truck parked a few feet away. Two big boys climbed out and leaned against it, chuckling—Bradley Martin and his younger brother, Blue. "Easy pickings. She's a generic watered-down can of beer dumped out of a car window onto the road. The cheap kind. Not the name brand. The kind you can take and nobody knows is missing. Or cares."

Austin's stomach dropped. Another young man emerged from the truck. Billy Tate—she recognized him from Uncle Bill's Last Stop Bar, the one who'd pulled a gun.

"She's the discounted, bargain-basement crap any old man who is a drunk might find off the side of the road half-drank," Abel said, rolling his tongue along his upper lip. "It's there. He'll grab it, drink it up. It's not the tastiest. Doesn't give much of a buzz. It's already been opened and drunk by a few people. But it's there for the taking. He takes it. Quenches his thirst when there's nothing else better around. And then that cheap beer comes back to haunt him. Leaves a big ol' hole in his kidney from drinking so much—and the man's stuck with that big ol' hole—"

"What do you want?" Austin cut him off. She was so tired she could have crumpled to the pavement and slept there. She felt ten years old again, sitting in the principal's office with a row of adults glaring down at her, waiting to list every failure and infraction. Powerless.

Abel lifted a brow, satisfied.

"My daughter planned on marrying that boy I was talking about. The one you whored up with a few years ago, then abandoned that retarded little girl on his front step." His lips stretched in a smug half-smile. "Lyndsey was worried about him. She said she'd come back to the farm at night—like she usually does—and he wasn't there. We followed him. Guess where we ended up?" He swept a hand toward the hotel. "Well, so this is where you set up shop? The next little whorehouse?"

Austin instinctively stepped back when Billy Tate edged around the rear of her truck.

"You might remember Billy from the bar?" Abel said casually. He reached into his shirt pocket and pulled out a cell phone. "Take a looky-look."

Austin stared at the screen—her fight with Billy at the bar, recorded by someone's cell phone, replaying in sharp, humiliating detail. Slow motion of her flipping him onto the table. God only knew how many times it had been shared.

"My boy over there's real sad about that," Abel muttered. "Got a million hits. He wants a little payback."

Billy grinned. He pulled a knife from his pocket, flicking it open with a showman's flair, then leaned down and jabbed it into the rear tire of Austin's truck. When it didn't penetrate, he kicked it—hard. Air hissed out in a slow, dying wheeze until the tire slumped flat against the pavement. Billy strutted up beside her, reached out, and shoved her.

She knew it was coming—could see it telegraphed in his shoulders—but her body was sluggish and unresponsive. She staggered, hit the truck, and dropped to her haunches. Limbs felt like jelly, heart hammering in her throat. Billy's soft smile twisted into something darker. She looked at Abel—and saw the same void. Both men fed on her fear as if it were oxygen.

"What do you want?" she asked again, breath thin.

"Pack up and leave. Stay away from that boy—or you're not the only one who'll get hurt. Use your imagination."

He scanned the lot. A single trucker sat in his cab far across the gravel, not paying attention. Abel stepped closer and extended a hand. Reflex—more than sense—made her take it. His skin was clammy, slick. The touch burned up her wrist like acid. Abel looked again toward the trucker.

Then, as quickly as a burst of cold wind, he slapped her. Hard. Austin spun, slamming into the side of the truck. Her stomach lurched; bile surged, and she retched, pavement spattered. "Bitch gonna beat me up now?" Billy laughed. "I don't think so." He lifted his phone, angling for a picture. "Here's one for me to remember you by."

His boot drove into her ribs. Pain exploded through her chest. She gasped—and vomited again.

The world blurred. Edges grayed.

Abel's arms hooked under hers, jerking her upright.

Austin blinked, her vision swimming, breath ragged.

"We know everything about you," Abel whispered, lips puckering in a self-satisfied grin. "Thanks to that Tremaine boy—talk, talk, talking. My Lyndsey's clever. She pulls secrets out of anyone. Even you."

A car trunk popped open.

Rough hands seized her arms. Her feet left the ground. The world tilted. She was shoved into the trunk like a sack of grain. The lid slammed.

Darkness swallowed her. Laughter muffled against metal. The thick smell of engine oil and fear pressed in. Austin clapped her hands over her ears and screamed, the sound swallowed instantly by the dark.

Chapter –35

"How can you protect me if you can't even fight off an old man?"

Austin was still in the bathroom, toweling off after her shower. Steam clouded the mirror. The air was thick with cheap soap and fear. The fluorescent light flickered, casting sickly shadows; the linoleum was cold and sticky beneath her bare feet.

She braced herself on the counter and groaned. Dammit, how did it even make sense that she was standing, let alone breathing? She examined her broken fingernails—splintered to the quick from clawing her way out of the trunk and crawling through the back seat to escape. The car they shoved her in wasn't just old—it was a field corpse. Martin must have towed the junker out of his pasture and shoved the keys at his son, who somehow managed to drive it here.

Her skin stung where she'd scraped it against the metal. *Still here, still me.* The taste of panic lingered on her tongue. A faint chemical tang from the motel cleaning spray burned her nose. *Can I ever wash this off?* Memories swelled. She had screamed herself hoarse—her voice reduced to a rasp, her breath caught in ragged gasps. Now, Starr had sat on the edge of the bed, keeping watch for an hour after the escape. Austin sat hunched and shivering, trying to hold herself together. *Can't fall apart. Not yet.*

She was still sweating bullets. The tonic from Aina and Starr did nothing to slow her heart. Why isn't it working? Her stomach churned. Her ears rang with the distant, muffled arguments from the next room. She pressed her palms to the towel—rough against her skin. *Breathe. Just breathe.*

Behind the closed door, panic clawed at her ribs. She needed a minute. She pictured River leaning his forehead against the door, Roo whining at the frame. Golem paced—each step vibrating through the thin linoleum, like distant thunder promising a storm.

"Can you guys just go someplace else for a few while I sort things out, huh?" Austin tried to sound upbeat and forced a smile toward the door, even though her voice wavered.

She quickly slipped into a pair of blue jean shorts and a tank top—her hands shaky, movements a little clumsy. Maybe putting on something casual could shift her from panic mode to a carefree state. "Go pack your bags or something," she called out, staring at her reflection for a moment before turning away.

"We're leaving?"

Oh, great. That was Hutch. He was in her room too. Austin dropped her chin and shook her head.

As she opened the door, her vision narrowed—too many bodies crowded the room, and too many eyes landed on her at once. The sudden press of people made her instincts scream to slam the door shut again, her hand jerking halfway before she caught herself.

"Yeah, we're leaving." Her eyes flicked around the room. Her heart pounded as she read the tension in every face. A faint, sour whiff of sweat and fear hung in the air. She avoided Starr's eye roll. She saw Aina's trembling lips, the way Golem's fists clenched and unclenched. Roo's old tennis shoes clicked anxiously on the linoleum. "What else can I do but run?" Her worst enemy right now was Abel Martin. He knew her weaknesses better than anyone.

"We're all going to die."

Every head turned to River. He trembled, pale, tight with panic. Austin pinched her temples. "We're not dying," she said, glancing at Starr. "Can you give him something for that?"

"You want a potion for common sense?"

"Common sense," Austin shook her head, hand out. "If that's what you call the anxiety you all had after adjustment, then yes."

"That was when we had Paolo protecting us."

"I protected Paolo."

Silence. Somebody was going to say it. And it was Aina who did. "And where is Paolo? Dead."

"Then we're all going to die."

"We are not going to die, River." Austin held up a grocery sack. "We're moving somewhere safer. Abel Martin threatened Tessa—if we stay, that's the risk."

"He almost killed you. The odds are certainly in our favor for dying," Stats noted. He was hunched at the table, poking the monitor of his battered laptop. The blue glow cast shadows under his eyes, making him look older, worn down.

"He didn't *almost* kill me—he threw me in a damn car trunk."

It wasn't his usual temperament. Considering the crap going on, Austin figured, what the hell. Everybody's going a little nuts.

"Shut up, Stats," Hutch said. "If you'd watched the GPS instead of porn, we'd have known that crazy dude was coming."

"It wasn't porn. Just naked women. All of them are over eighteen."

"If you don't get that girl from the commune, the senator sends people for me—we'll have two sides after us." River sat hard on the bed, pale.

"I didn't want this, River. Abel Martin was never my choice. I was ready to run." Austin moved to River and put a steady hand on his shoulder. "You're alive because I took this on. I could've walked away. I didn't. So, give me a break. Don't freak out. We move, Abel thinks we're running, and we gain time."

"We should just dump River and run," Aina said, stepping in front of Hutch, who glanced at Austin.

"I agree," Starr said, her voice frenzied as she patted her hands on her knees. "If everyone agrees, we dump him and go free."

"Dump him," Golem muttered. Austin looked from Aina to Starr, then caught Hutch's eyes. She finally noticed Golem halt, press his palms hard to his temples, and groan. He looked up with frightened, confused eyes—then shook his head, as if startled by his own words.

"Okay, something's off in here," Austin said, her voice quick and flat, the words vibrating with urgency. "None of us is right. We haven't been for days." She felt it—a prickling in her skin, a low ring in her ear, the air itself buzzing with something unnatural. "There's something in these rooms. We need to look for a spell bottle, a little bag, anything out of place. If it feels weird, bring it here."

It started slowly.

Nobody believed her—she could feel their eye rolls—but they still shuffled into rooms to look. Yet everything in their movements was off: jerky, irritable, twitchy, as if something was nudging their muscles. Aina pinched Starr—sharp, mean. Starr snarled and hurled a pillow at Roo. Roo's teeth flashed—he snapped at Austin's shoulder, not hard enough to break skin but enough to sting. Austin's foot kicked the bed frame—once, twice—before she even realized she was doing it. It wasn't funny. It felt peculiar. Like they were puppets tugged by invisible strings.

"There's something on that chair," Aina said.

Golem was holding it upside down, staring blankly. Sure enough, there was a small glass vial duct-taped beneath the pad. Aina dug it out and held it aloft. "Yeah, it's a potion. We have to break the bottle to release the curse."

"Hey! We got something in here!" Hutch yelled, running in with another bottle. Austin rubbed her eyes, half-laughing, half-exhausted, her nerves buzzing and skin clammy. The lingering throbbing in her hands reminded her how tightly she'd clenched her fists. Hard to believe she hadn't believed in magic four years ago.

"Keep looking. There's more somewhere," she called out, watching as the others methodically searched every corner.

~

"Frigging Wild American Garlic?" Austin muttered. "I eat garlic bread all the time. I had no clue it wasn't good for all powers. The movies just use it for vampires." She sat on the cool concrete curb in a fenced section of the parking lot behind the dumpster, elbows on knees. Aina was holding a hammer she'd gotten from the hotel office. She'd broken the glass vials—all eight of them—in a row. She looked up at Austin, a dribble of sweat slipping down her forehead.

"The idea of vampires came from the Celts. It comes from Dearg Due, a girly-girl vampire that attacks men." Aina leaned down, poked at something green. "My auntie used to tell me stories of her." She looked back down at the vials. "There's bergamot and barbary, hence the bad vibes going on. Ah—and the fighting. Lobelia. It makes people angry, and they take things out on each other.

I feel better already, like I tore off a wet wool blanket thrown on me on a hot night, right?"

Austin inhaled deeply—the air truly felt different. Lighter. Less thick. Like someone had opened an invisible window. "Yeah," she said softly. "Me too."

"The question is, who put them there?" Aina asked. She reached out and pressed a warm hand on Austin's knee. "The fighting was before River got here. I think it was getting bad at the farm, even. Nobody's left here but you. And you wouldn't do it. The place always has somebody in the rooms."

Austin nodded slowly, sadness pressing behind her ribs. "Brandon," she muttered. She rubbed her face, staring down at the filthy asphalt. Aina moved closer, wrapping an arm gently around Austin's shoulders.

"Maybe it isn't Brandon," Aina said softly. "Maybe somebody snuck into the rooms while we were asleep or—"

"No," Austin whispered. Her stomach dropped. The words tasted like poison. She hated saying them out loud. "Everybody knows the truth. I've just got to face it. He was the only one with access to the rooms, and no one would suspect him. Aina... he was long gone before we even got to Danville Station. Abel Martin has gobbled up the town, eaten up the area for miles. I just didn't want to believe it. Didn't think it was such a bad thing. It is the reason whatever is in that little bag my papaw gave me is calling for me." She had been warned by the letters that she still had not shown the others.

"You grew up with the commune there. It was just a part of your life. Who would have thought the dude would gain so much power?"

"I just wanted to see my kid." And she wanted to see Brandon. But she would only admit that to herself. "Tell Stats to search for a cheap motel outside a fifty-mile radius, can you do that?"

Aina nodded.

"And we need some sort of hoodoo to stop this if it happens again," Austin went on. "Maybe some signs that we can ward off evil so they can't find us. I should have been prepared."

"I can make us all some little bags with betony and hawthorn and a few herbs that will heighten our abilities. I've got a few magic things up my sleeve." Aina smiled. She liked doing those things. "I'll toss some rose petals in for you so you can find a new love."

"Last time you did that, I ended up confessing to things I never wanted to say out loud," Austin laughed. "Besides, there are already too many men orbiting me." She nodded toward the dumpster, where Roo peeked around with a bashful grin. Aina snorted. River was watching too, a pale face behind the curtain. "I'm like a magnet for trouble—and men, apparently. But—" She stood. "We're going to need your best work for payback. Abel doesn't get the last word."

"Oh, Austin's ready to fight?" Aina tipped her head. "I thought you just protected."

"Well, that's what Paolo had me do. Now—truth? I've always been a little bit of a wildcard. That's what pissed my daddy off about me. He tried to stifle it, tried to make me predictable. That's what makes this fun. Everybody thinks Austin is going to head out of town, a beaten puppy with her tail between her legs—just like last time. But I'm thinking I might be one of those little miniature Doberman pinschers. The ones that are about eight inches tall and bite the shit out of ankles. Tell everybody to pack. We're leaving in a few hours. I'm going to put in my notice at Crazy Jack's. Jack isn't going to like it. He's already a bit saucy because his dog ran off. But I'm going to see if he'll take me to the other truck—the one I used to follow Abel Martin in. It's still parked at the lot in town."

She glanced once more at the group, fatigue and adrenaline warring in her veins, but resolve hardening in her chest. The motel room felt too small for all of them, for all their secrets and fears. Outside, a siren wailed in the distance, reminding her that the world was far from safe. "Let's move," she said, voice low but certain.

As the door slammed shut behind them, Austin caught the faintest scent of cigarette smoke—someone had been standing just outside. Watching. Waiting.

She didn't know what waited for them at the next stop, but this time, she wasn't running—she was hunting.

Chapter −36

Brandon drove to Cherry Grove and pulled into the hotel parking lot. The place was nearly deserted, just a couple of compact cars squatting in front of the rooms. The pool was abandoned, the water a dull blue under the overcast sky. Austin's truck was gone. He sat gripping the wheel, sweat slick on his palms, the tacky leather pressing lines into his skin. His heart thudded with a hollow ache as he stared at the room she'd been staying in. The curtains hung open, nothing moved behind them—just stale sunlight and emptiness that settled over him like a damp blanket.

"She's gone, baby, I'm sorry."

He'd known she'd be gone eventually. Still, it gutted him to glance at the back seat and see Tessa craning her neck, her little arms pressing hard into the child safety seat, white-knuckled fingers digging into the faded upholstery as she tried to peer over the headrest and out the windshield. Then she twisted, nose smudging the glass, squinting through the window by the door, searching for any sign of Austin. She'd hugged that book all the way, the cardboard cover growing damp with sweat, singing some made-up song with Austin's name woven through every line—every hopeful note now dying in her throat. She seemed like a wide-eyed bird, searching for a worm that would never come.

"She said she'd read me a book, Daddy."

"Well, Austin is like a leaf caught in the wind, baby. She's wild and free. She'll blow back in again sometime. We just have to wait."

"It's all your fault, Daddy. I hate you!"

"Tessa—hey, that's not a nice thing to say." Brandon froze. He'd never heard those words from her before. It hit him like a slap.

But even as he said it, his voice felt thin. Something sharp twisted under his ribs. He'd betrayed the woman his daughter adored. Her mommy. The ache of it gnawed. Brandon let out a long, shaky breath, trying to steady himself. His fingers trembled against the steering wheel, leaving faint crescents in his palms.

In the rearview, Tessa's oversized glasses swallowed half her face. It was done. He'd followed Abel Martin's orders to the letter—taping those little vials beneath all the beds and behind dressers—even as he doubted the spell's purpose. Moving through the rooms had been easy at first; his farm-boy charm got him anywhere. But weaving Tessa into Austin's life, finding excuses to linger, took nearly a week and wore on him. Each night, Brandon lay awake, chest tight, guilt crawling beneath his skin.

Abel insisted the spell would drive out evil, and Brandon had complied, wanting to protect his family and perhaps prove Abel wrong. Brandon had laughed it off—evil? Austin was just a mess, not a monster. If she weren't evil, she'd stay. She left.

Brandon had seen enough strangeness lately not to dismiss Abel's warnings. Austin, using magic to send Starr up the ceiling, had rattled him. Abel claimed only witches or worse could do that, fueled by evil. Brandon found nothing online to contradict it—who else could walk someone up a wall? Only Austin.

Still, even that memory didn't sit right. It flickered behind his eyes like a faulty bulb—fear and awe tangled together. Something in him hesitated, doubted. And he hated that doubt.

Lyndsey made it all clear. She was cute, sensible, the kind of girl you could marry—just like Abel always said Brandon deserved. But he knew Austin too well. She always found ways to justify leaving Tessa, always claiming she had no other option, and he resented her for not taking responsibility. There were a thousand other options. Lyndsey was right: no decent person would dump their baby on someone else. Austin was just a mess of bad choices and unresolved issues. Her own dad called her a troublemaker.

Brandon felt relief settle in his bones—he tried to convince himself he was glad she was gone, even though part of him still wanted her to stay. Brandon filled his lungs with muggy air, the humidity clinging to his skin. He'd left feeling drained, but now a restless energy buzzed through his veins, making his legs twitch and his jaw clench. The drive had sharpened his senses, yet the dull ache for Austin twisted in his gut, a gnawing hunger that wouldn't leave.

He pressed his palm hard to his thigh, trying to shove it away and focus forward.

"Well, we've got to get back. Papaw Martin has asked everybody to help him burn more of the junk they've cleaned up on the mountainside. Then he's having a big picnic at church. *And* he offered your daddy a job working the well house at Canaan Mountain." He smiled. Tessa didn't smile back. "How about I buy you an ice cream, and you can go visit Aunt Kim?"

"I don't want to go to Aunt Kim's. There are too many kids. They all cry. I think she steals them."

"Ha ha, you're funny. She doesn't steal them; their parents pay her to watch them. Aunt Kim likes it when you come. And the other kids, they just don't want to be left without their mamas and daddies." He smiled as big as he could. "Aunt Kim loves Tessa!" he told her in a sing-song voice.

"No, she doesn't." Tessa mimicked his tone. "She says I look like a bug. She pushes me. She pinches my arms, too."

For one heartbeat, Brandon's stomach dropped. A cold prickle ran up his arms. "You're funny, Tessa," Brandon said too quickly, backing out. "Don't be mad at Aunt Kim just because you're upset with Austin. She doesn't push and pinch you."

"Yes, she does, Daddy." Her little voice shook. Brandon didn't want to hear it.

"You're not my daddy. You don't look like my daddy anymore."

Brandon's jaw clenched. He imagined how Abel Martin would deal with a recalcitrant child—how swift, how merciless that discipline would be. "Little girl, you don't say things like that to your daddy."

Tessa stared at him, unblinking. "You're not my daddy!" She kicked the seat hard, her legs thrashing and pushing.

He felt something cold slide through his chest. "Did Austin tell you to say that?"

Tessa shook her head. "No. You got mean eyes."

He turned then. Looked at Tessa.

And something ugly rose in him—hot, sharp, wrong. *Little brat.* Lyndsey's voice slithered through his thoughts. *She's a lot like Austin.*

His hand lifted before he even knew he was doing it.

Tessa's eyes went wide. She flinched—tiny shoulders curling in as she sat restrained in the child safety seat, unable to move and waiting for a hit. Brandon froze. The sight gutted him. His hand dropped like it suddenly weighed a thousand pounds. What was he doing? What kind of man even *thought* like that?

He turned, catching his reflection in the rearview mirror.

The face looking back was wrong—contorted, teeth bared in a vicious grin, eyes lit with a fury he didn't recognize. A stranger wearing his skin. His eyes drifted past his own face in the mirror and landed on Tessa in the back seat. She wasn't crying. She wasn't scared. She was *staring him down.*

"You're not my daddy," she hissed, every word sharp as a blade. "I want my daddy back."

Chapter −37

"Hey, Bradley." Brandon usually avoided him, but Bradley cornered him as soon as he arrived at the church and nodded toward his truck. Today was the day of the big community bonfire, and Brandon had volunteered to help. He dropped Tessa off at Kim's place and tried—failed—to shut out the betrayal in his daughter's eyes. She had kicked and bucked the entire hour back to the compound, wild with fury. Maybe she was just too worn out to fight anymore. When Brandon carried her to Kim's porch, Tessa stiffened, refusing to take the woman's hand. She stepped inside on her own—small, furious, untrusting—just as a pack of children burst out the front door, swarming the porch. They barreled into her, knocking her down hard on her palms.

Brandon instinctively stepped forward.

But Tessa scrambled up, recoiled from his touch, and lurched into the house, disappearing into the shadows before he could say a word.

"I hate you." She'd spat the words like poison, and he'd felt them hit. He'd never heard such venom in his little girl's voice.

Now, in the parking lot, the memory clung to him like an angry, oozing scab he couldn't stop poking—red, weeping, begging to be picked at even though he knew it would bleed again.

"Let's ride." Bradley Martin waved a hand at him. "Dad wants me to show you one of the chores you'll be taking over soon."

Bradley stopped the truck at one of the farm fields, got out, and Brandon followed. Heat shimmered off the dirt. Flies buzzed lazily around sweat-slick necks. In the distance, men moved like slow machinery—heads down, backs bent.

"We'll have them over working your farm soon to help out too." Then Bradley flashed a crooked grin. He made pudgy fists and feigned hitting Brandon in the jaw as they walked. "You know what happens if you ever hurt my sister, right?"

"I don't know what?" Brandon cringed as the words left his lips.

He knew better. Bam! Bam! Bam! Bradley punched him hard three times on the shoulder.

"That's what," he laughed heartily.

Brandon rubbed his shoulder, biting back a wince. Bradley jerked his chin toward the edge of the field. "Come on—Dad wants you trained on something important." He jerked his thumb toward a squat shed half-hidden behind a stand of dying pines. "Water duty. It's important. You'll take it over eventually."

He led Brandon to a padlocked pump house, popped the latch, and swung the door open. Inside, a thick pipe ran down from the rafters into a murky tank. Another disappeared underground. A chemical scoop sat on a nail.

"Every day we add a scoop of this stuff," Bradley said, handing it to him. "Keeps the water safe. Purifies it." He gestured toward the hill above Turtle Creek. "Comes straight from that pool Dad built when he dammed the creek. Best source on the mountain," he bragged—like it was something to be proud of.

Brandon nodded like he understood, but the chemical smell stung the back of his throat. The tank water had a flat, metallic tang. Something about it made his head swim.

"Don't sweat it," Bradley said, clapping his shoulder. "I'll train you properly later. Today's just the introduction."

Brandon set the scoop down—but the sour taste of the air lingered long after they'd walked away from the pump house.

"Dell, you and your boys finish up here," Bradley barked at the field worker across the lawn. "Then head over and start the bonfire—get the church lot ready for the picnic. We need tables, chairs, and a good stack of cut wood. Dad wants the pile six feet high."

Brandon looked around. The moment anyone glanced his way, they dropped their eyes and turned back to work. About twenty men, all shapes and sizes, shuffled in ragged clothes, hands raw, dirt ground into their knuckles from a day in the Martin fields. A faint smell of hot metal and sweat hung in the air.

"We don't want shit work, you got me?" Bradley huffed. "When you're done, you can finish up on the field work."

Dell nodded, offering Brandon a tired but warm grin. Brandon waved back automatically.

"Dude, don't wave at the help like we're equals, you got it?" Bradley leaned over, fishing a pack of cigarettes from his pocket. "There's a pecking order here. If you act like everyone's the same, pretty soon these folks will want the good jobs—or think they're good enough to marry my sister instead of you. I protect the family's status for a reason."

Brandon looked at Bradley, shrugged it off. "Isn't Dell going to the picnic? I thought Lyndsey said everyone's going to be there."

"No, the trailer people and the workhands don't go. Just family. That's everyone who matters. You're family. That's a big deal."

He smiled like he was joking, but there was no joke in his eyes.

"Rule one on Canaan Mountain: you do what the church tells you, which is what Dad tells you. Rule two: you don't mix with the help—they're here to serve, not to sit beside us. And rule three..." Bradley lowered his voice, almost conspiratorial. "You bed as many girls as you can before Dad transfers you to another community. Keeps loyalty fresh," he said with a shrug, "And the girls obedient."

Brandon swallowed. The heat felt heavier suddenly—pressing on his shoulders like a hand. "I'm not planning on leaving. The farm's been in my family for a couple of hundred years." He rolled the window down. "I've got my dad's old property to run. Hell, I've got two hundred head of cattle, and I'm planning to use the funds I make off them to get the farm running like a real farm again."

"Oh, okay." Bradley chuckled, rolled his eyes. "You'd better talk to dad about that then, because I think he's got a whole different direction he's got you traveling, buddy. He didn't talk to you?"

"About—?"

Bradley's tone softened, too casual. Too rehearsed. "He and your dad were talking about signing the farm over to the community, melding them together."

Brandon's stomach went hollow.

"They are going to put up a big plaque on the farm about the donation, kind of like they do at the big parks. Dad's a non-profit, private religious organization, you know."

The world tilted. Brandon stared out the window at a dirty, skinny child peeing beside one of twenty or so ancient campers gutted into homes—like it was the most normal thing in the world.

"He's set up like a conservation program," Bradley went on, shifting gears as if discussing the weather. He grabbed water bottles from the backseat. "Dad's all about saving the world. Conserving land. Don't worry, you'll reap the benefits. Lyndsey is your tie to the family—your contract."

Brandon opened the bottle, throat tight. The water tasted odd. Flat. Warm. His head pulsed behind his eyes.

It didn't feel like a conversation.

It felt like assimilation. It felt like being swallowed whole.

"Lyndsey's from his favorite wife, Stilts," Bradley shrugged. "You'll get sent someplace nice. Maybe Florida."

"How many wives does Abel have?"

"Dad?" Bradley squinted. "Six, I think. That's just the ones in the big houses. Trailer girls don't count." He stopped himself quickly. "You'll get filled in next week after you sign the prenuptial agreement."

Next week. Prenup. Wedding.

His pulse spiked. Breathing felt stiff—too shallow.

"Bud, I know this stuff seems strange at first. But you'll like it. I guarantee there's no going back once you get a taste of it."

Brandon's head spun. Brothers. Family. He'd felt shut out ever since Tessa was born—stuck, shackled, chained to one spot. Austin had dropped Tessa in his lap and vanished.

"She's a bitch." The words slipped out like a reflex.

"What's that, bud?" Bradley asked, slowing the truck near a shabby white house.

"Austin, she was a bitch."

"That's the chick that saddled you with the kid, right? The one at the hotel?"

"Yeah."

"Don't worry about it. We took care of her."

Everything in the truck went silent. Brandon froze, his heartbeat hammering so hard it shook his vision. "You took care of her?" His voice came out thin, hoarse.

"Nothing any brother wouldn't do for another, right?" Bradley slapped Brandon's shoulder with the back of his hand. "We just scared her a bit. She won't be coming back."

Brandon's stomach twisted. A cold, heavy dread crept into his throat. Still, this was family. This was belonging. This was—

Something dark and angry curled in his gut.

He realized he was getting pulled under faster than he'd expected, panic prickling under his skin like icy needles—like a four-year-old at his first swimming lesson. Bradley had just tossed him in the deep end and told him to swim.

"You're quiet," Bradley said. Brandon didn't answer. Sound felt muffled, distant. His fingertips tingled. He looked down. He had drained the water bottle completely.

He didn't remember drinking it.

"Yeah, I must be overheated. I'm feeling dizzy."

"Here, bud, have another."

Brandon watched Bradley reach back—flinching slightly, expecting another punch. He wasn't wrong. Bradley smashed his fist into Brandon's shoulder.

"Ha ha! You wanted that, I know." Then he tossed him another bottle. Brandon's hands shook as he twisted it open. The plastic crinkled loudly—too loudly. His vision sharpened unnaturally, then tunneled. A sharp scent—cigarette smoke, bitter and unmistakable—drifted through the open window, wafting into his nose and burning the back of his throat. Brandon turned, pulse thundering, but saw only shifting shadows beyond the tree line.

The skin on his neck crawled. Someone was out there. Watching.

Bradley's voice faded. The laughter in the cab thinned into a brittle hush. A dark shape shifted between the trees. For the first time, Brandon wondered if he'd ever really been part of the family— or if he was just another piece being moved across Abel Martin's board. Far up the dirt road, a single pickup eased into view, headlights off. Creeping. Patient. Off-kilter.

The hair rose on Brandon's arms. He tightened his grip on the bottle, throat dry, sweat chilling across his spine. He didn't know who was coming for him—or if they were coming for someone else. He only knew one truth now, cold as a knife's edge: No one ever really left Canaan Mountain. And he was one of them.

Chapter −38

From where Austin sat in the truck, she could see the compound spread across the lower stretch of the mountain. Abel Martin's house rose in the distance like a squat, brooding shape. Thin streams of smoke drifted upward from several controlled fires. Their glow flickered faintly in the gathering dusk. Somewhere behind the cluster of buildings, a mechanical hum throbbed. It sounded like generators or industrial fans working overtime.

"So—what does he do with these fires?" Austin asked, turning slightly toward Crazy Jack to gauge his reaction. Crazy Jack kept his gaze fixed ahead, his hands steady on the wheel as he drove and watched the compound.

She and her collection of misfits had settled into Crazy Jack's cluster of three tiny tourist cabins. Austin had known him half her life. Jack of *Crazy Jack's Pizza Barn was* the man who kept every teenager in Danville Station fed on greasy slices and unsolicited life advice. He gave them summer jobs and a place to hang out. He had black hair and a scrubby black mustache and beard. His vivid blue eyes—always reminding her of a hot August sky—glanced her way.

"We don't know. We only know the smoke never blows toward the compound." Crazy Jack sat back in the truck, his arms draped over the wheel and his chin resting on his wrists. When he said "we," he meant himself, his wife Martha, and most of the older folks from Turning Point Trailer Park and Cabins. They'd lived there long before Abel looked toward Whiskey Mountain. Crazy Jack jabbed a thumb toward the ridge. "See, just to our right—that's the wind turbine farm. Renewable energy, clean as it gets."

Austin followed his gaze. The white blades cut slow, steady circles through the hazy sky.

"Martin's smoke blows straight toward town," Austin said softly.

"Yep, if it weren't for those turbines stirring the air, that mess would sit over everything—the school, the Tremaine place, the whole damn valley—for a week." Jack snorted loudly in the truck.

"Most folks think turbines are just for power. Truth is, they keep the air moving. Cleaner. Safer. They're the only reason people down there aren't coughing up black sludge." He spat out the window into the dirt. "Martin's been fighting 'em from the start. Posts signs saying wind farms cause cancer, kill every bird in the sky. Lies. All of it. Man's got ties to fossil fuels, that's why he wants 'em gone. Wants his smoke to settle wherever it wants and wants the money that comes from keepin' things dirty."

"Propaganda," Austin muttered. "Smoking out anyone who won't join his church. Encouraging neighbors to report each other for 'disobedience.' Seizing inheritances, vehicles, property—calling it 'for the church.' Separating parents from their kids 'for discipline,' just like he's doing to Brandon Tremaine." Her voice thinned, but she kept going. "He's been at it for years—rotating boys and girls between communities to 'keep loyalty fresh.' Cutting people off from their families. Keeping everyone hungry, scared, obedient."

"A cult," Crazy Jack murmured. "Textbook stuff."

The adrenaline drained out of her all at once, leaving her legs shaky, exhaustion sliding in like cold water. The vinyl seat clung to the backs of her thighs.

The faint reek of old cigarettes tangled with engine oil. Beneath it all, she caught the acrid chemical tang of burnt plastics drifting from the compound's fires. Her fingertips still throbbed from clawing her way out of the trunk. Bruises wrapped around her arms and shoulders. Each flared when she shifted. Being this close to the compound made her feel drained in a way she couldn't explain. Her breath tasted smoky and metallic, as though the air itself carried something that worked against her. Her nostrils felt singed. A tightness crept up her throat. She made herself breathe evenly, planning step by step.

She had no idea Crazy Jack owned the Turning Point Trailer Park and Cabins until she stepped into his pizza restaurant earlier to give her notice. But he'd bought the property two years ago from Ansel Jones, who'd held it for forty years. Ansel decided to retire. Abel had been trying to buy it.

One night, while waiting for his usual half-pepperoni, half-anchovy pizza, Ansel let slip he was considering selling. Crazy Jack hadn't wanted Abel Martin near it. He snapped it up without hesitation. He figured it would make a fine retirement option once he wore out slinging pizzas.

The trailers sat there year-round. Tourists rented them. Migrant workers rented them. Hunters rented them. Jack collected the money and kept the lights on. He'd gotten himself into some debt, juggling both properties. He couldn't sell Crazy Jack's Pizza because most of his income came from dough and delivery. At sixty-eight, he grumbled about owning two businesses. Austin knew better. He loved talking to people too much to walk away. Between sunup and midnight, that man's jaw never rested.

"I don't want to put you in any danger, Jack."

"Baby girl, living here is dangerous every night. That asshole is the reason nobody wants to rent the campground in summer or come this way for pizza. The smoke. The creepy folk living there." he said gently. "We're a bit like kin, your family and mine. Both Cherokee. Abel wants this mountain. If you dent his plans, I'm behind you. Everyone here feels the same."

"Jack, you saved me back in high school when my dad was being...well, himself." She kissed his cheek. "I'd do anything for you. I'm just scared we're bringing trouble here."

"All hell's coming sooner or later." He chuckled, sniffed. "If Satan shows up on Whiskey Mountain, I hope you're the one standing there with the cross and Bible. Your dad couldn't hold anything off—he's too pudgy. You'd look cuter fighting them. Martha and I'll buy pom-poms and cheer from the porch."

~

"Alright, Roo," Austin said that night around ten. She knelt in the gravel behind the cabin she was staying in. Roo sat on an old cement block, staring at her like he already knew the plan. "Straight in. Straight out. You sniff Jenna Madison's shirt—this one I got from her mom—and see if you can tell whether she's here and where she might be kept."

"What if she's not in there?" Starr asked, working on a mosquito bite on her knee. She wore a long, wispy dress hitched up to mid-thigh, and River had been staring at her bare legs like he'd forgotten how to blink.

Eight minutes earlier, she'd dragged him off Roo when they nearly got into a scuffle over a donut. Somehow, the sight of Starr's skirt riding up shifted the tension immediately.

"Put it down, girl," Austin said, tugging the hem of Starr's dress. "You're going to kill the boy."

Starr blinked, feigning innocence, while River turned scarlet at the attention. "Sorry, River." Starr's voice carried no real remorse. She had been tossing him glances all evening. River, caught off guard, looked stunned and fascinated, as if this attention was something new for him.

River looked to Austin. She smiled, shook her head lightly, and waved it off. He grinned back, more relaxed than she'd seen him in days. He hovered close, nudging her arm or brushing her shoulder. He clung the way a child does to a favorite blanket. She didn't mind. Roo did. Whenever River stepped too close, Roo growled at him like a territorial house pup.

"It's not the donut," Starr had pointed out earlier when Golem hauled Roo out of the room. "It's you. They're sorting out a pecking order."

Austin didn't love the idea of being anyone's alpha. She also didn't love that if she left a bathroom door cracked while she used it—because shutting it still made her chest tighten—River drifted inside to lean against the sink like it was perfectly normal.

Roo dropped into a guarding squat at the threshold. "If Jenna's not there, we move on," Austin said, brushing off the incident.

"He's got like thirty compounds," Starr muttered. "Where does this end? We could be doing this for months."

"Well, he doesn't know we're here. That helps."

"And that's the only advantage," Starr said, letting her shoulders slump as she sat beside them.

River stepped forward and gently took the shirt from Austin's hand. She had driven five hours to meet Jenna's mom, Christina, and pick up the shirt, along with a necklace her father had given her last Christmas. River shook out the shirt, raised it to his face, and inhaled deeply. His eyes unfocused for a moment, and he tapped his foot, signaling he was processing something internally.

"Jay," he murmured. "Her grandma calls her Jay." His eyelids lowered in concentration. "She sits on a chair in her room to play guitar—not well, can't sing. Her grandpa—he's dead now—laughed at how her dad would hold his ears when she practiced."

Austin took a breath, letting the moment settle. River's gift was different from her own, rooted in his bloodline, not spellwork. But it left her unsettled. "Well, that's helpful," she said.

"It is," River replied with a small, proud nod. "Means she's close. If I get this much detail, she isn't far."

"See, Starr?" Austin said with a small smirk. "That's another advantage."

She turned to Roo. "Alright, buddy. Take the shirt. Find what you can. Don't get caught. If anything goes sideways, press the 9-1-1 contact I put in your phone—that's me."

After Roo left, the wait gnawed at her. Every tick of the cabin's wall clock echoed through the thin plywood walls. Outside, insects hummed, and the distant fires crackled in the night air. Leading meant pushing others ahead of danger while holding the responsibility herself. It sat heavily on her chest. She kept her expression calm, but beneath the surface, nerves pulled tight. Golem settled beside her, his hand warm and steady against her back. He smelled faintly of pizza and soap—grounding.

Across the yard, everyone tugged at the little leather protective bags Aina had made for them, filled with betony and hawthorn and a few other herbs chosen for each of their temperaments. Austin's pouch pressed warm against her heart. The scent wrapped around her like a quiet promise.

"He's in the middle of the compound," Stats said, eyes glued to the laptop at the picnic table. The little tracker she'd tucked into Roo's pocket glowed on the map. So far, Roo hadn't chased any rabbits or wandered toward water, both of which had a bad record of derailing him from missions.

"So—"

Austin jumped when River appeared beside her again, stepping out of the shadow like he'd been listening the whole time.

"Sorry," River said, pushing back his soft black hair. He looked like the type of boy she would have swooned over at thirteen—still too pretty to be real. "I'm starting to get a sense of everybody."

"That's good," she said, feeling his hand rest lightly on her shoulder as he stood next to her. "As long as nobody planted you with us as a spy."

"You don't sugarcoat," he said with a half-smile. "I wondered if you thought that." He didn't sound angry—just matter-of-fact. She didn't feel anything romantic toward him—he settled into her life the way a kid brother would, all nerves and need for reassurance.

River gravitated toward her like someone who'd been drifting too long and finally found a steady place to land, and he seemed to understand that the closeness between them lived in comfort, not interest. She'd watched him navigate everyone, gentle with Aina, careful with Golem, playful with Hutch.

"I'm here because they dragged me out of the hospital I was living in," he said. "Nobody told me anything except you collect freaks and monsters. You'd keep me safe. I probably can't convince you I'm telling the truth. Especially after what that guy did to you— the one you pretend you don't care about but still hope had some good reason for hurting you."

"Stop." Austin held up a hand. "River, don't pick through my personal stuff like that. My issues are mine."

"I know," he said, shrinking slightly. "You're tough to read. Your mind moves all over the place. Like an abstract painting. I like figuring people out. I'll try to dial it back." He paused, grinned shyly.

"Starr's pretty. Do I have to ask you before I sit with her? I'll come back."

Austin blinked, trying to interpret what he meant. "River," she said, "I meant what I said. You're free to do whatever you want as long as it doesn't hurt any of us. If something serious happens, we go into lockdown. I'll tell you when that is. And yes, you can sit with Starr. Just watch yourself—she's got a soft spot for pretty things and might put you in her pocket."

He beamed, eyebrows wiggling, then fell quiet. "My grandpa's the one I killed," he said in a soft, fractured voice. "He called me from up on the mountain. Said it was an emergency. Asked me to come. Said it was his time. I thought he'd finally lost it. People called him Naaldlooshii, but that's outsider talk. He wasn't a witch the way they treat it in stories. He was just my grandpa. He taught me to ride horses. Coached my soccer team. He was lonely. Grandma died fifteen years ago. Nobody visited him except me. He looked me right in the eye and said he was ready. So, I did it."

Austin leaned toward him, slow and steady. "I'm sorry you had to carry that. I had to leave Tessa. We all have our scars." She poked his leg gently. "We're here. We'll get you through it."

"That's it?" he whispered, barely audible. "You're not scared of me?"

She shrugged and smiled softly. "Scared? After the week I've had? No. We're good."

River swiped at his eyes, walked off, and settled alone at a picnic table. Starr noticed. Austin tipped her head toward him. Starr nodded and headed his way.

It was two in the morning when Roo slipped back through the gates of Crazy Jack's property. Austin heard the soft crunch of gravel and shot to her feet. Roo stopped a few feet away, shoulders hunched, his expression tight. "Roo, come here. Did you find her? What happened?" Austin asked.

"I found her," he said quietly. "She thought I was going to hurt her. You know...*hurt her.*"

"You got close?"

"She takes care of the dogs they use for fighting. Cleans their pens. Cleans up after the fights. Abel likes watching dogs tear each other up." He paused. "And people, too. He's got the girls fighting in cages. She was in one of them. A big one. I had to tell her over and over I wouldn't hurt her. Then I told her what River said about her singing loudly, playing the guitar, and her dad holding his ears. I mentioned how her grandma called her Jay. That's when she believed me." His face dropped. "She cried. A lot. I sat with her. Gave her the shirt you gave me. She kept it. She's tiny and looks like a kid the same as you."

Austin let the breath leak out slowly, tasting the bitter edge of coffee still clinging to her tongue. "Then we're in business. We need to move fast before Abel realizes we're anywhere near here."

Her mind was already mapping out the steps—routes through the woods, how fast guards rotated, which buildings the fires never lit, the time it took smoke to drift east.

A faint ribbon of cigarette smoke curled through the porch light, the same scent that had followed them for days.

Someone stood beyond the trees, watching.

Austin didn't flinch. She simply squared her shoulders and kept planning. The night wasn't done with them yet.

Chapter —39

"Hey, Pet, wake up."

Austin shot up in bed, heart beating hard against her ribs. The room blurred without her contacts—shapes pressing in too close, shadows crawling along the walls until she forced her lungs to open. Roo's warmth beside her grounded her, the familiar weight keeping her tethered to the present. "Hutch?"

"Yeah."

"What's up?" Austin pushed herself upright enough to swing her legs over the side of the bed. The cabin was crowded—Roo curled close, River at the foot of the bed, Aina on a nest of blankets, Stats somewhere under the mess, snoring like a clogged drain. She blinked up at Hutch, who leaned over her with his phone extended.

"Your ex-boyfriend just drunk-dialed me."

Austin rubbed her face. "Brandon...drunk-dialed you?"

"He has my number. We texted before he went to the dark side."

"The dark side." Austin sighed. "Just block him. Don't text him back." Hutch turned toward the door, and she nearly let herself fall back into bed before stopping. "What'd he say?"

"I don't know. He kept saying he still loved you. Something seemed...off. He wanted you to come back."

"Was he begging?"

"Yeah."

"Good." Austin snorted, but the reaction caught in her chest and turned into a bruised ache. She pressed her hand against the herb pouch hanging beneath her shirt.

"You want to hear it?" Hutch asked.

She didn't. But she did.

The message played—Brandon's voice slurred and desperate:

Austin, baby, I never stopped loving you. Baby, please come back. Did they hurt you? I'll hurt them back. I'll do anything. I love you—

"Oh, turn it off." Austin shoved out a hand, cutting it short right as he started a second voicemail.

"Wow, that's insulting to every man on earth." River's voice startled her. His tone was deeper than she expected, slipping from the corner of the room where he'd been sitting in the dark. She wasn't used to how silently he moved or how he blended into the cabin—close, but not threatening.

"You have to quit sneaking up on me, River."

"Sorry. I blend well." He shifted slightly, the faint gleam of his hair catching the lamp light. "I've been here all night."

"It's romantic," Aina mumbled from across the room. "You should go get him."

"Right," Austin muttered. "Sure, I'll just bring home the guy who dumped me for a commune chick in spandex and polos—the same one who is probably standing at the nearest airport handing out official Abel-Martin-brainwashing-your-boyfriend starter kits."

"He's a gentle soul, sweetie," Aina said, rubbing her eyes. "His aura is pale and white. Pure. He's not a good decision-maker. He's a follower. So what? He's hot. You're a leader. Deprogram him."

"He likes commune chicks. And you never said you saw his aura."

"You said not to freak you out. But that's why you're drawn to him. Opposites attract—"

"Opposites?" Austin shot her a look. "What? My soul is dark because his is white?"

Aina shrugged under her blankets. "I'm just saying yours is not white, exactly. He's gentle. Gentle people try to talk things out."

"The latter is right. He talked Bradley out of stuffing underwear in my mouth when they duct taped me to a wall in high school."

River lifted his head. "You're serious, somebody duct taped you to a wall?"

"I got shoved into lockers. Clobbered in dodgeball. You know what? It's two-forty in the morning. I'm not discussing childhood traumas." Austin nudged a pile of blankets aside with her foot, searching for a spot to lie back down.

"Ow," Stats muttered as her toe bounced off his arm. The small clock near the bed cast a dull glow across his tattoo. Two forty-five.

"Cripes almighty. What is this, a slumber party? Actually, no—slumber parties have structure. This is overwhelming. I need normal. For ten minutes, I just need normal."

"Is there such a thing as normal?" Roo asked, half-asleep.

"Yes. And at least Golem had the decency to stay in his own room and let me have privacy," Austin huffed, feeling River's hand as it rested on her shoulder. She let it linger for a beat—comforting warmth—before gently moving it away.

"No, he's in the chair. I'm in his lap," Aina said with a sleepy smile. "Admit you love us, Austin."

"Oh, hell." Austin dropped back onto the bed and knocked her head lightly against River's elbow. "What is my biggest fear?"

"That we will leave you," Aina answered.

"We won't ever leave you, Pet," River said. "I promise."

Austin grunted, not trusting her voice enough to answer. The faintest whiff of cigarette smoke drifted through the cracked window—thin, cold, familiar. Her nerves jumped, a prickling rising along her arms. Someone was out there. Watching. Waiting. She tried to tell herself it was the wind but doubt coiled deep and tight.

At ten after three, her phone rang. She hit the bureau, dragging half the charger with her as she grabbed it. "This is Austin."

Silence. She blinked at the screen. The call was real. PRIVATE flashed on the display.

"Austin, this is Ben. You need to come down to the police station. We've got a problem."

Her breath snagged. "H—how'd you get my number?"

"I'm a cop. I can get anybody's number. Just get down here. Now." He hung up. Fifty bad outcomes flashed through her mind. If she drove straight there, Ben would know her radius. She waited thirty minutes before pulling into the police station, sweating bullets in her business suit. If they booked her, at least she'd look professional.

Inside, the front lobby was empty except for Pamela Goodwin, the night dispatcher. Pamela never smiled, never blinked enough, and always looked like she'd smelled something sour. "In the back," she said, jabbing a thumb.

Austin walked down the dim hallway. Her heels clicked too loudly across the tan linoleum—echoes from her high school floors creeping back. A trap. It felt like a trap.

She passed an open office and heard Ben say her name. She backed up and peeked inside. He sat at a desk with only a small lamp on, cartoons flickering on a TV in the corner. He pointed at the floor. A blanket lay there.

Austin stepped forward and looked down.

"You know this *thing*?" Ben asked, voice low.

"Is it—Tessa?" she whispered.

"Yeah. Someone found her wandering around the old school playground at two this morning. Crying. Shaken up."

Austin knelt and brushed her hand through the little girl's hair. "She's okay?"

"EMS checked her. Bruises, cuts. They assumed someone had hit her. But she's intact."

"Where's Brandon?" Austin asked. "He wouldn't leave her."

"Don't be so sure." Ben rubbed his face. He looked worn down—not the cruel, short-tempered brother she'd fought with three weeks earlier. "We got a call from the compound. Brandon tore through a couple of buildings up there. Drunk. Wild eyes. You're not hanging out with those people, right?"

"No, Ben. Absolutely not."

"Look me in the eyes."

Austin pushed to her feet and leaned over the desk until their eyes were level. "Abel Martin is a lunatic with a cult on that mountain. He's dangerous. And I am *not* part of it." She tapped beneath her eye. "These are from exhaustion—not from whatever he's poisoning the water with."

"I thought you left town." Ben sighed. He scrubbed his face.

"Then one of my officers saw you Turning Point Trailer Park and Cabins. Hell, she looks exactly like you when you were three. I can't take her back to a drunk daddy and that mountain. I can't. I thought about calling Mom, but Brandon would just go after her. Mom couldn't protect her. This place is sliding downhill fast." He paused, looked embarrassed. "I'm so paranoid something's going on, I'm buying bottled water from two towns away."

Austin stared at him, unsure what to say. "Good idea."

Then, suddenly, his face hardened. "Get her and go. Now. Before the lunatics on that mountain come for her."

She blinked, thrown by the speed of his mood shift. Her gaze drifted to the wall behind him—pictures, plaques, shadowboxes. Arrowheads. And near the top, a small wooden case with a glass front. Inside hung a leather pouch.

Papaw's bag.

It tugged at her like a low, ancient heartbeat. Ten feet away, but pulsing in her chest as if it sat beneath her skin. She fought the urge to reach for it. Ben had called her, trusted her with Tessa—that needed to matter more.

She bent to scoop Tessa into her arms. The girl still clutched the book she'd taken everywhere.

"Tessa, baby. Wake up."

Tessa's eyes opened slowly. "Austin."

"Yeah, baby. It's me."

"I can't find Daddy."

"I know. You're coming with me for a while until we find him."

Tessa shifted, silent, then reached both arms toward Austin.

"Thanks, Ben," Austin whispered. He didn't respond until she reached the doorway.

"Hey."

She turned back.

Ben was standing on his chair, lifting the shadowbox off the wall. He hopped down and held the leather pouch out to her.

"Take it. I always figured you thought it was worth money and wanted to sell it. Dad—he was afraid you'd join the cult and use it against us."

Austin stiffened. "Why would I ever do that?"

Ben hesitated, then shrugged helplessly. "You were sneaking out to see Brandon. He was a time bomb. You always pushed Dad's rules. He thought Abel Martin would try converting you. Sending you away was the only way he knew to keep you out of it. He figured Abel passing you around to his sons and buddies was worse than you hating us." Ben exhaled. "But the pouch? It's not worth anything except remembering Papaw." He nodded at it. "Austin, there's nothing inside."

"Nothing?" she whispered.

"No. I opened it myself. Looked. It was empty."

The leather felt warm in her palm—too warm. A faint pulse hummed beneath her fingertips, quiet as breath. Empty or not, something in it remembered her.

And something in her answered in return.

Chapter −40

Brandon woke to a yellow ceiling he didn't recognize. Mildew webbed through the cracks. This wasn't his house. He didn't think he'd ever seen this ceiling in his life. A sheet covered him. When he pushed it aside, he froze—he was naked. His head throbbed like someone had wedged a steel vise around his temples.

"Hey, baby, you're awake."

The voice—soft, sugary, unfamiliar—made his stomach pitch. He turned his head slowly toward the sound. A woman stood over him. No—*two* women. Or he was seeing double. Both had sandy hair and brown eyes, but their blurred outlines made it hard to tell them apart. There was no sign of anyone with dark hair.

"Well, hello, sleepy head," the one on the left said. "You've been on a binge for three days. Ready to come back to reality?"

The other giggled. A high, flirty sound that scraped down his spine. The woman on the left plopped onto the bed beside him.

"Kim?" he grunted.

"Yep."

"Why aren't you—wearing clothes?"

"Because you told us not to get dressed two days ago." She shrugged. "We haven't had a reason to. You know." The other one giggled harder.

Brandon groaned. He remembered nothing after riding with Bradley Saturday night—"What day is it?"

"Wednesday."

He jerked upright, yanking the sheet around him. "Wednesday? Holy shit." His heart slammed into his ribs. "Where's Tessa? She's never been alone longer than a workday—what happened? Why am I—" His hands caught his attention then—raw, skin scraped open, knuckles swollen thick. A fat lip stung when he touched it. A split cheek. Bruises down his ribs. All of it hurt, but none of it sparked a memory.

Kim reached up and patted his cheek like he was a toddler. "Well, you little rebel, you got in a fight with Bradley and then Blue. Tore up one of the trailers on Root Road. Beat up Billy Tate, one of Uncle Abe's guards. He showed everybody a video of him beating up Tessa's mom. You called a bunch of people. Called 9-1-1."

"Aw, crap."

"It's okay, hot stuff." The other girl tried to crawl back into the bed and tug him with her. He pushed her away, palms out. Everything felt slippery and unreal.

"Uncle Abe told the cops you were just drunk. Said you'd never gotten drunk before."

"I haven't. An occasional beer—" His mouth was dry. "Was the cop who came Ben Jackson?"

Kim shrugged. "I don't know. Anyway, rebel, you're the one with explaining to do with Lyndsey."

"Oh my God."

"Oh, you don't even know the half of it. After Bradley knocked you to the floor—at my house—Lyndsey tried to calm you down. You told her you had two weeks to get married and you were gonna hit on every hot girl over eighteen. Then you walked out."

Brandon's stomach dropped to the floor. "Where's Tessa?" he demanded, voice cracking in a way he could barely choke down. His pulse pounded so violently, his vision blurred. He tried standing and nearly collapsed; pain shot up his legs, dizzying and bright. His breath hitched—shallow, panicked. He dropped back onto the mattress, hands numb and chest burning.

"Let me get you some water, sweetie," Kim said. "You aren't making it home without something in you."

"Kim, just tell me where Tessa is."

"I have no clue." She walked into the kitchen, filled a cup, brought it back, and held it out. "You didn't leave her with me. You didn't have her after the picnic. She wasn't with Lyndsey. Last time I saw her, she was wandering around outside the church. Haven't seen her since you ended up here on Friday or Saturday."

~

A faint waft of cigarette smoke drifted through the hallway—thin, stale, familiar. Brandon's skin crawled. Someone was always watching. Always.

By three that afternoon, he sat alone in his kitchen, staring at nothing. The silence pressed in so heavily that it felt like a weight on his chest. Abel wouldn't answer his calls. Lyndsey ignored him. Nobody knew where Tessa was. Worse—nobody seemed to care.

His hands trembled as he dialed. Sweat slicked his palms, breath sharp and cold. He had paced his floors raw, calling everyone he could think of, driving out to the compound, the farm, the outskirts of town. Every unanswered ring carved deeper into him. Every "no, haven't seen her" hollowed him out further.

He called, and called, and called. Someone had to have seen her. Someone had to know.

But they didn't.

And somewhere out there, Tessa—his little girl—was alone.

A thick coil of guilt wound around his ribs, squeezing until he couldn't breathe. He pressed a shaking hand over his eyes.

Maybe all of this was his fault. Maybe it always had been.

Chapter —41

Austin could floss, brush, and swish like a dentist's poster child and still need a root canal. Plans just didn't stick to her—ever. Which explained why she now stood dead center in Abel Martin's compound, whisper-yelling for Roo at three in the morning, so tired she could drop right there and let the world spin on without her. The only anchor right now was knowing Tessa was safe at the cabin with Golem and Aina. Austin kept that fact tucked against her ribs like a shield as she followed Hutch into the dark.

It was supposed to be simple. Roo would sneak in, use the saw on Jenna Madison's chain, and lead her out. Quick in, quick out. That had been four hours ago. Four hours, and Roo's GPS dot hadn't budged from a rust-colored blur of metal buildings and animal sheds on Stats's screen. Austin kept cursing herself for not getting a damn map—or at least figuring out the difference between one corrugated warehouse and another.

The compound was a maze of hay-stinking barns, chain-link pens, hulking steel sheds, and long rows of squat trailers glowing faintly under floodlights. Corrugated tin pinged under her boots with every cautious step. The scent of gasoline, urine, and burned plastic clung to the air like a sour fog. She didn't know where she was. Not in this maze, not with her heart tap-dancing with exhaustion and claustrophobia.

"Stats, where am I compared to Roo?" she whispered into her handset.

"I can tell you without asking, Pet," Hutch muttered at her side, digging a pebble from his sneaker. "About a hundred miles. Told you we took the wrong road." He had told her—about a hundred times. Hutch's voice was low, steady, not panicked, just resigned, the way he always sounded when she led them somewhere dense and crooked and terrifying. "You know, this sounds vaguely familiar to the first time we met." He nudged her with his elbow. "You don't want to bring that up?"

"Yeah, don't bring that up."

"But I distinctly remember you telling me: 'Mister Arias, there's been a little bit of a mix-up. My ride isn't here. Either he didn't show up, or I'm on the wrong street.'"

"Well, that was different."

"How was it different, Pet? You're lost now, too. You act like you've got all the answers, but you're the same woman who got lost trying to find the bathroom on a cruise ship. Uptight nanny. Same energy."

"Well, you're stuck with me. Your dad pays me to guard you. I guard you."

And he was stuck. Stuck in this chaos—chaos he preferred over his mother's champagne-drenched parties, or his father's security briefings and glass offices, or a half-dozen guards forming a wall around him every time he crossed a street. He just wanted normal. This madhouse was the closest he'd ever come.

Hutch's past pressed in on him—easy to see how it surfaced now, here, lost again with Austin in the dark. He never walked anywhere alone as a child. Forty-two kidnapping threats since he was two. He ran away at thirteen—straight into danger. Drained bank cards, shady bars, and Tomás Ríos, who had planned to collect a ransom after cutting off Hutch's ear.

He hadn't known any of that then—just that Austin's voice had pierced the noise of a Mexico City dive:

Hey, what's your name? You're cute.

She'd looked like a college girl in over her head, not someone sent to break him out. Somehow, the memory hit harder now—because right now Austin was doing the same thing: dragging him through danger with a half-smile and a terrified heart.

Hutch could still see the bar: Tomás's men closing in, Starr giggling like she didn't notice the guns, Austin flashing that casual, lopsided grin while her fingers curled around his wrist tighter than fear should allow.

He recalled her saying, *"Your mom says it's time to come home."*

He remembered the catacombs—the suffocating dark—how Austin hid her panic by shoving a broomstick under her arm and cracking a joke about flying off into the night. Starr had whispered prayers. Hutch had tried to look brave. Austin, white-knuckled and shaking, kept pushing them forward, even with the walls squeezing her breath out. That endless stone tunnel was the first place he'd ever seen someone fight through terror that raw.

She'd been terrified of closed spaces then. She still was. He'd seen her swallow hard tonight when she realized they'd stepped into a narrow cul-de-sac between two storage barns. The cramped angles, the echoing quiet—it pricked at her.

"Pet," he whispered. "Breathe."

"I'm breathing."

"You're not. You are gasping like you're under water."

She was gripping her pouch so tight the herbs inside crackled.

Roo was somewhere in this maze—Roo, who had been brave enough to approach Jenna Madison, to sit in a cage with her and convince her he wouldn't hurt her. He was stubborn and loyal and scared—but he'd never show fear, not when Jenna needed him.

Austin pressed a palm to the wall and breathed slowly, centering herself. Somewhere beyond the sheds, she caught a faint whiff of cigarette smoke. Not fresh—stale, drifting. Watching.

"Hutch," she whispered. "We're not alone."

"Yeah. I smelled it too."

A metal gate clanged somewhere far off. Dogs barked, low and angry. A chain rattled. The whole compound felt like it was holding its breath.

"We have to find him," Austin whispered. "Before someone else does."

"And before they figure out we're in here," Hutch added quietly.

Austin pressed on, turning left where she thought she'd turned right two minutes ago—corridor, shed, chain-link pen, another trailer, another shed.

Everything mirrored everything else.

Her claustrophobia clawed at her ribs as the path tightened between two rows of metal siding. The night pressed against her skin, too close, too tight. Mexico flickered at the edges of her vision.

"Pet," Hutch murmured again. "Breathe."

"I *am* breathing."

But her voice was thin, frayed.

When she finally stopped to orient herself, she realized the truth: She had no idea where she was. None. And Roo's dot on Stats's tracker might as well have been on the moon.

"Lost again," she muttered under her breath. "Story of my damn life."

And somewhere in the dark, cigarette smoke curled through the air like a warning.

Chapter –42

"I'm lost. Damn, I have no clue where we're at." Austin rubbed her bruised hand across her forehead, the sting a reminder of clawing out of the trunk. Next to her, Hutch stood rigid in the moonlight, arms crossed tightly, his impatience evident in his posture. "What?"

"Seems familiar. Every time you drive, you're lost. First time I met you. Now."

Austin exhaled, readjusting the pouch Aina had given her so it lay beside Papaw's scratchy leather bag against her chest. She steadied her breath. The familiar weight helped her control her nerves. Hutch's flannel shirt, snug in his jeans, hardened his frame, even if his scowl hadn't aged since thirteen. Her scraped palms pulsed, shoulders stiff, every breath tinged with the chemical reek from Abel Martin's compound pressing on her lungs. She checked her energy, wondering how much fight she could muster if needed.

"You lead," she said quietly.

Hutch blinked. "You want me to—lead?"

No, she didn't. She hated hinting that Hutch might lead better in this circumstance. But Starr had warned her two days earlier—burdened, serious—about the changes coming for Hutch. Now, Austin recognized she had to listen to the people who noticed things she might miss. Leaders didn't do everything alone; they handed off certain tasks to the right people, to lead beneath her. That didn't make her weaker. It made her better. "I need to talk to you." Starr had pulled Austin away from the cabins and into a quiet patch of grass, the moon high enough to silver their outlines.

"Hutch is getting ready to hatch."

Austin had stopped dead. "He didn't say anything to me. How do you know?"

"He came to me. Said he was having strange feelings."

It stung. "Why not me? He knows I went through this. I've known him since—"

"So have I," Starr cut in gently. "But he said the feelings were different. You understand? My job is fixing the skinned knees. Your job is leading. You can't do both. Nobody can. You delegated from day one: me with emotional stuff, Stats with research, Golem with safety, Roo with instincts. You know what everyone's strengths are. You asked me to tell you things like this. I'm telling you."

Austin had sighed, the sting fading. "Yeah. You're right. Thanks. So... what happens? How do we know?"

"That's the problem. We don't." Starr lifted a shoulder. "I'm digging through everything I can find—old translated tomes, whatever Stats can get into. But what I know is this: he's coming into manhood, whatever that means for someone like him. Leaders get restless, Pet. They test boundaries. He could push to take control if he feels it's his 'time.' Paolo kept trying to undercut you, but Hutch is too young. Too inexperienced. He can't lead us."

"And I already have the job."

"Yes. Which is why you need to mentor him. Let him taste leadership so he doesn't try to take it."

Austin wasn't fully convinced, but the logic made sense: mentoring Hutch now could stabilize group dynamics. Standing in the shadows of Abel Martin's maze, she decided to show trust in Hutch while silently retaining leadership.

"Lead," she said, steady now. "I'll walk with you and pull us back if needed."

Hutch absorbed that, jaw flexing. "I don't know—"

"We're different," she said. "I jump in, you calculate. Maybe that's your kind of leader. I make mistakes. You'll make mistakes."

"Like getting lost in the middle of Mexico?"

"Did you have to bring that up?"

He smirked, then tossed up a lazy hand, turning to stride ahead and claiming the lead. She kept step at his side, eyes sharp for trouble. They slipped deeper into the compound's outskirts. Austin touched Papaw's pouch, the warm leather reminding her why she was here—and not to let fear slow her down.

It hadn't occurred to either of them that someone would still be at the dog-fighting building at three forty-five in the morning. Just as Austin and Hutch tucked into a small stand of scrub trees, a gray car eased out—its window down, a thin wisp of cigarette smoke curling into the night. The engine hummed low. They held still until the taillights vanished.

They found Roo crouched in a patch of shadow, back straight and eyes fixed, perfectly still despite the cold. When he saw them, he stood slowly, gaze darting to the building.

Moments later, they made their move.

Inside, the acrid stench hit hard: urine, dirty straw, metal, blood. Roo slid to the cages and cut the plastic bands cleanly. Austin, hands throbbing with every movement, freed the girls and dogs. The sight jarred her—three girls huddled in dog cages, ten dogs pacing and whining.

They pressed through shadows, moving the girls quietly, every step calculated. Austin led them swiftly through the back, gravel crunching underfoot. The girls followed, sometimes sobbing quietly, sometimes bursting into wild, relieved chatter as freedom took hold.

The dogs followed, and only then did it become clear they weren't fighters at all. Just pets. Stolen ones. Roo stuck with them until a woman from two towns over arrived with crates and gentle hands, calling each dog "sweetheart" as she settled them inside.

Jenna Madison was tiny, brunette, her voice raw as she whispered to her mom on the phone. Katie Pierson and Jayce Wells trembled as Austin ushered them into a booth at a diner off the highway three hours later, where federal officials waited in plain clothes. The handoff was quiet, rehearsed, precise. Ten minutes later, Senator Madison met Austin outside in the shade of a faded awning and kept his word.

By three that afternoon, Austin pulled the truck into Crazy Jack's driveway. She had a thick wad of cash—payment she owed him for sheltering them—and she shoved it toward him.

"Ten thousand," she said. "Non-taxable. Take it."

He pushed her hands away. She dropped the cash on the table anyway.

"We're leaving."

"Leaving?" Crazy Jack followed her to the truck, eyebrows raised. "I figured you'd be here a while. We like the company."

"As soon as Abel Martin finds those girls gone, he'll get nosy," she said. "My crew sticks out like red balloons in a blue sky. All it takes is one person seeing them, and it traces back to us. Eventually, to you. I'm tired of being this close. I want to be a million miles away."

A crash echoed from the trailer where Starr was staying. Austin and Crazy Jack both jerked their heads toward the little cluster of homes. Aina sprinted across the gravel, stopped dead, looked right and left, then zeroed in on Austin.

"What the—?" Austin breathed.

Aina smacked a palm across her forehead, then spun and bolted back the way she came.

"That doesn't look good," Austin muttered, giving Crazy Jack a resigned wave before pushing her hair back from her face.

She was already too damn tired for whatever came next. She never got the peaceful lull before the storm—her sky always split open without warning, all lightning and thunder and no mercy. Tonight, would be no different.

Chapter −43

"Now—let me get this straight—" Austin planted her tennis shoes on the ragged blue carpet of the mobile home living room, jaw locked, hands flexing at her sides. The place felt smaller than usual. The ceiling pressed low, and shadows in the corners twitched like they wanted to fold around her. She forced herself to breathe through her nose—slow, steady, the way Aina's herb pouch taught her—but panic still crawled beneath her skin. She'd only slept a few hours—sun-up to early afternoon. Long enough for Hutch to talk, apparently. Long enough for the others to take his offhand comment about her "letting him lead last night" and turn it into a full-blown new command structure while she slept.

"You went over to Brandon's house to get Tessa some clothes—"

"She didn't have anything, but that ripped little pair of shorts and T-shirt," Starr said, wringing her hands and cutting a worried glance toward Golem, who was bear-hugging a raging Brandon tight. "We didn't think Brandon was home."

Brandon strained against Golem's grip, kicking, cursing, his face purple with fury. Golem's arms stayed locked around him.

"And when you walked into the house," Austin said through clenched teeth, "Brandon was there. Surprise. Why didn't you just walk out?"

"B—because he needs help," Aina stuttered, wide eyes darting between Austin and Brandon. Panic shone in them. "Look at him. He's crazy and—and sick. And he tried to hurt Golem."

Austin lifted one hand—sharp, commanding—to stop her. "At what point did any of you realize you were making a mistake? Surely—*surely* someone paused to think. Was there not a single moment in your little rebel outfit where someone said, 'Hey, maybe we should check with Austin before we cry mutiny'? Or were you expecting me to pat you on the head and whisper, 'Don't worry, sweetie, I can clean up your mutiny for you'?"

She swung her glare to Brandon, still thrashing. "Because I can't.

I have no clue how to fix this. Did it not occur to any of you that you just dragged Abel Martin's key asset onto the sound side of the mountain? You just exposed us to him."

Starr shrugged helplessly. "Um... no. We just thought—"

"Well, what you didn't *think*," Austin snapped, "was that Abel Martin was using dumbass here as bait. And you didn't think you were risking Crazy Jack's life. And you didn't think—at all—that we were finally home-free. Because if you had thought anything, you'd have let me order Tessa some clothes online, and we wouldn't have Satan's soon-to-be right-hand man foaming at the mouth and on to the carpet."

"Stats unhooked all the cameras in the house before we went in so nobody could see us," Aina said quickly.

Austin's head jerked toward the hallway—toward the sliver of shadow she knew Stats was hiding in. "He did, did he? Where is Stats?"

The man slinked another step backward, rubbing at the tattoo on his arm as if he could erase it. Austin's eyes narrowed.

"Dammit, Stats, even *you* defied my authority?"

"H—Hutch said it was okay."

"Hutch," Austin repeated, dangerous and flat. "That is not a surprise."

She cut her gaze to the couch where Hutch sat fiddling with his hands. "I was asleep for four hours. *Four.* And in that time you seized control of the group because I let you take a couple baby steps toward leadership?" Her voice rose, exhausted and furious. "We had a clean break. We could've left this whole bloody mess behind, vanished into some boring little Ohio town, played normal for five damn minutes. But now?" She jabbed a finger toward Brandon. "Now I have no choice but to stay, because this son of a bitch will run straight to Abel and rat Crazy Jack out—and Jack will be as good as dead."

"We weren't thinking," Golem grunted, tightening his grip.

"Where is Tessa?" Austin demanded.

"She's napping in your cabin," Starr said quietly. "Roo is watching her."

Austin pressed her hands to her face, thumbs digging into her temples until red marks bloomed. Claustrophobia and responsibility knotted tight in her ribs. Her eyes swept the room, lingering on the door—her instinct always pointing toward escape, even when she couldn't take it. "Good. Don't let her see her daddy like this. That's for damn sure."

"They were just trying to help," River said softly from the end of the couch. His shoulders hunched inward, voice uncertain. He glanced at Starr, then Austin, not meeting anyone's stare long. Emotions always passed through him like weather—visible in the set of his jaw, the tremor at his fingertips.

"Well, they didn't help," Austin said, sharper than she meant. "Their little bit of insubordination could cost us everything."

She pointed at Brandon, who was now spitting every foul word he knew in her direction. "Tie him up. Stuff a sock in his mouth. Then get out. I'll figure out how to fix this."

"You're not going to kill him, are you?" Starr blurted, eyes wide. "We did this for you. He's your safe place, right? Tessa's been crying for him—"

"Get out!" Austin snapped, stabbing a finger toward the door. They jumped as one. Boots scrambled. Apologies murmured. The room emptied quickly, leaving silence that felt heavier than the shouting.

~

Austin had seen chaos—gunfire, raids, catacombs—but never anything like this. Brandon thrashed like a rabid dog, heels pounding the carpet, spit flying as Hutch and River wrestled him into a wooden chair with a cracked vinyl seat. Ropes cut into his wrists as he jerked and bucked, dragging the chair until he toppled sideways and crashed face-first into the floor. The whole scene clamped down on Austin like a lid. Her chest tightened. Her fingers brushed Papaw's pouch at her collarbone. The faint warmth beneath the leather pulsed steadily enough to keep her breathing.

Still, Brandon rolled, kicked, cursed—rage ricocheting off every wall. "What can you do?" Austin asked Starr when the rest had fled. "What's wrong with him? Besides his brain being soft-wired to treat anyone but Abel Martin as the devil incarnate."

"He's drugged," Starr whispered. "Something in his system— something bad. His eyes are too puffy for booze and pills alone. Aina says his aura keeps flickering between white, gray, and black. I think he's been eating or drinking something he shouldn't."

"Can you purge it?"

"I can." Starr touched Austin's arm, hesitant. "We really did this for you, and I'm sorry. It was wrong. Hutch was just so convincing. He said you put him in charge last night. We only meant to grab her clothes. Then we saw Brandon's truck. Hutch said you loved Brandon—said if we brought him back and fixed him, you'd be happy. He had a battle plan—"

"No. He's fifteen and a pampered kid who's never had to shoulder real consequences," Austin said. "He cooked up some half-baked plan without thinking it through—and that's before we even factor in his favorite agenda: keeping me as far from his father as humanly possible. So really? He had two spectacularly bad ideas."

"It seemed so simple. And we followed his instructions. We thought he could lead us."

Austin's stare sharpened. "And how did that work?"

"Not...great."

"Starr, you know better. You're an adult and a doctor. He's a child," Austin said, voice low and controlled. "A fifteen-year-old doesn't have the wiring for this. They are like a car in the making. Their emotions hit the gas, and their common sense hasn't even finished building the brakes yet."

She tapped the side of her head.

"That part that thinks ahead? That plans? That sees danger coming? It's still under construction in him. So, the limbic part— the emotional, reward-chasing part—runs the show. He gets a feeling, he acts on it. No long view. No strategy."

She exhaled sharply. "Yes—I let him help. I let him taste responsibility. But last night? He *only led me to the barn*. I was holding his hand the whole damn time." She tapped her chest. "I was still the one person running the operation." She jabbed a finger toward the door Hutch had stormed through. "When I jump in feet first, it's because the situation is already on fire. A recon mission cannot be run by an inexperienced fifteen-year-old who's more interested in impressing the room than keeping the team alive."

Starr looked down, chastened. "You," Austin continued, softer but firmer, "are the one who knocks sense into me when I'm about to make a bad call. You make me rethink options. Recalculate when I'd rather sprint. And yet, you let a fifteen-year-old take control, making it look like you didn't trust me." She paused. "Do you trust my decisions?"

"Yes," Starr said so quietly that Austin almost missed it. "I just... wanted Hutch to explore the warrior growing in him. So... can this be fixed?"

"If you fix Brandon, I'll fix the situation." Austin poked her three times in the shoulder—sharp, playful, but firm. "It is not your job to train Hutch, nor is it your job to lead a mutiny against me on this leaky old tub of a ship I'm trying to keep afloat right now. Those are not your skills. Don't undermine me again. Or you'll find yourself working at a fast-food restaurant or something equally thrilling."

"You wouldn't." Starr giggled—weak, hopeful.

Austin didn't blink. "I would. You're either with me or against me. If you follow another captain, whether our ship is sinking slowly or not, you aren't part of my crew. That means one less person I have to protect now that Paolo is gone. It's always your choice."

Starr's smile slid away. "Why are you talking like this? I thought we were friends."

"You want to be besties with me, Starr?" Austin leaned in, anger rising hot in her chest. "Let me tell you something about friends. Friends don't stick a knife in your spine and then skip off after the next shiny leader. Friends don't abandon ship the second someone whistles."

She stabbed a thumb toward herself.

"And me? I don't exactly have time to braid friendship bracelets. I'm working two, three jobs at once—both hands in the water, paddling like hell to keep us afloat—while the rest of you lounge around like tourists on a rundown cruise ship. I'm the one making sure you don't fall overboard and drown tomorrow, but somehow every single one of you manages to toss your lifejacket overboard the second I look away."

Starr crossed her arms tightly. "Well, I wish Paolo weren't gone."

Austin's jaw tightened. "Do you think you were better off with him?"

"Yes. We got *everything* we wanted."

"As long as you didn't talk back. As long as the doors stayed locked. As long as you didn't cry or sneeze or drop a spoon—"

"We learned to live with his eccentricities."

"Except me," Austin said, voice low, "who got punished when you didn't behave how he wanted."

Starr looked away. Her voice, when it came, was barely a whisper. "The box."

"The box," Austin echoed.

The word sat between them like a bruise—one neither of them wanted to touch, but both still carried. Still, it lodged in Austin's mind, ugly and echoing: *Well, I wish Paolo weren't gone.*

It stung. And it lit something hot in her chest. She folded the hurt up, tucked it deep in her pocket, and made a quiet decision: If the day came when they left her paddling that damn ship alone, she wouldn't stop them. She would just keep rowing far, far away.

Chapter −44

"I'm going to get sick."

She knew he was lying again. The hard wooden seat bit into Austin's tailbone, her body curled, chin on her knees, the ache in her lower back sharp and constant. Every time her eyes closed, Brandon's voice clawed her awake—sick, bathroom, hungry, leg cramp, curses. The air felt thick with his presence, his sweat, and bitterness.

Brandon Tremaine twisted in his own chair, hands bound behind him, feet tied down, relentlessly provoking her. He hadn't slept. Starr had tried to ease his discomfort, but every time she loosened the knots, he worked free. The scratch of rope against skin had left angry red marks on his wrists. They anchored him to a kitchen chair in the room's center, then took shifts, passing the weight of responsibility back and forth.

He'd even said he loved her. *Baby, I love you.* Sound asleep, Austin had awakened, blinked. He was smiling over at her. It was soft and sweet. *But I'm going to get sick again.* She'd fallen for it, untied him, and stepped back.

Austin felt an unnatural heaviness around him—a fatigue that seeped under her skin, thick and numbing, like the crawling exhaustion Abel Martin brought, or when she crossed certain compound thresholds. She caught the first punch—her palm stinging from the impact, his knuckles rough and desperate. The second jab glanced off her forearm. The third slipped past—Starr gasped, Austin's head jerked toward the noise, and pain exploded as Brandon's knuckle slammed her cheekbone. Golem tackled him before he could bolt, the floor vibrating faintly with their scuffle. One full day and a half of this—Austin doubted he'd ever act normal again.

Austin untied his legs and then his hands from the back of the chair, but not from each other. She waited for his kick on her already-sore shins or the butt of his head against her chest.

She walked him to the bathroom. He didn't fight her.

Roo eased around the doorframe on his rear, watching closely. River had disappeared an hour earlier. The rest of them were sleeping.

"This is kidnapping, you know," Brandon growled right before she gave him a gentle push to his knees in front of the toilet. "When Abel sees I'm gone, he's going to come looking. You'll get arrested and sent to prison, or Abel will just kill you."

"Well, he hasn't looked for you yet. Just throw up. I'm tired." Austin eyed Brandon carefully.

It surprised her when he threw up. Starr had been forcing liquids through his lips, including some medicines, to make him throw up the poison. Most of the medicine ran down his shirt and to the floor. This last time, it must have worked. Austin had closed his nostrils, so he didn't have a choice.

"You stole Tessa, is that right?"

"Nope."

"Where the hell is she? She disappeared, you know that, right?"

"Shut up, Brandon."

"You must be really desperate for a man, Austin, to do this," Brandon spat between gags. "I take it Marco Arias isn't enough for you. Or—maybe there's nothing going on at all. Maybe it's because you're such an ugly bitch, nobody wants you. Nobody likes you. Nobody wants to be around you—just you and your freaks."

"Well, that makes you *nobody* because you're here right now," Austin spat back. "With us freaks."

He'd thrown up for a half hour more, then just fell over the side of the toilet in a dazed heap, sobbing for Tessa and begging Austin to find her. Austin cleaned him up and dragged him back to the chair. He just kept staring at her, then looking away.

"I woke up with two women in my bed the other day. I'm pretty sure we spent three days together without leaving the room. Jealous?" Brandon taunted. Austin rolled her eyes, but the words stung more than she wanted to admit. It shouldn't hurt, but it did.

An hour later, around seven, Austin left. She could still hear Brandon yelling, retching, and fighting his restraints as she walked to the cabin where Tessa slept.

She got Tessa up and made her breakfast. When the girl was awake, she clung to Austin, refusing to let her out of sight. Tessa cried when Austin tried to leave the room.

"Did you find Daddy?" Tessa had asked while she sat on Austin's lap, eating a piece of toast with jelly. Austin was staring at her cereal bowl, pushing her spoon into the little round pieces.

"We did. He is sick, but he is getting better."

"Are you sure you have the right one? Lyndsey hit me."

Austin's spoon stopped in mid-poke. "I am sure. And I'm sorry. Big people shouldn't hit kids. I won't let her hurt you again."

"Lyndsey's brother took daddy and got in a fight."

"I know."

"Kim says I'm ugly."

"You're beautiful, baby," Austin said softly, brushing a stray hair from Tessa's forehead before pressing a kiss to the crown of her head. The little girl's scalp was warm, the scent of sleep and jelly clinging to her skin. "You know why? Because you look just like me when I was little."

Tessa craned her neck to look at Austin, who was wearing her big glasses just like Tessa's. Tessa asked, "Are you my mommy?"

"I am."

Tessa didn't say anything at first. She just reached up with jelly-covered fingers and snatched a bit of Austin's hair.

"Daddy and I have waited for you for so long," Tessa whispered softly. "So long."

~

After comforting Tessa, Austin returned to her watch. The afternoon wore on, and Tessa napped, leaving Austin alone with her vigilance. As the house settled, River slipped quietly into the room, joining Roo.

"Guess what?" River slinked around the corner and settled next to Austin, nearly in her lap—close, but respectful, waiting for her nod before settling.

"What?" Austin asked him, eyeing him cautiously. "And I understand you two are trying to define social order, but you've got to figure it out soon. You are driving me nuts, throwing me off the bed in the middle of the night. By the way, what are you doing in the middle of the night before you come fighting it out with Roo?"

"That's what I wanted to tell you." River got a funny, half-grin on his face. "I woke up naked with Starr next to me."

Austin stared at him. She wasn't stunned. She just didn't really want to know who was doing what, when, or why. There was laughter across the room, pure laughter, and it was coming from Brandon. Austin ignored it, waited for some nasty remark. He'd been quiet since she sat down and started playing solitaire on her phone. Nothing came, so she nudged River with her shoulder.

"Why are you telling me this? There are some things I don't need to know. As long as you're consenting adults, and you are, I don't care if you all have an orgy as long as you don't wake me up."

"Because you're my person, you know." River's tone was earnest, like someone who'd never had a person before.

"*Your person.*" Austin tipped her head to check on Brandon. He seemed intent on the conversation. "You make it sound like you're a pet and I picked you up from the pound, River."

"Well, yeah. You kind of did."

Brandon sneezed. Austin jumped up, heart thudding, palms sweating as adrenaline spiked. Her skin prickled cold, breath catching, gaze snapping to him—her body still wired for any sudden move. She shot up, automatically jumping in front of River protectively.

"I'm going to get sick," Brandon suddenly burst out. He looked dazed, pale.

"Yeah, yeah, I've heard that story before—" Austin barely took three steps before Brandon vomited—choking, coughing, gasping.

The sharp, acrid smell filled the room. She rushed to his side, fingers trembling as she tried to untie the knots, the twine slick against her sweaty hands. Brandon's skin was clammy, his lips turning blue. She half-dragged, half-carried him to the bathroom, shouting for River to fetch Starr.

"You're okay, you're okay," she repeated, her voice shaky as she pressed her palm to Brandon's clammy forehead. He shuddered, coughed, his fingers digging into her forearm—cold, desperate, terrified. Their eyes locked, and Austin felt the raw panic in his grip.

"I'm going to die."

"No, you're not. You're going to be fine," she kept telling him, kept turning her cheek, waiting for him to slug her. He didn't. "You're okay."

By the time Starr and Aina got there five minutes later, Brandon was unconscious, breathing. He was lying half in the door, half out, and in Austin's arms.

Starr knelt down and ran her hands over him. She felt his breathing, lifted his eyelids, and peered inside. It seemed forever before she turned to Aina, who nodded her head.

"The black, it's going away," Aina whispered.

"That's what I thought," Starr added. "I don't smell it. I don't feel it. I think he needs to sleep this off, kind of like a hangover."

They cleaned Brandon up in a tub of water, the wet washcloth rough against Austin's fingers, his vomit clinging to the air. The three of them worked quickly, laying him in the bed. Austin jammed her chair under the doorknob, the wood pressing into her palms, barricading them inside. One by one, they took turns showering away the grime. Then Austin sent the others to sleep. She dug in, blinking heavy-lidded as exhaustion gnawed her veins, eyelids gritty and hot. Two hours later, sleep overtook her, heavy as a stone blanket. Light slipped around the curtains as she heard the toilet flush. Austin jerked to attention—Brandon stood not six inches away. Her eyes went wide. His hands came up. She raised her hand to shield herself. Nothing happened.

She turned her head, bracing for the blow she knew was coming. Her eyes squeezed half-shut, breath tight in her chest, muscles rigid and aching from hours of tension. But the punch never came. Instead, Brandon just wore that old lopsided grin—a look of defeat, his eyes dull and blinking slowly. He held out both hands in loose fists, knuckles raw and red, silently waiting for her to bind his wrists again.

"I had to use the restroom, so I wiggled my hands free," he said hoarsely. "I don't even want to know how I went with my hands tied. I'm assuming I'm under arrest or shanghaied or something because I know I did some bad things and—tell me Tessa's safe."

Austin nodded. "She's safe. You're detoxing. That's all you need to know for now."

"You're not lying? I looked everywhere for her. I thought—" His voice cracked. "I thought she was gone. I dropped her at Kim's. I remember that part. And then... Bradley. He took me to help with one of their bonfires. He showed me the well house—had me add chemicals to the water." He pressed a trembling hand to his head. "We got back in the truck and after that it's just... nothing. A blank. You think maybe I'm allergic to whatever they put in their water?"

"I don't know. Maybe." Austin unlocked her phone, thumb swiping through the dozens of pictures. But something in Brandon's words snagged her—*chemicals... well house... daily additions.* The words tumbled inside her head. The water. Not the drinking taps. *The source.* "Here," she said quietly, finding the series of Tessa in Crazy Jack's mom's old hats and giant wool slippers. Her voice sounded distant, even to herself. "Yesterday. I'm not lying. She's safe. She's with me."

He took the phone hesitantly, looked at her, then scrolled through the pictures one by one. A weak smile tugged at his mouth—relief so sharp it almost looked painful. Then his knees buckled. He crumpled before she could catch him. Austin lunged forward—half relief, half dread—because now she understood the part Brandon couldn't. What happened to him hadn't been an accident. It had been in the water.

Chapter −45

Golem knew he waddled when he walked. It wasn't his weight—just the way his massive hips carried him. Even with night covering him and only Austin beside him, he felt eyes on his back. The same old ache tightened his chest. People stared at him everywhere they went. He knew he was a freak. It made him sad. Sadder still that people like Austin and Aina liked him. He felt sorry for them for liking him.

"All the cattle are fed, right?" Austin asked softly.

She lingered in the open, posture tense, shoulders tight, hands curling and uncurling at her sides as she scanned the treeline—like even the night air pressed too close. Golem pushed aside the image she must see when he walked beside her and nodded.

He'd lugged out four extra round bales just in case the pasture grass wasn't enough. Then he'd checked all two hundred head one by one until he was certain they were maintaining weight. Well, one hundred and ninety-eight. Two were missing. He told himself he must have miscounted.

"Yes."

"You won't worry?" Austin touched his arm—a grounding gesture, but tonight her grip was too tight, fingernails dimpling his sleeve. She had trouble seeing in the dark, but this was more than that. Her breath came shallow as they moved away from the open field. Every shifting shadow made her jaw clench.

"I can't have you pacing and keeping everybody up again tonight. All the cows are fed. They're happy and healthy, alright? No worries."

"Yes." He smiled down at her. "You are nice to Josef."

They followed the creek bed at the far end of the property, heading toward the truck Austin had hidden off the roadway. The deeper they went, the thicker the night felt around them—dense, almost hushed. Crickets had gone silent, as if the land itself held its breath.

"It's because I love Josef," Austin said, stopping at the creek. She stepped deliberately into the open bank, boots on damp stone, shoulders easing with the space around her. "You are a link holding us all together. Without you, we'd break. Look at the moon shining off the water. Man, that is so pretty."

Golem stopped with her, staring down at the white ripples. The water sounded quieter than usual, muffled, like someone had thrown a blanket over the night.

He felt her hand slip into his—small, warm. She leaned lightly against him, her shoulder brushing his wrist.

"When I first met Brandon, he brought me here, where they put in the little pond. They call it Turtle Creek." She pointed across the gently running water. It was wide—wide enough to make a child pause—but shallow. "There's a spring and a little waterfall over that rise. We took off our shoes and went wading. You know... when I used to see him, I'd take a running jump straight into his arms. He'd always laugh."

"I know. You told us that before."

"Yeah. I suppose I did." She exhaled, slowly. "Feels like a thousand years have passed, even if it's only been three." Somewhere not far away, there was the sound of a waterfall.

Golem's skin prickled. Not from emotion—something else. A pressure in the air. The kind that made his instincts twitch. Every time the wind shifted, he caught a faint sour musk. Not cattle. Not creek. Something older. Something watching.

Then he saw something shiny at the water's edge. He knelt slowly, dragging Austin down beside him.

A sheetlike material lay half-buried—clear, ridged, and long. Much too long. "What you got?" Austin asked, watching him lift it. Only a small section came free; the rest stretched out like a flattened tube disappearing into the mud.

"I don't know. It looks like plastic."

Austin leaned in, running her forefinger and thumb over the texture. Then she snatched the piece from his grip.

"This—this looks—this looks like snakeskin."

She yanked gently and followed the length of it, peeling it inch by inch from the riverbank. It just kept going. And going. Four minutes of walking, tugging, lifting the ridged, translucent sheath from the mud.

Golem smelled it now too—musky, sharp, reptilian.

Austin didn't speak. She just crouched, holding the massive skin in both hands. The instant her fingers brushed it fully, she jolted— a tremor racing up her wrists as if the skin remembered whatever had once lived inside it.

She covered her mouth with both palms, eyes wide, unblinking. For a moment, even the open air failed her—her chest tightened, vision narrowing as she fought to anchor herself.

Golem had never seen Austin speechless.

"Are you okay, Pet?" he asked softly.

She didn't answer. She only stared at the skin, rolling it in her hands, examining the vast ridges and thick, translucent plates glowing under the moon.

Then—far off in the trees—a branch cracked.

Not loud. But deliberate.

Austin stiffened.

"We've got to go." She sprang to her feet. "We've got to get the hell out of here. This is snakeskin. Huge snakeskin. Like the kind my papaw used to talk about. The Uktena—the legendary snake with giant wings and great horns."

Golem stared at the long, pale coil in her hands.

"And whatever shed this didn't go far," she said. "Papaw said the Uktena slept beneath deep water. This one wasn't sleeping."

Chapter −46

"To have a skin membrane this enormous, a snake would have to be extremely large—" Stats stopped mid-sentence. He lifted the shimmering length of snakeskin high enough for everyone to see. The thing rippled like a translucent ghost under the kitchen light. "Pet... this isn't just big. This is *impossible*. Two feet wide and forty feet long. Minimum."

Stats refused to touch it with his bare hands. Instead, he pinched it delicately with the chewed end of a pencil, holding it as far from his body as possible. "Pet, snakes this size simply do not exist naturally in West Virginia. Or anywhere with a zip code."

"Okay, smartass." Austin leaned in, her voice low and worn thin. "If we toss out the odds and everything you say is 'impossible,' then what do we have left? Because right now I'm running on fumes and blind faith." Tessa was perched on Austin's hip in her pajamas, legs thumping rhythmically against Austin's thigh. "Baby, stop—that hurts," Austin muttered. Tessa giggled and wiggled a finger at her. Then she slowly slid it across her lips in a zip-it motion, her silent reminder that Austin had said a bad word.

"Alright, alright," Austin murmured before turning back to Stats. "Could it be something from the legends of Uktena? My great-great-grandfather swore he fought something like this. Dad always rolled his eyes." She pointed at the snakeskin, a long, iridescent strip that shimmered with an oily, rainbow sheen. "Tell me this is normal."

Stats breathed out slowly, expression shifting from curiosity to genuine unease. "Even Medusa—the largest recorded python—is twenty-five feet. This is nearly twice that. And thicker. And older." Stats let the skin slip from his pencil, the sound brittle and dry against the table. "But things go undiscovered. New species are found every day. What I thought was impossible five years ago doesn't seem so implausible now. Take Aina, for example. She now has two tiny feather buds on her scapulae—her shoulder blades.

In Irish lore, fairies had wings. When the Christian monks came to Ireland, they tried to erase Celtic beliefs, casting fairies as deities left behind on earth."

Austin looked toward the couch. Aina had frozen mid-episode, remote in her hand. Her cheeks flushed dark red. "You do?" Austin asked. "You've got feathers?"

Aina tugged her sweater across her shoulders, trying—and failing—to hide the faint swell beneath the fabric. "Stats, seriously, you promised you'd keep it secret. It's just a little feather bud. It doesn't mean anything." But her tone betrayed her uncertainty.

"She's a fairy," Tessa announced. "Like in my book."

Austin huffed quietly. "Yeah. She is." Then she turned back to Stats. "So... are you saying my papaw's snake stories could be true?"

"My point is, something this size shed this." Stats tapped the serpent skin lightly with the pencil. "There are things out there we don't know about. Odds are, it's a huge snake—house-sized."

Austin pinched the bridge of her nose. "Stats, I need you to do some checking for me." She watched him immediately grab paper and pencil, rocking with excitement as she listed tasks. "Get me a list of all the places Abel Martin has visited since we put the tracker on his vehicle. Then pull land assessments—old maps, anything with springs recorded—on Crazy Jack's property, Brandon's property, and Abel's. And go four miles out from there. I want to know if there's any significant water source we don't know about. Then, do a satellite sweep."

Stats paused mid-scribble. "For what?"

"Huge bird nests."

Aina looked up sharply. "Huge *bird nests*?"

"The Tlanuhwa," Austin said quietly. "The great birds in my papaw's stories—giant, fierce, the only creatures that could stand against the Uktena." A stillness settled over the room. "If the serpent's here, then the bird might be too." She paused, breathless, for a moment. "Papaw said these supernatural spirits fought each other—battling while people tried to survive between them."

Tessa screeched a bird call without warning, making everyone jump. Aina scowled. "I thought we were leaving. I'm tired of waiting. Everything here feels... heavy."

Austin's eyes narrowed. "I planned on leaving three days ago. But then you dragged back an anchor—Brandon Tremaine. If we let him go, he'll run straight to Abel Martin. Then Abel destroys Crazy Jack's property, and God knows what he'll do to Jack." She shook her head. "I'm stuck between choices that hurt either way."

"It's not like we've got money to do anything fun anymore," Aina muttered.

"Maybe if you all did a little work once in a while, got a job, you wouldn't be so bored."

"When I went with you, you promised I wouldn't have to work."

"No," Austin snapped. "Paolo promised you that. The same Paolo who controlled every breath you took. Maybe stop treating him like a missing vacation wallet. And me with some respect."

Aina's jaw tightened. "Well, I *wish* he were here."

Austin opened her mouth, ready to fire back, but the door creaked open. Starr stepped inside, her expression shadowed. "He's asking for you again. I think he's ready."

Tessa bolted upright. "Can I see Daddy now? Please? Please?"

Austin glanced at Starr. Starr nodded. "I think the worst is over."

Four and a half days of dragging Brandon to the bathroom, of watching him crawl there when he couldn't stand, listening to him cry for his daughter—Starr said some people were too pure, so the darkness clung harder. Brandon was one of them. Austin had seen it herself this morning—no trace of blackness on him at all.

Austin turned back to Stats. "One last thing. Check for disappearances—kids, teens, anyone. Ohio, West Virginia, and Tennessee. If the legends are waking up, we need to know."

Stats wrote faster, eyes bright with purpose. Austin held Tessa a little tighter, her stomach dropping like a stone. The monsters weren't just stories anymore. They were waking up.

Chapter −47

Brandon paced the room like a first-time dad on hour forty-eight—jittery and hollow-eyed. When he shot up from the chair too fast, Austin flinched before she could stop herself, a ghost-reaction from the last forty hours of blows, dodges, and shouted threats. But the old heaviness—the oppressive, Abel-Martin-type pressure that clung to him—was gone. Lifted. Dissolved like fog burning off under a rising sun. For the first time in days, she could breathe.

Starr had untied him before Tessa came in. He'd jumped to his feet so quickly Austin nearly jumped too, but when he saw her wide eyes, he backed up and sat down again, hands shaking. He'd asked what Tessa had said—what had happened. Austin didn't spare him the truth. She told him what they'd pieced together from Tessa's mealtime chatter and playtime whispers.

Kim had cared for Tessa because Brandon hadn't picked her up. The longer she waited, the angrier Kim became—pinching her, shoving her, calling her ugly. Soon, other kids had joined in. At the picnic, Kim brought Tessa along. Lyndsey wouldn't speak to her, telling someone she'd be better off without "that stupid kid." A fight broke out. After that, everyone scattered. Tessa wandered off, alone, toward town.

Austin set Tessa down gently. The little girl twisted back toward her, wiggling her small fingers in a silent plea. Austin nodded, took her hand, and together they moved forward.

"Is it Daddy?" Tessa whispered. Austin gave one small nod.

Tessa pushed her glasses up the bridge of her nose and crept toward Brandon, slow and cautious, stopping just outside his reach. Her eyes searched him—left, right, deep, as if trying to see past his face and into the man behind it. "Daddy?" she breathed. "Is it you?"

Brandon's voice cracked. "Yes," he whispered. "It's Daddy."

The relief in Tessa's tiny body surged so suddenly it nearly knocked Austin off balance. She released the girl's fingers and watched her run into his arms.

Brandon tried to stand but couldn't—too weak, down three pounds from his already-lanky frame, trembling with the effort of holding his own child.

Austin dropped into the battered old chair she'd befriended over the past four days. The cracked vinyl dug into the backs of her legs—warm, sticky, familiar. She curled her toes around the frayed edge to ground herself, refusing to let Brandon see any flicker of fear. Caution still gnawed at her; after what she'd endured, it would've been stupid not to be wary. But he didn't turn violent.

He sat quietly with Tessa tucked against him, voice soft, hands gentle, posture trembling with something like remorse. He listened. He whispered back. The tenderness replaced the edgy chaos she'd been wrestling with for days. Eighty hours. Maybe more. She'd stopped counting somewhere after the tenth vomit-run.

An hour passed. The shadows in the corners dragged long and thin, stretching the room into something somber and tired. Austin pushed off her knees to stand.

"I should get her to bed."

Brandon didn't argue. He only looked up, eyes hollowed by exhaustion and something deeper—fear, guilt, hope tangled so tightly she couldn't separate them. He held Tessa as if she were the last warm thing in the world.

Austin's throat tightened. "How about you two go lie down? I'll feel like hell all night if I rip her away now."

"Okay."

"I can't leave," she added, chewing her thumbnail—a habit she thought she'd killed years ago. "If you're feeling safe enough to—"

"Yes," he said softly.

He kept staring, and she tried to let his haunted expression roll off her back. It half worked. Brandon lay Tessa on the bed, slid in on top of the covers, jeans still on, eyelids heavy but alert.

"I know you didn't want to do this—get me out of there." His voice was thin, scraped raw. "Aina told me. Thanks for... not dumping me on the side of the road somewhere."

Austin tossed her legs up on the end table, leaning back. "Honestly, it's not that I didn't want to help you. I just didn't think it was safe. Not for anyone. Especially Jack and his family. You made your choice—I walked away." She exhaled hard. "And no, it won't be easy. But if you want Lyndsey out, I can get her out. Kicking, screaming—"

"She can rot in there with her family." Brandon's lip curled, bitterness carving harsh lines across his face. "I don't *want* her out," he said. "Austin, I've been walking in a fog for well over three years. This is the first time my head's felt clear."

Austin nodded slowly. She'd expected that.

"I thought you might be worried about her," she murmured.

He shifted, tucking Tessa closer under his arm. "I'm just worried you hate me. That you'll look at me like I'm some idiot who didn't see it coming—or a monster for letting it happen." His voice cracked on monster, and something in Austin's chest tugged hard—like a bruise pressed by accident.

"Well," she sighed, "A senator called me a monster collector. Maybe he's right." Her eyes drooped. "I'll add you to my collection."

Brandon huffed a soft, broken laugh. "I've got no gifts like everybody else. I'd just be the dumb guy standing without a cape when you all step forward."

"A cape," she scoffed. "Stats would have a spreadsheet cape. Mine would be made of Band-Aids and tetanus shots."

He snorted—almost a real laugh. The sound eased something inside her. "I feel like I went through hell," he said. "No glory at the end."

"Maybe, maybe not." Austin's voice softened. "Everybody feels safe with you—well, before you started drowning in that cult. I feel safe with you. You think you're not important because you can't throw people through walls? Brandon, you're the anchor. You're the one who keeps the rest of us from drifting straight into the storm.

"How can you say that?" Brandon whispered, horrified. "How many times did I hit you? I've never hit anyone."

"You're lying, or you've got a crap memory."

"I'm not lying."

"You punched Bradley Martin so hard he puked on you in high school. That was when he tried to shove his brother's underwear in my mouth while I was duct-taped to the wall."

"Oh... yeah," he muttered, embarrassed.

"Oh, yeah," she echoed with a thin laugh. "To you, it's nothing. But to an ugly little girl who got bullied, it was everything."

"You're not ugly," he said. "You were never ugly."

Austin rubbed her lower back; every joint ached from the damn chair. "I can't spend another night sitting here. If I come to sleep on the bed, are you gonna murder me in my sleep?"

"Nope."

Her knees cracked as she stood, pain shooting down her shins. Exhaustion drowned out every lingering instinct. She sat on the bed, then slowly rolled onto her side until her head rested on the warmth of his back—steady, rhythmic, grounding. She hated how good that felt. "Does that bother you?" she murmured.

"No." He shifted, rolled to his back. Tessa was still curled on one arm. He lifted his other hand, fingers wiggling for her to take it.

Austin hesitated. Then she closed her eyes and slipped into his arms, resting her head on his chest. His warmth soaked into her cheek, calming her more than it should have. "I'll deny this if you ever mention it," she whispered. "But it feels like I've waited my whole life to lie next to you. And damn it, I'm just gonna fall asleep."

"We could make a habit of it," he said quietly. "Wouldn't bother me."

A twist of old ache unfurled inside her. Funny—Brandon and Marco were opposites in every way that mattered. Yet they both wanted the same thing: a perfect wife to show off, plus someone like her on the side. And maybe she'd let herself fall into that pattern too many times.

"I'm not built to be second choice," she murmured, yawning. "Been there. Done that. Hard on the ego."

"Hit and run," he said softly.

"Pretty much."

Outside, a lone dog barked—brief and frantic. Austin's eyes flickered open, instincts twitching beneath her exhaustion.

Sleep wouldn't come easily. Not here. Not tonight.

But for the moment, she stayed.

Chapter −48

At twenty-three past four in the morning, Austin surfaced from sleep to the thin glow of a streetlamp bleeding through the curtains, casting pale bars across the bedspread. The room smelled faintly of wet fur and cold night air—odd, out of place. She vaguely remembered the door easing open earlier, the mattress dipping as someone—or something—had climbed onto it. Half awake, she'd drifted sideways toward Brandon's warmth.

Brandon's sudden sneeze—sharp, startled—snapped her fully awake.

Then came the sound that froze her blood: A hiss. Loud. Then a low, guttural growl vibrated through the mattress, up her ribs, into her bones.

Austin's eyes flew open.

She didn't turn her head all at once—just a small tilt, enough to glimpse the shadow pressed against her side. Her breath hitched. Something huge and furry lay draped halfway over her torso, its weight pinning her down, making the room's narrow walls feel even closer.

"Oh... shit," Brandon whispered beside her. He was trying not to sneeze again—holding it in like his life depended on it.

Austin exhaled slowly through her nose. "Brandon, be still. It's okay." She wasn't sure it was okay. But panic would get them mauled.

"You see what I see?" he muttered, barely audible.

"I do."

A massive black panther sprawled across her, yellow eyes glinting with eerie intelligence as it stared straight into hers. Its whiskers quivered. Its breath washed hot across her cheek. A single enormous paw rested on her stomach, claws half-unsheathed, gleaming faintly in the dark.

When the panther opened its jaws, Austin braced for teeth at her throat.

Instead...it yawned.

A wide, lazy, bone-deep yawn that showed every inch of river-wet fang before the beast lowered its head again and pressed its muzzle into the crook of her neck. Its whiskers tickled. Its warm breath puffed against her skin.

Then came the tongue. A long, sandpaper scrape from her jawline to the crown of her head.

Austin clenched her teeth, every muscle tightening. Comforting or not, a six-foot murder-cat grooming her was a different category of nightmare.

The panther flopped onto its back, belly exposed, tail thumping once against the bedframe. A purr erupted—deep, metallic, rattling her ribs like a power tool gone wrong.

Somewhere in the blankets, Tessa stirred and whispered drowsily, "Daddy... what's that?"

Austin's stomach plummeted.

"Be quiet, baby," Brandon murmured, voice shaking as he tucked her closer.

Austin gently peeled the panther's massive paw off her ribs and pushed it aside. "River?" she whispered.

The panther's ears perked. He blinked slowly—River's tell. Then he shoved his enormous head into her shoulder like a toddler demanding comfort.

"Yeah," she whispered, heart pounding. "Okay, buddy. We're going for a walk. Up."

She shoved at him again, firmer this time, but still gentle. The panther let out a half-grumble, half-chuff, then finally rolled to his feet, tail curling like an oversized question mark as he stepped off the mattress with unexpected grace.

Austin exhaled shakily. "Jesus, River. Next time, give me a warning."

The panther only flicked an ear, unimpressed.

And somewhere deep inside, Austin was certain of one thing:

He'd done this before.

Chapter −49

"I'm going home," Brandon announced two days later, his fork scraping against the chipped plate as he ate cold eggs at the cramped breakfast table in the trailer's tiny kitchen. The air was thick with the smells of old coffee and burnt toast. He looked up, catching Austin's attention through the blur of bodies—everyone reaching, the scrape of chairs, voices clashing and echoing off the thin walls. Roo and River squabbled over a fork, their movements sharp and restless. Golem and Aina laughed at something on the crackling radio by the sink. "I have to feed my cattle. I have to protect my land."

He expected Austin to argue. He knew he wasn't safe going back, but longing for home clung to him like sweat. Maybe Abel would leave him alone. Maybe Lyndsey would turn up, and he could end things for good. Maybe she already knew. "I've just got to go home."

Austin just nodded. "Figured you'd go back. We need to move on, too."

He didn't ask her to come. She didn't ask him to stay. They simply locked eyes for twenty or thirty seconds—quiet recognition, nothing else.

"Is it my fault?" River snapped the fork from Roo and shot Brandon a look—hurt, almost apologetic. "Sorry. It used to take me months. I just got comfortable." He looked at Austin with open adoration, which made Starr's lips tighten.

Brandon shook his head, sneezed into his wrist. After waking up to a black panther the size of the bed staring at him the other night, he should have known something was up when his eyes started getting red. He was allergic to cats. "No, buddy, you're fine."

Hutch grunted. "Yeah, until he coughs up a giant hairball."

Austin waved him off. "Once we settle, I'll visit Tessa on weekends. That'd give you a break?"

Brandon nodded, a pit forming in his stomach already. "Where do you think you'll go?"

"I figured New York. Somewhere we might fit in with the crowd. Where there are jobs."

Brandon realized he was making small talk with the only woman he had ever actually loved. It sucked that she didn't feel the same about him. *Hit and run.*

"Paolo is alive." Everyone froze. Stats stood at the end of the table holding up his laptop, his face pale behind the screen's glow. "He's alive," he repeated, deadpan.

"What?" Starr shot up from her chair so quickly that it rocked. She grabbed the laptop and pulled it close. She skimmed, then Aina leaned over her shoulder. "Read it out loud," she demanded.

Starr cleared her throat. "The title reads: *Eccentric Billionaire Paolo Bertinelli Found Alive.* Italian businessman Paolo Bertinelli, thought to have been killed in an attack by terrorists off a South American coast, has been found alive and well. His luxury yacht had left Chile and was heading northward, carrying his crew and business associates. It vanished and was later found adrift. Bertinelli said he extends his thanks to local fishermen for finding him floating in a small boat—"

The room erupted into chatter—overlapping voices, disbelief, excitement. The room seemed to shrink around them.

Only River sat still, watching with feline stillness, shoulders hunched like he was preparing for impact.

Austin sat frozen. Her knuckles whitened around her plate. Her face drained of color—almost as pale as the peeling wallpaper behind her.

She stood abruptly, her chair scraping the linoleum. She pressed her napkin to her mouth—her hand trembling—and brushed past Golem as she slipped out the door.

Starr hesitated at the threshold, shocked joy still half-lit in her chest. But concern clouded it. She followed Austin, the screen door banging shut behind her.

"And you're happy?" Austin said on the porch. "After all he did?"

"Not all the time," Starr murmured.

"So that's better than this?" Austin swept her arms toward the yard, the house, the world. "Being free? You liked being his pet?"

"That's not fair."

"No, what's not fair," Austin said, voice cracking, "is watching you all fall right back into his orbit like gravity pulls you."

Starr reached instinctively for River when she turned back inside—habit, seeking comfort. But River pulled back an inch, subtle but unmistakable, Hutch's stare heavy on him from across the room. Austin had already vanished into the yard.

Brandon watched her through the screen, Tessa adjusting her glasses as she tracked Austin's path with wide concern. Something in his child's expression twisted inside him.

Hutch, meanwhile, didn't look surprised at all. He sat tapping on his phone, eyes flicking up only long enough to assess everyone's reactions. Brandon saw the calculation there—quiet, unsettling.

He followed Hutch's gaze. Roo stared toward the door where Austin had disappeared, jaw tight. Hutch lifted a hand, palm out.

"Leave her alone," Hutch said quietly.

Roo paused—actually paused—and then eased back into his seat, throat bobbing as he swallowed something hard.

Brandon scanned the others. Aina hugged Starr. Stats scratched his arm like a nervous tic, eyes darting between Hutch and the laptop. River forced a careful smile for Starr but kept Hutch in the corner of his sight.

Something was wrong. Something was shifting under the floorboards of the group.

Tessa tugged at Brandon's shirt. "I wanna go with Austin."

"Yeah. Let's see if she wants company." He lifted her as gently as his shaking muscles allowed.

He reached the porch just as Hutch cornered Austin on the steps.

"My dad's paying for the hotel. Well—actually, it's a resort," Hutch said, thumbs flicking across his phone. "He texted me. Said he missed you. Thought you might want to land somewhere real. Where you could get your nails done. He said he liked the red ones."

Austin stared at him. "Get my nails done?"

"It was a figure of speech. You know—spa stuff. Nice place to stay. He said he'd help us out. Maybe even get a plane."

"He doesn't need to," Austin murmured. "I want you to go to a real high school. That's what you want, right?"

"I'm not in a huge hurry."

"You're not?"

"I mean—it's summer. School doesn't start until September, right?"

"End of August," she said softly. A reluctant smile tugged at her mouth. "Okay, let's pack. Getting my nails done sounds... nice."

Her voice sounded fragile, stretched thin by exhaustion and worry. Brandon saw how slowly she moved—how her shoulders curled protectively inward. He stepped out, the sun glaring off the worn decking. Austin blinked up at him, brushing sweaty hair from her forehead. She gave him a small, brittle smile and bounced Tessa lightly in her arms.

"Looks like we're headed out sooner than I thought," she said quietly. "Who would have thought Paolo was alive?"

"Maybe Hutch did," Brandon said.

Austin's head snapped up. "You caught that too?"

Brandon nodded.

"I saw the date on the article," Austin whispered. "They found Paolo five days ago. The news just hit here."

"You think Hutch has known that long?"

"I think Paolo trained him damn well," Austin murmured. "Better at mind games than Abel Martin, Five."

Her hands shook on Tessa's back. Her breathing hitched. She glanced at the doorway where Hutch's shadow lingered. "I never thought they'd go back to Paolo," she whispered. "But maybe they were always going to. Maybe I'm the one who didn't see it. Every night, they talked about what they'd do if they weren't in his luxury prison. Now they're free, and it scares me."

She hugged Tessa tighter. "For all I know, they're all in on it. I'd drive them back to Paolo myself, just to know the truth. I don't get why Hutch is playing this game. Who the hell do I trust?"

"You can trust me," Brandon said softly.

Austin didn't look at him. She stepped back instead, eyes dropping to Tessa. Starr slipped through the door behind them.

"What's the game plan?" Starr asked.

"I guess we pack," Austin said. "Hutch's dad got us a resort for the week. We can give everyone space. Then talk about Paolo."

"What do you mean?"

"If you want to go back."

Starr brightened instantly. "You wouldn't care if we did? Because oh my God, I would do anything to have my hair done—my toes done—"

"Satin sheets?" Austin finished for her.

Starr nodded eagerly.

Austin's tone cooled. "You're free to choose. But don't pretend Paolo won't notice you're sleeping with River now. He'll punish someone for it. Probably not you."

"Paolo doesn't care who I sleep with," Starr grunted.

Austin stared at her—cold, certain. "Then say no to him. Just once. Tell him no."

Starr's mouth opened, but no words came.

"Because here's the thing," Austin said quietly. "I'm not worried about you. I'm worried about River. He trusts you. And he'll follow you straight back into Paolo's hands. And Paolo will hurt him, Starr. I've seen him do worse for less."

She wasn't yelling. She wasn't angry. She was scared. And everyone on that porch felt it.

Chapter −50

When Hutch was thirteen, he used to pull blankets over his head to hide the blue glow of his cell phone so he could play games past midnight. No one ever checked on him back then. No one tucked him in. No one made sure he slept. That kind of absence taught Hutch something dangerous:

Control came from secrecy.

Power came from knowing things no one else saw.

Austin didn't realize any of that when he first came to her. She thought the grumbling and eye rolls meant she was simply annoying him. Then, one night, she leaned in, as she always did, and told him it was bedtime. Ten seconds of lingering told her something was off.

She heard the faint chirp of digital music under the pillow. She crossed the room, pulled the covers back, and exposed Hutch's eyes, defiant, phone clutched tight.

Even then, he wasn't embarrassed. Just calculating.

That same calculation flickered now, years later, when the mention of her fingernails gave him away. He'd said Paolo liked the red polish on her nails. But Austin's nails were nothing but chewed-down nubs—raw from a lifetime of clawing panic in too-small closets.

Marco was the only man who'd ever commented on her fingernails, joking that he was glad they weren't long when she dragged them down his back. And Stats... he noticed things. He'd been rubbing the bear tattoo on his left arm hard—his anxiety tell—ever since Paolo's photo flashed onto the laptop. Stats caught her eye, a silent warning. Roo made a low growl.

Only Marco, Stats, and Roo had ever truly had her back.

And they each knew something here did not align.

Marco had always been fluent in English, too—a fact Austin and only a handful of Paolo's closest ever knew. Hutch had no idea. Hutch never knew anything except what Paolo fed him.

Austin stepped into Candy's Taste of Sunshine Spa and Resort just inside the Virginia border at nine that night. The lobby lights were dim, curtains drawn tight. The air smelled like lavender oil and bleach. Paolo sat on a leather recliner, legs crossed casually, sunglasses on even in the dark. "Oh, surprise, surprise," he said, spreading his arms. "Look who it is! My pet. I missed you. I missed you so bad." He dragged out the last syllable, rolling it like something obscene.

Paolo was a thin-faced man with puffy lips, who pressed them together when he talked, like he was holding back a smirk. His eyes sat just slightly too far apart, giving him a watchful look—predatory only because of the calculation behind it, not because of any animal instinct. Every feature of him felt deliberate, curated, as if he'd practiced appearing harmless in the mirror until he got it right. He looked ordinary—blue jeans, a pale T-shirt, olive skin. Ten pounds lighter. Hair longer, moppier. He looked calm, but he was a storm wearing a human face.

Then he giggled behind his hand, tilting his head. "Nobody told you I'd be meeting you here? Funny thing, it was a surprise! They said you didn't want to come back to Paolo. You said Paolo was mean." His lip twitched. A thin smile cracked—too bright, too sharp. "I thought I wouldn't get my little darlings back."

He wiggled his fingers at Aina and Starr. They rushed to him at once, each grabbing a hand—like two frightened kids who'd finally spotted the parent they lost in a crowded store. He turned the wiggle toward River.

"And here's a new one. Look at you. You're *cute!*"

River froze, shoulders tight. His eyes flicked to Austin—wide, pleading. A low tremor ran through him, fur rising beneath human skin like something struggling not to burst free.

"Hutch," Paolo said lightly. "Bring that pretty thing to me."

Hutch nodded and strode toward River with slow, practiced confidence. "Come on," he said, voice unnaturally low, unnaturally steady. "Do what he says. Now."

River's spine locked. For a moment, he didn't budge an inch.

He only looked at Austin—her face drained, breath trapped in her chest.

Then Hutch's command hit him like a blow. River's pupils dilated. His nostrils flared. His hands shook as he took ten reluctant steps forward. Austin's stomach dropped. Hutch's influence was growing—some new line of loyalty Paolo had sown was taking root.

"Well, come here, little man," Paolo crooned. "Little Man. That's my name for you." He rubbed River's cheek like petting an animal. "What little curiosity are you? Let me guess. You're—"

"Paolo." Austin stepped forward, voice steadying. "His name is River. He's just eighteen years old. He's not yours to keep."

"Not mine?" Paolo's smile collapsed. The blanket slid from his shoulders to the couch. "Not mine? He's your little treasure now?"

He rose, peeled off his sunglasses, and walked straight to her.

"Well, sweetie, I figured he was a gift. You know...an offering. A little apology." His voice softened to a whisper. "Bitch."

The room tilted. Austin's stomach seized, lungs locking. The taste of copper filled her mouth. A phantom pressure pressed in on her ribs—the box, the airless dark. Paolo's hand settled on her shoulder like a spider claiming its web.

"You left me there to die," Paolo murmured, eyes narrowing in satisfaction as her body trembled. "Did anyone else know that? No? I didn't think so."

He looked up, checking the faces around him. Starr's smile faltered. Aina blinked rapidly, mirroring her. Roo stiffened. Stats's jaw clenched. River took a slow step back, shaking. Golem's eyebrows knitted, confusion growing.

Paolo inhaled thoughtfully. "No one knew you made it back to my room, did they? You got everyone to the boats. And then you came back for... something. What was it?"

He leaned in until his breath coated her neck. "WAS YOUR GODDAMN PURSE MORE IMPORTANT THAN PAOLO?"

Austin flinched, heart, crashing against her ribs.

"That's not true," Starr breathed. "Austin wouldn't do that."

"Tell them, Hutch," Paolo said. "Tell them exactly what our little Pet did."

Hutch rocked on his heels, hands in pockets, avoiding Austin's eyes like she was already discarded. "Paolo, it doesn't matter. I got them here. They're yours again."

"What was our little deal?" Paolo asked sweetly. "Go on. Tell them."

Hutch sighed. "Austin was working out when the rebels boarded—"

"Rebels?" Stats frowned. "I thought they were pirates."

"No," Hutch said. "A militant group. My father said they wanted Paolo for ransom. I heard the gunshots. I saw them beating Paolo. I tried to help. I threw punches. Then Austin came in. The lights went out. When they came on, she was over me. Paolo was unconscious. She dragged me to the lifeboat. She took me instead."

Paolo arched a brow. "You're forgetting something."

Hutch swallowed. He didn't want to say it. Which made what came next worse.

"She could have saved him," Hutch whispered. "There were only three left in the room. None of them had guns."

Stats' eyes widened, analytical gears spinning fast.

Golem's mouth dropped open.

Starr froze, uncertain.

Aina mirrored her stillness.

River shook—whole body trembling.

Roo took one step toward Austin, claws sliding from his fingertips—until Hutch shot him a look that made him stop, chest heaving. Austin saw it then. The shift. The line Hutch had crossed. He wasn't pleading for Paolo. He wasn't confused. He was performing. For approval. For power. And Paolo knew it.

Paolo beamed. "Good boy. We'll buy you a boat or a whore tonight. Or both."

Hutch managed a hesitant grin, still rocking on his heels.

"That said," Paolo continued, lifting his hands theatrically, "we're a family—a pack. And if one wolf turns rogue? The others tear it to pieces."

He pointed to Austin. "Hutch, you're the leader now. Do your job."

Hutch blinked. "You mean... throw her out?"

"You said you couldn't wait to get rid of her," Paolo reminded softly. "Don't let me down. Dog fight!"

Austin didn't expect the shove. Hutch walked up, pushed her back with one hand, like testing the weight of dominance.

"No fighting," Golem warned.

"Stay back," Austin ordered. She prayed none of them would move.

"You gonna fight?" Hutch taunted, lips stretching in a too-wide grin.

"No."

Hutch raised his fist and grazed her cheek. "Boom."

His other hand drifted toward her stomach, stopping just short. "Boom."

"You don't want to do this," she said. Breath shaking. "You're not using your brain."

His fist came fast. Then another. Hutch was quick, ruthless, and unpredictable. Austin blocked, absorbed, deflected. She refused to strike him. Not Hutch. Her forearms burned from the hits she caught. Two gut punches drove the breath from her. He flipped her hard into the wall. Her skull rang.

The floor rushed up. Pressure on her ribs—...no air......dark......the BOX...

Stale breath. Wooden walls. The tiny scraping of her own panic.

"You don't want to do this," she gasped, holding up a trembling hand. "I can't fight you. You're like my little brother."

"But you could leave Paolo to die," Hutch said, laughing. "That's why you went back. Just so you could get home, right?"

Paolo pumped his fist. "Do it! Do it! Do it!"

Hutch raised his hand and slammed it down on her head. A burst of white exploded behind her eyes.

Hutch's boot connected with her ribs. Pain flared sharp and electric.

For one terrifying heartbeat, Austin knew—if Paolo ordered it...Hutch would kill her. She had nothing left but one weapon.

Guilt.

"Te amo, hermanito," she whispered—*I love you, little brother*. The words fluttered out of her like the last light slipping from a candle. "Adiós, mi amigo... until we meet in heaven."

Chapter −51

"How do you say I love you in Spanish?"

Hutch recalled rolling his eyes when Austin asked him that question two months earlier. He recognized immediately why she asked—her motive was clear, since she was sleeping with his dad behind his mother's back. Knowing this, something hot and sour surged in his throat.

"You really don't know this?" he'd snapped. "Figures. You don't think anything's important unless it benefits you. But I'm not telling you—because you'll say it to my father. And then what? He'll leave my mom for the whore."

The word struck hard. He watched her flinch.

"Then you'll be my mom—*the whore*," he added, every word bitter. "Who wants that? Just say adiós, mi amigo. That means 'goodbye, friend.'"

Austin tipped her head, hurt flickering across her face before she masked it. That look always grated on him—soft guilt, the same expression his old nanny used to shame him into behaving.

"It wasn't for your dad," Austin said softly. "It was for you. You're like a little brother to me. If I had one, I'd want a way to tell him I loved him." Her voice grew gentle. "But if you think so little of me... maybe it doesn't matter. I'll figure it out."

~

"Te amo, hermanito," she whispered now—I love you, little brother—the words fluttering out of her like the last light slipping from a candle. "Adiós, mi amigo... until we meet in heaven."

Austin sprawled on the floor. Above her, Hutch loomed, his breath coming in sharp, ragged bursts as he hovered. His shoulders trembled with the thrill of being watched—being followed. Paolo's stare drilled into him, burning like a hot wire.

Hutch clenched his fist and slammed it down on Austin. Again. Again. The blows came sloppy and jagged, all adrenaline and something darker. He wasn't strong—just fast and self-absorbed.

He was young enough not to know there must be a reason to fight and inexperienced enough not to know when to draw the line. He felt power like he had never felt before, raw and unhinged. Unthinking. He wanted to show off his strength to all who would see it. Fear him.

"Done." Hutch rose, chest heaving, and nudged her limp shoulder with his boot. Pride surged hot through him. But something deep in the pocket of his soul screamed fear and sadness.

Why hadn't she fought back?

He swallowed the thought hard. *Because she's weak,* he told himself. *That's why.*

But the lie sat wrong in his gut, heavy and sharp.

With that new, intoxicating power came a weight he didn't expect—an awareness scratching at the edges of his chest, whispering that he had crossed a line he wasn't ready for.

Why hadn't she fought back? Because it wasn't weakness.

He pushed the truth down fast. Now wasn't the moment—not with everyone staring at him, wide-eyed, waiting. Her body rocked loosely when he nudged her again. "What do you want me to do with her?" Everyone froze.

Roo lunged first toward Hutch, claws unsheathing and pupils narrowing with fear. His chest heaved as he tried to decide whether to follow instinct or stay obedient. Hutch met Roo's attack by swinging his fist into Roo's jaw, then stomping Roo flat on the floor. Roo whimpered, curled tightly, and quivered, caught in indecision over who to obey, weight shifting side to side, the way a nervous dog circles before choosing a command. His breathing hitched—fast, shallow, like he was fighting the urge to bolt.

"I said listen when I speak," Hutch snapped. "Same as before. Same rules. I'm alpha. It's that easy."

Golem let out a guttural scream—raw, piercing, breaking open the room's silence. But he stood still, unmoving.

River shot forward, running in a blur. He reached Hutch but then halted, his body going completely still, frozen, and rigid.

He was like prey caught just before running. River locked up completely, every muscle going still in that predatory way—quiet, calculating, like a panther deciding whether to spring or vanish.

Hutch grabbed him by the shirt and slammed him against the wall. River sprang back to his feet, breath hitching, eyes flicking toward Roo as if waiting for someone else to make the next move. Starr darted in, reached out, and steadied River with shaky hands.

"Anybody else?" Hutch called out. "Roo? You want to go again?"

Roo shook his head violently, terrified. His nails scraped the floor but didn't rise. He couldn't look at Austin.

"Put her in the truck you drove in," Paolo said cheerfully. He produced a bottle of sanitizer, squeezed half into his palms, and rubbed briskly. "Take her body somewhere it can't be traced back. I can't believe you really killed her. I was joking," he added, letting out a giggle. "Let's get this ball rolling. Let's have a party."

Hutch exhaled, bracing for the next command—hungry for it. Paolo smirked, delighted.

"No, not you two," Paolo said, wagging a finger at River and Roo. "I've got different plans for you. I already called the pound—"

The lights flickered once. Twice. Everyone looked up.

And Austin was gone. Just... gone.

Paolo turned—for half a second—and she stood behind him, her hand poised on his shoulder.

"Oh, shit," Hutch breathed.

Paolo's mouth dropped. "You—*how*—"

"You might have used me as a punching bag once, Paolo," Austin said quietly, "but not anymore. And never my friends, my family."

Her fingers tightened. Paolo shrieked—high and shrill—and crumpled to his knees, arms flapping, legs kicking uselessly. "You look like a dying fish flopping on the beach," Austin hissed, her lips curling. "A helpless little, teeny-tiny, sickly fish about to be eaten by a gull." She paused, a sharp chuckle scraping up her throat, and spat on his head. Paolo whimpered and gagged. "By the way, I'm the gull. Flop, little fishy. Flop." She pinched his shoulder harder. "Do it."

Paolo instinctively writhed and wiggled, choking on fear.

"Hutch! Hutch! Save me!" he squealed, clawing at the floor. "Somebody help me!"

Nobody dared move.

Starr lifted a shaking hand, eyes darting between Austin and Hutch, but Austin snapped a glare at her.

"Stop, traitor," Austin said, voice shaking under the surface. "No... worse than a traitor. You're a Judas—someone who betrays the people who loved him for nothing but a handful of scraps."

Starr took in those words, and a thin, broken wail seeped out of her like rancid egg yolk escaping from a cracked shell.

"Don't you dare cry now—like you're just realizing the damage," Austin warned, turning toward Starr. The look on her face said she wasn't bluffing. She was done. Her expression held nothing but loathing, as if looking upon something filthy she wished she'd never touched. "You planned every bit of it. And what you've done, Starr? It can't be forgiven. It can't be undone. You can rot in hell now."

Then Austin's eyes swept the room. "I would suggest you all stay right where you are. Because in exactly two minutes, fourteen federal security agents will walk through that door. If this room stays clean, you walk out alive. If not... I won't be the only problem."

Starr froze. Tears streamed freely now, her entire body trembling. Paolo whimpered like a kicked dog.

Austin turned, crouching slightly. "Take your spoiled court with you," she murmured. "Except the ones I'm taking."

She straightened—Austin turned to Hutch, her voice low and steady as she stepped toward him. "Hutch, the reason you fight should never be for evil. Or for someone who uses you. You fight to protect. You fight for good." Her eyes hardened, all warmth gone. "But it's too late for that lesson now. You showed me who you are today. Your soul bends toward the darkest hand in the room, and you followed it without a second thought." She shook her head once—slow, decisive. "I would tell you to choose your allies more wisely next time, but men who betray easily never have true allies.

They are weak and only have the next master who snaps their fingers." She stepped back from him. "You're nothing but a cockroach. I hate cockroaches." Her voice didn't rise—it sank, cold and certain. "If I ever see you again, I'll step on you."

Austin slid one foot forward and ground it slowly across the floor, heel twisting as if crushing something fragile and crawling. "That's you," she murmured. "That's all you are now." Then she looked up at him—unblinking, merciless. "God, I'd do it right now," Austin whispered. "I'd end you without even feeling it." She leaned in, breath steady, voice like a blade. "But your father loves me so very, *very* much. I'm a saint to him." She straightened, heel still poised over the imaginary insect. "That's the only reason you're still alive." She stepped closer. "And here's one for the road—if you are fighting for Paolo, you are fighting in the name of evil. And I am no longer your ally... but your enemy."

She strode across the room and shoved him hard in the chest. Hutch collapsed to the floor in a tangled heap, unable to find his footing or get up. She leaned over him, one hand pressed firmly against his chest. Hutch's arms flailed as he tried to buck, but he couldn't move.

"Where is your strength, little hummingbird?" she hissed through gritted teeth. "Fly away, won't you?" But he couldn't rise— he just lay there, tears streaming down his cheeks.

When she finally released him, Hutch tried to push himself up, but his knee buckled. He caught himself on the dresser, fingers digging into the wood until his knuckles blanched. A tremor rippled through his hand—small, but not small enough. Aina saw it. River saw it. Roo saw it. Paolo definitely saw it. The truth pressed in sharp and sour: the fear wasn't from the fall. It was from the way she'd looked at him when she said those words. It was power seeping from her body, mind, and soul.

He curled his hand into a fist before anyone could notice, but Paolo always noticed. The power Hutch had soaked in minutes earlier drained out in a cold rush, leaving him hollow, scraped raw beneath the ribs. He tried to stand straighter, but his spine refused.

Tried to smirk, but his lips wouldn't shape it.

He felt twelve again—small, exposed, breakable. He shoved his hands into his pockets so no one would see them shake.

"Aina," Austin said, arms open in invitation, "I'll take your fairy on anytime. I know your weaknesses. They reek like rancid butter. Spoiled butter disperses quickly and leaves nothing behind." She leaned in. "But you don't know my power. Want to test me?"

Aina gagged, pale, vomiting on the carpet. No wings unfurled—only fear. "No."

"Good. Because I've wasted too much time on you and Starr already. You are dead to me. You're too much work and not nearly enough fun. I felt sorry for you, you know? Stupid, useless little bitches better off in the streets." Austin faced Hutch now, her voice hard as flint. "And you? You weren't ready. You've never had me fight you back before." Her smirk cut deep. "I'd smash you beneath the toe of my little size six shoe in two seconds."

She let the words settle.

"Eres un chiquito débil, Hutch." *You're a weak little boy.* "Nothing more."

Chapter –52

"Thanks, Marco," Austin said quietly. They stood near the black limousine, out of earshot of the agents. "Did you draw out shutting off the lights until he just about killed me?"

"It must have been lost in translation." Marco's grin was faint. He pointed at her cheek. "You should have a doctor look at that."

"I know."

He turned to go, but she nudged him lightly with her knuckle. Never too close—not with so many eyes tracking them.

"I just need a minute."

"Thirty seconds."

"Well, this is where I choose," Austin said, voice trembling. "I guess you knew it was coming. You're never going to marry me, right? Part of me hoped you'd say no, so I wouldn't have to face losing you. You've been there for me three years—sickness, health, and almost death-do-us-part. But you're married to her, and I'm tired of hoping for what won't happen. The tie we had was your son, and now that is severed. I love you—"

"I love you too."

"But I've got a chance to be with someone I love all the time," Austin said, "not just between flights and when your wife's in Italy."

Marco's gaze dropped. He couldn't meet her eyes. That told her everything.

"Maybe in another life," he said. Even he didn't sound convinced.

"In my world," Austin murmured, "we only get one."

Marco watched Austin walk away, her figure slipping under the parking lot lights until she blended into the dark. He didn't move. Didn't breathe. His advisor shifted beside him, impatient, but Marco lifted a single finger without looking away. "Un momento." The advisor fell silent. Only when Austin disappeared behind her truck door did Marco allow his shoulders to drop. The mask—polished, executive, unbreakable—slipped for just a breath.

He touched the spot on his knuckles where she'd nudged him. Then he looked at the ground, jaw tightening.

"Idiota," he whispered to himself. "You let the only woman who actually loved you walk away."

The limo door opened. He climbed inside and shut it behind him, the sound sharp as a coffin nail.

~

"Well, boys, it's just us," Austin muttered across the parking lot as she fumbled for her keys, hands quaking so badly she missed the ignition keyhole twice. Stats perched quietly up front, eyes tracking her shaking hands. Roo folded into himself, shoulders creeping toward his ears, a low whine slipping from his throat. His fingers curled like they were remembering claws he no longer had. River hovered near the shadows, throat clenching, eyes darting everywhere as if he expected Hutch to materialize.

"My God," Austin groaned. "I should've asked Marco for a car before I broke his kid."

Chapter −53

"Hey, Five."

Ten after three in the morning. Brandon nearly stumbled down the steps at the knock, heart drumming a frantic rhythm in his chest. The night smelled of diesel and dust from Abel Martin's trucks, the taste of adrenaline sharp on Brandon's tongue. The new knock wasn't loud—but it sliced through the hush like a blade, setting every nerve on edge. He peered out the upstairs window— only tangled tree shadows and empty dark. *Who knocks at this hour?*

"Austin?" Rifle in hand, he caught her eyes glancing to the weapon—a flash of calculation, not fear. A faint smear of dried blood streaked along her jaw, the copper tang ghosting the air between them. Her sleeve was stretched at the seam, fabric rough and sticky where someone had grabbed her hard. Sweat clung to her hairline, a cold sheen betraying how far past exhaustion she'd gone.

"I take it that's a no, we can't crash here tonight." Her voice scraped with exhaustion. She glanced back at the truck, posture wired and wary, as if bracing for another threat.

"No, I mean, yes, you can." He pushed open the door, watching as she signaled toward the truck—two sharp, quick flicks of her fingers. No one is visible in the back. "Who all do you have?"

"Just me, Roo, and River. And Stats." Her shrug was brittle, almost defensive. "The rest are on a fast track to Mexico with Paolo."

"I'm sorry."

"Yeah," Austin said, a humorless smile cutting across her face. "Me too. But flies are always drawn to shit."

The words snapped, sharp—then, abruptly, she broke. Tears came suddenly, silently, shoulders shaking with each ragged inhale. Salt stung her lips, and her fingers twisted into Brandon's shirt as if anchoring herself to something immovable—because for the first time since the resort, she felt safe enough to collapse. His warmth bled into her, steady and real.

Stats shuffled by with his computer, eyes fixed ahead, jaw clenched against the tense air.

He shot Brandon a look. "She's really done it now," he muttered, as Austin's grip tightened on Brandon's shirt.

Roo shuffled in after Austin, stepping tentatively across the threshold. His hands were jammed in his pockets, shoulders bowed, gaze glued to the floor. The air felt thick—heavy with exhaustion, the faint musk of sweat and fear clinging to every breath. The room seemed to contract around them, silent tension pressing close. His posture hunched forward—just slightly—but unmistakably the way a dog stands when it *would* tuck its tail if it had one.

"Hey," River said, voice low, stillness radiating off him like heat. His pupils were blown wide, jaw tight, shoulders rigid in a way that wasn't human. Without preamble, he summarized: "Long story short—Hutch, Starr, and Aina turned on her, set her up. Paolo tried to have Hutch kill her. But she knew. His dad tipped her off. She flipped it. Feds swooped in, Paolo's crew got shipped off. Didn't even get to say goodbye. Didn't really want to."

His throat bobbed. His eyes darted the way a panther's do when cornered—silky, watchful, waiting.

He hesitated, then continued, "While we were running, she called in health code violations at the hospital. On the drive here, we watched the FBI move in—Austin's phone, real-time. That's how we knew it was finally over."

"Cool, I guess. You know the drill. Make yourselves comfortable." Brandon's chuckle caught in his throat—a brittle sound, more relief than humor. He wrapped an arm around Austin again, steadying her trembling shoulders, feeling the chill of her skin through the thin fabric. She sagged into him, breath hitching, the sharp scent of fear and sweat caught between them.

"Let's go lie down. You can give me the long version if you want. I'll listen."

Chapter −54

"Will you walk with me?"

Austin leaned against the rough wood of Brandon's porch the next morning, exhaustion etched into the set of her jaw. Every muscle ached, and her hands shook faintly from pain and the adrenaline echo of the night before. Roo stood beside her, shoulders drawn inward, gaze fixed on the porch planks, juggling two tennis balls with restless, nervous movements—his sneakers scuffing soft, uneven tracks into the dusty boards.

When Brandon joined them, he nodded, wordless, and set off across the pasture with her. Austin paused only long enough to scoop up Tessa—settling the girl on her hip with a tight, protective grip—before slipping through the cattle gates and into the tall grass. The sun was already a heavy weight; sweat trickled beneath Austin's shirt, the scent of cut grass sharp in her nostrils.

As they walked, Brandon watched the pair: Tessa with one lazy arm looped around Austin's neck, small fingers tangling in Austin's hair as if she'd never left her side. Tessa's other hand mirrored Austin's every move—copying her expressions, copying her tension. Each time Austin brushed a bug from Tessa's face, her hand trembled—gentle, precise, but betraying the pain underneath. Tessa mimicked her, waving her small fingers in front of Austin's eyes, the two locked in a silent exchange that smelled of salt, sun, and something raw and new—family, fragile and fierce.

Austin stopped just short of the creek. She watched Roo slip off his shoes and start to wade near the edge. It hadn't rained in a week, and the water was lower than usual. "Show me where all the old springs are that used to come off the hills," she said to Brandon. Austin used the back of her wrist to swipe away the sweat on her forehead. It was only ten in the morning, and it was already hot.

"There are only two that I remember."

Brandon snatched up her free hand and tugged her along the sandy beach. "Come this way."

He saw her look down, see his fingers locked to hers. A smile played on her lips. Her eyes danced deep blue looking up at him.

They held hands for maybe ten minutes as they walked in quiet, their palms damp from heat and nerves. Roo always kept Austin in his periphery, his steps slow and careful, shoulders tight, eyes never lifting unless she glanced his direction—then dropping immediately again, submissiveness radiating off him in waves. Brandon tried to hide the goofy grin creeping up on his lips, but he couldn't. *Did she notice?* Maybe it didn't matter. His heart thudded so hard, he figured she could hear it a mile away—the pulse loud in his ears, the world narrowed to the hush and rustle of their little group moving through the sun.

He stopped just short of a bend in the creek. There was a small hillside they had to hike. Then, there was a teeny tiny stream. "Here it is. Look up." She turned, leaned into him, and handed Tessa over. Tessa reached out immediately, grabbed Brandon's neck, and settled against his chest. All three stared up at a small waterfall trickling down the hill.

"Golem and I found a snakeskin somewhere around here as we walked Turtle Creek. We could hear a waterfall. It was night." She turned her attention to the ground, used her foot to push away the grass, and exposed a huge footprint.

"Yep, size million shoes," she said. "This must have been the spot."

Austin sighed, her breath shaky, then slowly lowered herself to the ground with a wince, the stiff grass and leaves of stinging nettle biting at the bruises on her legs. The movement was careful, every joint protesting, a faint tremor in her hands as she patted the earth in front of her to signal Brandon down.

He settled, the scent of sun-warmed denim and salt sweat grounding her as Tessa crawled from his lap and walked over to watch Roo. Austin inched closer, knees brushing his—skin prickling at the touch, the contact both comfort and reminder of her injuries.

She forced herself to sit upright, posture rigid, hyper-aware of every movement, her control so tight it was almost a shield.

Still, Brandon caught the fresh cracks of emotion flickering behind her eyes—a glint of fear, and defiance, and something brittle that hadn't been there before.

"The Uktena is this huge creature that is said to have a snake's body and giant wings like the turkey vulture. They have antlers like elk. On its forehead, there is a crystal my papaw called the Ulunsuti stone that gives those who have control over it the power over light and dark."

She was poking the little bits of grass between them, not looking up at Brandon. "My great-grandpa once lived on this land your family claims. You and I both know there's no proof he lived here; you can't see his name on any of the plat maps in town because he was not white, and could not own land. Some wouldn't believe it is true, just like they wouldn't believe he fought a huge snake here. They can't see it with their eyes. Because they are words and not in some newspaper or book, they are considered folklore or legend."

"Yeah, I have heard the stories," Brandon told her. "It's a small town. They talk about it like it's an urban legend."

She looked up and rolled her eyes. "I know. It makes for a lot of drama. But I like the story that says your ancestors protected mine. I don't think my ancestors would have been allowed to stay otherwise, right? Everyone else was placed on reservations, shipped off somewhere else. I have family I will never know because they were torn from my family here and taken away."

"I'm so sorry." Brandon sighed.

"You shouldn't be. It's not your fault, but people long before us. This is a special place that needs protection by people like you, Brandon, with pure spirits and no ulterior motives, unlike greedy oil or lumber companies and evil men like Abel Martin. Aina says you have a pure spirit as white as snow. I think my ancestors saw this in your family. They knew the Cherokee could not protect the land, so they did the only thing they could." She looked at Brandon hard, taking in his eyes with hers. "They found the most worthy of the white settlers around them and made sure they moved here. They knew your family would protect the springs that flow into it.

Such was the Uktena, and its powers were safeguarded."

"Oh, that makes sense," Brandon said. "I'm seeing it now."

"I don't know if Abel Martin called upon the Uktena or fate brought the Uktena to him. I just know he was going to use the stone he got from the creature to stop people like your family from making them leave." She reached into the pocket of her jean shorts and tugged out a tiny leather pouch. "This is what kept drawing me back here, I suppose. I asked my dad where it was. He lied, said he didn't know. River said that my dad wouldn't give it to me because he didn't trust me. But Ben gave it to me." Austin reached out and snatched up Brandon's hand. "Ben was the one who got the call about Tessa. He called me to pick her up because—" She made sure Tessa was out of earshot. "Well, you were so sick then."

"Does the bag hold anything?"

"Well, legend says that those who have slain a Uktena hold a crystal in a bag. It holds power in the light and in the dark, for whatever that means. My grandfather was one of these warriors who allegedly did. But, Brandon, the crystal isn't in there. I'm not even sure there was ever anything in the bag. Still, I'm drawn to it. Why? I have no clue. There aren't any dimples to show that something has been set in there for a long time. Nothing. It was empty. I'm wondering if they didn't prepare the bag, and then Uktena was never killed. It makes sense. You own the land. My great-great-grandparents moved to live in shacks outside town. Maybe the process was stopped; he never got to kill it. The Uktena went away, and until now, it has never returned until Abel Martin called upon it. I think, Brandon, that Uktena saw the way to get into this world through your property. He has never gone away. He is still here."

"How did Abel Martin know he could steal this power?"

"I don't know. Stats seems to think Abel Martin can find places with strong energy. He's mapped them out and matched the history and legends to the areas to find the most powerful. He found that each of Abel Martin's properties has a spring and a certain amount of clean, impurity-free water. He is controlling the Uktena.

Perhaps he is breeding it. I don't know. I would assume that is the reason he goes to the places where people were killed in horrible ways. It leaves negative energy. He sucks it in, brings it back, and uses it for power. Negative power over the Uktena."

"How do you figure these things out, Austin?" Brandon leaned in and let his hand rest on her shoulder. "You're like this well-honed machine, just—"

"I just came up with the theories. Stats researches them." She sighed, rubbing the heel of her hand over her brow. "Without Aina, Golem, and Starr, I feel like half a person. Even Hutch—believe it or not, he throws wrenches into my ideas. That forces me to think harder, to find an answer so I don't look like an idiot. He was like another half of me, but after what happened, we'll never meet in the middle. I don't know." She shrugged, jaw tightening. "Hutch is special—very special. I may have screwed up, but some lines can't be uncrossed. Only time will tell if he chooses good or bad. I can't fix him. Each member of my family has an ability I lack, and they complete me. Do you know what I mean? But the old family is gone. It's just us now."

"I do."

"You too."

"Me?"

"Yes, you most of all. You pull me back from the edge, you make me feel light—happy, even." She jabbed his ribs, laughter shaky under layers of relief. "With you, I never feel like I have to fight for my place or order you around. You just know. It's like you're the only one who fits—the only one I can trust to catch me when I stumble."

"So, do you change like River and Aina?" Brandon asked quickly, afraid she might stop talking.

Austin blinked, looking more as if she'd found unexpected clutter in the sink than as if she was startled. She turned her head to the side and watched Roo leap, splashing water everywhere when his feet hit the creek floor. Tessa giggled and clapped for more.

"Would it bother you?"

"No," he laughed, rubbing a hand across his hair. "I just thought it'd be nice to know, so I was prepared for it. Unlike River. I've got to say, waking up to a black panther panting over your best girl in bed is on my list of things I'd never expected to happen."

"Best girl."

"That's what my dad would call you. Because you are the one here in my life right now. I'm not sure what you are, so I don't want to put a name on it, and then you run."

She furrowed her brow, narrowed her eyes. Then she ignored that part. "No, I don't alter my appearance like River. The closest thing you could compare him to is what White people call a Skinwalker or what the Navajo call Naaldlooshii. But Naaldlooshii is a witch, and witches are considered evil. River is not evil. We are not even sure exactly what he would be called—I'm believing now he is a medicine man, or Hatááłii. If he continues to use his powers for good, of course." Austin looked up to the sky thoughtfully. "But it appears that in his case, changing was inherited genetically from his grandfather. He says it always took him months to change. He would feel sore for weeks, find himself a little hairier for a month or two, his back would start to look deformed for a few more months, and he would end up resting in bed while his legs just kind of got smaller. The doctors thought he had a muscular disorder. No surprise. It wasn't written in their stupid textbooks. Sometimes... we tend to put a name to something we don't understand just to make sense of it. Sometimes, I just have to let my friends be themselves without defining them by some legend or monster."

She shifted and poked a finger into the grass. "The other night, that wasn't new, but it was much quicker. He had fully transformed before, but he said it was the first time he felt *good* in this skin. But I don't change. Does that disappoint you?"

"No, not at all." Brandon felt an urgency in his chest and a nervousness in the pit of his belly. "Now here's my next question. What about Tessa? Does she have what you have?"

"I don't know. My dad and Ben don't," She answered carefully.

"I don't see anything in her that makes me believe she does. My papaw always treated me differently. Maybe he saw it in me, I guess, is what I'm saying. And if Tessa has it, I would have seen—Brandon, I'm sorry. I didn't even think that might freak you out."

"No, really, it doesn't," he muttered. "I mean, I'd hate to have my fifteen-year-old daughter toss me over her head when I told her she was too young to date some guy in college, but I guess it would just be nice to have you around to help out if she does—or doesn't."

Austin turned her eyes to the ground. It was like she just shut down, her fingers stopping the nervous twitch of the grass tendrils.

"I'm asking you to stick around, Austin. I'm asking you to stay."

"To stay. Like for a couple of days?"

"Forever or whenever. You and your friends."

She snapped her eyes back at him. "They are your friends too." She nudged his knee with her knuckle. "I think River was excited to be back here. He's been cooped up in a hospital for three years. This is heaven. I think I can even get him to finish high school."

"You'll think about it?" he finally asked.

"Yeah." She beckoned Tessa over with a small snap of her fingers—a command, practiced, sharp as a drill sergeant's but softened for Tessa. Brandon watched Tessa skip from the creek and crawl into Austin's lap, tiny hands cool and clean against her battered skin. Austin leaned back, pulling Tessa with her, and tickled her sides until she squealed, the sound bubbling bright against the heaviness of the morning.

But Brandon's gaze caught the blue and black bruises blooming across Austin's ribs and belly, skin mottled and tender—the evidence of violence stark and intimate. He didn't say anything, but he saw her flinch when Tessa's elbow bumped a bruise; saw her jaw set and her breath hitch as she awkwardly tugged her shirt down. Every movement was a quiet mask over pain she refused to voice. The air thickened with the scent of grass and the sharp memory of almost losing her.

"I love you." Austin rolled her eyes and made a funny face at Tessa. "Blah, blah, blah."

"I love you." Tessa tried to roll her eyes, only managing a crooked tongue-out expression. "Blah, blah, blah."

Brandon laughed quietly, watching them, shaking his head. He had no clue what the blah, blah, blah meant—a sweet, private code that he didn't need to understand. He let himself sink into the moment: the hum of insects and Tessa's giggles.

The peace was shattered when Austin suddenly jerked upright. Every muscle went rigid, her breath catching sharply. Her hand shot behind her, eyes blown wide—pupils huge, her skin turning pale under the bruises. A wave of something primal flashed across her face: fear, then heartbreak, then that hardening resolve. "Do you feel that?" she asked.

Brandon *did* feel something. A vibration in the ground. Faint, but alive. He spread his palm flat against the earth. "What is it?"

"I don't know." Austin pressed her hand to the dirt, too, closing her eyes. "Does anyone dig or blast for mining here?"

"No. I mean—Abel mentioned if he got the land, he was going to dig for oil, but—" Brandon stopped. The realization hit him like a splash of cold water on his face. Maybe Abel had never wanted oil. Maybe he wanted something else buried here. Austin sniffed the wind. Her eyes moved to Brandon's. A musky scent drifted through the soft breeze over the creek. "Get up." Brandon grabbed Austin's arm, pulling her to her feet. He yelled for Roo and nodded toward the house. Austin clutched Tessa, whose eyes darted between them in fear. "What's the name of that snake?" Brandon asked.

"Uktena."

"I think," Brandon said, dragging Austin toward the house, "Uktena might be underneath us. It's like he's wiggling through the caves beneath us."

"Caves?"

"Yeah—they're small, collapsed mostly. But they're everywhere under the mountain."

Chapter −55

"Here."

Gravel crunched under Austin's boots as she crossed the yard, sweat stinging her brow. Late-summer sun pressed down, cicadas droning in the heat-thick air.

Stats stood rigid on the porch, jaw tight, eyes locked on her with that look he got when he'd been holding in information too long. As she and the others approached, he thrust a sheet of paper at her—his hand shaking.

Sixteen names. Children. Each marked in his sharp, uncompromising handwriting.

"What's this?"

"Missing kids," Stats said flatly. "Tennessee, West Virginia, and Ohio—last three months." He flipped a notebook open. "Add Kentucky, Texas, Indiana—six more. I excluded parental abductions."

Austin's pulse kicked. Her eyes skimmed the list as Stats reached behind him and grabbed a battered red shoebox from a porch chair.

"A local cop dropped this off—Officer Jackson." Stats studied her. "Your brother."

She passed the notebook and the list to Brandon, then pried the lid off the shoebox.

Letters—twenty-five, maybe thirty—stuffed inside, some yellowed and crumpled, ink faded from being handled too many desperate times.

"Those are pleas for help," Stats said. "People begging police to get family members out of that mountain compound."

He cast a pointed glance at Brandon.

"Stop," Austin snapped, catching the tilt of accusation. "It's not his fault. He's a victim too."

"How do you know?" Stats demanded. "How do you know he won't go back?"

"Because I'm not," Brandon said quietly. He set Tessa down. "Sometimes... you just trust."

"I thought I knew Aina. Starr. Hutch," Stats muttered. "But Aina and Starr lied, and Hutch attacked Austin. Never saw it coming."

"Sometimes people chase money or power and lose sight of what matters," Brandon said. "Like—"

"Like waking up with Starr curled up in bed beside me." The screen door slammed open. River grinned. "Oh yeah. That's worth more than money or power." He high-fived Stats on the head and flopped into a chair. Brandon tried—and failed—not to laugh.

"Laugh it up," Austin muttered, waving the binder. "Both of you will be getting lists of things I never want to hear again. *That*, River, is number one on yours. And Brandon—yours is 'I woke up with two women in my bed the other day.'"

She realized the stunned silence a moment late—Brandon staring at the floor, splinter between his fingers. River shot her a dramatic grimace.

"Well," she managed, throat tight, "um, we were talking about kids. Josh Smythe and Daniel Price disappeared last week—just an hour away."

"What's that got to do with us?" River asked.

"Because Abel Martin is gaining power. Fast." Austin pointed across the pastures. "He doesn't just have this commune. He has twenty more—stretching to Mexico. He wants this land. If he gets it, he connects his territory straight to town. The missing kids matter because they might be how he's building control. Kidnapping children breaks families, forces compliance. It's what dictators and cult leaders have always done." She swallowed hard. "I'm not letting anyone destroy people I care about. I'm not looking away while families get torn apart."

"So?" River shrugged. "How's that our problem?"

"Because we care," Austin said simply. "If we don't stop it, we become Paolo and Abel—selfish, apathetic. That's how people die. Need me to spell it out more clearly?"

She knelt beside Roo. He brightened instantly, shoulders loosening.

"Look," she said, running her thumb along the box's worn edge, "I think Abel Martin is abducting kids—maybe to feed them to the snake from my papaw's stories, maybe to build an army, maybe ransom. My papaw talked about the Tlanuhwa—giant birds that stole children. Legends repeat themselves if someone wants them bad enough."

She tipped her chin at River. "This is a puzzle. And you're good at puzzles."

"I like hanging with you," River said.

"That's great. But we need you. I know you don't want to sit on the windowsill like my grandma's spoiled old tabby, coughing up hairballs for excitement. You want to live, River."

"Okay, okay." He raised both hands. "I get it."

Austin straightened, spine tight. "We need a real plan. Not hope. Not waiting."

River arched a brow. "You think there's gonna be a war?"

"Yeah, you two talk it out," Brandon said lightly. "I'm putting Tessa down for a nap."

He vanished inside.

Austin faced River. "Yeah. I do, River. If we don't fight, he takes everything. And I'm not letting that happen. My family, this land—everything that matters is at stake. It's us against a tyrant, his followers, and whatever monsters he's pulling from hell. I won't be like the people who gave up." Her voice softened. "I know you didn't sign up for this. None of us did. And I'm not forcing you to stay. I'm not forcing you to fight. That part is yours alone."

She let that settle, let it breathe.

"But you are going to have to decide," Austin said gently. "If you want to be one of *us*... or go it alone."

Chapter −56

"I don't want a war waged in my backyard."

Austin stepped back as Brandon blocked the bottom of the stairs, hands out, tension rolling off him in waves. She'd only come inside to grab her phone—a text alert pinging—when he intercepted her.

He needed reassurance she couldn't give.

"Okay." She braced herself.

"That's all you've got to say?"

"I'm not the one waging war, Five. Abel is." Arms crossed over her ribs.

"Yeah, you are." He rubbed his face. "You're making plans. Abel drove by once. That was probably just Lyndsey."

"He poisoned you. She let him. Then she left our child at night. Now she's checking if you're dead," Austin snapped.

"They're not that bad."

"What about the missing kids?"

"It could be anyone. I think it's over. At most... plan a defense."

"We sit here and wait?"

"We'll just talk to him."

Austin closed her eyes. "My papaw always said strength was up here." She tapped her head. "He told me *I'd* lead—never Ben. He said my job was to see what people are capable of and bring out their best. When your family kicked mine off the land—"

"Great. Pulling that card again."

"Hell yes!" Austin exploded. "My ancestors didn't fight—I am, because they didn't."

"Not on my land."

"Fine! Dammit, Five, I'm trying to help you. Why are you—?"

"Zip it." Both froze. Tessa perched at the top of the stairs, finger wagging at Austin. "Daddy, I know that little boy," she said as she sat. "Daniel. He cried at the picnic. He lost his shoe."

"Sweetie, lots of boys are named Daniel."

"No. He said a lady took him from his mommy at the store."

Austin's phone buzzed again. She answered. "Yeah."

"Pet—listen," Aina whispered. "They took our phones. I borrowed one. We can't find Golem. He ran off at a rest stop on I-75. Paolo said leave him."

"I'm not *Pet* anymore. Don't call me that. How do you lose a seven-foot, five-hundred-pound man on a highway? He's your problem now." The line went dead. Austin groaned, pressing both hands to her head. Behind her, Brandon coaxed Tessa upstairs.

"How do you lose a seven-foot man?" he muttered.

Austin shrugged. "No clue. And it's not my problem." She lifted her hands. "Nobody respects my judgment until they're lost or shipped off to reform school."

"Or half-dead and drugged in a commune," Brandon muttered.

"You still don't respect my decisions," she said. "Or we wouldn't be fighting. But hey—sticking it out with Abel?" She smirked. "You had two women as an anchor. Most guys would do worse."

Brandon winced. "Okay, that's... not something I ever wanted to discuss with you. But here we are." He stepped closer. "I'm not that guy—the one who jumps into bed with anyone. Sure, maybe every man thinks about it. I'd never do it. I wanted you to see me as the one who wasn't cheating. The one who wasn't married. The one who wasn't Marco."

Austin softened. "You mean Marco and me?"

"I'm not Marco," Brandon said. "I wouldn't do that to you. When you came back, I realized Lyndsey and I were nothing. I kept my distance, waiting for you. But Abel—if I pulled away, he'd snap."

"You're with me now." Austin flashed a crooked grin. "Is it everything you hoped for? You know—since we're not fighting and we're all going to die."

Chapter −57

"Hey, Josef."

Austin stood in the fluorescent-lit waiting room of a Knoxville police station, exhaustion grinding in her bones. "I got a call—you were lost."

Golem sat hunched across two plastic chairs, massive hands folded tight, staring at the floor. Officers had told her he'd been crying for her for hours.

She'd spent six frantic hours pacing the highway by the rest stop, calling his name, then phoning every hospital and police station between Knoxville and Chattanooga until this one finally called back.

"I didn't want to leave you," Golem whispered. "Aina took my hand, but I didn't want to go." He rocked gently, voice trembling. "I was scared. Don't be mad at me."

Austin knelt, pulled a tissue from her purse, and held it out. "I'm here now. I'm not mad." She could feel everyone in the room watching them—the giant crying, the tiny woman comforting him.

She knew it hurt Golem when people stared. He never flinched or complained, but she saw the way his shoulders dipped, just a fraction, every time someone's eyes lingered too long.

She squeezed his hand. "Let's go back to Brandon's, okay? I missed you. I need you. The farm needs you."

"Okay." His voice was small, but he rose when she guided him up—gentle as a child, towering as a mountain.

Chapter −58

The clock on Brandon's phone glowed 1:00 a.m. He blinked sleep from his eyes, pulse pounding at the sharp tap-tap-tap splitting the dark. Roo stood at the foot of the bed—bare feet, pajama bottoms hanging loose, white T-shirt nearly phosphorescent in the gloom. He kept his gaze lowered, posture tight and anxious, fingers tapping the bedpost in a hesitant rhythm.

"Brandon... there are people in the backyard."

Brandon swung his legs over the side of the bed. "People?"

"Yes. I couldn't count them all." Roo's voice was low, slow, each word carefully shaped so emotion wouldn't twist it. "They're standing on the lawn. Maybe twenty... thirty... I don't know. When is Austin coming back? I don't like this. Can you call her?"

"Hang on, buddy. Let me take a look."

He skirted around Roo, giving him a wide berth since an incident earlier, and checked first on Tessa—curled beneath her blankets, breathing soft little puffs of air. Relief loosened something in his chest. Only then did he move to the upstairs room Austin had been using, pulled back the curtain, and looked out into the night.

"I don't see anyone," he whispered.

Wind brushed the trees; shadows swayed. Nothing else moved.

Roo stepped closer, fingertip tapping the window beside Brandon's hand. "Look. By the swing."

Brandon squinted. His focus sharpened—then dropped like a stone. What he'd thought were shadows coalesced into people. Dozens of them, still as fence posts, faces turned directly toward the house.

A cold ripple slid beneath his skin. He let the curtain fall slowly, as if hiding the sight might make it less real.

"Roo," he said quietly, "stay with Tessa. I'm calling the cops. I'll grab the bat and check downstairs. I didn't lock the doors, thinking Austin didn't have a key."

"Nobody is inside." Roo stepped back, voice steady in that way he had—emotion tightly held but not hidden. "I waited for Austin by the door. I walked the house every hour. Then they started showing up."

Brandon dialed 911. The dispatcher promised someone would come, but the county was tied up—an alarm at the Quick Stop, a domestic on Main, a grass fire burning toward the highway.

Of all nights.

He tried calling Austin. No answer. His stomach pitched with the fear she'd pull into the driveway while the strangers were still there. He grabbed his rifle, checked the chamber, then settled at the bottom of the stairs with it leaning across his knees. Every few minutes, he checked his phone again, thumb brushing the same unanswered text threads.

"Why are they standing there staring at the house?"

River's voice materialized from the dark. Brandon jerked so hard the rifle clattered against the step, and he nearly toppled sideways.

"Jesus—don't do that," he hissed.

"I was already here," River replied, slipping out of the foyer shadow with that eerie panther stillness clinging to him. "I see better in the dark. I counted fifty-two. Jeans, T-shirts. Just... watching the door. And I smell smoke."

Brandon's hands trembled—not from cold. The house sat at seventy degrees; it was fear crawling under his skin.

Time dragged. Thirty minutes. Then an hour.

The figures didn't move, barely even swayed. They just watched.

At 1:48 a.m., red and blue lights finally cut through the night, washing the curtains in color. A cruiser rolled up the drive, spotlight sweeping the yard. Brandon and River leaned forward, breaths held, until a dull knock rattled the door. Ben Jackson. Brandon's stomach clenched. The last time they'd met, he'd been drugged out of his mind on Abel Martin's "homebrew."

"You're back," Ben said, stepping in with authority. "You're not drunk again, are you?"

"No, sir. I—someone drugged me. I'm sorry for—"

"There's no one here." Ben's tone was firm. "Not now, anyway. Moon's bright. Could've been shadows. I'll drive the road."

He came back an hour later with an update: nothing but deer, a turkey, and—he gestured to the cruiser—"a young woman walking outside town. Says you know her."

Brandon peered through the back window. The interior light flicked on.

Starr.

"Yeah... I know her."

Ben asked if he wanted to take her or have her brought to the station. Brandon hesitated. Starr pleaded—she didn't want Austin to know, not yet. But Brandon refused to hide anything from Austin. Not after what Starr had done.

"I'm not going to keep secrets from Austin. You can stay in the basement until I talk to her, but I know what you did. Trust isn't something you get back that easily. Nor is it for me to decide."

By the time Austin pulled into the driveway an hour and a half later, Brandon hadn't even tried to sleep. He stood outside waiting for her, terrified she'd step out of the car and be mobbed again by unseen figures. Unsure how he would tell her about Starr's return.

"That's disturbing," she whispered when he told her about those standing outside. Her arm draped protectively around Golem, who followed her like a shadow. Brandon noticed the way she moved— slow, stiff, each bruise pulling at her skin. She kept scanning the tree line, ready for what might come out of it.

"They're trying to intimidate you," she murmured as he locked the door. "They are making sure you fear staying here."

She looked exhausted. Half broken. But still in charge. "I need to tell you something else—" Brandon opened his mouth to tell her about Starr as she shepherded Golem upstairs. But she noticed him nudging River and Roo toward their corners, then paused when she spotted a cut above Brandon's brow.

"What happened?" she asked, eyes working back and forth.

Roo instantly stepped forward. River braced. The tension was a living thing. "There was... an incident," Brandon said. "Roo—"

"He beat the crap out of me," River cut in, pointing at Brandon.

Austin didn't react. Not how Brandon expected, anyway. She just looked between them: Roo staring at his hands, River glaring daggers, Brandon bracing for impact. "You were beating the crap out of Roo," Brandon said, jaw tight. "He taunted Roo as soon as you left, and when I stepped out of the room—he pounced."

"Bullshit," River muttered.

Brandon stepped forward, palm flat against River's chest. "Do you want round two? Because I will."

"See?" River pushed Brandon's hand away and turned to Austin, his voice rising in a plea as she looked between them. Brandon braced himself, waiting for the moment she'd toss her head back and lose it. He didn't want to hit River—never had—but River had taken it too far, and Brandon had snapped.

Austin held up a hand. The room quieted.

"You got it under control?" she asked Brandon.

"Yeah," he said.

She exhaled through her nose. "Good."

"You're sticking up for them?" River demanded. "After everything—?"

Austin rubbed her eyes with shaking fingers. "River. I am so tired I can barely stand. I trust Brandon. And I know you've been riding Roo every time my back turns. Golem told me. Stats told me. Roo wouldn't say it because he's loyal to *everyone* in our family, no matter what stupid thing you do." Austin exhaled, long and tired. "You two fight like cats and dogs," she muttered. "And I'm too damn exhausted to referee tonight." She dug into her purse, pulled out a small box, and pressed a brand-new phone into River's hand. "Six hundred bucks," she said. "Golem spent three hours on the drive loading your contacts. All eight of them. And some ridiculous kitty-hissing ringtone. He wanted the lion growl, but every time he tested it, I jumped, and he'd start laughing. I told him no."

Austin's voice softened. "He worked his heart out because he likes you."

Silence spread like smoke. River stared—first at her, then at the phone. "If you want to stay part of this mess," she said softly, "just take it. We like you. I like the way you purr when I'm falling asleep. Stats won't admit it, but he likes that you don't chomp the cereal at the breakfast table like Brandon. Golem laughs every time you read the comics out loud. And Roo—yeah, he'd like you better if you tossed the ball once in a while."

River's composure cracked—just a hair, but enough.

He reached out—careful, almost reverent—and took the phone as if it were some strange gift he wasn't sure he deserved. River nodded, tried not to smile, and failed. It was in that moment that Austin turned and worked her way upstairs.

Brandon almost called after her to tell her about Starr, but stopped himself. Enough crises had been survived tonight. He couldn't bring himself to give Austin one more.

Chapter −59

Austin's body ached, exhaustion pooling in her bruised muscles, but her mind stayed sharp as she peered out the window the next night. Shadows hovered just beyond the spill of light from the house—people, or things shaped like people, with arms dangling and slack faces. The nearest was an older woman in blue jeans and a flannel shirt, her blank eyes fixed upward as if mesmerized by something on the roof. A tremor started in Austin's hands; the old fear of being trapped prickled under her skin, her breath catching as she willed herself not to freeze.

"So frigging creepy," she whispered to Brandon.

"Right? They were here three hours last night."

"You got the goggles?" she asked, and he handed her his dad's old hunting glasses.

"Got them."

Austin reached behind her toward Golem and wiggled her fingers, signaling for the spray bottle.

Golem extended his hand, gently placing the plastic bottle in her grasp. "Don't waste it, Austin," he warned softly. "I sanctified it myself—salt, scripture, and prayer. It's real protection."

She nodded, catching Brandon's eye in the dark. "He's an ordained minister. Are you ready? Open the window, put on the goggles, and I'll spray. Tell me what happens. And if anything moves toward the window, you'd better warn me. My arms will be outside—" Her voice broke with a thin laugh. "If something grabs me, I swear I'll lose it."

Brandon leaned down, unlocking the old hasp fastening the window tightly. Then he used his fingers to wiggle the window open about five inches.

"We look ridiculous," Austin giggled, thrusting the bottle outside.

"You're acting like this is fun." Brandon smiled.

"It is." She was concentrating so hard on keeping the bottle steady that she didn't notice Brandon shift behind her—until he gently poked her side.

Austin jolted so violently that she nearly sent Brandon flying backward into the dresser. He caught himself on the windowsill, swearing as he righted himself.

"Don't do that!" She giggled—then snorted—hands still clamped around the bottle. "Five, did you not remember me lifting that truck? One goofy move like that, and I could have—"

"Yeah, I didn't think that out." Brandon shook his head, half laughing. "You're wound tighter than a squirrel on five espressos."

Golem let out a sudden, booming grunt-laugh behind them. Both Austin and Brandon jumped like they'd been tasered.

"Holy shit, Golem!" Austin gasped.

Brandon clutched the window frame. "Warn somebody next time!"

Golem only grinned—broad, proud, clearly pleased with himself.

Their nerves cracked just enough for a soft burst of shared laughter—hushed, shaky, but real.

The laughter faded, leaving only the hush of the room and the distant, restless dark outside. For a moment, their little group felt almost normal—braver, even—sharing the kind of courage that only comes from facing fear together. But the windowsill was cold under Austin's arms, and the night pressed in, thick and waiting.

"This is the weirdest thing I've ever done—and that's saying something." She squeezed the lever, the bottle hissing a steady mist into the night. Her arms pressed so hard against the windowsill they ached, hands outstretched and exposed, her whole body fighting the urge to recoil.

Austin released her finger, blinked into the darkness. Only the soft breeze slipped through the small opening, making a ghostly wail. She sniffed. The scent of something burning wafted to her nostrils.

"Holy shit," Brandon breathed.

"What?" Austin asked, her head bobbing up and down, trying to see past a layer of condensation her own breath had left on the glass. She snapped her head upward, tried to see what Brandon was doing. He had the night-vision goggles shoved up to his face, pressed against the glass.

"Austin, you sprayed that woman's arm, and it is—smoking."

The words had barely registered before a sharp tickle brushed her wrist. Austin almost dismissed it—a bug, maybe—until it turned heavy: cold fingers, sudden and solid, clamped down on her wrist and yanked her toward the window.

She screamed. Her entire body was pulled forward, and her face smacked the glass with a bang. It happened so fast—just the lurch, the slap of cold glass against her skin. Almost instantly, Brandon latched his arms around her waist and jerked her backwards. Austin released the bottle and let it fall. Whatever grasped her wrist let go, and she toppled back onto Brandon; they skidded to a stop in a heap two feet away.

"Oh my God." It was all Austin could keep saying over and over, as her initial scream was followed by the deafening roar of screams outside. She shoved her hands over her ears, watched as Brandon did the same, and they lay there for nearly ten minutes until, suddenly, the shrill screeches just stopped.

"What the hell was that?" Austin sat straight up and rolled her fingers across her wrist. Whatever had latched onto it had squeezed tightly enough that it was still prickly from lack of circulation to her fingertips. She peered at her fingers, counted them mentally to make sure they were there. Brandon was still holding her around the waist, and she didn't care.

"Revenir." She didn't know how long Stats had been standing at the dark place between the living room and kitchen. His voice rang out, startling them all.

"Revenir," he said again while Austin pushed herself to her feet with Brandon's help. "That is French for revenant. The living dead. I think that's what they are. At least some of them. I think they are corpses brought to life."

"How do you know this?" Brandon asked. "The ones I could see looked like real, live people. Weird, but alive."

"Perhaps. But it appears the town's graveyard has been desecrated. I could see several people and looked up obituaries for the newly dead in town. Martha Peterson. That was the woman who was smoking. She lived at Abel Martin's and died recently. She is dead. Or, better worded, *undead*."

A hush fell, the word echoing in the room. For a heartbeat, nobody moved. Outside, the shadows seemed to press closer against the glass, as if they too were listening. Somewhere in the dark, something began to scratch.

Chapter —60

"Hey."

Austin looked up. Brandon knocked at her door. She was reading in bed. She'd found one of Aina's offbeat gossip magazines beneath the mattress. Perusing the latest star scandals was the farthest from her ideal bedtime read. But she needed something stupid, something incredibly distant from the material on Abel Martin Stats had given her tonight in a single bound report he'd printed out for her. Stats handed her the small booklet as if he were an administrative assistant delivering papers to a grand executive in a leather chair, rather than to Austin—who was perched on the kitchen sink in her pajamas, eating chocolate ice cream straight from the container in the dark.

"Hey, Five. Come in." She yawned and sat up. He was still in his jeans. It felt like everyone was waiting for something to happen. Austin blamed Abel Martin, even if Brandon denied it.

She patted her hand on the side of the bed, and he sat down.

"You have something on your cheek," he said, knuckling his upper lip.

"Chocolate ice cream. Sorry, I finished it off tonight." She wiped her cheek with her wrist and shrugged. Brandon hesitated in the quiet that followed, rubbing his palms down his jeans. Austin had just steadied herself, and the room felt brittle, ready to crack again.

"Austin," he blurted, the words tumbling out faster than he meant, "Starr is here. In the house. In the cellar."

Austin didn't flinch. Didn't blink. Didn't even shift her weight. Her expression stayed perfectly flat. "I know," she said.

Brandon's brow creased. "How? I didn't— I mean, she begged me not to tell you yet—"

"I'd expect that from Starr. She plays the scared rabbit with men—and with women, too—whenever she wants something."

"I wasn't going to hide it long, I just didn't want to dump it on you tonight. Then I felt like I was betraying you."

Austin looked at him, her voice low but certain. "I have safeguards established. Things I put in place after the resort. Nothing gets in or out of this house without me knowing. Not anymore. I learn from my mistakes."

Brandon stared at her, unsettled. "So... you knew the moment she came in? Before I even brought her down there?"

"I know my friends," Austin said quietly. "And I know my enemies. I know which ones try to sneak back in when they want something." She exhaled, shoulders tight with pain and exhaustion. "She can stay the night. After that? I'll decide."

"Thanks for not being mad."

"This is your house. I can't choose the guests."

"I mean, because I hesitated to tell you."

"I trust you."

"That said, I trust your judgement too. You're right." Brandon licked his thumb, leaned over, and scrubbed away the ice cream on Austin's cheek. She stifled a smile. She'd seen him do that with Tessa, too. "We need to be on the offensive. This is just out of my realm of thinking. I'm trying to keep an open mind and respect your decisions. You're right, I should. I mean, you respect my decisions regarding Tessa."

"And Roo and River." She feigned a couple of punches in the air. "And Starr." Austin blinked up at him. If she didn't know better, she would have thought Starr had given him one of her Respect-Austin-the-Warrior talks. He was so dead set against an attack earlier.

"Well," Austin scooted up in bed. "This is big, Five. It is bigger than little me." Austin nodded toward the little bound booklet on the bedside stand. "Stats seems to believe that Abel Martin is using this mountain as a central point. He has communes from Michigan to Florida, New York to California. He put little dots on a map where all the communes are located. Each of these dots has a legend associated with it: a battle or a legendary creature of the region. In our area, we followed him a couple of times, and he visited places where horrible disasters had occurred." Austin rubbed her chin.

"These small disasters—like areas of train wrecks and places where lots of people in a town were wiped out by cholera—appear, over time, to be a residual alteration of the battle or creature's existence."

Austin watched Brandon absorb what she said. "It seems that over time, Abel Martin has been buying properties with certain energies and sucking up that bad energy. Coincidentally, some of those families who have owned the property for centuries seem to just disappear or die under unnatural circumstances. Any families that were bequeathed the land in wills also vanished. Your family's farm is right in the middle, by the way."

"Why wasn't my family murdered then?" Brandon asked. "I mean, if we are right in the middle of it—"

Austin exhaled through her nose. "Because I don't think that's off the table. Not at all. "

Brandon swallowed hard.

"He's waiting," she said. "Abel Martin knows people would notice if you vanished. He sent Lyndsey to make you look bad—a drunk, a bad dad, maybe crazy. Then they kill you. When people ask, he'll say you sold your property and left for one of his communes. Everyone's relieved, since you were 'trouble' anyway." She shrugged, serious. "That's my guess. And it's a good one."

"You really think he would try to kill us?" Brandon let his head fall back, eyes searching the ceiling like it might give him a different answer.

"The undead outside your house every night aren't there by accident. They're meant to keep you awake. Exhausted people make mistakes. They give in. They're easier to control." Austin didn't soften it. "I think he's already rolling out the plan," she said. "Why do you think he almost drowned you in his poison last week? He put you in the cops' radar as unruly." She shrugged, but there was nothing casual in her eyes. "Your parents? They're next, Brandon."

Brandon swore under his breath, a tremor in it. "Damn. I shudder to think of the last few weeks. I was like a blind mouse walking around a mousetrap." He dragged a hand through his hair. "Isn't there a better way to resolve this than all the fighting?"

"Well, you could give him the land. It doesn't solve any problem outside your own. And nobody wants any part of it; they don't want to toss a rock at the hornet's nest. It is bad publicity in an election year, at least that is what a senator told me not long ago."

"Then you're saying we *could* just abandon the ship?"

Austin drew in a slow breath. "No. This isn't going away. If we run, he'll catch us eventually—and I'll feel responsible, because I see it coming." She swallowed. "People living under dictators—Hitler, Mussolini, even the ones we've had rise in the U.S.—they didn't recognize the danger at first. They ignored the signs. I think... we're standing in one of those moments." Her voice dropped. "Only Abel Martin isn't targeting one group. He's taking *anything* pure and good." She tapped Stats' binder. "Twenty-three children abducted last month alone—every one of them connected to someone in the Martin network. And that's just within the radius we checked." Austin's jaw tightened. "I called sixteen families tonight, said I was another parent looking for answers." Her eyes went dark. "They all told me the same thing. I didn't need to call the rest."

"What's that?"

"They lived within a two-mile radius of one of Abel's communes."

"So how do we stop them?"

"I was kind of hoping you weren't going to ask. It's much easier to blame somebody else for not getting involved."

"Austin, I know better. Golem said you bought out every bag of salt from every hardware store and grocery store from Tennessee to here. He was blessing each bag."

"Oh."

"Yeah, *oh.*" Brandon eyed her thoughtfully.

"I've got to be honest, it is both Aina and Golem that I usually seek advice from on matters of good and evil. Golem is more focused on protection against evil. Aina is much more assertive and hardline. She's the one who lets me know the most aggressive way to attack a problem. She uses magic, spells, and potions, and—"

Austin heard something soft—at first like a far-off whisper.

She tilted her head, rubbed a finger in her ear. It reminded her of the dog whistle Ben won at the county fair when he was eight, the one he blew all afternoon until it made her skull ache. A high, piercing note. Clear. Resonant. Ringing in her ears.

"Are you okay?" Brandon was staring at her. Austin blinked. Her head was aching suddenly, a horrible skull-splitting throb.

"Your nose, it's bleeding."

She reached up her hand quickly and caught a dribble of blood on her fingertips. Her eyes dropped. She felt strangely numb, tired, as if she were falling into the dark, oozy world of sleep.

"Austin!" Yeah, she could hear Brandon. "Austin, what's the matter?" But she also heard the ringing in her ears, the meld of voices outside. They were singing to her, singing a hushed lullaby of death and dying.

"Make it stop, Five." She could hear herself crying. "Oh, God, my head is going to explode." She was patting his arms, screaming. Crying, for God's sake, begging him to make them stop.

She felt her body falling forward, and just as the air around her turned to darkness, there was an explosion, a blast as if the house was a balloon that had gotten too close to a fire.

POP.

Austin barely heard the windows shatter in the bedroom; she only felt the coolness of Brandon's arms while she slipped through his hands in a wobbly mass on the floor.

"Holy hell!" Brandon yelled, and they both went rolling, skidding across the bedroom floor. Tessa's screams filled the air. Austin felt like she was looking through someone else's eyes, watching helplessly as she floundered there, hardly able to move.

She felt powerless, like her arms and legs had turned to jelly.

"Tessa." She could hardly say the name while Brandon lurched to his feet, staggered out the door toward Tessa's room. Austin dragged herself to the doorway and watched as Brandon's shadow disappeared.

She thought it peculiar at that moment; she recalled being ten or eleven and going to a beach in Fort Myers, Florida. She'd tossed a French fry into the air to one of the gulls flying past. In less time than it took for her to watch it fall, twenty more had darkened the sky above her head, swooping and screaming for her to toss more.

That was, until she saw the shadows of bird wings flapping against the bedroom walls, heard Tessa screaming and crying, and Brandon yelling for Roo not to let go.

"Oh my God! Roo, hold on to her!"

Austin pushed herself to a standing position, knees wobbling while she used the wall of the hallway as support to get to Tessa's room. She felt drunk, watched the dribbles of blood drop to her wrists. When she rounded the corner, she was nearly struck dumb with horror. Birds—huge, brown-colored birds—were wiggling their way through the window while Brandon tried to fend them off with his shoes and a lamp he held in his hand.

Tlanuhwa. They were the giant birds.

Then—darkness.

The trunk.

Austin blinked, and she was back inside that cramped, suffocating space: metal pressing all around, trapped in the ooze of her own fear. *I can't get out. I'm going to die.* The memory of the hotel trunk slammed into her—panic flooding her chest, her belly, her hands shaking so hard she couldn't catch her breath. The walls pressed in. She couldn't breathe. She couldn't—

"Hush, hush. You're coming with me."

It was just a whisper, deep and soft. Austin was holding her breath. She didn't know the voice. She turned, blinked into the darkness behind her. She felt a hand on her arm. She could see white teeth flash a smile at her.

"Okay."

Chapter −61

"We meet again."

Austin flinched before she could stop herself, the kind of startled reaction that came from fear trying to outrun logic. Sound sharpened strangely around her. The barn smelled of old hay and warm metal, stale sweat, and motor oil. Her vision carried a slight lag, like she had to catch up to what her eyes already saw. The concrete beneath her feet felt colder than it should have been. Somewhere behind her, water dripped in an unhurried rhythm that made her head swim.

She wasn't steady. She wasn't planning anything. She was trying not to sway.

"Sweetie, give her some more soda pop. I think she's getting ready to pass out again."

Abel Martin sat sprawled in a folding chair, fingers combing idly through his greasy hair as if nothing in the world could touch him. He flicked his hand toward Lyndsey, and she moved instantly, kneeling beside Austin with a bright, practiced smile and a can of soda fitted with a straw.

"Honey, take another sip," she urged. "You look dehydrated."

Austin lifted her shoulders in something that might have resembled a shrug if she weren't fighting the slow roll of vertigo behind her eyes. Her throat was dry enough to ache. When she pushed herself upright, the motion sent a dull pulse through her skull and a metallic tang spread across her tongue. She steadied one hand against her thigh, hoping they wouldn't notice.

"You're not bound," Abel said, raising his palms as though he were the benevolent one here. "You can stand. You can walk around. You can leave whenever you wish. But I'd appreciate it if you'd listen first."

Her voice came thinner than she meant. "Where am I?"

"One of my old horse barns," he said lightly, gesturing toward the dark row of stalls. "My grandkids ride here on weekends."

His eyes swept over her with a softness that didn't match the room. "One of my boys said you were petting a mare. You looked... confused. I asked Lyndsey to help. She's a nurse."

Austin swallowed and felt the movement catch halfway down. "What do you want with me?"

Abel's chuckle was small and patient and made her skin crawl. "Maybe the better question is what you want with us. You came across that pasture on your own. You walked right to my door. That tells me you're ready to talk about joining us. About unity. About peace."

She didn't feel peaceful. She felt sick. Hot behind the eyes, cold along her spine.

"I just want to go." The words came out unevenly, her breath catching at the end. Her head felt too heavy for her neck, and she pressed her teeth together to keep them from chattering.

"Of course," Abel murmured. "You can go anytime."

Lyndsey eased closer again with the soda. Austin pushed the can away, slower this time, because she wasn't entirely sure her arm wouldn't shake.

"I want to leave," she said again, more to keep herself conscious than anything else.

"Hush," Lyndsey whispered, fingertips brushing Austin's elbow. "If you listen, he won't put you back in your scary place."

The words hit her wrong—like hearing an echo of something she should have remembered but couldn't quite grasp.

And then a voice rose inside her mind, quiet but firm, a voice shaped like memory more than sound.

DON'T LISTEN TO HIM. YOU ARE NOT IN A BOX. THERE ARE NO WALLS. YOU ARE STANDING IN A FIELD. YOU ARE NOT TRAPPED. YOU ARE FREE.

Her breath caught. Not because she believed it completely, but because the voice felt familiar — grounding, steady, like a hand on her back. Abel's words grew warm and muffled at the edges, as though someone had stuffed cotton into her ears. She nodded once.

Then Austen pretended to follow the conversation, but she was clinging to that other steadying voice that had piped up to keep from sliding under whatever they'd dosed her with.

Lyndsey kept talking—something about forgiveness, something about Brandon—but it all blurred together until Abel's voice sharpened with sudden clarity.

"As a gesture of trust," he said, "we brought someone to see you. Someone important."

The metal door creaked open, and a young woman stepped out— tan skirt, blue blouse, head down.

"Laura," Lyndsey announced, smiling proudly. "Brandon's sister."

Austin blinked hard. Something about the girl's walk was off. The shape of her shoulders. The way her feet touched the floor without any real weight.

"I thought she left," Austin murmured.

"No," Abel said. "Laura has been with us for years."

Her stomach dropped, not from belief but from the lie. She caught the tell—the blink, the brush of his knuckle against his nose. He was lying because he always lied.

"If I don't join you," Austin asked quietly, "you won't let her go?"

Abel shrugged. "We keep our people. And yes—if you refuse us, then you die. I'd rather you choose life."

Her pulse throbbed painfully in her ears. Her balance was shot, the floor tilting in slow, nauseating waves—but she forced herself upright. Falling would give Abel too much satisfaction. She studied the girl again. Too still. Too smooth. Her face held that strange, glassy perfection people always complained about online—like those AI-generated images everyone could spot a mile away. The ones with eyes that didn't quite track, smiles shaped by a machine instead of a human, expressions that slid across the skin instead of living in it. The eyes didn't anchor to anything. The smile didn't quite reach its shape. Every movement felt rehearsed, weightless, like she wasn't fully part of the room.

Uncanny. Artificial. Not Laura. Not even close.

The voice returned, firm and unmistakable:

LOOK CLOSELY, LITTLE TURTLE GIRL. THAT IS NOT HER.

Austin inhaled slowly, willing the air to stay in her lungs this time. "What do you really want from me?" she asked, not because she expected truth but because she needed him talking long enough to stay on her feet.

"I want to be your friend," Abel said gently. She watched him blink. Brush his bulbous nose. Lie again.

The room tilted slightly to the left, but she forced her focus into a narrow line—past him, past the girl, toward the steel door. She lifted her hand, placed it against the cold metal, and stepped into the darkness beyond.

Not because she felt brave. Not because she was in control. But because moving forward was the only thing keeping her from collapsing at his feet.

"Well," Abel Martin called out just a little too sure of himself. "If you change your mind. Just send us a note. I'll be waiting."

Chapter —62

At three in the morning, Austin seemed to materialize out of thin air—or so Brandon said when she finally woke in her bed. He'd been keeping vigil in a chair only inches away, retelling how, after monstrous, human-sized birds crashed through the windows, chaos erupted throughout the house. Roo, who had been on watch outside her bedroom door, heard the glass shatter in Tessa's room and immediately rushed in. He wrapped Tessa in her blanket and threw himself over her, shielding her as the birds clawed and thrashed nearby.

Tessa had a few scrapes and a fear she tried to hide. Roo wasn't as lucky—a broken rib, stitches in his shoulder—but he never let go of Tessa.

Starr lingered in the hallway, her figure half-hidden in the shadows. She remained motionless, uncertain, like a child waiting to be told whether she was allowed to enter the room.

Austin fixed her with a cold, measured stare that silenced the room. "Step back, Starr. This isn't your place anymore. Not after what you've done." Her voice cut ice-cold through the room. "Brandon, get her out. Now."

Brandon hesitated. "She's been sitting by your bed for twelve hours, Austin. She's trying—"

Austin's hand stopped him dead. "I don't care if she stayed a year. She betrayed us. Loyalty's everything. She lost it the second she chose herself." Austin pushed herself upright in bed, moving steadily and deliberately. She never broke eye contact with Starr as she spoke. "You want to help? Then you remember your place. You don't speak unless you're spoken to. And showing up isn't forgiveness. Not now. Not soon. Maybe never." Starr recoiled as the words hit her, her face draining in the dim light. Austin didn't soften. Her voice was a blade. "We need strength, not dead weight. No more second chances for lazy spies and deserters." She turned her head slightly—toward the dark shape in the doorway.

"River. Take her back to the basement."

He stepped into the light, silent, expression carved from stone. Starr's face brightened for a heartbeat—habit, hope, the old reflex of reaching for the one person who'd always taken her side. She lifted a hand toward him.

River didn't move to meet it. "Stay away," he hissed. He shook his head once, stepping back just enough that she couldn't touch him. Hands raised—not in welcome, but in refusal.

Starr froze. The message wasn't just clear. It was final.

She hadn't only been pushed aside—she'd been stripped of rank, protection, belonging. Austin commanded. River obeyed. Starr was nothing in the space between them.

If she wanted trust again, she would earn it from the dirt upward—if Austin ever allowed that climb at all. The hierarchy was no longer unspoken. It had just been carved in stone.

Chapter −63

"The local news is reporting all the damage in town as an explosion at Weedlemeyer's Fireworks Store," Brandon said, talking too fast. "We weren't the only ones with windows blown out."

Austin ignored him, turning her glare on Starr. "When is my head going to feel better?" she snapped. It *was* easing, but she refused to hand Starr the satisfaction. "He's hypnotizing people. Every time I push the word *trunk* out of my mind, something in my skull screams." She told them about Abel Martin—about the fake Laura, the hallucinated commands, the words she couldn't say because they would manipulate Brandon somehow.

Starr lifted her chin. "Maybe if you relaxed—quit glaring at me, quit hating me—I could talk you down from it."

Austin stared at her like she'd lost her mind. "Why? So you can do it again? You knew my greatest fear. And you threw it in my face." She tossed a hand out. "All of us."

Starr snorted—an indignant, pampered sound, like a patron insulted at a spa when a worker forgot to hand her a warm towel. "Oh, please," she said, flinging her hair back. "You wear that fear on your sleeve so everyone knows not to leave you. Hutch was your bread and butter. And me?" She jabbed a manicured finger at her own chest. "I'm the one who's kept you alive after half your fights. You'd be a smear on the concrete without me patching you up." She folded her arms, chin lifting in a spoiled, superior tilt. "But you looked at us as if we were all just baggage to you. Dead weight. Except—" her eyes sliced toward Brandon, lingering with a curl of disdain, "they might be idiots." Her mouth sharpened. "He might be an idiot." Her gaze snapped back to Austin. "I'm not."

Brandon jerked, surprised by the venom, but he stayed silent. He looked at Austin who was staring at him pokerfaced. "Now you see the spoiled brat I deal with?" Austin's voice went hoarse and deadly soft as she turned to Starr.

"You're right," she sneered at Starr. "You *are* baggage. Paolo was the one who wanted you. At no point, did I really want to drag you around like an empty suitcase. I saved your ass. And how do you repay me? You don't. You won't get a job. You lounged around like a pampered Chihuahua while I worked two jobs. Then you leave me for dead when I most needed you. Why are you here?"

Starr's shoulders dropped. Her voice crumpled. "I don't know. I really... really don't know." She pivoted and walked out.

Austin listened to her footsteps hit the stairs to the cellar. Brandon rounded on Austin. "You're a bitch. You know that, right?" he hissed, raking his hand through his hair.

He rose to stand at full height, towering over her—but she didn't flinch. "You don't deserve any of them."

"She would have let Paolo kill me," Austin said, flat, factual. "You were not there. You did not see her face when she thought I was dead. It was as if she had finally trapped the mouse in her bedroom that had been getting into her snacks."

"Austin, she's not a fighter," Brandon argued. "She's like me. We don't always know what to do. But she loves you. The same way I do—deep, hard, messy love." His voice softened. "I understand her more than I understand you sometimes. Because neither of us knows how to get you to feel the same way about us. It's like we're a job to you. Work."

Austin drew in a slow breath, her expression cooling into a focused, level one. "Brandon... you're looking at this like friendship. I'm looking at it like leadership."

He blinked.

"I can't let people run over me," she said. "Not here. Not when we're fighting something bigger than all of us. If one person breaks rank and suffers no consequences, the whole herd goes wild. You know that better than anyone—you raised animals. One gets bold, tests a fence, and suddenly you've got chaos."

Brandon's jaw tightened with realization.

"These people look to me to lead," she continued steadfastly.

"If I let a traitor stroll back in with no structure, no accountability, then I lose control. And if I lose control, someone dies. I'm not being *mean* or a bitch. I'm enforcing order. Starr starts at the bottom," she said quietly, the room tightening around her words. "And she earns her way back up—*if,* and only if, I decide she's capable of being part of the team she helped break apart." Her eyes locked on his. "Don't undermine me again. Not when the stakes are this high."

Brandon exhaled a long breath—finally, fully understanding. Austin's next words broke the tension completely. "By the way, I love you too."

Brandon stared like she'd hit him with a bat. "R—really?" She nodded. He swallowed hard. "Then trust me when I say the right thing... is letting Starr stay."

Austin stared at him until her eyes throbbed. Finally, she nodded and rose—slow, steady, deliberate. "Fine," she said. "But she stays in the cellar. Like the rat she is."

A faint scratch in the hallway made her turn. River lingered in the half-light, shoulders slouched, gaze soft with a sadness he tried too late to hide. He straightened the instant she looked at him— mask snapping back into place, all obedience and stillness—but the flicker she'd seen was enough. It was why she led and Abel never would: she understood people. Even the broken ones.

She stepped toward him. "I suppose you agree with Brandon."

River shifted, jaw tight. "She is not my person. You are—"

"But?" Austin pressed.

He exhaled. "She makes me feel... happy. She makes me feel normal."

"Shit," Austin muttered under her breath. "Everybody deserves a little happy and normal." Her voice roughened. "But I make the calls. No sprinting down there like a lovesick fool. She earns her place back—if she earns it at all." Austin moved to the cellar steps and braced herself on the doorframe before calling down into the cold."If you want a place in my family again," she said, voice flint- sharp, echoing off stone, "you start at the bottom. You obey.

You rebuild what you broke. And maybe—maybe—you'll work your way back up. That's the only path you get."

Cold air bit her throat as she spoke. Her chest tightened. Her legs buckled without warning. She hit the floor hard, palms smacking wood. "Son of a bitch," she hissed, forcing herself to push upright.

River was under her arm in an instant, lifting her as gently as if she were made of ash. Roo crowded her other side, whining low.

"You don't need me," Starr called faintly from below, breathless.

Austin barked a ragged laugh. "Does it look like I'm okay?"

Her hands trembled violently. Her vision pulsed at the edges. Pain climbed her legs in slow, merciless waves. Still—she kept her glare locked on the shadows below.

"I'm not okay," Austin growled. "But trust isn't free anymore, Starr. Not from me. Not after what you did."

She steadied herself on Roo's shoulder, breath shaking.

"If you want to stay," she said, voice dropping to a command that filled the entire stairwell, "then you earn it. Starting now." Austin tightened her grip on the railing, eyes burning. "Heal me."

Chapter −64

Aina called from a diner in Hazard, Kentucky, at eight the next morning. Brandon picked her up and brought her back to the house. The ride was quiet except for the radio humming softly between them.

"She doesn't want me back," Aina mumbled when they pulled into the drive. She hesitated outside the truck door as if she were deciding whether to run or stay. She chewed her sleeve—a nervous habit she'd had since she was twelve. "I steal stuff. You know that, right?"

"I know, Aina."

"I can't help it." She lifted her wrist. "I have your watch."

His old wristwatch dangled loosely on her arm. Brandon only sighed, setting his keys on the hood, not angry—more relieved she was standing there alive.

"Is Golem safe?"

"Yes."

As Brandon turned toward the porch, the house looked battered—three bedroom windows still boarded up, splintered wood streaked with dirt and smoke. The air carried the taste of wet soil and the acrid ghost of bonfire wood, soaked and extinguished by last night's rain.

He blinked and squinted at the porch.

A young man sat hunched in his mom's old white wicker rocker, shoulders curled inward, hands twisting in his lap as the chair squeaked faintly, pitifully. It was Hutch, smaller and more fragile than Brandon remembered—road-weary, hollow-eyed, streaked with dust, looking like he'd traveled a long way on foot.

"Does Austin know you're here?" Brandon asked, slowing as he passed Hutch on the porch. Aina slipped quietly inside, avoiding Hutch's gaze and not speaking to him.

"Yes, sir." *Sir?*

Hutch kept his gaze down. "Pet—I mean, Miss Austin told everybody I should be alone. I'm in an adult time out." Shame weighed on his shoulders, which shook slightly with every breath.

Brandon opened his mouth to say something—to offer comfort, maybe—when Starr stepped out the door, interrupting him.

"Austin wants to talk to you."

~

"That poor boy looks like a pup that got kicked, Austin," Brandon said as he stepped into the kitchen.

The house felt like the walls were holding their breath. The roasted chicken smell battled the tang of bleach left from frantic morning cleaning. His glasses fogged as he stepped into the heat.

Starr pulled chicken legs from the oven. Roo and River sat stiff at opposite table ends: River drumming, Roo staring at a chipped plate. Golem cradled Tessa, her face in his shirt. Every sound—chair scrape, fork clatter—felt too loud. "I can't leave him out there," Brandon muttered. "It's going to be dark soon."

"You need to stand back and let him face the consequences. That boy nearly snapped my neck, Five," Austin said, waving an oven mitt. The mark on her elbow caught Brandon's eye. He ached. God, he missed her—and he'd only been gone six and a half hours.

Austin tilted her head as if expecting him to say something. When he didn't, she just smiled quietly. She wore a soft black dress with narrow straps—elegant and out of place against the old linoleum. It looked like something she wore to feel human again in the chaos. "He's in a time-out until his dad calls back," Austin said. "He's in 'yes, sir, and no ma'am' mode now, so make sure he addresses you properly. He's not allowed to talk to anybody yet; that includes you. He doesn't have his phone. I do."

Brandon blinked. Hutch, using honorifics. That was new.

"But before you say anything else, he needs to learn accountability. All of them do. He lied. He jeopardized everyone's life. He hijacked Starr, Aina, and Golem. He pushed past my authority, knowing I couldn't hurt him because he was in my care."

"I'm not questioning your authority—"

"Yes, you are," Starr muttered, arms crossed, pajama pants sagging, eyes swollen from crying. "You always do this."

"Now you're on my side?" Austin muttered. Austin eyed Brandon once, a wordless reminder that he couldn't undercut her authority—not with Starr, not with Hutch, not with anyone. Not now.

"I'm always on your side. Just... some days more than others," Starr said with a brief, humorless grin. Everyone chuckled.

~

"Can I go see Aina?" Golem asked softly.

Austin, who had slipped onto the steps between the rooms, nodded. "Because you're going to die if you don't, right?" she teased, exhausted. "Yes. I know you are not to blame for her decisions, but I ask you to keep your distance a bit."

Golem handed Tessa to Brandon; the girl clung to his shirt, her small hands trembling.

Austin's phone rang—a sultry Spanish ringtone Marco had set years ago. Austin closed her eyes briefly, already irritated. She stepped onto the back porch and shut the door.

"That's Marco's ringtone," Roo whispered.

"I'd pay money to hear this one," River muttered.

"Well, we know it's not sexy," Starr said, pressing her ear to the door. "She told him it's over, but maybe I can hear a little—"

She hardly needed to. The walls were paper-thin.

~

"Hutch is here—no, he's fine," Austin snapped outside. "Yes, he's safe. Yes, he walked God knows how far." A pause. "No. If you come and get him now, he'll never learn. And stop yelling. You can talk to your wives like that, but you don't talk to me like that—and DAMMIT, THAT'S WHY I WOULD NEVER MARRY YOUR SORRY ASS!"

River grinned. Starr shivered.

"No, I really don't want him back with us," Austin went on.

"It's the last damn thing I want. But he could have killed me. Maybe it was just me this time—but next time? It won't stop at one person." Her jaws were working hard. "You want your son to lead a region, right? Leaders who never face consequences start wars. Leaders who lose control burn whole countries down because no one ever told them no." Austin didn't blink. "He doesn't just need obedience. He needs compassion. He needs to learn how to work with people, not rule them like livestock. I'm trying to teach him to be something other than a spoiled little tyrant." She tilted her head, gaze razor-sharp. "But if you want him to grow up exactly like you? Fine. Come get him."

Austin grimaced, threw a hand to her forehead. "Oh, no, I didn't mean to call you a spoiled tyrant. I'm tired. But it's your call."

Silence. Then Austin slipped out the door, spoke in fluid Spanish—soft, soothing, a tone most of them had never heard her use. Starr closed her eyes as if listening hurt.

"She is telling him it won't happen again," Starr whispered. "She's consoling him. This is where he usually talks her into flying off for the weekend—"

Austin settled her rear on the porch. "This isn't about wanting more than our ridiculous, half-broken relationship," Austin said, voice cold steel under the words. "You're never here. I'm never there. Are you crying? Marco, stop. You need to listen to me right now: He stays. You will let him stay, and you will not interfere. Trust me. He needs this—and he needs me. I won't let you override my authority again."

Chapter −65

Hutch lay on the couch in the dim living room, shadows pooling in the corners like dust that wouldn't settle. Austin had allowed Brandon to bring him inside, feed him, shove him toward a shower, and leave him alone. Now, wrapped in one of Brandon's grandma's old quilts, Hutch stared at the ceiling fan turning slowly and unevenly overhead. The house creaked around him—old floorboards shifting, wind tapping the window frames, pipes ticking as they cooled.

He had never felt so alone, emptiness gnawing at his chest, the ache sharp and hollow all at once. And he knew exactly why.

Because for the last three years, he had tasted something he'd never known before—*family*. Not perfect, not soft, but real. People who saw him. People who cared. Austin had been the anchor of it all, even when she shoved him, yelled at him, and made him work harder than anyone else ever had. And he'd thrown it away. Let himself believe he could manipulate everything for Paolo. Let himself believe he mattered more than the chain of command Austin built. All for power that really was not there.

Now he felt the weight of that mistake pressing on him like Golem had sat down hard on his chest.

The journey from Texas to West Virginia had been long, bleak, grinding—measured more in dread than miles. He'd been wind-burned, grimed over with dust from sleeping under bridges and riding in the backs of pickups. His clothes still smelled faintly of exhaust and cold air. He'd walked farther than he'd expected, said no to more dangerous rides than he wanted to think about. Every step had pushed him forward with one question:

Would Austin take him back?

Or kill him?

Or worse... simply turn her back?

And the worst of those had happened earlier—she'd ignored him completely. Still, Hutch believed he could climb his way back.

Austin had taught him to fight for something he wanted. She'd taught him attention, accountability, and how to show up even when it hurt. She'd never let him off easy. But she'd also never abandoned him. So maybe—just maybe—she was showing him a harder lesson now: that earning trust back took time, and being part of a family meant taking consequences as much as comfort.

A soft sound—bare feet whispering across the old floorboards—pulled him from his thoughts.

"Forgiveness," Austin said quietly from the stairway's shadow.

Hutch swallowed. Her silhouette glowed faintly in the gray light as she stepped closer, the air shifting with her presence. She moved slowly, tired but controlled, a woman carrying the weight of the last two weeks with measured precision. She lowered herself to the floor beside the couch, sitting with her back against it. Her hand reached up, fingers searching in the dark. Hutch raised his, and they found each other automatically—muscle memory from all the nights she'd steadied him through storms of fear and nightmares. Their fingers linked, the ritual grounding them both.

"I left my daughter," Austin said softly. "Dropped her in her daddy's lap and walked away. Then one night, I came back and knocked on his door. He opened it wide. No hesitation. No questions. Just... let me in."

Hutch listened, his heartbeat thick in his chest, anxiety and hope battling inside him as Austin spoke.

"I can't teach you forgiveness," she continued, voice gravel-soft. "I can't pardon the man who left me alone in a city when I was a kid. I can't pity Paolo for what he's done. But Brandon—" she exhaled, eyes sweeping upward toward the dark ceiling "—maybe Brandon's actions will drag me along the path long enough that I can show you something close to mercy. I'm trying. So, Hutch... on the outside? I forgive you. On the inside... I'm working on it. Forgiveness is a muscle, and mine's weak."

Her honesty unclenched something in his chest, easing a knot of fear and shame. Warmth spread from their linked hands to his ribs, quieting the tremor of doubt.

He swallowed. His voice sounded older than he remembered. "I can't sleep. Will you tell me how the world was created?"

Austin huffed a tired laugh—part affection, part relief. "Of course." She shifted so their shoulders brushed. "In the beginning," she began, "there was nothing. Then there was God— Ometecuhtli. Good and bad, man and woman, disorder and order."

Her voice rolled softly into the room, warm and steady.

"Ometecuhtli had four children—North, South, East, West. They began to create land and seas, creatures of all kinds. One was Cipactli—part fish, part toad, part crocodile, always hungry. Everything they made, Cipactli devoured. Thus, the gods fought it, pulled it apart in all four directions. And from that—creation. On Cipactli's back the world rests. That's the earth we live on."

Hutch let out a slow breath, the weight of the story settling deeper into his shoulders. Fear intermingled with a fragile sense of belonging. "I feel the whole world pressing on me now," he whispered. "It's heavy... but bright, like I finally fit somewhere. And that scares the hell out of me." He rubbed the back of his neck, eyes flicking toward Austin. "Do you ever think I'll actually live up to my legacy? Because—God—it's supposed to be this huge, warrior-leader thing, and half the time I feel like a dollar-store action figure with the wrong body parts snapped on." He gave a strained little laugh, desperation slipping beneath the humor. "And a hummingbird. That's the creature I'm named for. Not a jaguar or an eagle or something fierce. A hummingbird—tiny, twitchy, and one bad day away from getting swatted into oblivion by a toddler."

"But the hummingbird isn't weak," Austin said softly. "It's fast. Precise. Fierce when it needs to be. People forget that something tiny can still carry enormous power. It only takes a sphere of plutonium the size of a softball—put together the right way—to unleash a nuclear explosion." She touched his arm, steadying him. "Small doesn't mean fragile, Hutch. Small just means concentrated." She held his gaze. "But you still have to earn the trust of whatever gods or legacies you follow. Power doesn't go to people who are careless with it." Austin leaned in, studied Hutch solidly.

"It usually chooses the ones who stay neutral or good—even when it's hard." She let that sink in before adding, "Start there. Do one kind thing every day. Quietly. Don't wait for applause or someone to tell you you're doing it right. Just do it... and walk away. That's how you'll know you're strong."

"Okay," Hutch said. "Tell me the story again, please."

She did.

When she finished, he whispered, "You know I'm not here for you to protect me. My father sends me to protect *you*, Austin. I knew you weren't dead."

"I know." Her voice gentled. "And I know you wouldn't kill me."

"I failed him," Hutch said, voice cracking under shame. "I failed you. I could see it in his eyes when he came to pick me up. It was— devastating."

She stood with a small grunt. "Listen to the story I just told you. Even gods screw up. They made Cipactli—a monster that ate everything. But they fixed it. That's what matters, Hutch. Not perfection. Correction."

He nodded slowly, letting her words settle over him like a blanket. She squeezed his hand once before stepping away. As Austin crossed the room toward the stairs, Hutch let his eyes drift closed.

The house settled. A pipe ticked. A board creaked. The scent of stale cigarette smoke wafted from somewhere. And then— from the far corner of the room, behind the coat rack, something breathed. Slow. Deliberate.

Hutch's eyes flew open. But nothing moved.

Chapter −66

Austin sat alone on cool grass. She let a blade slip through her fingers, its tickle grounding her. Eyes closed, she rocked gently, twirling another blade, then lay back. Sun burned her eyelids, turning the world pulsing orange-red.

She tried to empty her mind like Starr meditated—Austin's brain was a dumped junk drawer. Thoughts collided, scattered, tangled.

Did I lock the back door? When do the phones run out of data? Is Brandon in love with me or the idea of me? Did Aina steal my underwear again? Did I feed the barn cats? Where's Tessa? Why do I feel like I forgot something huge? Her thoughts snapped back to Brandon, the center of her restless cycle. Next came the ache behind her ribs, sharp and insistent.

Then food storage flashed across her mind, another worry tumbling forward. Hutch surfaced in her whirling thoughts. Just as quickly, Brandon again.

Her mind spiraled, jumping from one fear to the next, each new worry making her head spin faster as she tried to silence them.

"Crap," she muttered, sitting upright. She paced, glancing behind her. She'd ducked away from Roo for the first time in ages—bolting when he went to the bathroom—but still felt exposed, as if the world grew a thousand invisible eyes.

Papaw taught her to pray in the woods, Mama in church. Neither worked—no miracles, no clarity. Maybe she mixed her prayers, calling the wrong spirit by the wrong name. Maybe God was offended, or she just couldn't be still long enough to be heard.

The spring whispered faintly through the grass. Birds called overhead. Austin sank to her knees and clasped her hands in a clumsy prayer before popping back up again because her brain wouldn't stop spinning. Finally, she sighed, folded her hands with effort, and scanned the pasture to make sure she was alone.

"I don't know how to do this," she whispered. "God, Great Spirit—whoever—you—are. I need help. Please."

"You're good at a lot of things, but sitting still isn't one of them. And praying sure isn't your strong suit."

Austin dropped her head forward with a groan. "Aw, shit. How long have you been there, River?"

He stepped out from the treeline, sunlight catching in his hair. "Long enough to see why Brandon calls you Spaz." He held out a hand, and Austin accepted it.

"If my daddy hadn't been the judge, the doctors probably would've labeled me with ADHD. Everyone just called me 'hyper.'"

River dropped onto the ground, motioning for her to sit. "When Starr said you were dreamy, I thought she meant pretty. Turns out, you just get lost in your head." He waited for her snort. She almost smiled.

He plucked a blade of grass and twirled it. "Everyone else has skills. Golem, with his churchy magic, blesses every grain of salt from Tennessee to here. Hutch... well, Hutch has charm. Me? I just turn into a big cat. Big deal." He shrugged, gaze drifting down. "I just don't feel like I fit. But maybe I can teach you something—how to pray. I've had practice."

"Does it work?"

"I prayed a million times to get out of that hospital." His voice softened. "You came. So yeah, it works."

Austin huffed a quiet laugh. "If I'm a godsend, you'd think I'd get some dibs on miracles."

"Sometimes you *are* the miracle," River said simply. "Maybe your prayers are getting answered in ways you don't recognize yet."

He crossed his legs, elbows on knees. Austin mirrored him as he scooted closer until their knees touched.

"But you need to hear this," River said. "When Abel Martin attacked you in the hotel parking lot, he wasn't trying to kill you. He was testing you. Testing your strength against his."

Austin's eyes narrowed. "How do you know that?"

"I just do." He said softly. "He's coming here. To Brandon's land. You can't stop it—it's already set. I saw it in a dream."

She exhaled shakily. "Don't tell me how it ends."

"I can't. But I saw you facing him. Both of you know exactly what the other is. Just—don't run. If you run, he'll stab you in the back. Stand steady. Let him come."

"Stand steady," she whispered. "Great."

"Close your eyes," River instructed gently. "Just breathe. Listen to the wind."

Austin stared hard at River, at first cautious. But his gaze was steady. She drew in a long breath. The breeze lifted a strand of hair from her temple and cooled the sweat on her neck.

"Ask God to give you the strength of that wind," River murmured. "To face your friends—and your enemies."

She did so with slow uncertainty.

"Now feel the sun on your shoulders." His hand brushed her arm—cool, grounding—where the sun had sunk warmth deep into her skin. "Ask for power like the sun, to make decisions that matter."

Austin breathed again, the scent of clay and crushed clover rising around her.

"Now breathe in the earth," River said softly. "Pray your feet always move toward what's good."

She inhaled.

"Now picture yourself in a dark tunnel. And light at the end. Follow it."

The light unfurled in her mind—soft, pale, drifting like a glowing feather in the dark. Austin giggled quietly under her breath and chased it, feet kicking up behind her as if this were some secret game only she knew how to play.

The light drifted ahead, always just a breath out of reach.

Then it steadied.

Still, she followed the light toward the end of the tunnel. At first it was far off, then it drifted closer, bobbing ahead of her like a feather tumbling through the dark.

Austin came to a halt on the lip of a cliff.

River was beside her—not a boy now, but a black panther, shoulder warm against her hip. Her steps almost carried her over the edge before she caught herself, toes curling in her shoes.

"River," she asked softly to the black panther at her side, breath trembling as the wind tugged at her hair, "why did you bring me here?"

The wind howled up the face of the rock, threatening to pull her into the abyss. Austin looked down.

"Look."

She looked out over the mountain. Filmy curls of fog drifted through the trees and hovered over the creek. People moved below—some in buckskin and tan leather, others in white shirts. Women gathered in dresses, children splashed in the water.

Austin watched, silent. A vibration crawled up her fingers and into her feet. The ground shook. Children screamed. A man in traditional clothes looked up—his gaze locking with hers across the distance.

And though he didn't speak aloud, a voice thrummed through her skull, deep as bedrock:

It is not the serpent beneath the mountain.

Austin's breath hitched.

It is something deeper. Older. From the bowels of the earth.

The land split. People scattered. Dirt and stones rained down. The man lifted his arm, holding her papaw's old medicine bag in his fist.

"Run, River!" she cried, grabbing the panther's ear. "Run!"

But River wouldn't move. Austin's heart slammed against her ribs. She took a step back, then turned. "River!"

His eyes burned into hers—not human, not soft, not steady. Wild. Angry. Ancient. He crouched, haunches flexing.

A cat about to pounce.

"River, it's me," Austin whispered. "It's Austin." But he lunged.

Chapter −67

The porch boards still held the late-afternoon warmth when Brandon settled onto them, paper plate on his knee, a hot dog and chips balanced carefully as he crunched down on the first bite. The air carried the sweetness of cut grass and the faint hush that sometimes settles before dusk—one of those uneasy summer pauses where even the insects seem to hold their breath.

Austin joined him with a posture sharper than it had been days earlier, fingers tapping against her thigh in restless little bursts. Her eyes kept darting toward the yard's edge, as if she expected something to move there.

"What's going on between you and River?" Brandon asked, brushing chip crumbs off his jeans.

"What do you mean?" Austin replied too fast, the clipped edge in her voice giving her away.

Roo and Golem sat next to Austin, sharing a low chuckle. The porch swing creaked beneath them. The two along with Aina, Starr, and Brandon had watched River appear around the side of the house with his plate—only to jerk to a stop the instant he spotted Austin, his body twisting in a fast, awkward pivot, almost stumbling in his haste to whip back around the corner and vanish. A faint breeze stirred the hair at the nape of Austin's neck, raising goosebumps.

"You two have been dodging each other like middle-schoolers at their first dance—standing on opposite sides of the gym pretending the other doesn't exist."

Austin exhaled. "We had a moment, I guess." The words were already cast before she could reel them back. Starr's eyes narrowed—jealousy, fear, and something harder tightening her jaw. Aina rubbed her thumb faster over her knee, watching Brandon for his reaction. "Not that kind of moment," Austin added quickly. "I got into his head. He got into mine. It was an accident. A personal place, not physical. Now it's just... awkward."

"Is there something I should know?" Brandon pressed.

"I don't know. Maybe not." Austin poked at her hot dog with her fork, jaw tight. "He is like a brother to me. It wasn't sexy—just... in our heads, not our bodies." She winced, glancing at Starr, whose eyes took on an anxious gaze.

"Austin, please explain yourself," Starr said quietly.

"It was spiritual," Austin muttered, fork scraping a rut into the flimsy paper plate. "Is that worse? It felt like he saw the bones beneath my skin—all my secrets on display. Not naked, not like that. Like when you walk in on me in the bathroom, Brandon—just humiliating. I want to forget it."

She didn't add the truth: waking from the vision tangled with River, skin clammy, the taste of copper lingering long after she'd sat up gasping. Both had snapped awake silent, shaken, static crackling across her nerves for hours afterward. The silence around them thickened, settling over the porch like damp cloth. Austin's appetite flickered out. She watched Tessa mash a shredded bit of hot dog into her doll's stiff pink mouth, the plastic squeaking in protest. The tiny, strange domestic act pressed against Austin's frayed nerves.

A chill skated across her foot. She looked up instantly—because River had a way of appearing out of nowhere.

"It's going to happen tonight." His voice dropped into the hush, low and rough as gravel. A cicada whined out in the dusk. He didn't seem to notice the eyes turning toward him, but Austin felt the truth of his words settle into her gut like cold stone. Her heartbeat stuttered, one painful skip.

"Okay." She nodded. She felt everyone watching the two of them.

"I think I should go away for a couple of days." River's gaze slid to the ground, then flicked toward Brandon—something unspoken hanging between them. "Maybe you're better off without me."

"You can't," Austin said, voice firm, fingers curling tightly around the paper plate. She didn't want to say it aloud, but the truth sat heavy in her chest: she didn't trust Hutch, Starr, or Aina with anyone's life. So, she did the only thing she could at quick notice.

She paired each traitor with someone she *did* trust, someone who could watch them, contain them, and keep the rest of the family alive. "Starr's inside the house. You, Aina, and Roo are my only line of defense if it comes to a fight. We're putting salt around the house. Aina, you'll have to be outside the circle—"

"Are you saying I'm—evil?" Aina cut in, wiggling her head, equal parts mockery and hurt.

"You break out in hives around blessed salt. You hiss when I hold up a cross with holy water, and iron burns your skin. What do you think?" Austin told her—gently, matter-of-fact. "Not evil. Just... otherworld. Sensitive to those things."

"It's a medical condition," Aina huffed, though her shoulders trembled briefly before she masked it with bravado.

"What about me?"

Austin snapped her attention to the screen door. Hutch stood there—the silhouette of someone who had been listening longer than he planned, his shoulders sloped, eyes tired. "You're guarding Brandon and Tessa," Austin said. What she did not tell him was that Brandon was carrying a small handgun with him should he need to protect himself from Hutch.

Her gaze locked onto River again. Her thumb brushed a scar on her wrist—a grounding habit she barely noticed. "Please stay."

"For your safety, I can't, Little Turtle Girl." River's tone softened, almost reverent. The name scraped something deep inside her— Papaw's voice echoing behind his. "Yeah, it was him in the vision. He was warning you. About me, I think. I'm sorry. I have to go."

He turned. His fingers twitched at his sides, like he was holding himself back from reaching for her.

Austin stood too, voice measured. "Did it occur to you to look at all angles, River? Maybe you're protecting someone else from me. Maybe—" She bit down the rest, jaw tightening. "Maybe I'm not the one who should hold the snake's crystal."

River paused, finally looking at her fully. "That's a lot of maybes, Austin," he murmured—but he didn't look away.

Chapter –68

"It's time."

Austin had dreamed it moments before she felt the first quiver beneath the house—an almost imperceptible shift, like the ground bracing itself. She sat on the edge of the bed, hand steady as she laid it on Brandon's shoulder. He blinked awake, eyes focusing on her face. Whatever he saw there—fear, resolve, inevitability—he understood. He nodded without question.

Earlier that evening, long before the tremor, Brandon had been perched on the front porch, Tessa curled and sleeping against him, when Austin stepped out. She had changed into a black dress, sharp at the edges, lace whispering warnings in the porch light. Keys dangled from her fingers like a decision already made. Brandon's eyes tracked her, uncertain.

But she wasn't leaving—she had changed the plans again. For the last hour she'd been turning over one plan after another, fumbling with the idea of dropping Roo off down the road and having him keep an eye on the tower. Austin had already set the charges herself, wired and placed exactly how she wanted them. But at the last moment she backed out of assigning Roo to guard it—too risky, too many variables, too many ways it could go wrong.

Fewer moving pieces. Fewer targets.

With everything tumbling through her mind, she barely registered the keys in her hand. She'd been turning them over and over—mindlessly, endlessly—as if her body needed something to hold while her thoughts tried to sort themselves. Another anxious reminder that focus mattered. And that focus had never been her strongest point... and absolutely wasn't tonight.

He exhaled hard. "I figured something out. And I hate it." His hand shook as he ran it through his hair. "I know I was being trained to poison everyone. I didn't see it—God, I didn't see it—but it hit me two days ago. The day everything went south? That's when Bradley took me to the water house. He showed me how to add the chemical.

Like it was nothing. Like it was normal." His voice cracked. "They were grooming me. Teaching me to do it myself."

He pressed the heel of his palm to his eye, as if trying to push the memory back out. "I would've poisoned the whole compound. Maybe the whole town. And I thought I was helping."

Austin's hand closed over his shaking knee.

"Brandon," she said softly, "they manipulated you. They drugged you. This is not on you."

"If you wouldn't have come back—"

"But I did." Her voice was steady. "Listen to me: you are the reason we even caught it. You are the link that brought us together, that brought me home. Without you and that link, none of us would have known the water was laced. None of us would have traced it. None of us would have understood the pattern." Austin smiled. "You didn't doom this town, Brandon—you saved it."

He swallowed, throat tight.

"Well, saving it might be an overreach. Stats says the odds are only thirty-seven percent we survive this," she added with a humorless breath. "But those odds would be zero without you."

His eyes glistened with the weight of finally understanding his own place in the war that was being fought in his backyard.

Brandon's gaze slid down her dress, paused at the keys. "Are you meeting someone?" She exhaled, glanced down, and seemed almost surprised to find her keys still in her hand. A quick, self-conscious chuckle escaped her as she set them aside. She kicked off her shoes and slid in beside him.

"No. A date. Kind of a breakup, really."

"Oh." Brandon stared ahead.

"I fooled myself," Austin said quietly. "Thinking Marco and I could do casual. But neither of us fit that shape. We dragged the end out because it was easier than admitting we were pretending. I don't want that with him—never did. He has obligations. So do I."

"I was your second choice," Brandon joked weakly. "Isn't that what you said about Lyndsey and me?"

332

"You were never my second choice." Her voice sharpened, unwavering as she sighed. "Not once. You always felt out of reach. I figured you didn't want someone like me—too much, too loud, too scattered. Troubled and troublesome. You never really looked at me."

"I listened to every word," Brandon murmured. "Just... badly, I guess." He flushed. "I'm not relationship material. I lost my job at the hardware store."

"You're a farmer," Austin insisted. "Farm and stuff."

"Farm and stuff." Brandon snorted. "Great résumé. And I've lost fourteen cows."

"A big snake?" she asked lightly.

"It's either that or Abel Martin's stealing them. His whole place is in lockdown."

Austin's heart hammered. "Lockdown?"

"Yeah. Quiet over there. No fires. Nothing."

Her breath caught. "Okay," she said softly. "Then it's time."

"Time for what?"

"I know you don't always believe me," she told him, fingers brushing gently over Tessa's hair—a grounding ritual. "But my grandfather—he was in Abel Martin's barn the other night. I saw him. He told me I have something nobody else does. Something called me here. Something Abel wants."

Brandon stared at her, no longer skeptical—just afraid.

"I can call Uktena," Austin said. "The snake. He's here. We've heard him beneath the ground. I felt him move. Abel conjured him to draw me back so he could steal the crystal from the snake's head. That's what he's after. The crystal Abel wants—it's missing from my papaw's medicine bag. The one controlling light and dark. And me."

"Controlling *you*," Brandon whispered.

"Unless I get it first and hide it."

"Teeny-weensy you against big him," Brandon murmured. "There has to be another way."

"No, Brandon. She is strong. She is a warrior," Starr said softly from the doorway. For once, no sarcasm touched her voice. "Austin comes from a line of fighters. That power is in her blood. She might be small, but her strength is here." Starr tapped her temple. "When it's time, she'll know what to do." She reached for Tessa. "Let me put her to bed. Sit with her while she sleeps. Austin dressed up for you, you know. Tell her you see her. Tell her you believe in her. She needs that more than she says."

Brandon flushed. "I... I did notice," he admitted awkwardly.

Austin nudged his shoulder with her knuckles. "Don't listen to her." Starr slipped quietly inside with Tessa. The screen door clicked shut behind them. Roo emerged from the shadows, silent and ready. Austin angled her head toward the door. He understood immediately: watch Starr. Never let her out of your sight. Especially when Tessa was anywhere near her.

"Do you want me to tell you you're a warrior?" Brandon asked, head cocked like he was trying the idea on for size.

"What I want is simple," Austin murmured. "I want to go upstairs, lie down with you, watch TV, drink hot chocolate, eat popcorn, and wait for Tessa to sneak into bed with us. Just one moment where we're like a normal family."

"You make it sound like you're about to die," Brandon teased gently. She didn't laugh. The silence stretched, heavy. He looked at her—really looked at her—as if this might be the last time.

"You know she's trying to sell me on you," Austin said. "Chicken dinner, dresses, makeup. She thinks I can't manage the basics you want in a woman. I can't cook real meals—your cows terrify me, and I hate cleaning. I'm not that girl. I fight. I don't hide behind anyone. And yeah, Starr knows it. You always pick the girly girls—the Lyndseys—over me."

"I don't like girly-girl," Brandon countered. "If I wanted that, I'd have married one of 'em."

"You like girls who flirt with guys and stab their friends in the back and run," Austin muttered. "Like Caylee Wesley. I'm a bitch— you said it yourself. I stab and stand my ground."

"You're wrong." Brandon's smile was crooked. "I want you just as you are. Not fluff. Not fake. You. Always you."

She didn't argue when he leaned in and kissed her.

Later—before she left the note—Austin sat up and watched Brandon sleep. Wind battered the window. Lightning flickered at the edges of the blinds. Her heartbeat stuttered.

She wrote the message by hand.

To Whom It Might Concern,
I will be a quarter mile beneath the water tower along the creek
before dawn.
We will meet.

She walked straight into the compound without anyone stopping her. No alarms. No questions. She crossed the yard, went up onto the porch of Abel Martin's big house, and tucked the note where he would find it. She watched the door open, a hand coming out to snatch it up. He had been waiting. She was gone less than thirty minutes. But she knew, deep in her soul, that the note was probably pointless. Abel Martin would have sensed her, sensed the calling long before she left the safety of Brandon's house.

Austin returned to Brandon's room, lay down beside him, and dozed for maybe ten minutes.

Her dream was full of little black creatures—darting, swarming, whispering at the edges of her vision—but above their chaos came her the steady voice: *Turtle Girl. He comes.*

Austin shivered. Something ancient was rising.

She shook Brandon's shoulder, voice low and urgent.

"Brandon. You have to take Tessa and go to your parents' house. Take the black jacket in your closet. It has a handgun in the pocket. If I had a choice, I would not send you with Hutch," she whispered. "But my army is small. He is the strongest, and can protect you and Tessa. But he is no match for a gun should you have to use it. Abel Martin is waking the snake. I can feel him moving. Please, Five. Wake up—"

Chapter –69

Austin hadn't slept. She'd tossed and turned all night, every version of the plan unfolding behind her eyes and failing in a dozen different ways. Each time she thought she had it right, something shifted—one wrong move, one blind spot, and Abel Martin would take everything from them.

By dawn, she'd stopped pretending rest was possible and sat up in bed, elbows on her knees, breathing through the familiar ache behind her sternum. Planning was how she survived. It was the only way she stayed ahead of evil that wore human faces.

By the time the sun rose, she had the shape of it.

Not perfect. But workable.

Roo and Golem would move first. Roo had slipped out before daylight, not to fight and not to interfere—but to watch. His job was the children. The compound. The dorms. He was there to keep eyes on the youngest ones while the adults moved about their rituals and routines, to make sure nothing changed suddenly and no one was moved without warning. If Abel tried to relocate the kids, use them, or hide them, Roo would be the first to know.

He was an early warning system. Nothing more. Nothing less.

Golem's role was quieter but just as vital. He would bless every water source he could reach—creeks, troughs, spigots—anything people might drink from. Sanctified water wouldn't neutralize the chemical itself, Stats had been clear about that. But it would burn anything else moving through it. Anything dead. Anything summoned. It would give them boundaries. Lines that couldn't be crossed without consequence.

Stats would stay at the farmhouse, running intel and monitoring movement. Not because he wanted to—but because he was, as Starr had bluntly put it, "a thinker, not a hitter." The salt circles and wards around the house were insurance, not confidence.

And Brandon...Austin swallowed hard.

Brandon wasn't part of the fight. Not tonight.

Hutch had left with Brandon and Tessa early—before the tension reached the point where it would spook a child. Brandon had headed toward the outskirts of town, to his mother's place, where the lights still worked and the roads stayed busy enough to discourage anything strange. Hutch hadn't argued when Austin told him. He'd just nodded once. That was his job tonight: protect them. Keep them alive. Keep Tessa asleep and unaware that the world was cracking open.

Austin, Aina, and Starr would drive one of Crazy Jack's old trucks to a pull off and down an old logging road to the creek, far below the water tower, where the shed snake skin had been found.

Aina would stay in the truck, watching the treeline for his approach. She would not cross the salt unless Austin gave the signal.

Austin's role was simple on paper—and deadly in practice. She would draw Abel Martin out.

Starr would lay an open arc of salt along the bank, wide enough to look like hesitation, not a trap. The circle would remain incomplete at first—an invitation disguised as desperation. Abel needed the snake. He needed Austin. And he would step inside to claim both. Once he crossed the line, Starr would close the circle behind him. No retreat. No slipping sideways. No shadows left to hide in.

And Austin would do what she'd come back to do.

Call Uhktena. Get close enough to take the stone.

End Abel Martin before he could touch it.

That was the plan. It was clean. It was brutal. It depended on Abel coming alone. Outside, something shifted and changed.

The earth shuddered—once.

And not far away, Abel Martin and Paolo changed the rules.

Chapter −70

The road into town was closed.

Maintenance crews in reflective vests clustered around six ruptured water lines. Brandon eased his truck onto the muddy shoulder at Road 665, tires grinding through wet gravel. Ahead, Bill Thomas's white maintenance truck idled, yellow caution lights flashing through the drizzle.

Brandon glanced sideways at Hutch. The boy's hair shot up in wild tufts, sleep clinging stubbornly to the corners of his eyes. He sat up, suddenly alert—watchful, tension thrumming beneath his small frame.

"What's up? Which roads are open?" Brandon asked.

Bill threw both hands into the air. He laughed sharply, then his face grew serious. "Some kind of gas leak. An explosion under Mister Salty's Gas and Carryout. The gas must have slipped through the caves, right under half the town—so now, the whole region looks like a war zone. The asphalt buckled from here to Main Street. Electric's out for a few thousand. Water's shut off because of the breaks. We didn't expect this mess, so we're still trying to get ahold of employees to help clear the roads. Most can't even get to work."

He scratched his jaw. "You can try Tucker Road. Or go around Canaan Mountain if you're not scared of power lines coming down from the wind. But we're getting calls from everywhere. And the storm hasn't even hit yet." Then he peered past Brandon and smiled into the cab. "Is that a nephew? Didn't see him at church Sunday."

"He's a friend of the family," Brandon said.

"We need to go, sir" Hutch thumped Brandon's arm. "Anywhere but Canaan Mountain. What is the deepest backroad that will take us up the mountainside so I can see if I can get satellite reception?"

Brandon nodded. "Hey, you don't gotta call me sir. Brandon's fine. And that would be Mine Hollow and then up Tucker Road. But that is so far from civilization—"

"No, sir. I do." Hutch jabbed a finger at the dirty windshield.

"You're undermining Austin's authority. We're on lockdown. Follow her orders. Tucker Hollow is where we need to head."

Brandon flicked a glance toward the backseat. Tessa clutched the book Austin had given her so hard her knuckles shone, fingers ghost-pale. Her small, tremulous voice kept asking where Austin was, why she wasn't there. Each question twisted deeper, twisting pain beneath Brandon's ribs until he could hardly breathe.

"Okay," Brandon murmured to Hutch. "Safest route."

He backed the truck up, turned toward Tucker Road as thunder rumbled overhead. "I'm sorry," he muttered after a moment, jaw tight. "It's just... hard taking orders from a friend. Someone I'm close to. It's not that she's a woman. Or that we, you know, date. It's just weird."

Hutch let out a small laugh, tapping a restless rhythm on his sneaker. "You don't have to take her orders," he said. "She doesn't expect it. That's why she hesitates when you push back. She respects your input, but if she disagrees, she's doing the math in her head. Seeing if your plan's better." He turned his gaze to the window, his voice steady. "But you gotta respect the orders she gives us. She trusts me to follow them, and I can't let her down. Don't ask me to cross her, sir."

Brandon shook his head. "Damn. She's right about you. You're really sharp."

Hutch's mouth twitched. "Yeah. Did she tell you how she found me?"

"No."

"Tomás Ríos kidnapped me when I was twelve. Confederation of Red. Terrorist group." His tone flattened, matter-of-fact. "Three government teams tried to rescue me. Tomás was gonna mail my dad three of my fingers and an ear. Austin walked into the bar where they were keeping me. Walked out with me without a scratch."

Brandon's fingers froze on the steering wheel.

"Later," Hutch continued, "Rios and six of his men were found dead under an old Catholic church. The government called it a hit."

He didn't blink. "It was Austin."

Brandon swallowed. "She... did that?"

"If she has to," Hutch said. "Paolo gave the orders. She got everything ready. Led the attack."

"Why are you telling me this?" Brandon whispered.

Hutch's answer came without hesitation. "Because Paolo's paying me a million bucks to isolate you from Austin and bring you and your kid to him," Hutch said directly, revealing the truth. He shrugged slightly, eyes still on the road ahead. "Austin's got Abel Martin on one side and Paolo on the other. And you? You're stuck in the middle with me. I want you to know where I stand, even with all this mess."

Silence settled. Brandon flushed as a dizzying, swooping dread hollowed his chest. For a heartbeat, he thought he might actually pass out from the fear twisting in his gut. Brandon's elbow brushed the gun hidden under his jacket, and a cold realization crept up his spine. The weapon wasn't reassurance—it was a burden. If Hutch lunged, Brandon might have to shoot a boy. A boy barely old enough to drive. And Tessa would see everything. If he even survived long enough to pull the gun free.

Rain ticked against the windshield in frantic, skittering patterns. Brandon's grip on the wheel tightened; his knuckles turned bloodless, every muscle straining as his chest filled with dread. Austin. God, she was so damn trusting—too trusting, maybe. The fear for her twisted through Brandon, sharp and raw.

He saw her last night—sitting curled under the soft glow of the bedside lamp, shoulders hunched, breaths catching like she was bracing for a blow she knew might come. Vulnerable in a way that clawed at him. "You want to make out or something?" she'd whispered. He'd laughed—until he realized she wasn't joking.

Her cheeks had burned. "I'm awkward with this stuff," she'd muttered. "Without my crew, I'm just a geeky girl in thick glasses talking too much when I'm nervous." Her fingers twisted in the bedsheets. "I wanted a clean slate. A new diary. But Abel Martin and Paolo—they won't let me throw the old one away."

And Brandon had kissed her—quietly, gently—pulling her into him until every laugh, every breath, tangled together.

Her hands were trembling as she unbuttoned his shirt, her dress slipping over her head, their bodies warm and clumsy, almost rolling off the bed in a knot of limbs and laughter.

The ache still lingered across his back where her fingernails had raked him.

"What do I have to do so we don't get hurt?" he asked quietly now. Hutch finally looked at him, all humor gone from his face. "Pull off on the side of the road," he said, tone flat.

Chapter –71

The ground trembled beneath Roo's feet—subtle at first, then rising through his bones like a low warning hum only a half-shifted Rougarou could sense. Pads thickened beneath the skin of his palms, nerves sharpening. Tension typically sparked a slight change to his form if it was close to a full moon—like now, when the shift itched just beneath his skin, tugging at his bones and sharpening every instinct. The anxiety meds never helped; they didn't slow the partial change. They only made him itchy, exhausted, and prone to those strange patches of fur and half-phases breaking out along his arms and back.

The vibration crawled up his spine, a predator's premonition, the kind that makes animals freeze before avalanches or quakes. He hated it. It made him jumpy, restless.

As he slunk under the compound's gate, his elongated fingers brushed gravel. He glanced up at the security camera Stats warned him about. No red blink. No slow pulse. Nothing but dead plastic.

Relief flickered—thin, fleeting. Good. Austin must have clipped the power line. If she hadn't, he'd already be lit up on Abel Martin's screens. Roo inhaled sharply and let out three clipped, urgent barks. A summons.

The replies rippled back through the dark—the anxious bay of a beagle, the low chesty rumble of Rottweilers. His old friends. Jittery. Afraid. Not because of the storm.

"Come on, boys," he murmured, voice rough with the gravel of Rougarou's throat. He jogged along the cracked asphalt, which crumbled into gravel at the crossroads. A weather-beaten wooden sign read Maintenance. Roo pulled a creased map from his jeans, finger tracing the red circle Stats had drawn around the long dorm-like building. "That's where Brandon says the kids sleep," he whispered. The dogs approached, but their hackles were up, tails low, whining in uneasy rhythm. Something in the wind made them drop their heads even lower.

"It's okay," Roo soothed—though even he didn't believe it. He stuffed the map away. He took three steps—then froze.

A stench slid through the air. Not the roadside reek of a single dead deer in August heat. This was worse—a thousand carcasses layered together, rot stacked atop rot. Old paper. Wet earth. Grave-dust stirred too soon. The smell coated the back of Roo's tongue like moldy velvet. Something ancient had crawled up from below. He dropped into a crouch, one palm raised in command. The dogs melted into the ground, bellies flat. No sound. Not even a breath.

Then he heard it—voices. Children's whimpers. Soft cries. Little sniffles swallowed down to avoid punishment.

Roo's throat tightened. He pressed a hand to his chest, breath thin and sharp. The fog shifted—and shadows materialized. He squinted, his night vision sliding into perfect clarity. A procession. Children walking in a line, hands clasped in pairs. A single man at the front.

Abel Martin.

Roo trembled—not from cold, not from fear, but from the pure, razor-edged sense of true evil. His spine felt carved from ice.

Some of the adults walking beside the children weren't alive. Only the ones holding the children's hands did not have the stench of death. The undead's skin sagged. Faces were half missing. Teeth bared through rotted cheeks. Clothes stiff with dried mud. Hands blackened at the fingertips. Joints grinding like bone on stone. The children clung to the living just to stay away from the dead.

Roo swallowed a growl threatening to spill from his wolf-man throat. He slipped backward into the brush—leaves trembling against his back. His breath went shallow, jaw locked to keep from panting. No one noticed him. They didn't even sense him.

Fifteen minutes dragged past, suffocating and endless. Roo's muscles cramped. A dog whimpered once—Roo pressed a palm to its snout. A little girl cried softly, tugging at the hand of her escort. One corpse paused, turning its ruined face toward Roo, sniffing.

Roo didn't breathe. Thunder rolled overhead. The procession moved on.

Only when the last child vanished into the mist did Roo's control snap. Tears streaked down the fur-shadowing his cheeks—something he hadn't done in this shape since childhood.

Then he bolted. Crashing through the brush, heart pounding, lungs burning, he sprinted down the mountain—toward anyone who could stop this.

Chapter −72

Golem stood beneath the leaning water tower, its rusted frame silhouetted against a bruised-purple sky. The air held a metallic tang, damp with the coming storm. Goosebumps prickled his arms as a shiver traveled up his spine.

In his calloused hand, he clutched a battered Protestant Bible Aina had "borrowed" from the rickety dresser in her room at Cherry Grove Hotel. Its pages fluttered in the wind, the leather cover slick with sweat. Golem's job was twofold: track down whatever was physically contaminating the water, and protect anyone near it— blessing every creek, trough, and spigot he could reach, asking for protection over every person who drank from them.

He'd started at sunrise, clambering across Brandon's dew-wet fields until the cold soaked into his boots. Because something had poisoned the water, and not just with herbs or medicine. Something darker. Something that made Golem's stomach twist.

Three days earlier, Austin had crept out at dawn and filled four red plastic picnic cups at different water points. She'd taken them straight to Stats, who squinted at the samples through thick glasses, the steamy smell of coffee and bleach clinging to the cluttered kitchen. Two cups showed trace amounts of Rohypnol—street names: roofies, Mexican Valium, as Stats was quick to point out. The kind that wipes your memory clean. The third sample, drawn closest to the water tower, held enough to drop a grown man. Stats had taken off his glasses and muttered a curse. Brandon had suffered every symptom: dizziness, nausea, confusion, and muscles turning to jelly.

It wasn't an accident. Abel Martin wasn't just drugging the adults. He was drugging the children, too—keeping his people docile, compliant, pliant. And someone kept refilling the supply. And that was the part that chilled Golem: This wasn't old contamination sitting in the pipes. Someone was actively adding the drug every few hours.

chth

Roo had tracked the physical source: the well house that pumped water from the dam-created pool on Turtle Creek. But Stats had pieced together the rest after Brandon's confession of tainting the well water: once the water left the well house, it fed straight into the elevated water tower, which pressurized it and pushed the drugged supply through the entire community. The only way to break the cycle was to dilute the contamination faster than Abel could replace it—which meant disrupting every point the water passed through.

And blowing the tower.

If the tower fell, the pressure dropped, the flow slowed, and the drug's concentration wouldn't spread fast enough to overtake the community before they could intervene. It wasn't perfect—but it bought time.

Golem climbed the rutted forestry road, breath fogging, before dropping down to a narrow feeder stream that joined the creek like a thin silver vein. Every step was slow, deliberate, searching for the place where the poison entered.

Now, at the base of the water tower beside the squat cinderblock pump building, Golem lifted his face to the churn of dark clouds overhead. The sky roiled, swollen with rain, the air thick with electricity.

He laughed under his breath—thin, exhausted. If Austin asked, she'd probably expect him to bless the rain itself.

Suddenly—Something skittered up his feet. A cold, frantic shock. Like something small and electric had raced straight over his toes.

He looked down. Then recoiled. Rats and mice—hundreds of them—poured across the creekbed, their slick bodies glistening like wet stones. A living tide. A frantic stampede. Their claws scraped over rock and mud, their high squeals slicing through the thickening air. Golem shuddered so violently that the Bible nearly slipped from his hand. He hated rats—their twitching tails, their darting hunger, their too-clever eyes. His skin crawled.

They're fleeing. But from what?

The earth trembled once again—this time much deeper, older.

A vibration thrummed through his bones, low and grim, a warning from the ground itself. "Lord, give me strength," he whispered, voice tight. Half prayer. Half plea.

The exodus grew. A white-tailed deer burst from the treeline, hooves clattering, nearly clipping his shoulder. Golem flung his arm up instinctively, heart pounding. Then came a raccoon. Two foxes. A mottled skunk barreled past like a runaway boulder.

And beneath it all—the sound no one should ever hear at the surface—the wet rustle of earthworms bursting upward, soil churning as if something below pressed them out in terror.

Golem's breath hitched. Something massive was coming. Something deep. Something that made even the worms flee.

"Golem!" The voice cut through the storm-thick air like a blade.

He spun. "Roo?"

Roo emerged from the trees—half-shifted, trembling. Now the partial shift tore at him, jaw tight, eyes feral, breath ragged.

"I need your help," Roo gasped. "They're leading the pups—I mean, the children—somewhere. I tried to stop them, but there are too many of them. Humans... and the dead ones mixed with them."

His voice trembled.

"I can't do it alone, brother."

Golem's heart slammed against his ribs. "What direction?"

Roo pointed toward the mountain—toward Abel Martin. And toward the thing beneath the earth that made even the worms flee.

Chapter −73

"Do. Not. Move."

Bradley Martin's eyes snapped open. The world tilted, spinning in a nauseating swoop. His breath came fast, metallic and hot. He froze—every muscle stiff—as the cop's voice buzzed up the steel frame of the billboard. He was duct-taped naked to it. Thirty feet in the air. High enough that a fall wouldn't kill him, but it'd make him wish it had.

Tape cinched across his chest, biting into his ribs, pinning his arms uselessly. Sticky edges ripped hair out with every breath. The metal sign radiated heat from the floodlights; sweat trickled down his spine. Bugs landed on him like sparks of hot ash, drawn to the light.

"Dude... dude, what's going on?" Billy Tate whimpered somewhere to his right, voice thin and cracking. "They're ripping stuff out of your truck. Hazmat suits. Hazmat suits, man. What did we *have* in there?"

Bradley heard him, but his brain sloshed—fogged, slow, off. The billboard swayed in the breeze, worsening the vertigo.

"For the love of—shut up," Bradley hissed. "They're going to shoot us if you don't." Billy sobbed louder.

Below, headlights swept across gravel as Deputy Cotter climbed out of his cruiser. He didn't bother raising the loudspeaker at first— just stared up at the billboard like someone examining something unpleasant stuck to their boot. Then his disgust sharpened.

"Bradley Martin." He didn't hide the venom. "Well, well. What you got yourself into this time, boy? Didn't expect to scrape you off a highway sign tonight."

He turned to the growing crowd behind him. "Alright, folks—get your pics, then get along."

People already had their phones up. Recording. Laughing. Livestreaming. A woman shouted, "Already on Facebook! *Hashtag Billboard Boys!*"

Another: "Channel 12 just picked it up!"

A teenage girl cackled, "My Snap is blowing up—Brad Martin's wiener has its own group chat!" There was great laughter after that.

If Bradley could have crawled inside the metal skin of the sign, he would have. Billy let out a broken sob. "Oh God. Oh God. We're viral. I can hear the notifications."

And Bradley felt it then—deep in his gut, cold and brutal:

Austin Jackson did this on purpose.

And she wanted him to know the whole town was watching him pay.

His humiliation wasn't a punishment.

It was a warning. And she wasn't done with them yet.

Chapter −74

Austin stood on the rise above Turtle Creek, the night thick with humidity and the smell of wet earth. Moonlight slid across the water in a pale ribbon, bright enough to shimmer over the thin circle of salt Starr had poured in a huge arc. Just outside the ring, Aina jabbed a stick into the mud as if she could pry courage out of the ground.

"Aina, you should be in the truck." Austin kept her voice smooth, calm, and unbothered—hiding the dread slithering beneath her ribs. Her eyes tracked the rambling, sad excuse for an arc of salt—a line so crooked it looked like a drunk snail had been in charge—while a faint smile twitched at the corner of her mouth. "I don't want you turning full fairy if we don't need it. And there's salt everywhere. Starr apparently thinks the difference between trapping evil spirits and prepping a holiday roast is just a matter of the amount of seasoning."

"It's everywhere," Aina added. "I think she's aiming for 'protective barrier' but landed somewhere closer to 'salt explosion at aisle five.'"

Austin laughed. Inside, though, a cold weight pressed against her lungs. Every choice tonight rested on a knife's edge—one wrong step and Abel Martin would have them all. Torture them. Twist them. Break them apart piece by piece. The brief panic flickering across her face burrowed hard into Austin's mind—what that salt alone could do to Aina, what Abel Martin could do, was unthinkable.

If that wasn't enough, the ache of what Hutch, Starr, and Aina had done still pulsed under every breath.

Trust didn't break loudly—it bled out slow—and she wasn't done bleeding yet.

Aina stepped close to the ring's edge, extending a small pouch on a cord. Her fingers shook, and she flinched when the wind stirred the salt at her toes. *What if Aina turns fairy and then turns traitor on me again?*

Austin forced those thoughts into a dark corner and locked them there.

She reached from within the circle and took the pouch with some hesitation, slipping it over her head. Lavender and lichen brushed her collarbone—warm, soothing—but it couldn't quiet the tightness gathering behind her sternum.

"There are protections inside," Aina murmured.

Austin's laugh was soft and razor-thin. "Yeah? Shame I didn't have something like this *last week*—might've protected me from you and Paolo."

Aina's jaw flexed, but she pretended not to hear. "I prayed over it," she continued stiffly. "The pouch for the crystal—you have it?"

"I do." Austin tugged the leather pouch from her pocket just enough to show it. "We're set. Stick to what we talked about."

Wind whipped her hair, stinging her cheeks with grit, thunder muttering somewhere north like a warning rumbling through the hills. A storm pressed close, carrying a strange bite of ozone that made her stomach tighten.

Aina glanced toward Starr, who knelt inside the ring, marking sigils into the grass, her movements careful, deliberate. "I don't want to be useless out here," Aina whispered.

"You're not," Austin said, and her voice did not waver. "But you're not crossing this line. The salt hits you wrong, and I'm holding wrought iron." She lifted the old iron bar. "You know the drill. Only in an emergency. Iron and fairies don't mix."

Aina's shoulders drew tight. "Let me change when he gets close."

"No." Austin's answer was quick and firm. "Doctor's orders—and mine."

"I'm stronger that way."

"You're also dead if your wings outpace your bones or your thoughts outpace your body because the salt messes with your judgment." Her tone stayed even, cool. "We're doing this my way."

"You will never trust me, will you?" Aina looked down, defeated.

"Doubt once planted is like wild rose," Austin said softly.

She lifted her hand and pointed to the thorny brush beside them, tiny red flowers peeking through the snarled branches. "Invasive. Hungry. It grows exactly where it shouldn't, and every thorn it puts out makes it harder to cut back. Nearly impossible to kill."

Her heartbeat thumped hard and off rhythm, a strange double-pulse that made her lightheaded for a moment. This was supposed to be clean: call Uktena, destroy it, take its power, crush Abel Martin, save the kids. Now everything felt uncertain, the plan pulling apart thread by thread as doubt clawed at her concentration.

Her phone rang. She answered instantly. "Pet... I mean Austin," Golem whispered. His voice trembled. "Roo is with me. Dead people walked down the road. With a bunch of little kids. Maybe twenty. Abel's people, Kim and Lyndsey, are leading them straight to you. He's with them. One little one's crying so hard..."

Austin's breath stopped short. The children. Abel had the children. He'd wrapped their tiny bodies around himself like armor.

"He's using them as a shield," she whispered. The words tasted harsh, bitter. Her head throbbed with a sudden, sharp pressure—Abel pushing at the edges of her mind, muddying her thoughts, fogging her focus.

She forced a slow inhale. She could not unravel.

Aina sniffed loudly, wiping a bug from her nose, and the small ordinary gesture cracked through Austin's spiraling fear long enough for her to steady herself. *There has to be a way. Pull it together.*

"Stay behind them," Austin said, keeping her tone level. "If anything happens, we neutralize by placement. Roo takes Kim. You handle Lyndsey. Keep them off him."

"*Neutralize?*" Golem echoed weakly. "I can't hurt anyone."

"Then sit on her," Austin said, and hung up.

She turned toward Starr, who watched her with a deep crease between her brows. Anger flickered in Austin's chest—steadying her, giving her something solid to grip besides fear.

"Did River tell you where he was going?" Austin asked.

Starr shook her head. "No." Her voice was small—regret, guilt, and the weight of everything she'd shattered between them. "He's been... standoffish since the—incident."

"You mean the betrayal," Austin said flatly. "You mean he stopped worshipping the ground you walk on. I guess he finally saw the darker side of you."

Starr sniffed, the sound brittle. It satisfied Austin—just a little—until the satisfaction twisted into something that almost hurt.

"Don't read into whatever bond we have," Austin muttered, looking away. "We just need more hands. Abel got the kids first. That changes everything."

Starr nodded once, subdued. "Then tell me what I need to do. I will do anything to make this up to you."

"We're doing what we planned," Austin said. She stood straighter. Her tone settled into the certainty of someone giving orders on a battlefield. "Stick to your role. Watch the treeline. Don't cross the salt." Her certainty was a polished mask. A perfect one. Underneath it, her stomach knotted so violently she thought she might be sick—but she didn't let so much as a breath show it.

Starr didn't question her. Aina didn't either. If nothing else had come out of their bitter lesson with Paolo, it was this—they no longer undermined her every decision. And somehow that made the weight of this battle even heavier. If she screwed this up, it made Paolo right. She could almost hear him laughing at her, smug and certain in the dark.

Austin knelt within the circle and prayed silently, jaw tight, pushing words through the haze Abel had smeared across her thoughts. Nothing answered. Not the waterfall whispering beside her. Not the sky tightening overhead. Not the earth shifting beneath her knees.

A hush rolled through the creek bed as if the world were drawing breath. "Now?" Aina whispered. "Do we move?"

"Hold." Austin kept her voice steady. "Not yet."

The earth shuddered—deep, close.

Thunder shivered across the hills. The grass trembled as though something massive moved just under the soil.

Austin drew a long breath through her nose. The air tasted metallic, like lightning about to strike. She didn't blink. Fear churned so fiercely inside her she thought her bones might splinter from the pressure, but to Aina and Starr, she stood unbending.

She had to. Because Abel Martin stepped over the guardrail.

He walked down the bank without bending a single blade of grass. The air around him buzzed faintly, an electric hum that crawled over Austin's skin like cold sparks.

His shadow stretched long across the ground, sliding ahead of him in a twisted, impossible shape. Behind him, the children moved in eerie unison—silent, pale, their eyes emptied of anything human. Their small feet made no sound in the grass.

Austin straightened, lifting the iron bar. She looked carved from stone—steady, fierce, immovable.

Inside, her heart slammed so hard it hurt.

Silence folded over the creek like a lid sealing shut.

Then—from the direction of Brandon's farm—a scream ripped through the night.

Stats.

High, sharp, and full of fear. It cracked the darkness open.

And everything shifted.

"Aina," Austin hissed, snapping her gaze to the young woman who had started to slink off toward the truck. "Change of plans—"

Austin jerked her chin skyward.

Aina caught the gesture, and the glimmer of the most evil smile crept across her face—like she'd just been handed an entire box of matches in a fireworks factory.

Chapter −75

Stats sat on the roof of Brandon Tremaine's farmhouse, the shale slates digging sharply into places he did not wish to reflect on. His laptop wobbled on his knees, glowing faintly in the thick summer dark. Beside him—balanced with questionable stability on the steep, slanted roof—were Brandon's parents.

Olivia Tremaine clutched the kitchen broom like a medieval halberd. John Tremaine gripped a baseball bat with the grim determination of a man who had probably used it only on slow-pitched church league ballgames.

Both were still panting, eyes huge, twenty minutes after they'd scrambled out onto the roof to escape the revenants banging at the doors and windows below.

"So—so those *things*," Olivia stammered, peering over the gutter into the half-light, "they're dead people from the cemetery?"

A dozen revenants wandered the yard, slack-jawed and stiff, their movements dreamlike and confused. They circled beneath the roof as if compelled but too uncoordinated to figure out the slant.

A dull scatter of salt ringed the house—messy lines across the porch boards, windowsills, and doorframes. Golem and Starr dumped entire bags of salt around the exterior for "Stats's protection," because while he excelled at analyzing risk, he was physically incapable of surviving it. Hutch had added that Stats couldn't fight his way out of a slow hug.

Stats had ignored their snark. Statistically speaking, he was indeed the softest target. He pressed his lips together. He'd told them—very politely, he thought—that salt worked better in horror movies than real-life undead management, but they hadn't listened. And now, of course, the revenants were happily trudging right through the salt circles as if they were wading through spilled popcorn at a movie theater.

Stats exhaled through his nose, half-scowl, half-smug.

Naturally. Naturally, he was right.

"Yes, Mrs. Tremaine," Stats whispered. "They are what we call *revenants*. The undead." His throat still ached. His scream—the one Austin, Aina, and Starr had heard from the creek—hadn't come from terror, exactly. He'd simply slipped when climbing onto the roof and nearly skidded right off. It felt important that the record reflect this. But no one asked.

"There's a small cemetery in the compound," he continued, shifting carefully. "Old church. 1834. Been tracking its perimeter all week."

"Oh my," Olivia whispered. "I wonder if Grandma Lilly is among them." She turned to her husband. "John, we probably know some of them. Do you think they'd recognize us? If Grandma Lilly is out there, she might listen if I tell her to go back to her grave."

Stats stared at her. She was either optimism in combat boots or a singular force of nature. He was leaning toward superhero. She hadn't even broken a sweat after everything that had happened thirty-two minutes earlier—

Thirty-five minutes earlier, Stats had been sitting at the kitchen table. To his eternal annoyance, absolutely no one ever believed him when he said he wasn't always looking at porn. At that particular moment, he was researching explosives—a far more respectable interest, in his opinion.

He was proud of the small charge he had engineered for Austin—strong enough to shatter the water tower without leveling half the county. He'd watched the girls hang upside down from the tower, pointing gleefully at the explosives he'd mounted in clay. He expected a cue from Austin at any moment to detonate it.

He was practically vibrating with anticipation when the knock came at the door.

By the time he reached the living room window, a hand was already waving at him from the porch. "Sweetie, can you open up?" Olivia Tremaine called. "The power's out in town, and the air-conditioning's off. It's so hot. We thought we'd stay at the farm tonight."

Stats opened the door. Three minutes later, they were at the kitchen table.

"So, Felix," Olivia said politely, smoothing her flowered skirt. "What's your profession?"

Stats cracked his knuckles. "I have six master's degrees in computers and science, a PhD, and two doctorates. But Aina tells me when I say that to people, it intimidates them, so I've been instructed to say: Austin calls me the Best Computer Hacker Ever."

"Oh," Olivia nodded. "That explains very little. Do you know when Brandon will return? It's so late."

John checked his watch again. "He should be home with Tessa by now..." It happened precisely then. A dull *smack* against the door. Then another. Stats drifted toward the living room window, curiosity tugging him forward. Something pale and shriveled pressed against the glass—ragged lips, a caved cheek, eyes like wet stones. He jolted backward—straight into Olivia.

"John. Olivia," Stats said, breath thinning. "If you would kindly choose a weapon—or any blunt object—that would be ideal. Our discussion is encountering... a minor complication." He honestly couldn't decide which was worse: their awkward questions or the creatures approaching. Olivia stared into the window for nearly two minutes, studying the face—then the three more that smashed in beside it. "Hmmm. I don't recognize any of them," she said calmly. "Should I crack the window and call out for Grandma Lilly? She might be with them. Although I daresay she was always quite prudent, and most of these people are dressed in their nighties."

"That would be extremely ill-advised." Stats dabbed at his forehead, voice tightening. "Might I suggest that you and Olivia relocate upstairs while I formulate an appropriate response downstairs?"

"Nope," John said, planting his feet with the solid calm of a man whose glory days peaked at eighteen. "I'm not a fighter by trade, but I'd never leave a man to fight a battle alone. I was in the Junior Corps in high school—I've been waiting for this my whole damn life. What's the plan, son?"

Stats shoved tools into their hands—a baseball bat for John, a broom for Olivia—and snatched up his laptop. He herded them up the stairs, slammed Brandon's bedroom door, and maneuvered them out the window onto the roof. It seemed logical. Revenants couldn't reason. Couldn't climb slate. And couldn't fly—he double-checked that one.

Stats immediately texted Austin. No answer. A cold fizz trickled down his spine. Austin always answered. He puffed out his cheeks, hesitated, then texted Brandon.

Hi Brandon! This is Stats. Remember me? I am on your roof with your parents. There are revenants on the porch. We are well armed. Just thought you should know. LOL 😊

He added the smiley face because he didn't want Brandon to worry. Now, balanced precariously beside the Tremaines, Stats peered down at the revenants circling below.

"Oh dear," Olivia murmured, swatting at a bug flitting around her hair. "Are they... getting closer?"

"They're... confused," Stats said. "But drawn here. Probably because Abel Martin is moving. Revenants follow disturbances they recognize."

John gripped his bat tighter. "This Abel fella better not hurt my boy." He paused, then winked at Olivia. "Or my best girl."

"I'm trying to reach Austin," Stats said. "She'll know what to do."

Thunder rolled in the distance. The air thickened—the same unnatural heaviness Austin felt at the creek. The revenants paused. Every single one of them. Their heads turned—slowly—toward Brandon's fields. Stats felt his blood chill. "Oh no," he whispered. "They felt something."

"What?" Olivia's voice trembled for the first time.

Stats stared toward the dark stretch of farmland, dread crawling over him like frost. "I think," he said, "that was the pre-echo of something bad." A moment later, across the black fields—from the direction of Turtle Creek—Stats heard the distant scream of a child. And all the revenants began to move.

Chapter −76

Flashlights bobbed in the dark like wandering fireflies, weaving through the trees toward Turtle Creek. Austin watched from her stance near the salt ring, her eyes tracking every shuddering movement below. The undead clustered at the far bank—a dozen or more—gray-footed, slack-jawed, stepping in those stiff, dreamlike lurches. Their stench hit her next, sour and sweet like a rotting animal corpse beneath wet leaves. She forced back a gag.

They crept toward the water, toes brushing the shallows, but none crossed. A few tried—bare feet or ragged burial shoes sinking into the creek mud—then reeled back, shrieking in pain. Golem's blessing held like a burn barrier.

Across the water, adults shouted, shoved, cursed—nothing worked. The revenants stumbled along the bank, circling, baffled by the water's invisible wall.

Behind them, the Canaan Mountain adults and their hostage children broke through the treeline in a ragged march. The rain had not yet raised the creek, leaving a slender, shallow stretch down the center. Austin narrowed her gaze. Some adults released their children and turned back toward Abel's side, fear and confusion slicing through their dumbed resolve. Others trudged on, tightening their grip on small hands. Starr stepped up beside her, breath sharp.

"The ones turning back... they can't cross blessed water," Austin whispered. "That means they're like him." She leaned in close. "We have to cut off the adults who can't cross," Austin went on. "Get the kids inside the salt semi-circle. When they're in, you close it. Then get them to the truck. Fast."

"There's no way," Starr whispered. "I'll be running straight through the middle. There are at least twenty kids to round up."

"Then shove them if you have to. Aina can fly and keep them back from Martin's side." Austin interjected, raising her hand to halt Starr's protest. "I trust your judgment. More than you think. If you trust me even a little, back me up."

Starr swallowed, her eyes bright with fear but steady. "Your ADHD doesn't limit you except your focus, my love. You're wrong about the rest. I'm the one overcompensating. Do it." She squeezed Austin's hand. "Do what you think is right."

Stand steady.

River's voice from days ago whispered in memory. Now she knew why. If she moved too soon, she wouldn't catch the children inside the salt. Austin stepped into the posture she learned in church greeting lines—feet splayed, hands behind her back, calm on the surface. And she stood steady.

The march thinned. So many adults abandoned ship that only six or seven remained to herd the children forward. Twenty-three kids in all. Some were barely Tessa's size. Some were nearly Hutch's age.

Kim barked orders at the adults, her voice slicing across the creek. She herded the little ones toward Austin with sweeping arms until they were well inside the salt arc.

Austin stayed still. A stone sentinel. Abel Martin strode down the bank toward her—suit coat and dress pants slick with rain, hair plastered tight to his skull. His eyes burned with the kind of holy fever that didn't come from God but from something deep, wicked, cracked, and hungry inside him. Mud clung to his cuffs; shadows gathered at his back as if they knew him, folding around him like a mourner's shroud. "Praise me, Lord!" he screamed, hurling himself upward in a convulsive jump, fist driving at the heavens. His followers flinched at the vibration of his voice. "All praises! Raise your hands and witness the beginning!"

No hands raised, but Abel Martin did not care. Five steps separated them. No more. As Abel leaned in, his coat dripping rain beside her cheek, the scent hit her—sharp, stale, unmistakable. Cigarette smoke. That same faint curl of cigarette smoke she had sensed for months outside doors, windows, even when no one else was awake. And the shadow that fell across her now it was the same one she had glimpsed on porches, across gravel drives, beside motel curtains.

Her breath snagged.

It had been him. All along. Not a phantom. Not some dark spirit pressing at the edges of her mind.

Abel Martin had been *physically* there, lurking just out of sight, listening, learning, hunting. The smoke wasn't some hallucination. The shadow wasn't a trick of fear. It was Abel pacing the darkness like a man checking pig pens before slaughter.

With that realization came a sharper clarity: even if Abel Martin had some psychic reach, it was limited—he wasn't godlike. For all his danger and hollow soul, he was still only human.

She hadn't realized she'd been holding her breath until it left her in a slow, shaky exhale. Her gaze swept the scene again, sharper now. Because he *was not reading her now*, he had not sensed the maneuver she'd been building—and his people had unknowingly driven all of the children straight into the open arc of salt.

The darkness around her pressed close, touching her skin like cold ash before sinking deeper—through muscle, through bone—stopping just shy of her soul. Heat climbed through her at the same time, thick and stifling, rolling over her like an open oven door and stealing the air from her lungs.

God, Starr. Please be watching. Please be closing the circle along the outside edge—creek to bank to property line—with that cheap Thrifty Value salt they'd picked up from Brandon's pantry. If she didn't connect it full circle, this trap meant nothing.

"Call the great snake!" Abel's command exploded like a gunshot. "Do it now. I will feed it. You will take the stone."

Austin flinched. His scent—musky and dead—twisted through her senses. Sickening, seductive at once. His presence hit like a toxin: heavy, oppressive, suffocating.

Austin's knees buckled. She hit the ground and vomited, whole body shaking. He oozed corruption. Blackness clung to him—dust, smoke, something alive—as if the very air rotted around his skin.

"No." The word rasped out, barely audible. She needed time. She needed Starr to finish the circle. She needed anything, but he pressed himself against her. *C'mon, Starr, faster! Faster!*

"Can't or won't?" Abel's boot came into view—six inches from her hands.

He kicked her. The toe of his muddy boot cracked against her jaw. Her head snapped back. She hit the ground, tasting blood, seeing the storm twisting overhead in a whirl of dark clouds. His gray hair whipped in the rising wind. Rain caught on the bulbous tip of his nose. His pale blue pig eyes locked on her.

He lifted a hand, fingers splayed. "Little bitch," Abel hissed. "You can call him. DO IT. Or I'll kill these children one by one until you do."

Lyndsey appeared beside him, clutching a small boy in her arms. He shivered uncontrollably. Sobbed.

"That one first," Abel snarled.

"Please don't." Austin's voice broke. "I'll do it. Please—I'll do it."

"You're begging," he yelped, delighted. "You're weaker than I thought."

His palm hovered over her forehead. A ringing burst behind her eyes. Burning pressure crawled from her nose into her skull. She needed him inside the salt. *Needed the children inside. Needed him farther still, just a few more steps...*

"I'll... do it," she gasped.

He booted her aside like a rag doll. She rolled on the ground hard. Austin pushed herself to rise. Elbows and knees held her up. Skinned elbows. Skinned knees. Before she could get her breath and rise, Abel seized her by the collar and yanked her upright, then slapped her. Heat flashed across her cheek.

"One stupid-ass move, and you're dead."

Austin nodded shakily. "I know what to do." A lie. She tightened her fist around Aina's pouch—mint, herbs, useless comfort.

"I need to pray," she whispered. "Ask Uktena to rise. Back up. I can't do it when you're draining me."

Abel motioned, and his people stepped back three paces. Lightning flashed to the west. She counted: one, two, three, four, five, six, seven, eight. Eight seconds. The storm was close.

Another flash: seven seconds.

Austin scanned the scene when the light flared—sharp, brief frames of reality.

She caught Aina's silhouette perched above, nearly invisible against the sky, waiting for the signal.

Another flash: six seconds.

When it blinked again at six seconds, Austin mouthed, *Three seconds.* Aina blinked in acknowledgment.

Austin closed her eyes. Sweat trickled down her temple, halting below her brow.

"Listen to the wind."

She jolted. River's voice—low, deep, familiar—drifted from the edge of the creek where darkness pooled. Her heart soared. She didn't open her eyes. Couldn't risk it.

"It's no different than last time," River murmured. "Listen to the wind and ask God for the strength to call Uktena."

"You're here," she breathed.

She felt him move—not seen, only sensed—as if the shadows themselves thickened. Something darker than the dark stepped close, no more than an arm's length away. The faintest outline of man and panther appeared when mist curled across the bank.

"I can't stop destiny," River said. "I'm sorry. I can't stay hidden long. Only you feel me. The others don't see a damn thing. Everything around you is heightened now—the sounds, the air, the storm. Use it. Focus. Call Uktena. Slay it. Take the power before he does. I'm right here."

Austin swallowed. Without River, everything could have fallen apart in five directions. Maybe it still would.

"Pray that hell doesn't break loose," River whispered, "and pray I don't turn on you—"

"Pray!" Abel roared.

River shuddered beside her.

"Please, pray," he murmured. "I'm not strong around him."

Austin sucked in a breath. "God—give me the strength of the storm to battle. The strength of the wind to call Uktena." Power prickled through her skin—River's, hers, something older. "Put power in my weapon from the lightning. Let thunder guide my strike. Let the rain help me choose the right enemy."

She opened her eyes. Aina was gone from where she'd perched.

Austin felt the earth shift—a deep tremor rising from the ribcage of the world. River's shadow faded and reformed. She glanced across the creek and saw him again—this time in the shape of the black panther lounging low in the brush behind Abel.

"Rise," Austin whispered. She extended her arm and slammed her foot down.

The ground vibrated.

"Rise!"

The earth split.

AND HE ROSE. Uktena burst upward—a massive serpentine body with antlered horns, earth flinging off them in sprays. His snout gaped wide, yellow fangs glistening. Twin golden eyes rolled above her, irises tightening to slits as his head swept side to side.

"The power!" Abel shrieked, spinning to face the creature.

Black dust poured from his pores in ecstatic waves. Gooseflesh raced over his wrists and neck. Darkness spiraled around him like a living storm.

The snake lowered, raised, tasted the air. Austin inhaled its musk—sharp, earthy, recently shed skin. He was hungry. Watching her. Waiting. The crystal—she finally saw it. A multi-colored shard nestled between the beast's eyes, gleaming like a living gem.

Austin lifted her hand, palm out. The snake followed the motion with hypnotic grace. She leaned right. He leaned right. She leaned left. He mirrored her. A strange kinship flickered between them— two creatures shaped by the dark, misunderstood, pulled toward power they never asked for.

Come closer. He obeyed.

The iron stave in her hand felt heavy, slick with sweat.

Little Turtle Girl. Her grandfather's voice. *Who is the monster? The serpent? The man? Why take a life for power? Sometimes, child, you must step away.*

"Step away," Austin murmured. "I need the power. I can't fight him and the undead and his converts without it."

You are not alone.

She blinked hard. She felt alone. Had always felt alone. Sweat trickled again—she wiped it from her temple.

You are not alone.

Austin's eyes lifted over Abel Martin's shoulder toward the mountain. And she saw them—the dark shapes from her dreams. The shadows. The watchers.

You see? We are always with you. You say you must look past the fuzzy baby shit-colored skin of kiwi fruit to reach the sweet inside.

"Yes," she whispered.

What you see as darkness isn't dark at all. It is the shadows of their souls. Their spirits. Their ghosts.

"Kill the monster! Get the crystal!" Abel Martin screamed, shattering the moment.

He lunged in front of her, seizing her shoulders, shaking hard. He released her and raised his hand to strike.

"No," Austin said.

Her voice was steady. Cold. Final. "No."

Uktena snapped free of his trance and whipped his great head back—and dove straight toward her.

Chapter −77

Hutch had been tapping furiously at his phone for twenty-two minutes. Brandon knew because he'd been staring at the green digits on the truck's dashboard clock crawl forward with painful slowness. The cab felt like an oven; sweat pooled in the hollows of Brandon's armpits and slipped down his temples. Every time he shifted to wipe it away, Hutch's eyes flicked up—dark, unreadable, unsettling. Occasionally, he cracked the door open an inch, then shut it again, as if testing the air or checking for something unseen.

Brandon slid a look into the back seat. Tessa's head had flopped sideways against her car seat; she slept soundly through the storm gusts that buffeted the truck. Wind rocked them in hard pulses, rattling the windows, making the door seams hiss.

Storms used to terrify her; she'd cling and sob at thunder. Brandon's mother would show up, rocking Tessa and telling stories about rain on the tin roof and angels bowling in heaven. He'd thought her overbearing, but tonight, with danger pressing in, he felt only gratitude for every minute she taught Tessa not to fear storms.

Quiet—unnatural, heavy—settled around them. Brandon's heart thumped in his throat. For a moment, he wondered if he should just punch Hutch, grab Tessa, and bolt. But there was no way he could get her unbuckled before Hutch reacted. No way to run far enough. Or fast enough if Hutch *did* hold something like the power of the gods within his grasp.

"You know my father has asked Austin to marry him six times," Hutch said suddenly, eyes still on the phone, voice flat as stone.

Brandon stiffened. "I... didn't know that."

"Yeah. I used to think she was just too ditzy to learn Spanish. Too shallow." Hutch's voice tightened, eyes narrowing at his reflection in the wet glass. "Then I find out she's fluent. Has been all along."

"I mean, I think she took Spanish classes in high school," Brandon said carefully.

Hutch lifted his head, peered beneath dark lashes, and stared at him—slow, incredulous—as if Brandon had just proposed the dumbest explanation imaginable.

"Yeah, right. She learned all that from the American public school system. I doubt that. Anyway, my father told me he was going to ask her again. He was ready to divorce my mom." He exhaled sharply, anger tightening his jaw. "Which is insane. My mom's a saint."

Brandon swallowed hard. Great. Another reason Hutch might want him dead. He loved her too. God help him, he did. He just wished he'd live long enough to tell her.

"So," Brandon said quietly, fingers pinching the bridge of his nose, "how does this go down?"

Hutch huffed out something that might've been a laugh. It was hard to tell. "*Go down...* yeah, that's funny."

Brandon's skin crawled. The kid was off tonight—too calm, too blank.

"I'm working that out right now," Hutch added, lifting his phone. Brandon opened his mouth—to ask *who* he was talking to, to protest—but Hutch put out a flat hand without even looking at him, a quiet, sharp command to hold his tongue.

"Yeah," he said into it. "Same truck. Corner of Canaan Road and the state route. Yeah, that's us. You got the plates. We're sitting in the truck. The little girl is—gone where I said I'd put her."

The little girl is gone? Brandon's eyes narrowed; he snapped them to the back.

They weren't anywhere near Canaan Road. And Tessa was still asleep.

Hutch had given the wrong location—intentionally. But why? Was he stalling? Setting them up? Keeping Austin away?

Lightning hit the horizon—or something like lightning. Brandon leaned toward the windshield. The flash had been orange-red, blooming upward like a fireball. "What was that?" he breathed, scrubbing condensation from the glass with his palm.

But Hutch wasn't listening to him. "Yeah, dumbass, I'm still here," Hutch snapped into the phone. "Surprise." He raised a finger at Brandon—*wait*—warning him off again. Then he kept listening. "Good news for us, right? Bad news for you, Paolo. Because..." Hutch lifted his free hand where Brandon could see it, palm out, showing the countdown with his fingers.

Five. Four. Three. Two—

Another explosion tore through the horizon—brighter, louder, shaking the truck. Hutch lowered the phone.

Brandon stared, stunned. "What—what just happened?"

Hutch dropped his last finger. "One. And boom." His voice was quiet, worn. "That was Paolo getting blown up." Hutch didn't look triumphant. Didn't even look relieved. Just hollowed-out tired. "It was me," he said quietly. "Not letting Austin down again. Not screwing up this time."

He reached up, flipped the visor down as Tessa squirmed sleepily in the back. A tiny camera dropped with it. "Paolo and whoever he hired have been listening the whole time," Hutch said. "Had me put a mic up there days ago so he could monitor every conversation. Paolo was never going to let Austin go. Or me. Or you." A muscle jumped in his jaw. "Or her." He jabbed a thumb behind him. "He wanted the little girl as a pet, a reminder of Austin. You know, like a serial killer keeps trophies. That's why I opened the door earlier. I was supposed to put her in a box he left in the woods."

Brandon felt his stomach drop.

A cold sweat broke across his spine.

Hutch rubbed his face, exhausted. "I called in a few favors with my dad. We figured Paolo would try something. Austin told me someday I'd have to make a choice—the kind that feels awful but saves more good people and gets rid of someone rotten." His voice softened. "Paolo was rotten."

Brandon stared at the horizon where the fire still fanned upward. He felt strangely weightless—shaking, drained. "And Austin's old truck...?"

"First explosion," Hutch murmured. "His men rigged it. We detonated it before he could."

His eyes flicked to Tessa. "She's safer now. All of us are."

Brandon let his head fall back against the headrest. He didn't know whether to thank Hutch or strangle him. Maybe both.

"Kind of like Austin leaving Tessa," Hutch continued softly. "Her dad kept telling her she was bad. Broken. Couldn't raise a kid. She spends way too much time trying to prove he was wrong." He gave a small, tired shrug. "You don't remind her of all that."

For the first time all night, Brandon believed him.

"Let's go," Hutch said. "We need to drive. Keep moving. Oh—no. No, no—dammit."

Brandon tensed. "What now?"

Hutch scanned his phone, color draining from his face. "Starr texted me ten times. She's in full emergency mode and needs Stats to blow the water tower." He refreshed the screen. "She can't reach him. I can't either."

He exhaled sharply. "The last message he sent was twenty minutes ago. He said he was sitting on your roof... with your mom and dad." Hutch's hand shook slightly. "Now his phone's not working."

Brandon's pulse throbbed in his ears.

And the storm outside pressed harder against the windows, as if waiting.

Chapter −78

Brandon bent over with his hands braced on his knees, gasping for breath, sweat burning his eyes. His arms throbbed from swinging the only weapon he'd been able to grab—a four-way tire iron from his trunk. He and Hutch had been forced to abandon the truck on the main road after a fallen tree blocked the way, its splintered limbs littered across the asphalt, still sharp with the smell of fresh breakage. They had jogged the last stretch toward the house, feet slipping in mud, branches snapping beneath them. They reached the top of the driveway just as Hutch grabbed Brandon's upper arm, breath hot against his ear.

"Get ready," Hutch said. "The shit's about to hit the fan."

Tessa clung to Brandon's neck, her arms tight and trembling, her breath quick and warm against his skin. Hutch covered them, barking orders into his radio for Stats to blow the water tower. Brandon didn't know why he started counting bodies—it was something to hold onto, something to keep his mind from fracturing under the sheer horror of what they were charging into.

He tore through eighteen undead before he stopped bothering to count, murmuring to Tessa that they weren't real. "Just dead dummies, sweetheart," he choked out, as if that made any of it less horrifying.

The tire iron slipped in his hands, slick with gore, and the reek of decay clung to him in waves so strong he gagged. Somewhere behind him, a blast tore through the air—Stats must've blown the tower. It echoed across the valley like a cannon.

Hutch had nearly reached the porch when another tide of undead stumbled from the shadows, twenty more staggering forward in stiff, jerky movements. The world became nothing but blows, screaming, wet impacts, and the relentless grind of survival.

Then Brandon heard them—his mother and father—shouting encouragement from the rooftop, their voices rising above the storm as they had at his third-grade little league games.

Their familiar whoops and hollers cut through the night, absurd and strangely comforting. Hutch waved wildly from the porch, slicing the air with his arms and pointing behind Brandon, eyes wide.

He barely had time to turn.

An enormous plank—ripped from his own barn—was already swinging toward his head. The undead man wielding it was massive, shoulders sloping, one milky eye staring straight at him with eerie accuracy. The plank hissed through the air, rough wood splintering in the wind. Brandon's stomach dropped. He couldn't dodge. This was the moment he was going to die.

Time slowed.

Tiny sparks flashed in the darkness—brief flickers of gold like fireflies. The sight tugged a fragile memory from somewhere deep inside, bright enough to cut through the terror. Fireflies on the lawn. Tessa's laughter rose like music as Golem, Austin, Roo, and Hutch darted barefoot through damp summer grass, chasing glowing butts of light with an old Ball Mason jar. Austin's soft smile as she encouraged the kids. Starr shrieking with excitement, dragging Aina and Austin after her. Aina giggled as a firefly crawled up her arm. The night had felt enchanted, the kind of simple magic he'd never gotten to keep.

For once in his life, Brandon had felt like he belonged. Like this strange little group of misfits had made room for him without hesitation. He remembered rising from the porch and crossing the lawn, slipping his hand into Austin's. She had looked down at their joined fingers with something sharp and tender in her eyes. He could have sworn she was crying before she tugged him forward to join the chase. "I know we can't," she whispered, breath trembling, "but I want to be with you forever."

"Daddy!" Tessa screamed now, her voice slicing the chaos.

Brandon ducked and threw himself around her, dropping to his knees so she wouldn't take the hit. The tire iron slipped from his grip. The plank should have caved in his skull and scattered him across the dirt. A sudden rush of wind slammed into Brandon— hard, forceful, unexpected.

Not storm wind.

A downdraft, powerful and rhythmic, like the beating of enormous wings sweeping low across the lawn.

The force knocked him sharply sideways, just enough to throw the swing off course. He twisted mid-fall, curling his body around Tessa before they hit the ground. The earth was cool beneath him, soft with wet grass and mud.

For an instant—barely a flicker at the edge of his vision—Brandon saw something dart overhead. A shimmer of shifting light. A tiny silhouette with frantic wings and a sharp, temperamental tilt of its head before it flitted aside.

A hummingbird, small and fast, a darker shadow running beneath it as if something larger walked in its wake before disappearing into the storm.

Something in the movement felt familiar. Protective. Always irritable.

Hutch.

His fogging mind made the connection before he could stop it. He couldn't see clearly—not with rain and smoke and chaos tearing through the sky—but the rhythm of the wind, the sudden lift in his chest, the strange safety washing over him...

It was him.

A faint smile curved Brandon's lips.

"Oh... hey, Hutch," he murmured, voice slurring as darkness crept in around the edges. A cool quietness spread through his mind, soft and strange. "Fireflies," he murmured.

That single word drifted through the darkness as it swallowed him whole.

And then everything went black.

Chapter −79

Austin held her ground inside the open arc of salt on the rise above Turtle Creek. The blessed water was behind her, the children clustered in a trembling knot at her back, and the storm pressing low enough that every breath carried the taste of wet earth and metal. Starr was somewhere along the outer bank, racing to finish the salt line before anyone noticed the gap.

But the salt was not working. The undead shuffled around in it unheeded. Only Aina, hovering above the treetops, her gray silhouette weaving through the wind was keeping them at bay by soaring downward and knocking them with her feet. Abel Martin and the last of his followers stood across from her inside the arc they had unknowingly entered, all of them framed by the storm's flickering light. Austin didn't move. She couldn't. Her stance—feet braced, iron staff slick in her grip—was the only thing keeping the trap intact.

Uktena snapped out of his trance, golden eyes tightening to blade-thin slits as he reared back. A burst of hot, ancient breath rushed across Austin an instant before the serpent lunged. His antlered horns caught the lightning, fangs flashing as the ground erupted in a shower of wet soil and torn roots. Austin braced herself, her pulse hammering against her ribs. A scream cut through the storm—child or adult or wildcat, she couldn't tell—and the wind shoved her so hard her knees nearly buckled.

Then another sound rose through the downpour: wings. Not one pair—many. Heavy. Rushing. Violent.

"*Ho—ly* shit," Austin hissed. The Tlanuhwa dropped out of the black sky in a spiraling descent, talons flaring as they aimed straight for the children huddled behind her. Their cries tore across the creek like metal ripping. Austin's breath seized in her chest.

A shadow eclipsed the sky. Aina plunged downward in a streak of gray and bone, wings snapping wide as she slammed into the first monstrous bird with enough force to knock it spinning wildly.

There was nothing delicate or storybook in her form—only ash, sinew, and a terrible determination that sent her colliding into the Tlanuhwa again and again, holding them back by sheer will, then dropping down to force back the undead.

Austin couldn't help her. She couldn't help the children. She couldn't even look away—because Uktena's massive head was almost upon her.

Abel lunged into view, gripping both of Austin's shoulders and shaking her so violently her teeth clattered. "Kill the monster! Get the crystal!" he bellowed, his spit hitting her cheek. "NOW!"

He released her and raised his arm to strike.

Austin lifted her chin. Her voice came out low, cold, unshaken. "No."

The wind from Uktena's dive slammed past her first, a pressure wave that rippled through her skin. She smelled earth, musk, and old power just before something barreled into her from the side.

A dark shape launched from the grass—swift, heavy, controlled.

River.

He didn't come with claws or fangs. He slammed his shoulder into Austin and knocked her clear of the strike, rolling her through the wet sand as Uktena's jaws clamped onto empty air and Abel's iron bar smashed down where her skull had been.

Abel spun, nearly slipping as he recovered. He lifted the iron again, aiming for River. He never connected.

Uktena's head swept sideways and struck in a single, explosive snap.

Abel Martin vanished between the serpent's jaws.

A spray of black liquid erupted, thick as tar. It vaporized midair into a fine red mist that glittered as the storm winds carried it away. Austin blinked back the sting of it as flames burst overhead—the Tlanuhwa igniting one by one in sudden, startling flares before collapsing into drifting ash. A pulse of raw power rolled off Uktena, sharp and electric. Austin felt it skate across her skin and settle deep into her bones. It tugged at her—inviting, intoxicating.

Her shadow-spirits gathered at her ankles, restless and insistent. Their forms flickered in the lightning, urging her in the only language they knew.

Take it. Kill the serpent. Claim what he carried.

Austin's hand trembled. Power shimmered in the air, bright and sweet and dangerously easy to reach for.

One strike would be enough.

One choice, and all of that strength would become hers.

POWER!

But beneath the clamor of the spirits came something quieter—steady, ancient. Her ancestors. Their presence brushed her mind like a hand on her shoulder. They had walked away from Uktena generations ago. They had refused strength purchased with blood. They had chosen restraint when taking power would have been simpler, faster, easier.

Their pull reached her now, guiding her toward mercy.

And with it came a familiar ache, shaped like loss—like watching Aina throw herself into danger, or feeling Starr pour herself hollow to protect others.

Creature or human, scaled or feathered, life was still life.

River's voice cut through the storm beside her. "It is time," he said quietly. Rain dripped from his whiskers; he stood half-panther, half-shadow. "It's either you or the snake."

Uktena lowered his head until his snout hovered inches from her forehead. His breath warmed her face through the cold rain. His golden eyes watched her—waiting.

Austin reached out with steady hands and pressed her forehead gently to his. His scales were warm beneath the storm's downpour, humming with a deep, ancient vibration.

"You won't be finished with us," she murmured. "But you're no monster. No more than I am."

Her fingers slid into River's fur, steadying herself.

"You have to kill him," River urged, urgency tightening his voice. "Austin—he will not walk away."

"No," she said softly. "This isn't our war. Not mine. Not his. My ancestors walked away—and so will I."

Uktena's pupils widened. A long, low breath escaped him—almost a sigh.

He drew back, his massive body rippling. The ground shuddered as it opened beneath him. Soil rolled over his scales as he slipped downward, sinking back into the deep earth from which he'd risen.

The storm shuddered. The wind broke. Silence fell—heavy, humming, unreal.

Austin stayed on her knees, one hand in River's fur, the other pressed to the damp earth. Behind her, the salt line held.

And Abel Martin was nothing more than glitter drifting on the wind.

The silence didn't last.

A flat, distant *whump* rolled in from the ridge above town—low at first, then swelling into a deep-bellied boom that bounced off the hills. Light flared white-orange against the clouds. Austin's head snapped up.

"The tower," she breathed. *Stats.*

A second later came the metal scream—the hollow, groaning shriek of old steel giving way. Austin's gut dropped. Every horror-movie image she'd ever hoarded detonated at once.

"Run!" Her voice cracked across the creek. "Big boom coming! Get the kids up the bank—now! Go, go, GO! BIG BOOM COMING!"

Starr didn't hesitate. She grabbed two little ones by their wrists and hauled them toward higher ground. Aina dove low, half-fairy silhouette cutting through the thinning rain, shrieking at the older kids in Spanish and English both to *move*. River hooked an arm around Austin's waist and dragged her backwards as she stumbled, still half on her knees.

Austin pictured it in a flash: the whole tank letting loose at once, a roaring wall of poisoned water barreling down Turtle Creek, wiping out the church, Brandon's pastures, half the town. For one wild heartbeat, she was sure they'd miscalculated everything.

The roar never came.

A thin hiss reached them instead—more like a giant radiator letting off steam than the judgment of God. Austin squinted toward the ridge through the broken clouds. The tower's silhouette was crooked now, top buckled, side peeled back like a sardine can. Instead of a killing wave, water sprayed out in a high, pathetic arc before pattering down in a glittering drizzle.

Not a flood.

A leaky shower.

The creek below them burped, rose... and settled into a slightly fatter, muddier flow.

"That's it?" Austin gasped, chest heaving, kids clinging to her legs. "All that math for... a glorified sprinkler?"

One stray drop—cold, muddy, and extremely unimpressive—landed on the back of her neck.

River snorted, breath still rough. "Looks like your hacker blew up a water tower with the caution of a ninety-year-old church lady," he said. "Broke the tank, vented the pressure, didn't drown a single cow."

Aina hovered above the bank, wings beating hard, eyes wide as she took in the gentle sheet of water spilling down the far hillside like a small, lopsided waterfall. "Well," Starr called out, "it's not exactly cinematic... but it did the job." She let out a shaky laugh she tried to pass off as a cough. One of the smallest kids—face streaked with tears and mud—looked up at Austin.

"Is... is the big boom over?" he whispered.

Austin swallowed, wiped her mouth with the back of her hand, and forced her lungs to slow. The tower sagged on the horizon, bleeding out the last of Abel's control in a sulky drizzle.

"Yeah," she said. "That was the big scary part."

A distant *plink* carried on the wind and made them all flinch—metal giving one last, defeated complaint. "Mostly."

Chapter –80

"Okay, which one of you broke my boyfriend?"

Austin stood at the bottom step of the porch, arms crossed, dried sludge streaked across her shirt in mottled green and red. Roo pressed against her leg, gaze lifted in his quiet, loyal worship. She craned her neck around Evan Tate, trying to see past the EMS flashlight he was shining in Brandon's eyes.

Up on the porch steps, John Tremaine sat with Tessa perched in his lap. She'd refused to move from Brandon's side since the battle ended—eyes on her father, clutching his shirt like it was the only thing anchoring her to the world.

But the moment she saw Austin? "Mama! You found your way home!"

Tessa slid off John's knee and barreled toward her through the wet grass. Austin barely had time to drop her posture before the little girl slammed into her arms. Austin pressed her face into Tessa's hair, breathing her in, steadying her heart.

Evan—an old acquaintance of Brandon's family—glanced up and nearly lost his composure when he caught sight of what stood behind Austin: Golem holding Aina's hand, Starr and River limping with exhaustion, Roo at Austin's ankles like a silent shadow. For a split second, he almost gasped.

Then training kicked in, and he pasted on a steady, professional smile. "He's not completely broken," he said. "Holy hell, —are you alright?" Austin was a disaster. Bruised nose, swollen eye, bottom lip fat and puffy on one side, and streaks of green and red gore drying in cracked lines across her clothes.

"I'm fine," she said, voice rough. "Except I think some of this got in my mouth." She held out her arms to show the crusted mess. "This is them. Not me."

"So, I'm your boyfriend now?" Brandon said from where he sat, Evan's flashlight still in his eyes. His laugh was thin but real.

Hutch groaned loudly from the porch.

The farmhouse door slammed open.

Stats burst out and ran straight into Brandon's shoulder. He skidded to a stop at the steps, chest heaving.

"I-uh—I can't remember the proper protocol," he panted. "When you think someone is deceased and then you find out they are *not* deceased."

"It's a hug," Austin said, wiggling her fingers at him.

Stats stepped down two steps, halted inches away, and pointed at her shirt. "Is that stuff gonna hurt me?"

"It's dead-people goo. You tell me."

He pushed his glasses up and rubbed the snake tattoo on his forearm. "I'm supposed to say I don't care, right? Even though I do?" When Austin rolled her eyes, Stats made a strangled noise, leaned over Tessa's little shoulder, and patted Austin's back in three quick, awkward taps. "I did good, right? The emergency medical staff person said half the valley's bone-dry now," Stats added proudly. "But it stalled the undead long enough for the church folks to get the kids."

"You tell me," Austin said. "You saved Brandon's parents. You blew up a water tower. You basically lived your weird little dream— minus half-naked girls floating around you while you detonated things. You deserve a medal."

Stats puffed up... then froze. "It was Hutch who saved Brandon. He *turned*."

Brandon's mom rose and squeezed Stats' arm, her voice shaking as she whispered a thank-you, but he pretended not to hear.

Austin's head snapped toward the porch.

Hutch lounged in a rocking chair, dazed but smug, arms draped over the armrests. Olivia Tremaine pressed an ice pack to the side of his head and kept patting his shoulder. Each pat made him wince, but he didn't pull away.

"I feel like one of those stretchy toys you got me for Christmas," he muttered. "The ones Golem ripped the arms off to see how far they'd go."

"*Turned*?" John Tremaine echoed. "All I know is—Brandon was pinned with Tessa on his back. One second, Hutch was at the door... the next—boom! Gone. He hit that thing so hard they both vanished into the dark. Saved my boy's life. I owe him an ice cream cone!"

Hutch barely looked conscious of what he'd done—like the power had borrowed him for a moment and wasn't finished deciding whether to give him back. Austin's chest warmed. "I knew you'd figure it out."

"Oh, don't look like I'm your first batch of cookies you didn't burn," Hutch said. "And you stink like death, Austin. Real bad. I can smell you from here."

"Join the club." Austin exhaled. "There are twenty-three kids accounted for. Ben called half his church—they've been tending to them. Mostly skinned knees and confusion. Somehow... most of them thought they were at some kind of strange church camp." She rubbed her forehead and winced. "Kim was... weirdly kind to them. Whatever Abel did to her... it didn't touch that part of her. She kept them alive."

"Ben's guys burned what was left of the undead," Brandon added quietly. "Nothing's moving out there anymore."

She hesitated, then looked at Brandon. "Well, now Ben's got Lyndsey and Kim in the patrol car. Lyndsey wants to talk to you. She seems normal again. Or normal for Lyndsey. Her dad put chemicals in the water. I don't think she knew—she's not very bright." She took in a breath, puffed the air out. "That last part is jealousy."

"You're good to go," Evan told Brandon. "If you want to see her. But the hospital's full—commune folks are vomiting, freaking out. Everything's on generators. Might not be where you want to be."

"Ben said they've got the whole group under observation," Austin added. "Detox, psych evals, the works. They're going to be okay once that stuff clears their system."

"Lyndsey didn't have anything to do with this?" Brandon asked quietly.

Austin sucked in a breath, shifting her weight, automatically nudging up glasses that weren't on her face anymore. "You all need to know something." She turned in a slow circle, meeting every pair of eyes. "I got a letter six months ago. Someone is begging me to get them out of Abel Martin's compound. There were photos of you, Brandon, with Lyndsey and her brothers. One of Tessa. Everything pointed to you being trapped there." She swallowed hard. "I begged Paolo to let me go help. He wouldn't let me. Then he started tormenting me with the letter. Using it against me."

Hutch straightened a little. "My dad handled Paolo," he said quietly. "He's... gone. He can't hurt you again."

Austin froze. "Gone how?" she asked, voice sounding thin. "Gone like... hiding? Gone like—"

Hutch sighed. "Dead, Austin. Dead. We'll talk later." He slumped back as Evan stepped away from the porch, giving them space. A cold weight settled in her stomach—final, immovable. Paolo's shadow had reached the end of the road.

Starr blinked as realization hit. "So that's why you let the rebel soldiers take him."

Austin nodded once. "I waited until they boarded. I knew they were coming. I never wanted anyone hurt. I just needed us away from him."

The porch went dead still. "You what?" Starr asked, incredulous.

"It sounds like she set everything up to annihilate Abel Martin," Stats said bluntly.

"You put our lives on the line without telling us?" Starr snapped.

"Tell them what he did," Golem said softly. He stepped forward, slipping his hand from Aina's.

"It doesn't matter," Austin whispered.

"It does," Aina said. Her small voice carried iron. "I knew. Golem told me. Paolo sold him to a fighting ring. He was angry at Austin. He planned to blame her. We were on our way to finalize it when... everything happened." Her eyes were rimmed red—exhaustion and leftover fear bleeding through her usually bright composure.

"You should have told us," Starr said—and then shoved Austin lightly. "And for that, I get the first shower."

"That's it?" Austin blinked.

"You leap first, flounder second," Starr said. "We know who we're dealing with." She scooped Tessa up. "Come on, baby. Let's make sure you're really okay."

Tessa waved at Austin over Starr's shoulder before disappearing inside with Aina and Golem. Golem shot Austin one last reassuring nod over his shoulder—tired, scraped up, but very much alive.

Austin sighed. "Should we tell her there's no water until the electric comes back?"

"No," Brandon said. Austin hugged Roo, who gave her a comforting shoulder bump, then looked at River standing in the shadows—human, but darkness clinging around him like smoke.

"Can you give me a minute with Brandon? Before this goo dries and I start gagging again?"

River nodded, nudged Roo toward the door, and the two bickered softly, brotherlike, as they vanished into the house with Olivia and John.

But as River passed, Austin felt it before she saw it—a faint tightening in the air, a sense of him brushing against her thoughts. Even drained, his presence tugged at her—soft, grounding, familiar. When their eyes met for the briefest heartbeat, she pretended she didn't feel him that strongly and offered only the smallest nod. But he knew. As he went by, he let one corner of his mouth lift—a quiet, weary confirmation that he was still with her.

"It was Lyndsey," Austin said once they were alone. She reached down and helped Brandon stand. "She wrote the letter. Ben says once she detoxes, she'll probably just face minor charges. She wasn't the mastermind—just caught in the crossfire."

"What? Lyndsey? There's no way—"

Austin handed him a folded slip of paper. "Ben let her write you a quick note before they drove her to the station. Same handwriting. Same hearts over the i's. She knew her dad was dosing the water.

Took a sample to the hospital. They tested it. She tried to warn someone... but fear got her. By the time we showed up, she was too far gone."

Brandon stared at the little-hearted *i still love you*. "You're kidding."

"No," Austin said softly. "She tried to save you and Tessa."

The EMS truck pulled away, leaving them in the cooling hush of night. Austin groaned and tilted her head back. "Brandon... we're a package deal. I'm not leaving them. Hutch is incredibly powerful now—God help us when he has a teenage meltdown. Stats spends half his time googling naked women. Aina's diving headfirst into her fairy identity. And River and Roo..." She shrugged. "They're always going to end up in my bed."

Brandon laughed. "Yeah. Waking up with a black panther paw across my stomach was... something."

"See?" she said, nudging him. "This is normal for us."

"You stink," he said.

"You stink worse."

Brandon crushed the note in his hand. "I'm not talking to Lyndsey. I'm throwing this away. I'm here—with you. Literally." He tugged her closer, grimacing as their shirts stuck together with dried gore. "Tessa and I... we've been waiting for you. Stay with us. We'll figure out the farm. The rest of it. All of it. All of us."

"At this point," Austin muttered, "I don't have a choice. You're going to have to peel me off."

"So, you figured something out?" he asked softly. "When you called me about Tessa—you said you wouldn't take her until you figured something out."

"I did," she whispered. "I figured out I love you."

Brandon cupped her jaw gently. "Yeah," he said. "I love you too."

Austin leaned her forehead against his. The porch lights flickered back on, and for the first time all night, the farmhouse felt like a place people lived in—not a battlefield. A faint vibration shivered through Turtle Creek—low, deep, ancient.

Not enough to knock anything over. But enough to be felt. Enough to say something wasn't as finished as the night wanted them to believe.

Austin stiffened slightly. Brandon lifted his head. The tremor faded into the earth. The night held its breath. Austin sighed deeply, chuckled softly. "I am glad the battle is over. I am done fighting for a while." And somewhere far below the soil...something shifted in return.

www.ingramcontent.com/pod-product-compliance
Lightning Source LLC
Chambersburg PA
CBHW031143270326
41931CB00006B/131